WORK, ORGANIZATION, AND POWER

Introduction to Industrial Sociology

Ramona L. Ford

Southwest Texas State University

Allyn and Bacon, Inc.   Boston   London   Sydney   Toronto

Brief Contents

Contents

Tables

Figures

Preface

Most of us will have to work during the major part of our lives. We will probably have at least one family. We will join associations, choose from among candidates with varying social policies, and pay taxes to support those policies. We will all be affected in numerous ways by the structure and functioning of the political economy.

Do we really understand how our "private troubles" are often "public problems"—to paraphrase sociologist C. Wright Mills? This understanding has not become easier as societies have become more technologically and organizationally complex and more interlocked into the international economy.

This book is intended to give you a broad framework of national (and some international) social institutions, especially the economic and political systems. Within those systems are located the organizations and associations where we as individuals will play most of our social roles. If you have looked at the Contents, you may have thought, "What are all of these different subjects doing in one book? Hunting and gathering societies, United States history, management theory, political and economic power, multinationals, union history and problems, social classes, work and health, organizational structure and culture, alternative workplace organization, future scenarios? This looks like three books." This is what you should get from reading the chapters—an idea of how all of these pieces relate. In fact, you should come away with understanding more than one view of relationships of the parts to the whole, since opposing views are presented.

Why should you want to know how you are affected by larger systems? First, it is a boost for mental health—getting the "big picture" may help you maneuver in the world with more understanding, hence with more effectiveness. Second, it should alert you to events and ... not noticed before or throw a new light on puzzling subjects. If this book does its job, you will end up with more questions about, and interest in, your environment—from the family to the international scene. It should stimulate you to pursue more historical data on how we arrived at the current situation, on current events and questions, and on where we may be headed in the future. Finally, if this interest in questions and knowledge occurs, it may lead to involvement in trying to influence our future options.

No book is ever really the product of one author, no matter what the copyright says. I owe much to the hundreds of students in my industrial sociology courses over the last eight years. Acknowledgement and gratitude must be expressed to the outside reviewers of the entire manuscript, whose suggestions I have taken seriously and sometimes followed. My thanks goes to colleagues Susan Day, Jim Garber, David Jorgensen, Keith Kirkpatrick, John O'Connell, Al Short, and Mike Smith whose comments on various chapters were most helpful. Special thanks goes to Robert Heilbroner who read the manuscript in its earliest rough draft and provided much encouragement. Needless to say, they are not to be held accountable for the final form in which the material is presented.

Finally, this book could not have been written without the twenty-one years of ongoing debate and discussion about the political economy with the late Arthur M. Ford, Ph.D. (1935-1977) to whose accomplishments and memory this book is lovingly dedicated.

Bringing Macro and Micro Together by Means of History

1

Introduction

The theme of this book is power. Every chapter deals with it in some manner, whether it is power differentials in male and female roles in the family, power in the organization, power distribution in the community, power in the national political and economic spheres, or power among nations with differing degrees of industrial development in the global economy. The subject of power is of special interest to political economists and other social scientists who approach it from what we will refer to below as the power/conflict approach to analyzing social relationships.

Power itself need not be a zero-sum entity. For example, giving workers more autonomy and power may enhance the power of an organization, which thereby becomes more successful, giving its management more power in the wider society. In definitional terms, however, *power* is usually defined as zero-sum—one gains it at the expense of another. We use Perrow's definition:

> Power is the ability of persons or groups to extract for themselves valued outputs from a system in which other persons or groups either seek the same outputs for themselves or would prefer to expend their effort toward other outputs. (Perrow 1986:259)

Simply stated, power is the ability to get one's own way—even when met with resistance.

Even though we are studying power and its effects on all aspects of society from the family to the international scene, we should keep the following four underlying points in mind.

1. This text presents both of the dominant Western views on how our society operates: (1) the order/consensus assumptions underlying

the more specific ideas of power pluralism, structural functional social stratification, the human capital argument on how wages are set, and neoclassical economic view; and (2) the power/conflict assumptions underlying power elite theory, conflict social stratification, structuralist institutional discrimination argument, and a political economy view.

2. The power/conflict approach examines and is more critical of the political and economic systems. This approach is emphasized here because it is less familiar to the reader and because the author feels it helps us understand relationships and processes in the social system. Data and arguments for the order/consensus view should be commonplace to anyone familiar with U.S. culture. The reasons we get so little exposure to the critical power/conflict perspective will become apparent in subsequent chapters.

3. Even though most of the data and arguments presented here support this second view, we cannot make simplistic arguments to negate the first view. Good arguments can be made from both perspectives. In any case, any social situation can best be understood when alternative interpretations are considered.

4. Caveats: Since we are trying to integrate so many aspects of society around opposing worldview frameworks, this book pursues a wide range of topics. There is not space in one volume, however, to cover all topics in depth or to present all opposing arguments on all issues introduced. This means that you, the reader, must take what is here and pursue it to satisfy your own curiosity about the questions raised. This book is a place to start and to be challenged. The bibliography provides sources with which to begin, and the library indexes to journals, books, and other media offer additional materials. As you gather information on the world economy, do not neglect press clippings. As economist Howard Wachtel has noted, sometimes "the best source of information has been economic and financial journalists who have produced a rich body of factual and analytical material on the world economy" (Wachtel 1986:xiii–xiv). Even though the popular media are helpful, the investigative reporting in the "alternative press" should not be neglected.

To make sense out of the bits and pieces gleaned from various sources, however, we must have that knowledge of alternative theoretical frameworks or worldviews mentioned. We return to this important area of differing frameworks after a brief look at the history of industrial sociology and some basic terms, including levels of analysis. These levels of analysis—macro, mezzo, and micro—are intimately connected with the framework/worldview through which one views society.

A BRIEF HISTORY OF INDUSTRIAL SOCIOLOGY IN ITS MANY FORMS

The Late 1900s to World War I

People have always tried to understand society and predict where it is going. The social sciences (economics, psychology, sociology, anthropology, and political science), as we think of them today, are attempts to build systematic bodies of knowledge based on empirical data as well as theories. These fields grew out of people's attempts to understand the effects industrialization was having on societies in the nineteenth century. In this broad sense, industrial sociology has been around as long as the discipline.

Sociology as a discipline has been defined as the study of patterns of behavior of groups in society, and of the antecedents and consequences of these patterns. *Industrial sociology* as a subdiscipline has many definitions, as we will see. Industrial sociologist Curt Tausky's (Tausky 1984:2) broad definition is the one we use: industrial sociology is concerned with "the work-related features of life in industrial society." The term *work-related* covers quite a lot. Students of the *sociology of knowledge* (the study of how ideas become shaped by occurrences and social forces in societies) tell us some interesting changes have taken place in industrial sociology since its beginnings—assuming it began quietly as one of the early aims of sociology.

As a separate discipline, sociology itself did not appear until the latter half of the nineteenth century. Beginning to be recognized by the 1880s, it came in slightly later than most of the other social sciences. The industrial revolution was well under way by then, having started in Great Britain by the second half of the eighteenth century with the application of new mechanical means of power to the production of goods. Industrialization did not reach the United States to any great extent until the Civil War. As Tausky (1984:2) points out, in 1860 there "were more slaves than factory workers, and the waterwheel, not the steam engine, powered half of the country's factories until the last three decades of the nineteenth century." In Europe social thinkers, such as Saint-Simon, Comte, Durkheim, Marx, and later, Toennies, Pareto, Simmel, and Weber, had been writing on the effects of industrialization, its early capitalist relations of production, its rationalization and division of labor, urbanization, and the bureaucratization of societies.

In the United States the early sociologists in the late nineteenth and early twentieth centuries until World War I were also concerned with holistic examination of the effects of industrialization on society. They hoped their work would improve social conditions. In this early period the line between political economy and sociology was very weak and their concerns and research projects were sometimes mutual. For example, economist John R. Commons, who was yet to develop his institutional labor studies, and sociologist E. A. Ross had both been trained as political economists and sometimes shared ideas as colleagues at Wisconsin. They were "preoccupied with the problem of social integration within an increasingly centralized national economy based on a democratic polity" (Cohen 1983:49).

Their ideas surfaced on projects such as the first big urban survey in the United States, *Pittsburgh Survey*, for which Commons helped develop some of the interview questions (Cohen 1983:48–49). In this study, a multidisciplinary team of sixty field researchers examined the effects of U.S. Steel activities on the work, family, and political rights of the steelworkers in the community from summer 1907 to fall 1908 (findings reported in Fitch, 1911; Eastman, 1910; Byington, 1910). The team was led by Edward Devine and Paul Kellogg and funded by the Russell Sage Foundation. Taking a holistic approach, the researchers had reform of a politically active, democratic participatory nature in mind. They wanted to do something about what they felt was the "choking of democratic institutions" (Fitch, quoted in Cohen 1983:50).

The 1920s and 1930s

This reformist political economy approach to industrial sociology ended for most sociologists with World War I and the end of the Progressive era. In the 1920s with the preeminence of the Chicago School of Sociology, holistic community studies remained but the political nature of the industrial influence had disappeared in favor of human ecology and the search for ecological equilibrium. The Bolshevik Revolution in Russia and the Red Scare of the Palmer witch-hunts after World War I may have contributed to the loss of importance of the political nature of industrial development—the conflicts it brought and the limits it put on the quality of community life (Cohen 1983:54). The study of power waned.

One eventual major direction of industrial sociology was influenced by the now well-known Hawthorne studies at Western Electric's Hawthorne plant in Chicago from 1924 to 1933. Elton Mayo of the Harvard Business School and his multidisciplinary team conducted the research. The studies focused on the small work teams and on worker fatigue, morale, boredom, and productivity. The emphasis of the studies was to give management some tools with which to increase productivity rather than to study wider politically oriented issues. Political and economic concerns of the worker in the writings of Progressive era sociologists gave way to the social concerns of the worker and participation in the life of the small group. These studies are discussed in more detail in Chapter 4 for their contribution to human relations management.

Mayo's studies influenced sociologist Talcott Parsons at Harvard. Parsons, in turn, greatly influenced the direction of sociology. In his own theoretical work on the social system and social action, Parsons expanded Mayo's concept of social concerns to a wider cultural base, including workers' motivations into which they are socialized in the home (Cohen 1983:59). In practice this often put the focus back on the characteristics of individuals in groups at the micro level.

Parsons also felt that the changes in industrial society, with its differentiation of work and division of labor, had changed the role the social scientist should take. These changes had taken the following forms: worker-led conflict was no longer important in industrial society, even when assisted by politically active social scientists; and the professionalization of social scientists now meant they could pursue knowledge in a disinterested scientific manner, advising industrial firms and government agencies, if called on. A few social scientists began to consult with or be hired by organizations to work in this new professional capacity. For example, the new personnel departments of large companies hired industrial psychologists to match worker aptitude to the job.

By the eve of World War II, sociology had progressed from its holistic reformist beginnings to more specialization, more emphasis on the smaller group/micro level of research, and a nonpolitical, professional role for sociologists.

The Post–World War II Years

In the post–World War II period industrial sociology had to be rediscovered, and this time it became a recognized subdiscipline. This postwar burst of interest in industrial relations in the United States saw industrial departments, institutes, and committees set up at such universities as Chicago, Yale, Cornell, California, Michigan, and Illinois (Faunce 1967:9–10). These new organizational features appear, in part, to have been a reaction to the Hawthorne studies completed by 1933 but not well reported in the literature until 1939 and 1945 (Roethlisberger and Dickson 1939; Mayo 1945), except for Mayo's short summary at the Lowell Lectures (Mayo 1960). Because of this belated influence on academia, Elton Mayo has sometimes been referred to as the father of industrial sociology, although he was not a sociologist (Faunce 1967:6). Others (Form 1979:2) grant Wilbert E. Moore, the author of the first industrial sociology text, *Industrial Relations and the Social Order* (1946), the title of father of the subdiscipline. Actually, the influences at this time came from a wide variety of sources, and the field expanded in several directions.

Postwar industrial sociology, sometimes called the sociology of work and occupations, depending on its emphasis, does not have a single definition or focus. It has grown from and contributed to a number of bodies of research. These bodies include the study of current or historical social institutions (especially the interaction of the political and economic systems), labor history, institutional economics, occupations, bureaucracy, industrial relations (the relations between employers and employees), stratification and social mobility, intra- and interorganizational structures, industrial psychology, community organization, cross-cultural comparisons of organizations and worker attributes, and economic development of Third World countries (See Miller and Form 1980:3−37; Faunce 1967:1−19; and Form 1979:1−25 for early contributors to these areas).

Not all sociologists in the post−World War II period saw the entrance of Parsons's professionalized, disinterested, scientific sociologists into the field of industrial consulting as a good thing. Sociologist C. Wright Mills (discussed later as seminal in the study of power and interest group conflicts) castigated these applied sociologists in a 1948 article (Mills 1970:11−32). In the vein of the Progressive era sociologists, he abhored the pseudoparticipation approach he felt was being taken. When it worked, it turned the workers away from real political and economic concerns. Mills felt the workers became cheerful robots rather than actual participants in decision making in the workplace (Mills 1959:171−176). Managements' agenda, not the workers', were being served. Industrial sociologists should be careful not to lend themselves to this self-serving enterprise. We return to Mills's arguments in Chapter 11 in the discussion of alternative workplace organization.

The 1980s

Where does the field of industrial sociology stand now? According to industrial sociologist William Form (1979:1) current attention in the field has "shriveled" to remnants based around the study of human beings and technology, including the interesting area of the cross-cultural impacts of technology on organizations and on worker personal attributes. (*Technology* can be defined broadly as the study of both the equipment and techniques used and the distribution of tasks involved in practical solutions to the material problems of social life.) Form here excludes the areas of complex organization, occupational sociology, and the sociology of political economy institutional relationships at home and abroad, which he seems to be classifying as other subdisciplines. This author feels these excluded areas have a place in industrial sociology, as broadly defined. Parsons accurately recognized the differentiation and division of labor proliferating in industrial societies—including academic disciplines, which splinter and lose sight of the whole. Our task here is to reintegrate these splintered parts into a larger picture.

Today, a book on industrial sociology might reflect any, never all, of these areas. British texts tend toward the social history, macro-institutional emphasis, carrying on the European nineteenth-century social history approach. Texts published in the United States often tend toward organizational analysis within the firm, industrial relations, and the sociology of occupations, following the lead of Mayo's work-group studies, the case studies of individual plants, or the more general works on organizational theory undertaken in the 1940s and 1950s. Mainstream works have not often been involved with the wider industrial society issues of power and conflict seen in some of the earlier works from the political economy approach.

In addition to these orientations in the current literature, there is a growing body of work on both sides of the Atlantic, with influences from Japan, dealing with alternative workplace organization in the context of the broader global economy. In general, these alternatives embody some form of worker participation in decision making in varying degrees. The motivation behind the experiments, research, and theorizing in decentralization varies from attempting to increase worker satisfaction, commitment, productivity, and company profits to a more activist position compatible with some Progressive era sociologists, worker participation in decisions in the workplace, or even worker ownership and control over the means of production. In the face of multinational corporations, plant shutdowns, offshore sourcing, and the influence of these corporations on domestic and foreign policy and on the development of Third World countries, some industrial sociologists have been attending to both cross-cultural studies of industries and Third World economic development literature. This broad perspective is carried throughout this book.

In this introductory text many of the areas mentioned—historical and current, and macro, mezzo, and micro (defined below) —are encountered briefly. Again, the main goal is not to explore each subject in depth, but to help the student begin to develop a broad framework and to gain some idea of the interrelationships among the parts when analyzing social structure and processes in industrial society and the ways they affect the quality of life. The reader is reminded at the outset that all chapters examine the concept of power and how it affects all levels of our society and the global economy.

INDUSTRY, WORK, AND LEISURE

This book uses the term *industry* more broadly than just the application of mechanical means of power to the production of goods. That definition, found in the older dictionaries, would limit us to the study of manufacturing. In the more broad use, an *industry* refers to any specialized area of productive work, its capital, and workers. Hence, we can speak of the steel industry, the communications industry, the education industry, the chemical industry, the banking industry, the auto industry, the fashion industry, the real estate industry, and even the agricultural industry. An industry in this sense is more than a plant or a group of firms; it also includes any associations, governmental regulatory bodies and agencies, legislation and court decisions, unions, and trade journals, for example, associated with that particular field. Remember—we are interested in all work-related features of life in industrial society.

Like the term *industry*, the word *work* has had many meanings in different times and places (See Chapters 2 and 4 for examples). For our purposes, *work* can be losely defined as the production of any good or service that has value for other people (U.S. Dept. of Health 1973:3). Note that this definition does not limit work to activity for which one receives pay, although that definition has been used many times. Our definition includes the housewife, who is not recognized by the Bureau of Census as being in the labor force and whose production of goods and services is not counted in the gross national product. It also includes the unpaid worker in a family enterprise, who is recognized as being in the labor force if working fifteen hours a week or more and whose production is added to gross national product. This definition also includes the volunteer worker.

By the same token, *leisure* is defined here as an activity that produces something of value for the individual doing it. Leisure is usually defined as a residual category, rather negatively, as "freedom from the demands of work or duty, spare time" (Funk and Wagnalls, 1958:729). These definitions of work and leisure are not entirely satisfactory since they are not mutually exclusive in many instances; the reader can quickly think of many grey areas. The motivation of the actor may muddy the waters. Is a woman who builds a doghouse on the weekend working for her dog as a duty, or is she enjoying a creative leisure pastime? Does the person who pursues a craft because he or she enjoys it but then sells the products at a little profit to an admiring buyer pursue work or leisure in the production? You might want to call these leisure activities because they are not "job-" or "occupation-" related, but are done more by unsolicited choice.

LEVELS OF ANALYSIS

Macro Level

The terms *macro*, *mezzo* or *meso* (middle), and *micro* are used here to refer to levels of analysis used by social scientists. Social scientists concentrating on the overall patterns of a culture or the social institutions are working at the *macro level* of society. A *society* or *social system* is the largest unit of analysis that shares a common social structure and culture, although it may contain subcultures with distinctive traits of their own. A *social structure* is made up of the interrelated social institutions of society. *Social institutions* are patterns of behavior in the broad problem-solving areas with which every society must deal. These broad areas include such subsystems as the economy, the political system, the educational system, the military system, the religious system, the family system, the legal-justice system, the medical system, and so forth. Chapter 2 contrasts examples of these social institutions in hunting-gathering societies and industrial societies.

Culture, a term favored more by anthropologists when studying societies than by sociologists, has been defined broadly as the way of life of a people or society. More specifically, culture includes all the material (the more concrete modes of architecture, dress, food, tools, etc.) and nonmaterial (ideas such as values, mores, social norms, and attitudes) aspects of a society passed on to subsequent generations through the use of symbols (language, gestures, writing) that have meaning for that culture.

Mezzo Level

At the *mezzo, meso,* or *middle level*, sociologists look at organizations or associations founded for specific purposes. These associations or organizations might include a school, a business firm or corporation, a church, a social club, a professional or trade association, or a government agency. They exist within the larger social institutional framework, that is, within the economic system, the political system, and the educational system.

Micro Level

For sociologists the *micro level* includes the primary and secondary groups, sometimes imbedded within an organization. A *social group* in this sense consists of people who interact frequently according to an established pattern and who usually define themselves as members of that group. This definition sets a social group apart from a collectivity, such as a theater audience or a crowd on a busy street, who are not interacting on enduring relationships with each other. Statistical categories, such as all female heads-of-household or all unemployed teenagers, are not social groups as the term is used here in that they do not interact as a unit. However, you may hear social scientists frequently use the term *group* instead of *category* because of its use in everyday language. Whether the social group is a *primary group* of family or friends interacting on emotional, personal, social bonds, or a *secondary group* that is more impersonal and utilitarian in nature, the actors will be playing *social roles* they feel are appropriate for that social group according to *social norms*, or rules, for specific situations. Every society passes on its culture by socializing its members into social norms and roles.

Groups can also be thought of as *formal* or *informal*. A department in a company may be though of as formal, in that the workers have been formally hired and interact much of the time on the basis of formally established job specifications and work routines. Informal groups can also arise within the formal setting. These groups are often based on friendship preferences.

Figure 1.1 is a brief sketch of the macro, mezzo, and micro levels of analysis.

Levels of analysis are important to keep in mind when reading about or doing research. First, understanding levels of analysis is useful in examining the problems of organizations. A simple example of this is the study of a large firm in the United States to see what is causing it to fall behind in industry competition. A case study of the internal workings of the organization, its structure, corporate culture, communications, worker commitment, productivity levels, investment in equipment and research and development, waste, quality control, and so forth, might be very enlightening. The competitive position of the single firm, however, cannot be fully understood in a vacuum. The national and perhaps international economic conditions may be the most important factors within which to understand the firm's position.

Second, knowing that there are different levels of analysis helps us understand how social structure affects our personal lives. Individuals are affected by their organizations and by the broader institutional struc-

Figure 1.1 Levels of Analysis

Society/Social System	
Macro	
Social Structure (made up of social institutions, e.g. economy, polity, education, etc.)	Culture (material and nonmaterial aspects of society passed on through symbols)

Mezzo
Organizations and Associations
(founded for specific purposes)

Micro
Social Groups (primary, secondary, and
formal or informal)
social roles
social norms/rules

ture and culture of their society. Since people interact on a face-to-face basis, it is more intuitive to place credit or blame for occurrences on the human characteristics than on the influences of more distant and less discernible social institutions. For example, in times of rising divorce rates individual marital partners might fault the personality traits of their respective spouses, rather than analyze their personal problems arising from the stresses of economic recession or the changing of cultural definitions of social roles. Some understanding of the larger picture is not only a boost for individual mental health, but it also helps an individual become a more effective problem solver in society.

OPPOSING WORLDVIEWS/*WELTANSCHAUUNGEN*

Understanding possible levels of analysis is also a first step toward understanding the worldviews (*Weltanschauungen*) or ideologies of people who attempt analyses of society—philosophers, politicians, editorial writers, the friend at the local bar, and social scientists. Behind every specific theory lies a worldview with a set of values and assumptions, sometimes unstated, on how the society operates, on the nature of human beings and what motivates them, on how the world ought to be, and sometimes on how to get to what ought to be. In fact, we all operate on such values and assumptions, whether we realize them or not. The idea of a value-free social analysis might better be replaced by an attempt to be value-aware so that social scientists and the general public would be in a more favorable position to judge what was included and what was left out in the analysis.

Western cultures have two predominant clusters of assumptions about the way societies operate, and most of us tend to lean in the direction of one of these two opposing camps. It can be argued that existentialism in the West does not fit either of these worldviews, and certainly many Eastern and pre-industrial societies have alternative systems.

Throughout this book are references to opposing views on many subjects—how political and economic power is distributed, how wages are established, the effects of multinational corporations on the United States and the Third World, and alternative theories of management and organizational structure, for example. Each side of the argument will have its own idea of the problem, studies and facts supporting its view, and recommendations for solutions as that view sees it. In a general way these alternatives are related to one or the other of the two worldviews. Two individuals using these opposing analyses of society can look at the same situation, and even the same data set, and interpret it quite differently, arriving at social policies that are contradictory in means and often in goals.

The Order/Consensus Worldview

The worldview frequently referred to as the *order/consensus* view tends to focus on problems at the micro level of analysis. This worldview contains the following five basic ideas (See Horton 1968:34–51 for expansion on some of these ideas).

1. Society is a system of interrelated parts (social institutions).

2. These interrelated parts maintain a moving equilibrium (the social institutions may change slightly to adjust to each other, but stability is maintained) and any large degree of social change is not viewed favorably.

3. Stability is kept by (a) everyone adhering to traditional social values and social norms which all agree to (consensus) or (b) functional interdependence which is imperative for individuals to survive (without collective action); the greatest good for the whole society will accrue from each individual pursuing his or her own interest according to these values and norms already in place.

4. Persons who wish to rise in the social system will be accepted when they adhere to these values and social norms.

5. If there are social problems it is because individuals have failed to learn or follow these values and norms or to pursue with sufficient motivation their own interests and may require a remedial social policy of re-education or resocialization through the intervention of professionals (educators, professional psychologists, sociologists, social workers, and so forth)—the individual or group must adapt to the on-going social system.

The emphasis in this worldview is on order, stability, or a slowly changing society always straining toward equilibrium. This view is based on individuals agreeing and adhering to an accepted set of values and behaviors while working to further their own interests. Eighteenth-century ideas from the classical economics of Adam Smith and nineteenth-century thoughts of social Darwinism (the rise in society of those who are fittest to survive) are present in this ideology. It is micro-oriented because any social problem is seen as being something amiss with the individual or his or her group, not with the structure of the social system. Therefore, the problem, the research, and the resulting social policy recommendations will be focused on changing the micro level units of individual, family, or group.

The Power/Conflict Worldview

A second worldview, often called the *power/conflict* view, which focuses on the macro social institutional level, contains the following five assumptions.

1. Society is a system of interrelated parts.
2. There is conflict among groups that have differing interests (*social categories* is a better term than *groups* unless the members recognize themselves as such and begin to interact).
3. Stability is maintained by coercion or manipulation, convincing people who have less that they are inferior and that the unequal distribution of scarce resources is fair; hence, social change in the appropriate direction (redistribution of wealth and power) is viewed favorably.
4. People of low status/less power can expect to be exploited by the more powerful who control the institutional structure—until the less powerful recognize their situation and organize to do something about it.
5. The problem is seen as not so much with people of low status—unless it is their lack of awareness and their failure to organize—but more a problem with institutional discrimination and exploitation built into the social structure; hence, the focus of remedial social policy is on changing discriminatory institutional barriers at the macro level.

This second worldview does not believe that society is self-regulating, is based on consensus, and distributes rewards on the basis or merit alone. People who hold this ideology see exploitation and manipulation of the subordinate by the dominant through the use of the latter's power to influence social institutions.

Chapter 2 summarizes some generalizations on power distribution in various types of economies and some limitations and possibilities for social organization in those economies.

PLAN OF THE BOOK

Section I examines how societies change in their general institutional structures over time, given the limits and opportunities of differing economic and technological bases. Chapter 1 has given us a common set of terms and alternative views of society. Chapter 2 reviews types of economic organization from hunting and gathering to industrial societies. We see some general patterns of social organization that can be anticipated, given a society's particular economic system. The institutional patterns discussed are basically in the political, educational, family (including male/female relationships) systems. Chapter 3 surveys the changing nature of the occupational structure and work force in the United States from an agricultural society in 1800 to a mid-1980s mature industrial society, making a few comparisons with other industrial nations. Like other social creations, management theories grow out of their time periods, and Chapter 4 traces the development of four basic types.

Section II discusses the concentration of power—political and economic—in the United States. First, in Chapter 5 we see the growth of oligopolies in the primary/core sectors of the economy and how the centralization of economic power of conglomerates across industries influences domestic public policy in the political system. Chapter 6 illustrates this centralization of power outside the United States through the influence of multinational corporations on the Third World and on U.S. foreign policy.

Section III relates several areas in which U.S. workers are affected by the distribution of power and wealth in society. Chapter 7 summarizes the history of the labor movement and the problems unions face today. Chapter 8 continues with a review of the social class structure and its varying lifestyles. Chapter 9 relates some ways in which workers' mental and physical health are affected by the influence of power over the occupational structure and health-related policies. Chapter 10 includes consideration of bureaucratic organizations and the problems for long-run economic growth that concentration and centralization of power have helped create in the political economy.

Section IV asks what can be done to alleviate the problems posed by the concentration of political and economic power in the United States. Chapter 11 outlines a number of attempts at alternative workplace organization intended to decentralize some of the decision-making power and/or ownership to the workers. Chapter 12 presents views of the future from various perspectives, including the conservative, the postindustrial liberal, and the democratic left views. The latter is particularly concerned with some decentralization of power.

SUMMARY

By now you should have some orientation as to:

1. Why this book was written and what you should get out of it. It was written to help the reader pull together a number of areas in industrial sociology and to try to construct a framework for understanding

our industrial society and its effect on the quality of life of its members. Even though the text basically focuses on the U.S. system, it also offers glimpses of Japan, other industrial nations in Europe, and the developing areas of Central America and the Caribbean.

2. A short history of the subdiscipline of industrial sociology—from where it came and its changes in orientation over time.

3. Definitions of some basic terms used in the book—*sociology, industrial sociology, work* and *leisure, levels of analysis (macro, mezzo* or *meso,* and *micro), society/social system, social structure, social institutions, organizations* and *associations, social groups, social roles, social norms,* and *culture.*

4. Assumptions behind two basic competing worldviews in western industrial societies—order/consensus and power/conflict.

5. The perspective taken in this book. The text's emphasis is on a power/conflict worldview that pays particular attention to the macro social institutional/structural relationships and how they are influenced by a concentration of power.

BIBLIOGRAPHY

Byington, Margaret. 1910. *Homestead: Households of a mill town.* New York: Russell Sage.

Cohen, Steven R. 1983. From industrial democracy to professional adjustment: The development of industrial sociology in the United States, 1900–1955. *Theory and Society* 12, 1:47–67.

Eastman, Crystal. 1910. *Work-accidents and the law.* New York: Russell Sage.

Faunce, William A., ed. 1967. *Readings in industrial sociology.* New York: Appleton-Century-Crofts.

Fitch, John A. 1911. *The steel workers.* New York: Russell Sage.

Form, William. 1979. Comparative industrial sociology and the convergence hypothesis. *Annual Review of Sociology* 5:1–25.

Funk and Wagnalls Standard Dictionary of the English Language, International Edition. S.V. "leisure."

Horton, John. 1968. "Order and conflict theories of social problems." In *Radical perspectives on social problems: Reading in critical sociology,* edited by Frank Lindenfeld, 34–51. London: Macmillan.

Mayo, Elton. 1945. *The social problems of an industrial society.* Cambridge, Mass.: Harvard University Press.

———. 1960. *The human problems of an industrial society.* New York: Viking Press (reprint of 1933 edition).

Miller, Delbert C., and William H. Form. 1980. *Industrial sociology: Work in organizational life,* 3rd ed. New York: Harper & Row.

Mills, C. Wright. 1959. *The sociological imagination.* New York: Oxford.

———. 1970. The contributions of sociology to studies of industrial relations. *Berkeley Journal of Sociology* 15:11–32 (reprint of 1948 article in *Proceedings, First Annual Conference of Industrial Labor Relations Research Association,* edited by Milton Derber. Urbana, Ill.: University of Illinois Press).

Moore, Wilbert E. 1946. *Industrial relations and the social order.* New York: Macmillan.

Perrow, Charles. 1986. *Complex organizations: A critical essay,* 3rd ed. New York: Random.

Roethlisberger, F. J., and William J. Dickson. 1939. *Management and the worker: Technical versus social organization in an industrial plant.* Cambridge, Mass.: Harvard University Press.

Tausky, Curt. 1984. *Work and society: An introduction to industrial sociology.* Itasca, Ill.: F. E. Peacock.

U.S. Department of Health, Education and Welfare. 1973. *Work in America.* Cambridge, Mass.: MIT Press.

Wachtel, Howard M. 1986. *The money mandarins: The making of a supranational economic order.* New York: Pantheon.

2

From Gemeinschaft to Gesellschaft

Among the social institutions or subsystems of any society, possibly the most important is the economic subsystem and its accompanying technology. The *economic subsystem* is how members of a society organize to produce, distribute, and consume goods and services, that is, items of vital subsistence, such as food, clothing, and shelter. Anthropologists have helped us understand this importance through the comparative study of the remains of earlier societies and the cultures of current nonindustrial societies. Historians have furthered our understanding of societies that have left written records. Other social scientists have observed complex modern societies and their social institutions and cultures. Our understanding of the importance of power relationships in a mature industrial society can be enhanced by a review of other societies with differing economic bases.

Even though many important cultural differences exist among societies with similar economic and technological bases, certain features are common in the social organization of these societies due to the limitations and opportunities provided by the nature of the economic subsystem. This influence on society by its economy has been referred to as "the long shadow of work" that falls across all areas of life, including the division of labor and specialization of tasks, the mode of family organization, social stratification, the political format, the legal-justice system, the kinds of education required for members to function in the society, and so forth.

On the other hand, economic organization is not complete destiny. Sahlins (1968:39) reminds us that in some areas where nature has been particularly bountiful, such as the fishing tribes of Northwest America, a hunting and gathering society may form more settled villages and more complex social institutions usually found in settled agricultural societies. In other cases relationships with powerful neighboring societies may also influence social organization. The need for military protection and trading strength, for example, requires more political organization than the society's economy would otherwise need.

Because of the common features in social arrangements in societies with similar economies, social scientists often use a classification system of societies for purposes of analysis that reflects the societies' modes of economic subsistence. These categories are (1) hunting and gathering, (2) horticultural and pastoral, (3) agrarian or settled agricultural, (4) preindustrial urban merchant, and (5) industrial societies.

FIVE CATEGORIES OF SOCIETIES ACCORDING TO ECONOMIC BASE

Hunting and Gathering

The Earth is four billion or more years old. Plant and animal life appeared about half a billion years ago; early humanity (hominids, which preceded modern man) appeared during the Pleistocene period 2.5 to 5 million years ago; about 2 million years ago our own genus *Homo* appeared; and our species *Homo sapiens*, about 300,000 years ago (Brace 1967:5, 60–62; Fagan 1977:29; Kottak 1982:52; Leakey and Walker 1985; Weaver 1985: 564–623). (See Table 2.1 for a timeline of events mentioned in this chapter.) For several million years hunting and gathering societies, roving in bands of fewer than fifty people, appear to have been the form of human social organization. Hunting and gathering bands were organized around the extended family, which provided all the functions of subsistence, training the young, medicine, religion, and so forth. Relatively simple but often handsomely crafted tools included stone choppers and scrapers, the spear, snares, and, perhaps 35,000 years ago, the bow and arrow. Possessions were limited to what could be easily carried.

The diet provided by hunting, gathering, or fishing varied with the environment. For most groups over the ages, the major part of the diet was probably vegetable rather than animal. Peoples of the North, however, may have relied on hunting megafauna (large animals) for as much as three-fourths of their food until the end of the last Ice Age around 8000 B.C. By 7000 B.C. most of the large animals had been decimated by climate changes, receding ice and encroaching forests, and overhunting, perhaps in an effort to keep up the standard of living with increasing population and decreasing animals (Harris 1977:21–23). In North America thirty-two genera of large animals became extinct, including horses, giant bison, elephants, oxen, pigs, ground sloths, camels, and giant rodents. Harris (1977:29) hypothesizes that the extinction of suitable draft animals became a cultural development detriment to the New World.

Table 2.1 Cultural TimeLine

4 billion years ago	Earth being formed
5–2.5 million years	Pleistocene period—early hominids
2 million years	*Homo* appears
300,000 years ago	*Homo sapiens*
12,000 B.C.	Settled villages in Middle East
8000 B.C.	End of last Ice Age
8000–3000 B.C.	Neolithic period
5000 B.C.	Irrigation in Mesopotomia
3000–1000 B.C.	Bronze Age—ox-drawn plow; 2900 B.C. Egypt unified; 1200 B.C., iron making spreads
250 B.C.–A.D. 250	Late Preclassic Mayan period
250–900 A.D.	Classic Mayan period
410 A.D.	Fall of Roman empire
500–1450 A.D.	Middle Ages in Europe
700s A.D.	Invention of stirrups
1000–1200s A.D.	Crusades; foreign trade encouraged; padded horsecollar and horseshoe for rapid plowing
1300s–1500s A.D.	Renaissance in Italy—new view of joy of work
1500s–1700s A.D.	Commercial Revolution—preindustrial urban merchant societies in Europe; exploration, foreign trade, early colonies acquired by Europeans; Reformation in Northern Europe; Protestant ethic view of work
1600s–1800s A.D.	Enlightenment
1750 A.D.	Industrial revolution begins in England.

American Indians invented the wheel for toys, but they did not have animals to harness as energy for farming and transportation and thus did not invent some of the technologies, such as the ox-drawn plow, important in the rise of complex civilizations later developed in the Old World. The complex advanced horticultural civilizations of the New World had to rely on other technologies, such as irrigation and terracing.

In general, hunters and gatherers relied on plants for their diets. The first more or less permanent villages appeared in Jordan and other Middle East sites around 12,000 B.C. These villages were situated near fields of wild grain, and plants were already a large part of the menu. In other less-favored areas, such as the Tehuacan Valley of Mexico, smaller animals were hunted to extinction as people attempted to maintain a high meat level in their food supply (MacNeish 1972).

Division of labor in hunting and gathering societies was by sex and age. Men hunted the larger animals. Women, burdened with children, gathered plants and hunted smaller game closer to camp. Children and the elderly had tasks around the camp, such as gathering firewood and preparing food and clothes. The elderly also served as "repositories of accumulated wisdom—the 'libraries' of a nonliterate people" (Haviland

1987:176). Evidence from modern hunting and gathering societies indicates little social stratification, little division of labor, and little accumulated wealth or surplus. Groups that relied on women's gathering for much of their diet may have had little inequality between the sexes. Foraging kinship systems are usually *bilateral* (kinship traced from both mother and father with inheritance from both sides). These societies have a variety of residence choices for individuals and couples. Customs regarding premarital sex, adultery, and divorce are more nearly the same for both sexes than they are in other economic systems (Kottak 1982:246).

Foraging societies made little distinction between the work and leisure. In areas with a generous environment people spent much less time on subsistence than they do in modern agricultural or industrial societies. For example, the Kuikuru of the Amazon Basin work 3.5 hours a day to meet subsistence needs (Carneiro 1961:4). The Kung San of the Kalahari Desert average 2.4 days a week in hunting and gathering and seem to stay well-nourished and healthy, since 10 percent are more than sixty years old (Harris 1983:44–45). Presumably, if they lived in a more lush environment, they would require even less effort.

Horticultural and Pastoral Societies

In the Neolithic period (8000 to 3000 B.C.) *horticulture*, using simple farming technology, and the domestication of animals were developed in the Fertile Crescent of the Near East, Mesoamerica, and Southeast Asia, spreading from there to other parts of the continents. Low-technology horticulture was once widespread and may initially have been a supplement to hunting and gathering. However, these horticulturalists were subsequently pushed off the best land and out of the more temperate zones by the encroachment of either advanced horticulturalists or settled agricultural societies with higher technology and more complex social organization. Today most horticulturalists are slash-and-burn farmers found in tropical rain forests in Oceana, the Amazon Basin, the Congo Basin, and the forests of Central America and Southeast Asia. *Milpa* is the term used for slash and burn in Mesoamerica, *ladang* in Indonesia, and *swidden agriculture* by some anthropologists.

Anthropologists feel that men, familiar with animals from hunting them, may have domesticated stock. Women, familiar with plants from gathering, probably developed agriculture. Cultivation was with simple tools—the digging stick, the ax, and later the hoe. Because the low-technology horticulturalists did not have the plow of the later settled agricultural peoples, nutrients could not be brought up from deep in the soil and weeds could not be controlled. In two to four years the crops would begin to decrease and a new patch would have to be cleared and burned. In some forest areas it might take twenty years or more for land to recuperate and gain enough second-growth vegetation to be cultivated again. The only fertilizer was the layer of ashes provided by the burning to the trees and other vegetation.

Low-technology horticulture requires societies to be more sedentary than do hunting-and-gathering groups. Small villages, usually no larger than 250 inhabitants, can lie in the center of the large area required for cultivation, given the length of time often required for rejuvenation of the land. A permanent or semipermanent residence enables the construction of better housing and the accumulation of more possessions, such as mats, pottery, tools, clothes, ritual objects, furniture, and other "neolithic kicknacks" (Sahlins 1968:31). Some domestic animals can be kept to enrich the diet. Population must usually be kept at a low density (ten people per square mile is common among forest peoples). This low density has a disadvantage in limiting communication, trade (especially if the neighboring groups are growing the same things), and more elaborate political organization. Hence, we see why low-technology horticulturalists fell easy prey to more organized and powerful economic systems.

An average adult might spend 500 to 1,000 or more hours a year in low-technology horticultural production, excluding food preparation. Men generally had the task of clearing new land, sometimes with the help of others in the community. Women often did much of the planting and weeding, and the family participated in harvesting. In many areas a hectare (2.47 acres) will feed a family of five to eight for a year. This expenditure of labor does not seem significantly different from some hunting-and-gathering societies in terms of work hours, but the more reliable food supply and the advantages of a sedentary life-style seem to have given the horticulturalists a somewhat higher standard of living.

The status of women in low-technology horticultural societies varied greatly. Martin and Voorhies (1975) found that women contributed more toward agricultural production in 41 percent of the 515 horticultural societies they studied, that men dominated cultivation in 22 percent, and that this work was shared equally in the other 37 percent. In *matrilineal* (ancestry and inheritance through the female line) societies, women dominated agriculture in 64 percent of the cases, and the *patrilineal* (kinship and inheritance through the male line) groups, women produced more in 50 percent of the cases (Kottak 1982:247). Dominating production may help women in some societies gain more equality, but other factors also are involved. The control over what is produced is also important. The matrilineal Iroquois are an example of a horticultural society in which women were able to maintain control over the distribution of what they produced, so much so that the men who served in the tribal councils were nominated and recalled at the pleasure of the matrons who headed the female clams. When women disapproved of men's plans for a long-distance war party, women withheld the food supply and the men stayed home (Harris 1977:60–61; Kottak 1982:247–248; Niethammer 1977:139–140).

Pastoral societies are groups that obtain 50 percent or more of their diet from meat and dairy products. Herders who are also horticulturalists are more sedentary. Others, such as the classic nomadic pastoralists of the semidesert and grassland regions of Asia and Africa, have given up agriculture entirely and rely on their animal herds and trading with, and raiding of, horticulturalists and settled agriculturalists. The nomads (for example, the Mongols and Turks of Inner Asia, the Bedouin of Arabia, and the Fulani of the West African savannah) appear to have taken to herding in these regions that are inhospitable to farming when the horse and camel were domesticated for carrying human beings and their belongings. This discovery made large-scale herding in these areas more feasible. Sometimes the deserts and steppes appear to have been a place to which to escape when more powerful settled agricultural civilizations threatened horticulturalists. This seems to have happened in 1500 to 1000 B.C., when pressures from an encroaching exploitative Chinese civilization drove farmers into the Inner Asia area to become nomads.

Mounted nomadic pastoralists and their herds may cover more than a thousand miles in their annual cycle between pastures and waterholes. Some contacts and agreements with other nomadic groups are necessary to decide who will be where and at what time, and warfare between these groups and on settled agricultural societies is frequent. Mobility also allows some tribal cohesion. Some tribes may elect a chief to coordinate raid and trade plans among the bands belonging to the tribe. Despite this seeming political organization, the band chiefs under the head chief remain independent and alliances are constantly shifting. These groups do not develop permanent and complex political organizations and substructures (Sahlins 1968:32–39).

Pastoralists tend to be male dominated—*patrilineal* and *patrilocal/virilocal* (the bride moves in with the husband's kin). The status of women is relatively low. Some of the Pueblo Indians, Hopi and Navajo, are matrilineal-matrilocal pastoral horticulturalists. These societies were matrilineal horticultural before the introduction of stock by incoming Europeans put them in the "pastoral fold" (Sahlins 1968:33). More usual is the social organization of the Balkan Peninsula (Greece, Yugoslavia, Albania, and Bulgaria) pastoralists. Women reside with their husband's family, isolated from their own kin, deferring to husband and his kin in all things, beaten for anything, and killed if adultery occurs (Kottak 1982:251–252).

Both low-technology horticultural and pastoral societies are able to generate more stable food supplies and surpluses than do hunting and gathering groups. Some members of the society acquire more wealth, portable wealth in the case of nomads, and a ranking system or stratification system may become apparent. Chiefs may arise, and a few specialized roles appear, such as shaman, trader, or craftworker. Warfare and the taking of slaves appear in both types of societies, now that other groups have more to steal and slaves can be put to work creating more surplus. Religious institutions become more developed than in hunting and gathering groups. Pastoralism developed a god or gods who took an active interest in the group who worshipped them—much as the shepherd tends his flock (Lenski and Lenski 1978). Judaism, Christianity, and the Islam religions all have pastoral roots.

Settled Agricultural Societies, Including Advanced Horticulturalists

Anthropologists studying the socially complex civilizations of the Old World have long felt that *settled agriculture* was made possible by irrigation and by the invention of the plow. This conclusion left some questions about how to explain the complex social organization and the population density of some New World groups who practiced various forms of intensive agriculture, such as raised fields and terracing, but were classed as horticultural societies. Late Preclassic (250 B.C. to A.D. 250) and Classic period (A.D. 250 to 900) Mayans were once thought to have been only slash-and-burn horticulturalists. However, they developed advanced civilizations in the Yucatan in Mexico, in the Peten of Guatemala, and in Belize, Honduras, and El Salvador. How could they have done this on such low-technology horticulture?

Recent fieldwork has helped resolve the question. Radar technology has detected the raised fields (soil platforms) that enabled Mayans to farm seasonally flooded lowlands. They also built canal networks, dams, and cisterns for rain water and they drained swamps and terraced the hillsides (Adams 1986:445, map 437). Intensive agriculture and, in this case, some irrigation allows for at least *advanced horticulturalist* status, even though the Mayans apparently did not form an empire with a dominant capital.

Other advanced horticulturalists are the Aztecs, who irrigated by bringing the land to the water. They built *chinampas*, or artificial islands, in the shallow lakes of the Valley of Mexico, canals, aqueducts for drinking water, and dikes (one was ten miles long). Also included in this category are their predecessors of the Teotihuacan culture, from whom the Aztec may have learned island building (Leonard 1967:39, 122).

Teotihuacan (A.D. 300 to 700) had between 50,000 to 100,000 inhabitants at its height. Tenochtitlan had 300,000 residents in the city in 1519 when Cortes arrived to plunder Aztec gold—five times the size of London at that period (Leonard 1967:66). It is possible that the earlier Olmec and Zapotec/Mixtec cultures should be in this advanced horticulture category as well. Advanced horticulturalists with intensive agriculture techniques and complex social organization have, therefore, been included in this section with settled agriculture.

In irrigation societies, initially, perhaps, people planted in areas in which seasonal flooding replenished the land's nutrients. Ditches were cut to carry water from rivers to dry areas further from the banks. Simple irrigation systems with ditches, damming and flooding, and terracing were used as early as 5500 B.C. in parts of the Fertile Crescent (Leonard 1973:135). Such small irrigation systems are still found, for example, in the American Southwest among the Pueblo Indians, in Hawaii among the Polynesians, and in many parts of Southeast Asia. Hydraulic agriculture, with elaborate canals, sluices, and clay-lined basins for trapping river water, was the basis for the early civilizations of Mesopotamia, China, Egypt, Mohenjo Daro in the Indus Valley, the Incas of Peru, and now, as noted, for some portions of Mesoamerica. An insured abundant food supply made larger permanent settlements possible, created great wealth and power for the new elite, and freed many people for tasks other than farming.

Division of labor in settled agricultural societies became more specialized, with artisans and traders found in the larger towns. Jericho, for example, had from 2,000 to 3,000 inhabitants in 7000 B.C. These societies appear not to have had much social stratification, however, until the increase in warfare and bronze weapons in the late Neolithic period (Tausky 1984:7). As warfare increased, towns became walled, and warlords, officials, and priests formed a protecting, governing elite.

Wittfogel (1957) pointed out the importance of complex political organization to administer the large hydraulic operations. Smaller irrigation systems need less central political direction. The Pueblos did not organize above the city level, and they seem to have had an underlying turbulence despite Benedict's (1934) analysis of them as entirely peaceful. Elaborate religious ceremonies calling on cooperation of all clans seem to have been useful in mitigating open hostility (Sahlins 1968:42–44). Advanced irrigation or hydraulic societies in Sumeria (modern Iraq) and Egypt are good examples of the more complex administration required by the emerging city states. By 3000 B.C. the Sumerian city of Ur had a population of around 24,000; Uruk, a populace of 20,000; and Umma, about 16,000.

At the beginning of the Bronze Age (3000 to 1000 B.C.) the wooden plow appeared, pulled by oxen who also supplied fertilizer. Pictorial word symbols from Egypt and Mesopotamia around 3000 B.C. indicate what their ox-drawn plows looked like by that time. The man-drawn plow certainly must have proceeded this. Eventually plows were equipped with a wheel in front to keep the point from digging too deeply, and a mold board was added above the plowshare to turn the soil over, add air, and bury weeds in one operation. These simple forms of the early plow are found today in developing countries and occasionally in developed countries for small jobs (Leonard 1973:140–142).

During the Bronze Age the wheel and wind power made transportation easier; writing, copper and silver money, and taxes were developed in Sumeria. Egypt was unified about 2900 B.C. and developed an elaborate theocracy, political administration, and hieroglyphic writing for keeping track of administration and business (Krader 1968:52–63). With the formation of elites in these highly stratified societies the view of physical work as degrading appeared. Manual work was for slaves and the lower classes.

When the Hittite empire (Turkey) collapsed around 1200 B.C., their secret for making iron began to spread. By 800 B.C. tools and plowshares were being made of this stronger material. When the armies of Alexander of Macedonia (Greece) conquered Sumeria and Egypt in the fourth century B.C., the combatants were armed with iron weapons.

After Rome conquered Egypt in 31 B.C., the Roman armies marched across Europe to Britain. In their wake followed Roman roads, trade, and taxes. The nobility lived well and towns grew around the manor or estate. Artisans in larger towns congregated in areas according to craft and formed mutual assistance guilds. Wages were kept low, partly because of competition from slaves. A craft shop of twenty-five freemen and slaves was large; most shops contained only one artisan with one helper. The Roman government provided bread for the increasing number of unemployed and circuses for the general population, whose purchasing power and quality of life was generally low.

By the third century A.D. civil war raged in the Roman Empire. Small farmers left the countryside for the protection of the town, and estates became self-sufficient as trade broke down. In the fourth and fifth centuries Rome was sacked twice by invading Huns, and a new era began in Europe.

The period called the Middle Ages in Europe covered a span from about 500 A.D. to 1450 A.D. Life during this period was based on the more or less self-sufficient manorial economic system already in existence and on the feudal political system of loyalty between lords and vassals. More than 90 percent of the population were serfs bound to the land; others were free persons and church officials, and 1 or 2 percent were nobility. Serfs farmed the lord's half of the land as well as their own half. They paid in kind for the use of the lord's grain mill and ovens. Each person subsisted on about 1,600 calories a day (Wolf 1966:9–10). The lot of the masses was justified by the early Church Fathers, who saw work as necessary to keep idle hands from doing evil. By the time of St. Thomas Aquinas (thirteenth century), work was an obligation with somewhat more positive qualities—"a source of grace along with learning and contemplation" (U.S. Dept. of Health 1973:1).

In the eighth century, the stirrup was added to the saddle, and mounted armored knights, now able to stay on their horses, revolutionized warfare (White 1962). By the eleventh century the horseshoe and padded horsecollar (which allowed more rapid plowing than by oxen), the heavy wheeled plow, windmills and gears, and the more efficient three-field crop rotation system were in use, freeing more people for warfare. From the end of the eleventh century to the end of the thirteenth century, the knights and their men were off on the crusades to the Holy Land.

These adventures spurred trade. Craftsmen and merchants formed *bourgs* around castles and ecclesiastical cities around cathedrals and monasteries. Craft guilds of weavers, tailors, carpenters, and shoemakers emerged to regulate hours, tools, materials, quality, and price. Trademarks of the individual artisans were required on products for easier quality checks, and fines or confiscation of goods were the penalties for failure to obey regulations. Eventually some guilds became less democratic as they fell under the control of wealthier craftsmen, and the idea of a just price gave way to making profits and charging whatever people would pay.

Despite the variety of intensive agricultural societies discussed, we can make some generalizations. Settled agricultural societies produce a surplus that allows population to grow, cities to emerge, and new social stratification to develop. New roles increase—including the king (occasionally, the queen) and his (her) bureaucrats, powerful religious leaders, traders, artists, and warriors. States come into existence, and empire building becomes possible. Advanced horticulturalists also developed human sacrifice to appease their capricious gods. It has been suggested that this ritual was an outgrowth of their experiences with the harsh realities of increased social inequality (Swanson 1960).

Settled agricultural societies tend to become male-dominant with the use of the plow. Men's production is outside in the public sphere; women's production is inside the home in the private sphere. Women have fewer rights in divorce, and their sexuality is more strictly controlled. They become dependent and subordinate. Some exceptions can be found—for example, in state societies in which a woman of the elite might occasionally wield some power and even become ruler.

Urban Preindustrial Merchant Societies—England and the United State

As the feudal ages ended with the rise of the urban merchant preindustrial society, a number of developments took place and hastened the process. The Renaissance in the Mediterranean; the Reformation in Northern Europe; the exploration of the New World and subsequent influx of gold to Europe; the rise of both stronger European states and mercantilism; the enclosure movement in England; the beginning of colonization of parts of Africa, Asia, and Latin and North America by European nations; and the development of scientific experimentation and invention during the European Enlightenment—all occurred between the fourteenth and mid eighteenth centuries.

The Renaissance (fourteenth to sixteenth centuries) was a burst of artistic and scientific activity in the prospering merchant states of Italy. To the artisans and merchants there, work was a joyous, creative activity that made life worth living. This Renaissance view of people and work was at variance with the earlier view of work as necessary pain and Heaven of where there would be no work. People such as Leonardo da Vinci—painter, sculptor, architect, scientist, musician, and natural philosopher—typified the ideal Renaissance person. Da Vinci wrote about and experimented with ideas on power-spinning looms and the turbine, which were considered amusements for the wealthy in his day, but which would be reinvented and perfected three hundred years later for mass production. With the trial and conviction of Galileo (1564–1642) for heresy, scientific activity seemed to drift from Italy toward northern Europe.

In the North, the Reformation had been taking place with Martin Luther (1483–1546) and John Calvin (1509–1564). Out of their activities grew what came to be called the Protestant ethic (Weber 1958). Work was still seen as a duty, as God's calling, but now prosperity showed that one was predestined to be among the Chosen at the right hand of God in the afterlife. Frugality and reinvestment, rather than ostentation, were also called for. This entrepreneurial activity suited mercantilism with its emphasis on increased production for export and the accumulation of gold bullion for the benefit of the coffers of the rising nation states as well as the merchants.

Merchant capitalism grew with the putting-out system or cottage industry. The merchant capitalist would hire workers to produce in their cottages, supply them with raw materials, and distribute the products. The system was particularly prevalent in Great Britain and the Low Countries. Cottage industries can be seen as an important precursor of the factory system. The worker was subject to the control of the capitalist, who set the wages and terms of employment and provided the raw materials and the market for what was produced.

In the years following the voyage of Columbus in 1492, the prosperity of Spain and Portugal from their New World colonies furthered consumer demand for northern products. In some cases gold, silver, and other valuables came north even more directly, as smuggling and buccaneering flourished in the seventeenth and eighteenth centuries. Pirates have probably been around as long as ships have sailed, the term *pirates* refers to sailors on a vessel that will attack any ship of any nationality to obtain its cargo. The buccaneers were French, English, Portuguese, and Dutch sailors who preyed on Spanish ships and on property on land in the New World in the sixteenth, seventeenth, and eighteenth centuries. Privateers are pirates who are hired or commissioned by governments to attack the ships of enemy nations. This, too, was prevalent during this time. Sir Francis Drake, working as a privateer with a royal commission, received his knighthood in 1580 from a grateful Queen Elizabeth I for circumnavigating the globe and for his successful raids on Spanish galleons and colonial towns. Later Charles II of England knighted the popular Henry Morgan after his adventures on the Spanish main and the sacking of cities in Panama and on the west coast of South America.

The collecting of dependent colonies by European states began in earnest in the seventeenth century. Anxious to enjoy the trade and status privileges that colonies had brought to Spain, England began nibbling at Spanish holdings in the Caribbean—Bermuda, Barbados, Jamaica, the Bahamas, and British Honduras (Belize). They also picked up areas in the Far East and Africa—India, Tangiers, Madagascar, the Gold Coast. The French West Indies Company, founded in the seventeenth century, gained trading spheres and colonies in Southeast Asia. Eventually, France also came to have large holdings in French West Africa.

The Dutch (the Netherlands) began their colonial holdings after they threw off Spanish rule about 1572. In 1580 Portugal and Spain had united, and the Dutch trading vessels were shut out of Spanish-Portuguese ports. The Dutch West Indies and Dutch East Indies Companies were very successful in fighting their way into these ports and establishing colonies and plantations of their own in the New World and Indonesia. Various ports of call along the trade routes were incorporated into the Dutch Empire, such as Cape Town in 1652. These companies dominated trade with the Far East until the nineteenth century.

The effects of European colonialization in Africa, Asia, and the Americas were to supply the mother countries with raw materials from the colonies using cheap native labor and also to provide outlets for marketing manufactured goods—at terms of trade favorable to the mother countries.

In England new agricultural technology (such as the seed drill), new methods of crop rotation, new animal husbandry methods, and other innovations speeded up the enclosure movement in the eighteenth century. This movement, begun in the sixteenth century, had moved slowly until technology and some entrepreneurial fervor gripped the landed aristocracy. More than 1,300 enclosure laws were passed in the period from 1790–1819 alone. The laws forced the closing of the commons and woodlots, thus removing tenant farmers and yeoman freeholders into urban areas to compete for emerging industrial jobs.

Industrial Societies—England and the United States

Industrial revolution is a term applied to the remarkable change from tools to machines and the substitution of other forms of power for animal power. Even though the word *revolution* sounds as though the change happened overnight, the changes actually were incremental. As we have discussed, the *commercial revolution* from the 1500s to the 1700s had expanded trade for foreign markets. Merchant capitalists had used the putting-out system to increase production and as early as the sixteenth century began establishing shops where they gathered fifty or sixty craftsmen or less-skilled persons and supervised them in an early form of the factory. Whereas the early wind- or water-powered mills required only a few people to tend the grinding of grain, the factory system called together a number of persons to tend looms and spindles in simple, routine jobs. For the sake of convenience, however, historians place the start of the industrial revolution in England at 1750, specifically in the textile industry. The U.S. industrial revolution occurred about 100 years later.

Several factors interacted with the increase in foreign and domestic commerce. One amazing factor was in technological innovation. The European Enlightenment of the seventeenth and eighteenth centuries, with its emphases on scientific experimentation, applied technology, rationality, and mathematical cogitation, was particularly alive in England. Before 1760 twelve new patents a year had been the average number filed. In 1761 there were thirty-one, in 1783 there were more than sixty, and in 1825 there were 250 patents filed. A partial list of inventions is impressive: John Kay's flying shuttle in 1733; Hargreaves's spinning jenny in 1764; Watt improved Newcomen's atmospheric (steam) engine in 1765; Arkwright's waterpower frame in 1769 (a factory using it in 1771 employed mostly children in the production of the first cheap calico); Crompton's spinning mule for making inexpensive muslin in 1779; Dr. Edmund Cartwright's power loom in 1785; and in 1794 Eli Whitney's cotton gin (reputed to have been designed by Katherine Greene, who could not obtain a patent in the United States because she was a woman). All of these inventions stimulated an increase in the importation of cotton and an export trade in the finished goods. Between

1720 and 1795 exports from England quadrupled. France, which was somewhat behind England in the mechanization and factory processes, managed to increase exports fivefold from 1715 to 1789.

During the same period improvements in travel abetted both trade and invention. Hard surfaces were being applied to turnpikes, and a boom in canal building occurred from 1760 to 1830, giving England 3,000 miles of these water highways. Moving raw materials, and displaced workers, to the cities and marketing products thus became easier. As the burgeoning textile factories required additional supplies of coal, iron, and steel, new inventions and processes occurred in these industries. New ideas in coal mining helped production rise from 2.5 million tons in 1700, to 10 million tons in 1800, to 57 million tons in 1861. In 1760 a blast furnace to smelt iron more cheaply was developed. Nearly 100 years later Sir Henry Bessemer developed a blast process for the steel industry and Siemens invented the open-hearth method. With these developments, steel replaced iron in industry.

Building on previous discoveries, nineteenth-century inventors made tremendous strides in transportation and communications. In the United States in 1807, Fulton, following on the heels of earlier steamboat inventors, constructed the *Claremont*, which traveled up the Hudson River to Albany. Steamships were crossing the Atlantic in 1838; the voyages of the *Sirius* and the *Great Western* took eighteen and fifteen days, respectively. Regular transatlantic service began the next year with the establishment of the Cunard Line in England. By the 1830s railroad building began to expand rapidly. In 1850 there were more than 6,500 miles of track in England, and by 1870 some 15,000 miles of track.

Many of the laws of electricity had been discovered in the eighteenth century; it thus was not surprising that the electric telegraph was invented independently by a German, an American, and an Englishman at about the same time in the 1830s. Samuel F. B. Morse, the American, went on to patent his invention and organize his own company. By 1851 more than fifty companies using Morse telegraph equipment were operating in the United States, and within ten years the Morse telegraph was found throughout Europe. By 1866 the first transatlantic cable was in place between England and the United States, and soon all major areas around the world were connected. In 1899 Marconi's wireless, using radio waves first discussed in the 1860s, made communications even easier.

The turn of the century also saw the spread of another important social change agent—the automobile. In 1903 the Wright brothers made their successful flight at Kitty Hawk, North Carolina, and the era of the airplane began.

By the late nineteenth century what some people refer to as the second industrial revolution was taking place. On the social side the deplorable conditions in early factories, mines, and urban slums were being addressed by many social reformers in England and the United States, and, eventually, by government regulations. Three-fourths of the workers in the early textile mills in both England and New England had been women and children. Early deaths of many indigent children stirred protests. The conditions of women and children in the mines also demanded reform. Women were hired in place of dray animals to pull heavy coal carts because it was cheaper to hire a woman than to feed a horse. Children were used to retrieve coal from tunnels too small for men to crawl into (Deckard 1983:210).

Unions had been organizing since the early days of industrialization in an attempt to shorten working hours and to improve working conditions and wages. The bust period of recurring business cycles added to the difficulties of organizing and holding gains made in the boom periods when workers were in demand. These unions were unlike earlier guilds in that union members were hired labor, not craftpersons working in their own shops. Chapter 7 presents a short picture of the labor movement in the United States.

Public education was becoming more available as the occupational structure began to shift from agriculture to urban blue- and white-collar employment. A literate and disciplined workforce became desirable to employers. A discussion of the shift in occupations and the changing nature of the workforce in the United States continues in Chapter 3.

Related to the interest of government (mentioned above) in some social reform and public education was the spread of the franchise (the right to vote) from the propertied owners to all men by the end of the Civil War in the United States. In England it was 1918 before this right was extended to all men at age twenty-one, even men without property, and to all women at thirty years of age. In 1920 women in the United States gained the vote in all elections. Lipset (1959:48−75) feels that stability in politically democratic societies is made increasingly likely by industrialization, where a high standard of living for all members is made possible by mass production and there is a large middle class. Other social scientists argue that even though these societies are formally democratic, the influence of elite classes continues the oligarchic tradition popular in some nonindustrial societies. Chapter 5 summarizes these debates, and Chapter 8 examines the shape of the class structure in the United States.

Businesses in England and the United States grew increasingly larger in the nineteenth and twentieth centuries, encouraged by mass production and marketing technology and the increasing cost of fixed capital and made possible by new forms of organization, such as the joint-stock company and growth of financial establishments. In the United States there were virtual monopolies in petroleum, steel, and rails by the end of the nineteenth century. In the twentieth century oligopolies (three to seven firms controlling more than half of their industry's market) have added to economic concentration in chemicals, electronics, communications, automobiles, rubber, and copper, among other industries.

Since World War II giant conglomerates with subsidiaries and holdings in diverse products and services have developed and done much to centralize power across the economy. Along with the growth in size of organization in the late nineteenth-century United States came a professionalization of management and schools in which to train them. These points are picked up again in Chapter 4, which discusses theories of management and the social conditions out of which they appeared, and in Chapter 5, which discusses economic and political power.

Another feature of industrial societies that affects the family is the phenomenon of *demographic transition*. In societies that have already industrialized, it has been noted that initially a population increase has accompanied industrialization. This increase is due to a fall in the death rate, attributable to improved sanitation, medical care, and diet. Family size does not immediately change, hence more members of society live to adulthood and reproduce. Eventually, however, as people become increasingly urban, as expectations for the standards of living and education rise, as social security systems for the elderly are introduced, children began to be seen as an economic liability rather than an economic asset. People have fewer children. To state this in a less negative way, parents tend to become more interested in their children's quality of life and thus begin to limit the size of their families. This decline in birthrate is somewhere near the death rate level, slowing the rate of population growth. In some industrial societies at some periods this has meant zero population growth or even negative growth—people are not replacing themselves and the population is declining in numbers.

Finally, industrial societies accentuate the dichotomy between the public sphere of office and factory and the private sphere of home. When the farm or cottage is no longer the scene of basic production—the *domestic mode of production*—the status of women as economic producers declines. There are no matrilineal industrial societies. Even though industrial societies are frequently *bilineal* (inheriting and tracing lineage from both sides of the house), they are also patriarchal in varying degrees.

GEMEINSCHAFT AND *GESELLSCHAFT*

The previous broad classifications of societies by their economic and technological subsystems presents a general social evolution pattern. By this pattern, anthropologists are calling to our attention that through new technology and social adaptations societies tend to become more complex over time. Individual societies can be forced to back track from more complex to simpler organization through ecological failure or conquest by a more powerful society.

Looking at the earlier forms in comparison to industrial society, there seems to be a dichotomy—bridged perhaps by the preindustrial urban merchant societies that have the beginnings of some industrial patterns. In 1887 German sociologist Ferdinand Toennies (1855–1936) described these differences, labeling them *Gemeinschaft* and *Gesellschaft* (Toennies 1957). *Gemeinschaft* societies are based on communal and kinship relationships. The small group is intimate and face-to-face, shares common values, and operates on tradition and custom. The extended kinship group provides all of life's necessities. There is little division of labor, as people in the same gender and age group perform the same tasks. There is little status difference; roles are usually ascribed, although there are exceptions, such as the achieved headman position in many hunting-gathering societies and in some tribal and horticultural groups. Group membership, patrilineal or matrilineal, on which these types of societies are based is also ascribed.

Gesellschaft societies are based on association. Communal and kinship loyalty gives way to individualism. Contacts are mostly impersonal as an individual plays a different role in each association belonged to. These associations perform the functions the family once provided— economic, political, social, religious, educational, health, and so forth. Cohesion on traditional values is no longer taken for granted in the large, complex industrial society; subcultures, other ethnic groups, social classes, and other religions now crosscut the solidarity of values and even of some behavioral norms. Laws must be written and enforced to ensure that everyone knows what is expected. Governments and other agencies such as media and education work at creating common identities and beliefs for members of the society. Division of labor is highly specialized, and myriads of jobs and social statuses call for efforts toward individual achievement of one's position.

Other writers have observed this dichotomy and given it different names. French sociologist Emile Durkheim (1858–1917) referred to it as *mechanical* and *organic solidarity*, emphasizing that the common values and roles that held society together have been replaced by specialized roles held together by dependency, much as the organs of the body rely on each other to perform their functions. American anthropologist Robert Redfield (1897–1958) called these differences *folk* and *urban*, emphasizing the personal versus impersonal relationships of the traditional countryside and the city, respectively. American sociologist Howard Becker (1899–1960) used the terms *sacred* and *secular* to denote the change in solidarity from common belief in traditional ways supported by religion to a more rationalized, self-interested, science-oriented willingness to experiment, to change, and to entertain a variety of possible values.

A negative tone is evident in some of these earlier writers. Toennies and Durkheim, writing in the nineteenth century, were observing problems caused by early industrialization and were concerned that the rapid social change would cause societies to fly apart—that the common value center "would not hold."

The questions may now be: What next? Chapter 12 addresses future possibilities given the current late twentieth-century situation. Here we note that attempts at supranational organizations above the nation-state have appeared more frequently in the twentieth century. At the global level the League of Nations, followed by the United Nations, were attempts by nations to take action on common concerns. Various regional associations (the European Economic Community, the Organization of American States, and Organization of African States, for example) have arisen and sometimes fallen. In addition, private profit or nonprofit international groups have also appeared. Examples of these groups include the World Council of Churches, Amnesty International, international trade union organizations, and the Trilateral Commission. In the last quarter of the twentieth century, we have seen an increase in multinational corporations from different countries joining each other in joint ventures such as General Motors and Toyota. These supranational organizations represent an addition to the list of ongoing general social evolution.

SUMMARY

1. Human societies can be categorized according to their economic and technological subsystems as:
   a. Hunting and gathering: small bands of foragers organized around kinship; little division of labor except by gender and age; simple tools; little social stratification.
   b. Horticultural and pastoral: domestication of plants and animals; more permanent villages for horticulturalists; simple digging stick and hoe tools; slash-and-burn cultivation techniques; more division of labor with some specialization of tasks, such as potter; agricultural surplus possible; some social stratification may begin to appear; horticultural societies may be either matrilineal or patrilineal; pastoralists can also accumulate degrees of portable wealth; some social stratification and chieftanships may arise; warfare among nomadic pastoralists common; pastoralists tend to be patrilineal; religions with a god or gods who intervene in human affairs may arise.

    c. Settled agricultural, including advanced horticulture: advanced horticulture (classified by some anthropologists with the horticultural and pastoral, as discussed above) identified with intensive agricultural techniques, such as raised fields and terracing, but can develop complex social organization, including the state, similar to settled agriculture; settled agriculture made possible by plow and/or irrigation; more dependable food surplus freeing many for urbanization and other occupations; accumulation of wealth; social stratification increases; complex political, economic, military, and religious bureaucracies may arise; development of crafts, trade, writing, coinage, the arts; public construction of irrigation systems and monuments; female—male inequality may be underlined with paid production outside the home and use of new technology by males.

    d. Urban preindustrial merchant: increases in trade, science and technology, urbanization, exploration, and rise of the nation-state during the Renaissance; Reformation, Enlightenment, and colonization periods in Europe, allowing increased division of labor, complexity of social organizations, and generally inequality between the sexes.

    e. Industrial: increases in growth rate of science and technology in production, transportation, and communications; introduction of the factory; growth in size of businesses, financial capitalism, oligopolies, professional management, unions, government intervention in commerce, urbanization, private versus public spheres in male—female inequality, and the occurrence of a demographic transition.

2. *Gemeinschaft* and *Gesellschaft*: Attention has been called to a dichotomy in social organization and relationships between societies based on *Gemeinschaft* (communal, personal, and seemingly immutable traditional relationships) with *Gesellschaft* (industrial, rationalized, impersonal, associational/contractual relationships).

BIBLIOGRAPHY

Adams, Richard E. W. 1986. Rio Azul: Archaeologists explore Guatemala's lost city of the Maya. *National Geographic* 169, 4:420—450 (April).

Benedict, Ruth. 1934. *Patterns of culture*. Boston: Houghton Mifflin.

Brace, C. Loring. 1967. *The stages of human evolution: Human and cultural origins*. Englewood Cliffs, N.J.: Prentice-Hall.

Carneiro, Robert L. 1961. "Slash and Burn Cultivation Among the Kuikuru and its implications for cultural development in the Amazon Basin." The evolution of horticultural systems in native South America: Causes and Consequences. *Antropologica*, Supplement number 2, edited by Johannes Wilbert.

Deckard, Barbara Sinclair. 1983. *The women's movement: Political, socioeconomic, and psychological issues*, 3rd ed. New York: Harper & Row.
Fagan, Brian M. 1977. *People of the Earth: An introduction to world prehistory*, 2nd ed. (formerly *Men of the Earth*). Boston: Little, Brown.
Fried, Morton H. 1967. *The evolution of political society: An essay in political anthropology.* New York: Random.
Harris, Marvin. 1977. *Cannibals and kings: The origins of cultures.* New York: Random House.
———. 1983. *Cultural anthropology.* New York: Harper & Row.
Haviland, William A. 1987. *Cultural anthropology*, 5th ed. New York: Holt, Rinehart, and Winston.
Kottak, Conrad Phillip. 1982. *Cultural anthropology*, 3rd ed. New York: Random House.
Krader, Lawrence. 1968. *Formation of the state.* Englewood Cliffs, N.J.: Prentice-Hall.
Leakey, Richard, and Alan Walker. 1985. *Homo Erectus* unearthed. *National Geographic* 5:624–27 (November).
Lenski, Gerhard, and Jean Lenski. 1978. *Human societies*, 3rd ed. New York: McGraw-Hill.
Leonard, Jonathan Norton, and the editors of Time-Life Books. 1967. *Ancient America.* (Great Ages of Man Series). New York: Time-Life Books.
———. 1973. *The First Farmers.* (Emergence of Man Series). New York: Time-Life Books.
Lipset, Seymour Martin. 1959. *Political man.* Garden City, N.Y.: Doubleday.
MacNeish, Richard. 1972. *The prehistory of Tehuacan Valley*, vol. IV. Austin: University of Texas Press.
Martin, M. Kay, and Barbara Voorhies. 1975. *Female of the species.* New York: Columbia University Press.
Niethammer, Carolyn. 1977. *Daughters of the Earth: The lives and legends of American Indian women.* New York, NY: Collier (Macmillan).
Sahlins, Marshall D. 1968. *Tribesmen.* Englewood Cliffs, N.J.: Prentice-Hall.
Swanson, Guy E. 1960. *The birth of the gods.* Ann Arbor: University of Michigan Press.
Tausky, Curt. 1984. *Work and society: An introduction to industrial sociology.* Itasca, Ill.: F. E. Peacock.
Toennies, Ferdinand. 1957. *Community and society (Gemeinschaft und Gesellschaft)*, translated and edited by Charles P. Loomis. New York: Harper Torchbooks/Harper & Row. (First edition in German, 1887.)
U.S. Department of Health, Education and Welfare. 1973. *Work in America*: Report of a Special Task Force to the Secretary: Cambridge, Mass.: MIT Press.
Weaver, Kenneth F. 1985. The search for our ancestors: Stones, bones, and early man. *National Geographic* 5:561–23 (November).
Weber, Max, 1958. *The Protestant ethic and the spirit of capitalism*, translated by Talcott Parsons. New York: Charles Scribner's Sons.
White, Lynn, Jr. 1962. *Medieval technology and social change.* London: Oxford.
Wittfogel, Carl A. 1957. *Oriental despotism.* New Haven: Yale.
Wolf, Eric. 1966. *Peasants.* Englewood Cliffs, N.J.: Prentice-Hall.

3

The United States from 1800 to 1985: Changes in Occupational Structure and the Labor Force

In the previous chapter we gained some idea of the changes taking place in technology, urbanization, communications, organization, education, and family size in England and the United States during their industrial revolutions. In Chapters 4 and 7 we return to look at this period from the points of view of management theory and of labor history. This chapter deals in a general way with some of the changes in the U.S. occupational structure and in the characteristics of the work force from 1800 to the present.

OCCUPATIONAL STRUCTURE AND EMPLOYMENT, EDUCATION, AND EARNINGS OF THE WORK FORCE

Occupational Structure Since 1800

At the beginning of the nineteenth century, the United States was still largely an agricultural society. Approximately 73 percent of the work force was engaged in agriculture. An early factory in the United States was build in 1815 at Lowell, Mass., by Francis Cabot Lowell, who had brought the plans for a textile mill from England. As we have discussed, the majority of the early mill workers were women and children, the women typically receiving one-fourth to one-half of men's wages. Industry continued to grow during the 1800s, particularly during and after the Civil War. The division of labor (specialization) increased in both manu-

facturing and in white-collar occupations. This specialization has proceeded so far that today the *Dictionary of Occupational Titles* lists more
than 20,000 occupations. Accurate statistics on occupations and industrial sectors before 1890 are not available (the Bureau of the Census
began the decennial census in 1890). However, some estimates have
been made from the earlier, less systematic censuses. Figure 3.1 approx-
imates the distribution of the labor force in three broad categories.

The three industrial groupings in Figure 3.1 can be divided into what
economists call the *goods-producing industries*, which contain the primary and secondary sectors, and *service-producing industries* of the tertiary sector. The goods-producing industries include such areas as farming, fishing, lumbering, mining, manufacturing, and construction. The
service-producing industries include all other occupations; that is, people who produce services, such as lawyers, insurance, real estate dealers,
salespeople, and so forth, in the private sector, and also the public service sector, which contains government workers, most of whom produce
services under the broad definition of the term.

Table 3.1 divides the occupational structure somewhat differently,
into four categories rather than three, and mixes broad occupational categories ("white-" and "blue-collar") with more industrial headings
("farm" and "service"). The "farm" category is similar to the primary
sector in Figure 3.1, but without fishing and lumbering. The "blue-
collar" category contains basically the blue-collar workers of the secondary sector, but includes some services, such as transportation.

The tertiary sector has been divided into "white-collar" and "service." The category of "service" as used by the Census Bureau in Table
3.1 includes private domestic service and a few of the "nonprofessional"
services, such as waiters, dishwashers, cooks (bakers are counted as
skilled workers), guards, porters, barbers, beauticians, fire fighters, police (despite the fact that many have undergraduate and graduate degrees), practical nurses (who have less certification than registered
nurses), and so forth. This "service" category contains only a small part
of what economists and the Bureau of Labor Statistics call the "service
industries" that we saw in the tertiary sector of Figure 3.1. Some of the
confusion can be resolved if you remember that the Bureau of the Census has tried to divide blue-collar service, which they call "service,"
from "white-collar," most of which is also in the service sector.

Looking at both Figure 3.1 and Table 3.1, we can see some major
shifts in occupations. After the rise of manufacturing in the last half of
the nineteenth century, the blue-collar work force remained fairly stable
at well over one-third of the work force, until it began a decline in the
late 1960s. The decline is expected to continue in heavy manufacturing
and mining, where the better paid blue-collar jobs have been. Overall,
this blue-collar category is shifting in structure. Some of the slack in

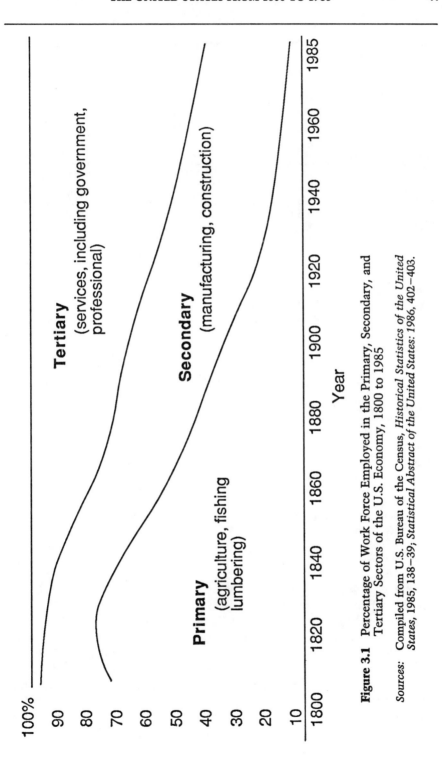

Figure 3.1 Percentage of Work Force Employed in the Primary, Secondary, and Tertiary Sectors of the U.S. Economy, 1800 to 1985

Sources: Compiled from U.S. Bureau of the Census, *Historical Statistics of the United States, 1985*, 138–39; *Statistical Abstract of the United States: 1986*, 402–403.

Table 3.1   Employed Persons Sixteen Years of Age and Older, by Occupational Group, 1800 to 1984, and Projections for 1995

	White Collar: prof., tech., mgrs., clerical, sales		Blue Collar: crafts, operators, trans., nonfarm labor		Service: barbers, fire, domestics		Farm: owners, farm labor	
	Total (000)	%	Total (000)	%	Total	%	Total	%
1800[a]	na		57	3.0	40	2.1	1,400	73.7
1820	72	2.9	349	14.0	110	3.5	2,500	79.6
1840	183	3.8	881	18.4	240	4.2	3,600	73.6
1870	1,191	9.5	2,707	21.6	1,000	7.7	6,800	61.2
1900	5,115	17.6	10,401	35.8	2,626	9.0	11,700	37.6
1910	7,962	21.4	14,234	38.2	3,562	9.6	11,800	28.6
1920	10,529	24.9	16,974	40.2	3,313	7.9	10,800	27.0
1930	14,320	29.4	19,272	39.6	4,772	9.8	10,600	21.2
1940	16,082	31.1	20,597	39.8	6,069	11.7	9,600	17.4
1950	21,601	36.6	24,266	41.1	6,180	10.5	7,900	11.8
1960	28,522	43.4	24,057	36.6	8,023	12.2	6,000	7.8
1970	38,024	48.3	27,807	35.3	9,719	12.4	3,100	4.0
1980	51,882	52.2	31,452	31.7	13,228	13.3	3,100	2.8
1982	53,470	53.7	29,597	29.7	13,736	13.8	2,700	2.7
1984	57,334	54.6	29,921	28.5	14,151	13.5	3,600	3.3
1995[b]	66,971	52.5	37,376	29.3	20,793	16.3	2,550	1.9

Sources: Compiled from U.S. Bureau of the Census, *Historical Statistics of the United States: Colonial Times to 1970*, 138–139; *Statistical Abstract of the United States: 1986*, 1985, 402–403.

[a]**1800**   1,900,000 total labor force (1,370,000 free and 530,000 slave). Note that the 19th century occupational categories are not strictly comparable, since industries are moved from one broad classification to another with each census.

[b]**1995**   Projections from U.S. Bureau of Labor Statistics, *Handbook of Labor Statistics*, December 1983; Ritzer and Walczak, *Working: Conflict and Change*, 3rd ed., 22.

na not available

this category may be picked up by light manufacturing, high tech and defense industries, and transportation; short-run projections to 1995 are for some leveling off of the decline (Kutscher and Personick 1986).

As the farming sector began contracting from more than one-third of the work force at the turn of the century, the white-collar category expanded. Service, with the narrow Census Bureau definition, held fairly steady in this century but is growing slowly as a percentage of the labor force and is expected to increase in the foreseeable future. White-collar and service together, a loose approximation for the tertiary sector in Figure 3.1, represent more than two-thirds of all occupations and are expected to continue expanding in the future. This expansion may be slowing as a loss in real income and the baby bust period of 1965 to 1979 produce some drop in demand (Newton 1987). As we can see by adding white collar and service in Table 3.1, almost 70 percent of the new jobs projected between 1984 and 1995 are in the tertiary sector, and a more recent Department of Labor revision places the figure at nearly 90 percent (Rudolph 1986:58). The news is not all good, however. As the blue-collar and secondary sectors shift in nature and as jobs increase in the service sector, which includes white-collar workers, we get some mixed reports on what is happening.

What does this mean for today's worker? Your first thought probably was, "Don't plan on farming for a living." The second thought might have been, "What is happening to the goods-producing sector?" Or, stated another way, "Are we all going to be engaged in providing services for each other for a living?" More important for both workers and society, "Will I be able to maintain middle-class status in both occupation and income?" What does this mean for the quality of life in the United States for the average person?

People who look at occupational status find shifts out of occupations that have been traditionally lower status (blue-collar) into traditionally higher status (white-collar) ones. People who look at earnings find the bad news. Many of the traditionally better paying occupations are declining in median weekly earnings (McMahon and Tschetter 1986). In other words, the jobs being created in the largest numbers in both the goods- and service-producing sectors in the 1970s and 1980s are lower paid. For example, median earnings by some industrial categories in 1985 were as follows: service (narrow definition) $262.44; retail trade $174; eating places (excluding tips) $109.98; manufacturing $394.23; construction $467.31 (Newton 1987:78). In fact, 44 percent of the jobs created between 1979 and 1985 paid poverty-level wages and only 10 percent paid $29,000 or more (Bluestone and Harrison 1987:15).

Researchers warn us to be aware of the possible effects of the business cycle and of the entrance into the work force of baby-boomers and women. The new entrants to the work force have less experience and might account for some for the lowered earnings. This is the optimistic view. Other researchers note that since 1979 three-quarters of the jobs taken by white men, not all new entrants, were at "the low end of the spectrum" (Bluestone and Harrison 1987:15). We comment on women's wages later in this chapter, on the effects of plant shutdowns on workers in Chapter 6, and on the possible implications for the social class structure in Chapter 8.

Before we continue discussing jobs and workers in the United States, let us satisfy our curiosity as to how the United States compares in terms of occupational distribution with some other industrial countries. Table 3.2 lists four broad categories similar, but not identical in all respects, to the categories in Table 3.1.

From Table 3.2 it is clear that no matter what other differences exist in their economies, industrial nations share a marked similarity in occupational distribution among broad sectors of their economies. The agricultural sector has noticeably shrunk with the mechanization of agriculture—keep in mind that "agriculture" in this table also includes forestry, hunting, and fishing.

In the data set from which Table 3.2 was taken, figures were given for all countries from 1960 to 1982. During this twenty-two year period, some countries had definite shifts out of agriculture. Japan, for example, dropped from 29.5 percent of the labor force in agriculture in 1960 to the 9.4 percent shown in Table 3.2; France went from 23.2 percent to 8.6 percent; Italy declined from 32.5 percent to 12.4 percent. Manufacturing by itself accounts for less than 30 percent of jobs in all countries except West Germany. All countries except Japan (up 3 percent) and Italy (up 1.9 percent) lost percentage points in manufacturing in the twenty-two years, although West Germany lost less than 1 percent. The average loss was 6 percent. The service sector, which uses the broad definition of the term we recognized as similar to the tertiary sector in Figure 3.1, is more than half of the jobs in all countries, with the United States

Table 3.2   Occupational Distribution of Workers in Ten Industrial Countries, by Percentage in 1982

	Services[a]		Manufacturing[b]		Mining, Construction		Agriculture[c]	
U.S.	69.2%		20.4%		6.8%		3.6%	
Canada	69.3		18.2		7.2		5.3	
Australia	64.8	('81)	19.6	('81)	9.0	('81)	6.5	('81)
Japan	56.0		24.7		9.8		9.4	
France	57.1	('81)	25.1	('81)	9.3	('81)	8.6	('81)
Germany (F.R.)	52.7		33.7	('81)	8.1		5.5	
Great Britain	62.4	('81)	26.7	('81)	8.1	('81)	2.8	('81)
Italy	50.4		25.9		11.3		12.4	
Netherlands	64.3	('81)	20.9	('81)	8.9	('81)	5.9	('81)
Sweden	64.9		22.5		6.9		5.6	

Source: Complied from U.S. Bureau of Labor Statistics, *Handbook of Labor Statistics*, 1983, 424–425.

[a] Services: Includes transportation, communication, public utilities, trade, finance, public administration, private household services, and miscellaneous services.

[b] Manufacturing: Includes only manufacturing; excludes mining and construction.

[c] Agriculture: Includes agriculture, forestry, hunting, and fishing.

and Canada leading, approaching 70 percent. This sector is growing decidedly in all countries. The average growth in the service sector for the twenty-two-year period was nearly 15 percent. The range was from a low of 10 percent in Australia to a high of 20.8 percent in Sweden. Government services may account for some of this growth, but this cannot be verified from this particular data collection.

Minorities' Work

From an overview of the occupational distribution in the United States and a comparative perspective of distribution and changes in other industrial societies, we now look more closely at who gets what jobs in the United States. Table 3.3 looks at jobs held by whites and by two of the minority groups in the United States, blacks and Hispanics. *Minorities* in the social science meaning of that term refers to groups that have less power in the society, are identifiable by physical or cultural differences, and have received unequal and unfair treatment by the groups that dominate the society's social institutions. *Minority* here does not refer to size of group. For example, under this definition, women have been referred to as a minority, even though they outnumber men. By the same definition, blacks in South Africa are a minority, even though they comprise about three-fourths of the population.

By looking at the percentage of the group in the total work force at the top of Table 3.3, we can get an idea of how underrepresented or overrepresented the group is in each occupational category. A quick look reveals that in the more highly skilled jobs and farm ownership, whites are overrepresented. In the lower-skilled and labor jobs, minorities are overrepresented. These facts probably are not surprising, but it is interesting that this is the case after more than twenty years of increases in years of education for minorities, affirmative action, and various manpower programs.

The question of why so many minorities (including women) seem stuck in low-status, low-skilled, and/or low-paying jobs is discussed next. There are opposing views on how this has happened.

Women's Work

We note in the previous chapter that when industrial societies turn from the domestic mode of production on the farm or in the cottage, a sharp status distinction appears between the public sphere of the factory and office and the private sphere of the home. As England and the United States began to industrialize, the patriarchal cultures fostered the idea that a woman's place was in the home. Actually, there was also

Table 3.3 Occupational Distribution of White, Black, and Hispanic Workers, by Percentages, 1984

	White	Black	Hispanic	
Total labor force: (105,005,000 workers)	84.2%	9.6%	6.2%	
White collar:	88.8	7.0	4.2	100%
Prof., tech.	90.2	6.7	3.1	100%
Mgr.	91.5	5.0	3.5	100%
Clerical	84.2	10.2	5.6	100%
Sales	90.5	5.0	4.5	100%
Blue Collar:	80.3	11.2	8.5	100%
Skilled	85.6	7.2	7.2	100%
Semiskilled	76.2	14.3	9.5	100%
Laborer	75.0	14.8	10.2	100%
Service:	74.5	17.5	8.0	100%
Domestic	59.7	30.3	10.0	100%
Other service	74.9	16.8	8.3	100%
Farm:	82.1	7.7	10.2	100%
Farmers	97.9	1.0	1.1	100%
Laborers	70.8	12.2	17.0	100%

Source: Compiled from U.S. Bureau of the Census, *Statistical Abstract of the United States: 1986*, 1985, 402–403.

a very practical reason for someone's needing to stay home in those days—the tremendous amount of time and effort necessary to produce goods and supply the services for the home. Unless the family was well-off and could afford to hire help, the wife was busy making clothes, hauling water, firing up the stove, scrubbing on the washboard, hanging clothes out to dry, heating the heavy iron on the fire and ironing with it, trimming and cleaning the lamps, baking bread, canning, pickling, preserving, and sometimes growing the food if there were a backyard. Then there were the children—and no day-care centers. It was nearly the end of the nineteenth century before technological changes in the home and mass retailing in department stores lightened the housekeeping burden. Meanwhile, the man's place was seen as in the public sphere, earning a living for his wife and children.

Other factors besides the time-consuming nature of housework also fed the cultural ideal/stereotype of women and their place in the home. Under English common law, as explained by Blackstone in his *Commentaries on the Laws of England* published in 1765, the wife's identity disappeared on her marriage—she became a *femme couvert* or *couvert-baron*, under the protection and influence of her husband, her baron, or lord. During her marriage her condition is called her *couverture*. She and the children, and any property she brought with her to the marriage, became the property of the husband. The children stayed with the husband in the case of a divorce. One odd side effect of this situation was that the husband was responsible before the law for his wife's actions, except for murder and treason. The legal point was that she was a part of him, but since he did the thinking for both of them he had to control her. If she transgressed, he was liable, much in the way that parents are sometimes liable today under contract law for the actions of their minor children.

In addition to being almost a nonperson under the law, married women also received a negative image from the medical profession. Doctors promoted the image of women as frail, delicate, and not rational once a month. Obviously, women were too emotional and unstable to be trusted with duties in the public sphere—either working in responsible positions or voting. Apparently many middle- and upper-class women who patronized doctors took advantage of the sick role as well as of the new methods of birth control. The birth rate dropped for these groups in the second half of the century. The declining birthrate of middle- and upper-class women seems to have led, in part, to the passage of the Comstock Law in 1873, which outlawed the dissemination of birth control information and devices. The bill was backed by the American Medical Association (AMA) and the Young Men's Christian Association (YMCA).

We have noted that patriarchal societies are very restrictive of women's sexuality and hold to a double standard for men and women. The last half of the nineteenth century, the Victorian era, enforced this cultural value. (This time was also rife with pornography and child prostitution.) During this period, England and the United States were particularly circumspect about sex and women had to be exceedingly careful of their reputations. Young women who did work outside the home were expected to quit when they married. Black women and poor immigrant women often worked all their lives, black women as domestics, immigrant women as domestics or factory workers. However, working was not respectable in the cultural ideal/stereotype of the family roles of the day, and few American-born white married women were in the paid labor force, no matter how poor they were.

Given these expectations on appropriate roles for men and women, the historical occupational differences between men and women in industrial society are not difficult to understand. Most of the early textile workers were young New England farm girls working until marriage and motherhood. Later, in the 1840s and 1850s, the mill workers were immigrant women and children. The Civil War allowed a few women into new fields (running the family business or the farm, for example), but most returned to the home after the war. Women also entered the professions of teaching and nursing during the Civil War, and they stayed with these fields—to the point that these are now traditional women's jobs.

By 1900 we see in Table 3.4 that more than 8 percent of working women were in the professional/technical category. A few women had entered professional schools, such as medicine, alongside men. Six percent of the doctors in 1900 were women. (Historical notes: A few women had been in the field for a while; the first white woman doctor was Elizabeth Blackwell, M.D. 1849, and Rebecca Lee became the first black woman physician in 1864. By 1890 there were 155 black women doctors.) Most of the professional women were not in men's professions, however, but were public school teachers, nurses, and, as of the reform era around the turn of the century, social workers—the low-paying professions. More than half of the women employed outside the home were still in the familiar categories of factory worker (23.8 percent) and domestics (28.7 percent).

Looking at the participation rates for women in the labor force for this period (Table 3.5), we see 20 percent of women over sixteen years of age were counted as employed. *Labor force participation rates* are the percentage of a particular category in the working years—usually sixteen to sixty-five years of age—who are employed or actively seeking work. Then, as now, this is undoubtedly an undercount since it does not include all the piece-rate workers in the home or the illegal shops that avoid reporting to the government. The undercount also includes persons who work only an hour a week as fully employed and workers who have become discouraged and have not looked for a job in four weeks. The Center on International and Public Affairs in New York City estimated the number of people who wanted jobs and could not find them at twice the official rate of 7 percent in 1986, including 5.6 million discouraged workers (Strautmanis 1987). This undercount is probably highest for marginal workers, who include minorities, many immigrants, and women.

For women workers the big shifts in employment in this century are apparent in Table 3.4. The typewriter had just been introduced in the late part of the nineteenth century and the manufacturer had trained young women to demonstrate how easy it was to use. Until that time office workers had been men, who could rise from the position of clerk into administration, if they were apt. Into the office with the typewriter came the young women. As office jobs expanded with growing corporations and governmental agencies, women's jobs in this area increased so

Table 3.4 Occupations by Sex in Percentages, 1900, 1950, 1980, and 1984

Occupation	Men				Women			
	1900	*1950*	*1980*	*1984*	*1900*	*1950*	*1980*	*1984*
White Collar:	17.6	30.0	40.9	44.2	17.8	51.1	65.6	68.1
Prof. & tech.	3.4	7.1	13.3	14.4	8.2	12.0	16.6	17.3
Mgr.	6.8	10.3	12.1	13.0	1.4	4.2	7.2	8.5
Clerical	2.8	6.4	6.7	5.7	4.0	26.7	30.6	29.1
Sales	4.6	6.2	8.8	11.1	4.3	8.4	11.3	13.1
Blue Collar:	37.6	47.2	45.2	41.3	27.8	21.7	14.8	12.0
Skilled	12.6	18.7	20.9	20.2	1.4	1.5	2.4	8.5
Semiskilled	10.4	20.1	17.4	14.9	23.8	19.3	10.1	2.4
Laborers	14.7	8.5	6.8	6.2	2.6	0.8	2.3	1.6
Service:	3.1	6.1	9.3	9.4	35.5	20.8	18.1	18.7
Household	0.2	0.2	0.05	0.1	28.7	8.6	1.3	2.1
Other	2.9	5.9	9.3	9.3	6.8	12.2	16.8	16.7
Farm:	41.7	14.7	4.3	5.1	19.0	3.6	1.0	1.2
Farmers	23.0	9.8	2.0	2.1	5.9	0.7	0.3	0.4
Laborers	18.7	4.8	1.3	2.7	13.1	2.8	0.5	0.8
	100.0%	98.0%	99.7%	100.0%	100.1%	97.2%	99.5%	100.0%

Sources: Compiled from U.S. Bureau of the Census, *Historical Statistics of the United States: Colonial Times to 1970*, Part I, 1975, 139; *Statistical Abstract of the United States: 1986*, 1985, 402–403; *World Almanac and Book of Facts: 1986*, 1985, 108.

that more than 30 percent of women workers today are in clerical occupations—the so-called "pink-collar ghettos."

Another area of growth not readily identified in Table 3.4 is the increase in the numbers of professional women. In February 1986 they outnumbered professional men for the first time—6,938,000 to men's 6,909,000 (Mann 1986:C3). Most were in the usual women's professions, but in a few areas, such as psychology, statistics, editing, and reporting, women outnumbered men in what had been traditional male fields. Women have also made some recent gains in the area of management. Most of these positions are in the middle-management ranks and in industries employing a large number of lower level women—retailing and trade, media, and financial services (Blumenthal 1986).

Another major change in occupations in this century is the decline in domestic employment, largely the exodus of black women from these jobs during and after World War II as better opportunities became avail-

Table 3.5 Participation in the Labor Force, by Sex and White, Black and Hispanic, 1880–1985, and 1995 Projections

| | Men | | | | Women | | | |
	Total	White	Black	Hispanic	Total	White	Black	Hispanic
1880	79%	na	na	na	15%	na	na	na
1890	84.3	84.0	86.6	na	18.2	15.8	37.7	na
1900	85.7	85.4	88.5	na	20.0	17.3	37.7	na
1910	81.3	na	na	na	23.4	na	na	na
1920	84.6	84.1	87.5	na	22.7	20.7	40.6	na
1930	82.1	81.7	86.1	na	23.6	21.8	40.5	na
1940	82.6	79.7	80.0	na	27.9	24.5	37.3	na
1950	83.2	79.2	76.6	na	32.8	28.1	37.1	na
1960	83.3	83.4	83.0	na	37.7	36.5	48.2	na
1970	79.7	80.0	76.5	na	43.3	42.6	49.5	na
1980	77.4	78.2	70.6	79.9	51.5	51.2	53.2	48.0
1983	76.4	77.1	70.6	79.2	52.9	52.7	54.2	47.7
1984	76.4	77.1	70.8	79.0	53.6	53.3	55.2	49.6
1985	75.9	na	na	na	54.2	na	na	na
1995[a]	76.1	77.0	70.5	na	60.3	60.0	61.2	na

Sources: Compliled from U.S. Bureau of Census, *Historical Statistics of the United States, Colonial Times to 1970*, Part II, 1975, 127–128, 132; *Statistical Abstract of the United States: 1986*, 1985, 391, 392, 396.

na not available

[a] 1995 Projections

able to them for the first time. There has also been a decline in semi-skilled operative work. Many of these jobs have been automated or exported to foreign countries. And, of course, women left the farm along with the men.

Participation Rates

Table 3.5 shows some changes in participation rate in the labor force for years in which rates were collected for that group. *Participation in the labor force* includes people who are working on a job; people who are unemployed but have been actively seeking employment for the past four weeks; people who had jobs from which they were temporarily absent because of vacation, strikes, illness, or temporary layoff; or people with new jobs that would start within the month. The *participation rate*, as you recall, shows what percentage of the group who are in the usual working years fits the above categories, on the job or looking for a job. Individuals not in the labor force are people who do not choose to enter the labor force—students, housewives, the severely disabled who are not institutionalized, the independently wealthy—or people who have looked for work, become discouraged, and given up the search.

Also it should be noted that there may be a sizable group of people who have for some reason given up trying to earn a living in the traditional manner and decided to work in the underground or subterranean economy. Their work and income are not reported to the Internal Revenue Service, the Bureau of the Census, or other governmental agencies collecting statistics. This work may be either legal—except that it is not reported—or illegal activity. It can range from someone working on construction for cash (the work itself is not illegal), to selling drugs, pimping and prostitution, numbers running, and so forth. For some persons, this hustle on the street possibly seems more respectable in terms of money and self-esteem than do the kinds of jobs available in the legitimate labor market.

The labor-force participation rates for men and women are noticeably moving in opposite directions—the percentage of working men declining slowly through the century and women increasing rapidly since World War II. Until after World War II black men had the highest participation rate of any group studied by the Census or Bureau of Labor Statistics. Some reasons for the subsequent decline are discussed in the next section on unemployment—the shift in the occupational structure, automation of jobs, plant shutdowns in industries in which many black men were employed, and early retirement. Many of these workers may have become discouraged and joined the underground economy and so do not appear in the official participation statistics.

The rise of the participation rate for women has been partially discussed—increased education and expectations. In addition, we see that working is a matter of economic necessity for about two-thirds of women workers. Table 3.5 supports the comment that black women were less affected by the cultural ideal of the housewife in the late nineteenth century. White women did not approach the 37.7 percent rate of the 1890 black women until the 1960s. It is unfortunate that we do not have government data on Hispanic women until recently. The research studies on small samples indicate, in general, a much lower participation rate for Hispanic American women than the general rate for women, until the 1970s.

While looking at the participation rates of women workers and pay of full-time, year-round women workers compared to men in the United States, we can note some aspects of the employment situation of women in other industrial countries. Using comparative data on twelve industrial countries in the early 1970s, Roos (1985) found some striking differences in the shape of the participation rate curves by age group. In some countries there was a slight dip after initial high participation while women had and cared for young children; the rate then returned to the initial level. In one country (the United States) the rate was virtually flat—meaning that women entered the workforce and stayed while they were raising their children (Roos 1985:45). In terms of numbers, this means that half of all women with children under three years and 70 percent of women whose youngest child is from age six to thirteen are in the labor force (Austin NOW Times. Large gap separates work place, family 1986:3).

In one country in the Roos study, the women were paid more than the men. This occurred because the participation rate for women was fairly low after the initial high entry. The well-educated women stayed in the work force, holding more professional jobs and being more educated than their male counterparts, in general. Since there were fewer women in lower-skilled jobs, the median earnings stayed high. This was in Israel. Women in Finland hold the record for the highest participation—around 80 percent. Three of the Scandinavian countries—Denmark, Finland, and Sweden—had the highest participation rates for women (Norway is the exception). The Netherlands, West Germany, Ireland, and Israel had the lowest participation rate of the twelve countries. Italy was not in the study. Table 3.6 indicates that it has a low rate.

Both cultural (values) and structural (political and economic) factors influence the status of women in the work force in industrial countries. Countries in which the cultural ideal is a woman in the home do not enforce affirmative action, equal pay for the same job, laws for equal pay for work of comparable worth, and do not provide social supports for the working woman. For example, in Japan, where the cultural ideal has been characterized as the courtesan role playing to the sumarai male role, the tax laws are punitive for women's wages (O'Kelly and Carney 1986), daycare is not made readily available, and companies usually do not offer on-the-job training and promotions or life-time employment. Conversely, in Sweden the tax laws do not penalize women who work, public day-care is available in most places, and it is assumed that women will be working throughout their lives—hence, training and promotions are more readily available. Also, parental leave is granted for birth or adoption (males are included in this, although apparently few take advantage of it).

As economist Sylvia Hewlett (1986) has graphically pointed out, women in all industrialized countries (with the exception of Japan) are supported more in terms of child care, maternal benefits, and other career-oriented options than they are in the United States. In fact, maternity leave, which more than a third of working women in the United States do not have, is a basic guarantee in 117 nations of the world; it is

Table 3.6 Participation Rate of Women in the Labor Force and Percentage of Men's Wages in Ten Industrial Countries in 1960 and 1982

| | Participation Rate | | Percentage of Men's Wages in Year Specified | |
| | | | Hewlett | |
	1960	1982	1982	Morgan
U.S.	37.7	52.6		64.7% (1983)
Canada	30.1	51.6		50−66% (1978−79)
Australia	na	45.4		76% (1979)
Japan	52.7	47.0		53% (1983)
France	41.6	43.1 ('81)	78%[a]	69% (1980)
Germany (F.R.)	41.2	38.9	73%[a]	
Great Britain	39.9	48.1 ('81)	74%	
Italy	32.2	29.9	86%[a]	74% (1978) 91.8% [b](1975)
Netherlands	na	33.3 ('81)	75%	77.9% (1980)
Sweden	46.1 ('61)	60.9	90%	70% (1982)

Sources: Compiled from U.S. Bureau of Labor Statistics, *Handbook of Labor Statistics* (Bulletin 2175), December 1983, 422; Morgan, ed., *Sisterhood is Global: The International Women's Movement Anthology*, 1984; Sylvia Hewlett, *A Lesser Life: The Myth of Women's Liberation in America*, 1986, 415 (Hewlett's source: Eurostat, "Hourly earnings—hours of work," various issues, Luxembourg: Statistical Office of the European Community).

[a] Manufacturing only

[b] Agriculture only

na not available

a part of the law. Further, maternity leave in the United States, when it is available, is usually without pay. In the European industrial nations, maternity leave includes some percentage of one's wages. Hewlett appears to blame the women's movement in the United States for not pushing for these benefits but merely demanding equal opportunity. However, the reasons may go deeper into U.S. culture. The European women's movements chose to work on formulating practical policies through the women's bureaus of political parties, unions (which are more widespread in Europe than in the United States), and professional, social, and religious organizations. They did not work on consciousness raising because that tends to rivet attention on the individual rather than on society's responsibility (Hewlett 1986:165).

The reason U.S. working women are behind all other industrial societies (except Japan) on all the economic and social indicators for working women may be that the United States itself—and not just the women's movement—is not culturally geared to analyzing social problems from a macro point of view. Cultural norms and values in the United States tend to view any problem that a category of people has as a problem of theirs that they must change and solve. This attitude may be a holdover from the nineteenth-century credo of social Darwinism (survival of the fittest), discussed in the following chapter. Meanwhile, the working woman in the United States is doing a juggling act between home and workplace, without support in most cases. The 50 percent divorce rate gives some indication of the strains the family is under. Part of this strain is due to the changing social roles inherent in women entering the workforce.

Why do women in the United States work? One-third are the sole support of their families—divorced, widowed, separated, husband unemployed (Council on Interracial Books for Children, 1982:4). Another one-third of the working women are married to men whose earnings are close to or below the poverty line; the income is needed to raise the standard of living to a modest level. The other third work for reasons other than attaining a modest family income; they want a better standard of living and self-fulfillment, and/or they enjoy their work. In any case, more than half of all married women in the United States work. Today's reality is a long way from the nineteenth-century stereotype of the working father, the homemaker mother.

Unemployment

Now that we have some idea of what working people are doing, we turn our attention briefly to people who are looking for work. As noted on previous tables, information on minorities has not been available until fairly recently. In these recent years, however, there seems to be fairly constant ratios among black, white, and Hispanic unemployment, as shown in Table 3.7. Black unemployment runs more than twice as high as white, and Hispanic is in between at one and a half the white percentage. Why should unemployment hit these minorities harder than the general public? The reason is not, apparently, the phenomenon of "last hired, first fired" but the types of jobs they are most likely to be in. These occupations in the laborer, operative, and low-skilled service sectors are likely to be the first to be eliminated in cutbacks and automation.

Economists also talk about the type of unemployment that seems to be increasing in the Untied States—structural unemployment. *Frictional unemployment* means that workers are without work because they are changing from one job to another. This state is usually short-term, and the rate of about 3 percent is considered normal even in the best of times. *Cyclical unemployment* is also normal in many industries, such as agriculture and tourism, and in some regions that rely on such industries. *Structural unemployment*, however, is long-term and sometimes permanent; it occurs because of technological change or de-

Table 3.7 Unemployment: Black, White, and Hispanic, 1940–1985

	Total	Black	White	Hispanic	Ratio: Black to White	Ratio: Hispanic to White
1940	14.6	na	na	na		
1950	5.0	9.0	4.9	na	1.8:1	
1960	5.5	10.2	4.9	na	2.1:1	
1970	4.9	8.2	4.5	na	1.8:1	
1980	7.1	14.3	6.3	10.1	2.3:1	1.6:1
1981	7.6	15.6	6.7	10.4	2.3:1	1.6:1
1982	9.7	18.9	8.6	13.8	2.2:1	1.6:1
1983	9.6	19.5	8.4	16.3	2.3:1	1.9:1
1984	7.5	15.9	6.5	11.6	2.4:1	1.8:1
1985	7.1	15.1	6.1	10.5	2.5:1	1.7:1

Sources: Compiled from U.S. Bureau of Labor Statistics, *Handbook of Labor Statistics,* (Bulletin 2175) December 1983, 71–72; *Historical Statistics of the United States, Colonial Times to 1970,* Part II, 1975, 135; *Statistical Abstract of the United States: 1986,* 1985, 396; *World Almanac and Book of Facts: 1986,* 1985, 108; *Employment and Earnings* March 1986, 39.

na not available

cline in an industry. Workers' skills are no longer needed. If training is not readily available or geographic mobility not possible, or if the worker is too old or too untrainable, this situation is a serious problem for both the worker and society.

Obviously, structural unemployment hits minorities particularly hard. Many minority workers have been employed in the declining auto, steel, and textile and apparel industries. The educational level is somewhat lower for minority groups as a whole, and the quality of their education also may be lower. Economists express concern that structural employment is growing steadily and perhaps creating a permanent underclass of structurally unemployed people. A large percentage of this group may live in inner-city ghettos and one-industry towns of the so-called rust belt. We return to some causes of structural unemployment in Chapter 6 in the section on plant shutdowns and in Chapter 7 in the discussion of computer technology and robotics and the worker.

A comparison of U.S. employment rates with rates in other industrial countries (Table 3.8) might raise some questions about why such differences exist among capitalist nations. Some of the later chapters shed light on possible reasons. Although worldwide recessions in the global economic system affect everyone, unemployment is not equally affected in all countries. Differences can occur because of the stage of countries' economic development, the nature of their industries, and so forth. More important, perhaps, are the differences in public policy and private company policies adopted by various societies. Some societies

Table 3.8 Unemployment Rates in Ten Industrial Countries, Adjusted to U.S. Concepts, 1960–1982

	1960	1965	1970	1975	1980	1981	1982
United States	5.5	4.5	4.9	8.6	7.1	7.6	9.7
Canada	6.5	3.6	5.7	6.9	7.5	7.6	11.0
Australia	1.6	1.3	1.6	4.9	6.1	5.8	7.1
Japan	1.7	1.2	1.2	1.9	2.0	2.2	2.4
France	1.6	1.4	2.4	4.2	6.5	7.6	8.6
Germany (F.R.)	1.1	0.3	0.5	3.4	2.9	4.1	5.8
Great Britain	2.2	2.1	3.1	4.6	7.0	10.6	12.3
Italy	3.2	3.0	2.8	3.0	3.9	4.3	4.8
Netherlands	na	na	na	5.2	6.2	8.9	12.2
Sweden	1.7	1.2	1.5	1.6	2.0	2.5	3.1

Source: U.S. Bureau of Labor Statistics, *Handbook of Labor Statistics* (Bulletin 2175), December 1983, 419–420.

push for full employment as an important value. Others leave employment and unemployment to the vagaries of the market.

Education and Earnings

One of the most profound effects of the growth of industry and technology on society is in the area of education. As long as most people were engaged in low-technology agriculture, there was no need for widespread education, from an occupational point of view. Until the industrial revolution even public school education was only for the few and higher education was for the elite or the very lucky. In 1870 there was one public school teacher (average annual salary, $189) for every sixty individuals aged five through seventeen in the United States. In that year only 2 percent of the adult population had a high school diploma. By the turn of the century 6.4 percent had high school diplomas. In the last half of the nineteenth century, and particularly the last quarter, some interesting things were happening in education.

As we have discussed, the second half of the nineteenth century saw technological innovations in industry, transportation, communications, and even in the home. Organization size and the mass marketing of new products were increasing. Immigration was spurred by problems in the old country—such as potato famines in Ireland, political upheaval in Germany, and agricultural problems in Scandinavia—and by the attractions of new land and of gold and political freedom. Apparently people all over the world heard about the gold rush; even the Chinese heard of *Kim Shan*, the Mountain of Gold, and came. Many of these immigrants swelled the urban areas in the New World. Migrating westward was too expensive, farming too different, the risks too high for some, and many had recently left lives of farming. After about 1890, all the best land was already taken. By then the Native Americans held only small pieces of what once had been theirs—only 140 million acres in 1890 (further reduced to 50 million acres of tribal trust lands today). This era was the closing of the frontier. Thus, in this hustle and bustle of immigration, urbanization, and industrialization, education became gradually more and more useful occupationally.

The content of higher education also reflected this change in the structure of the basic economy. As long as higher education was for the elite and not necessary for occupational purposes, only the classical humanities curriculum and religion were taught. The purpose of higher education was to give a man a general background for such gentlemanly pursuits as politics, the law, or the clergy. Most occupations were learned in apprenticeships on the job. Daughters of the elite were sometimes tutored at home, if they were educated at all. Consider, however, the following demands of the last half of the nineteenth century:

Industry needed more scientific and technological information.

The cities and a more complex *Gesellschaft* society called for an understanding of social problems (suicide, urban crime, poverty, socialization of immigrants, exploitation of workers by the factory system, public health, and urban planning, for example).

The new corporations wanted to hire people who knew something about business management.

Public education was expanding and wanted teachers with more than a high school education, although in many rural areas this level was enough until after World War II.

Women began demanding higher education, both in areas opening to them in the Civil War (such as nursing and teaching), and later in the century (such as social work), and also as a general right in the growing suffrage and liberation movements.

The professions began to demand formal higher education certification for admittance to practice.

We can see why new departments and even new types of schools began to be created. The natural sciences, social sciences, and business departments developed their new disciplines. Women's colleges and normal schools (teachers' colleges) appeared. Land-grant colleges emphasizing agriculture and technical education were established. The new states, anxious to vie with established Eastern universities, set up systems for their own citizens. Black colleges were established for students who found white college doors closed to them. Black colleges even opened their doors to women, who often outnumbered the male students after the 1890s.

The post–World War II era experienced a push toward education that rivaled the seminal changes in the late nineteenth century both in participation and in curriculum changes. The GI bill offered returning veterans a chance for higher education unthought of by even their immediate ancestors. Women and other minorities had obtained better jobs and pay during the war. Apparently some saw education as a road to keeping and improving their status gains. The civil rights movement, from about 1955 to 1970, also encouraged these groups to aspire. Women and other minorities entered or stayed in higher education in increasing numbers until the recession of the 1980s began to cut into higher education for blacks.

The postwar period also experienced some incentives to improve the quality of the higher education curriculum. The Soviet Union's launching of Sputnik in 1957 riveted attention on the need for more science and technology throughout the public school and university curricula. The loss of premier status in U.S. competition on the world market, apparent since the late 1960s, again increased the emphasis on science and technology in some large universities. Many states are now openly trying to attract and subsidize scientific and technical research. Such research gains them government and foundation research monies for the universities and also attracts high-tech business and research people to the area, creating jobs for local residents. Faculty and graduate students often find it necessary to pursue topics of interest to the corporate and military establishments, thus pointing themselves, their disciplines, and society's knowledge base in certain directions. In pursuit of occupations many more students today are following business and computer careers, adding to the growth of interest in higher education in these fields. The economy thus has had a profound impact on the knowledge industry.

How has this increase in participation in education affected the general population, both in public school and in higher education? By 1980 there was one public school instructor (average annual salary, $18,404) for every nineteen young people in the five through seventeen age group (World Almanac 1985:195). In 1984 more than 73 percent of the population over twenty-five years of age had a high school diploma and 34.9 percent had at least some college, as indicated in Tables 3.9 and 3.10 (World Almanac 1985:195). The education level in years attained had dramatically increased with industrialization. At the same time a reported 20 percent of the adult population in the United States are functionally illiterate and another 10 percent are "marginal" (King 1985:18; Ehrenreich 1985:54). Despite the increase in educational attainment, other problems exist in addition to the functional illiteracy rate, as we will discuss.

Table 3.9 Median Years of Education in the Labor Force, by Sex and White, Black, and Hispanic, 1983

	Men	*Women*
White	12.8	12.8
Black	12.5	12.6
Hispanic	12.1	12.3

Source: Compiled from U.S. Bureau of Labor Statistics, *Educational Attainment of Workers, 1982-83* (Bulletin 2191), April 1984, 26–28.

Table 3.10 Educational Attainment of Persons over Age Twenty-Five by Sex and White, Black, and Hispanic, and Young Adults (Eighteen to Twenty-Four Years) in Percentages for 1984

	Less than 4 years of high school	*High school, 4 years*	*College, 1–3 years*	*College, 4 or more years*
Total population	26.7%	38.4%	15.8%	19.1%
Men	26.3	34.6	16.1	22.9
Women	27.0	41.8	15.6	15.7
Young adults	21.7	45.1	26.4	6.7
White	25.0	39.1	16.1	19.8
Men	24.6	35.1	16.3	23.9
Women	25.4	42.8	15.8	16.0
Young adults	20.5	45.3	26.9	7.3
Black	41.5	34.3	13.8	10.4
Men	43.0	32.9	13.8	10.5
Women	40.3	35.4	13.9	10.4
Young adults	28.3	46.3	22.8	2.6
Hispanic	52.9	27.3	11.6	8.2
Men	51.4	26.2	12.9	9.5
Women	54.3	28.2	10.5	7.0
Young adults	44.5	35.8	17.8	2.0

Source: *World Almanac and Book of Facts: 1986*, 1985, 195.

From Tables 3.9 and 3.10 we can see some surprising changes in education. Table 3.9 includes the median years of education only for people in the workforce, which usually means people with better educations than the population as a whole. The higher one's education, the more likely one is to be employed or looking for work, and hence counted in the labor force. Looking at median years—the midpoint in educational attainment if the entire group were ranked from zero to the top number of years of education—is usually more reliable for estimating the group as a whole than is using the average. The average or mean—everyone's years added up and divided by the number of people—is likely to represent a more distorted picture, since extreme cases (perpetual students) can make the group look more educated. (Note: The same is true for income, or any scale that has a limitless top. The median, then, is likely to be somewhat lower than the average and thus more representative of the population.)

The surprise in Table 3.9 is how close the median years of education are for the workers in the three racial/ethnic categories and the two genders. Even though this is encouraging, it does not address the quality of education or the curricula pursued by persons in the various categories.

The single median years figure also evades the educational attainment of individuals not in the work force. It also does not disclose the possible skewedness of the distribution on either side of the midpoint. From Table 3.10 we can see that for blacks and Hispanics in the twenty-five and older group there are sizable percentages who did not finish high school—41.5 and 52.9 percent, respectively. Apparently many of these persons are not participating in the work force. For the young adults we see some improvement; 28.3 percent of blacks and 44.5 percent of Hispanics have not finished high school. The school dropout rate, which had been becoming lower over the years, currently seems to be rising slightly, and in 1985 it stood at 11 percent for whites, 15 percent for blacks, and 40 percent for Hispanics.

In terms of quality and type of education for minorities, we immediately see the high functional illiteracy rate mentioned above. Those people in this category, some of who were graduated from high school, may find entering the work force exceedingly difficult. We saw in the occupational distribution figures earlier in this chapter that unskilled labor jobs are on the decline. We also noted that structural unemployment is on the rise and that it is long-term or permanent. Even the low-paid low-skilled service sector jobs often require some literacy (e.g., making change, filling out reports) including the forms required in applying for a job. When 20 percent of the adult population is in this predicament, the situation becomes critical.

Other aspects of the quality and type of education are more subtle than is functional illiteracy. Inner-city schools are sometimes serving more of a custodial function than an educational one, not giving their students the best possible start in the job competition. Inner cities are where so many black children live today. Minority children, girls, and lower socioeconomic children often get tracked into courses that are traditional for their group rather than into courses for which they might be well suited and that could lead to better jobs (Bowles and Gintis 1976; Feagin and Feagin 1978). Lower socioeconomic status young people, for example, are more likely to be found in vocational tracks in high school than in the track preparing for college entrance. Young women have frequently been socialized by parents, friends, media, and even by teachers and counselors into taking courses that lead to traditionally acceptable women's careers, resulting in both crowding and lower pay (Lengermann and Wallace 1985:Chapter 4 on socialization; Scott 1984).

Putting aside for the moment the problems with the kinds of education people may often be getting, let us consider what happens to workers who followed the advice when told to get more years of education. Do these workers get higher quality jobs than their less well educated forebearers had? Have the skill level, the responsibility, the challenge of the job kept pace with the increase in education? For the majority of workers, the answers seem to be, no. For professional, technical, and managerial jobs, the skills required today may call for more years of formal education. For many other jobs in blue-collar, service, and non-managerial white-collar areas, increased credentials are required in order to be considered for employment, but the nature of the jobs may not have changed that much. We noted that these low-paying, dead-end jobs are the ones increasing most rapidly in the current economy and the foreseeable future. Ivar Berg (1970) has referred to this demand for increased education without an increase in skills required by the job as "the great training robbery."

Why does a worker now need a high school diploma to work on an auto assembly line at a routine, entry-level job? The diploma is used as a screening device and, since the majority of potential workers have one, companies can use this as a cut-off point in the hopes of getting the best workers. Sociologists Ritzer and Walczak (1986:53) note that this tactic may not work in the employer's favor. Studies indicate that overeducation for a job can "adversely affect job performance, the physical and mental health of workers, and lead to higher rates of absenteeism, strikes, drug problems, and sabotage in the workplace." Education for its own sake is good, but expectations for better work have been raised and not met (Guzzardi 1976:128). More people are finding themselves underemployed in this manner. The clerical worker in the typing pool with a bachelor's degree in literature is a common example of the phenomenon. In fact, when critiqued on their writing style by professors, students have been heard to remark, "Don't worry. When I get into business I'll hire a secretary with a degree in English."

We return to this problem of increased expectations and of routine jobs in Chapter 11 on alternative workplace organization, discussing some ways in which organizations have tried to do something about the situation by improving job content.

As noted, in 1983 women's wages were almost 65 percent of men's.

The median income of males, regardless of race/ethnicity, is higher than that of females, regardless of their ethnic group (See Mellor 1986 for comparisons of men's and women's earnings in more than 200 occupations). Tables 3.11 and 3.12 show comparisons of occupations and educational levels against earnings for men and women. Earnings gaps can

Table 3.11 Occupations and Median Weekly Earnings of Full-time Workers, by Sex, 1982

	Men	Women	All Workers
White Collar:			
Prof. & tech.	$489	$338	$411
Mgr. & officials	520	310	436
Clerical	337	236	247
Sales	397	222	326
Blue Collar:			
Skilled & forepersons	380	232	370
Semiskilled	315	201	305
Laborers	256	208	250
Service workers:	247	174	201
Farm:	191	160	189
All occupations:	$370	$240	$308
Women's earnings as percent of men's:	65%		

Source: U.S. Bureau of Labor Statistics, *News*, Tables 4, 5.

Note: The earnings do not include fringe benefits, which may equal 20 to 30 percent of income.

Table 3.12 Income and Education by Sex, 1980, for Full-time, Year-round Workers.

Educational Attainment	Income, Men	Income, Women	Female as % of Male
Less than 8 years	$11,753	$ 7,752	66%
8 years	14,674	8,857	60
High school, under 3 years	16,101	9,676	60
High school, 4 years	19,469	11,537	59
College, 4 years	24,311	15,143	62
College, 5 or more years	27,690	18,100	65

Source: U.S. Department of Commerce, 1981, cited in *Fact Sheets on Institutional Sexism*, New York: Council on Interracial Books for Children, 1982, 11.

readily be seen, both in every occupational category in Table 3.11 and at every level of education in Table 3.12. In Table 3.12, for example, a woman with graduate education can expect to earn more than $1,000 a year less than a man with a high school diploma. What is not easy to explain is why this is so.

TWO VIEWS ON THE EARNINGS GAP AND THE LOWER OCCUPATIONAL STATUS OF WOMEN AND OTHER MINORITIES

Human Capital

The *human capital argument,* as it is termed by economists, takes a micro supply side, neoclassical economic theory approach to explaining the gap in earnings between dominant groups and minorities and between men and women in our society. *Human capital* is what the worker brings to the labor market—his or her investment in skills, education, on-the-job training, years of experience in the work force, and attitudes toward work that show up in such behaviors as absenteeism, turnover, and low productivity and effort. The older line of thinking held that workers have freely chosen not to invest in themselves in appropriate ways to compete for better jobs in the marketplace. A less harsh view among more recent advocates of the human capital argument is that premarket factors have incorrectly socialized some workers into developing less of their human capital than they might—for example, the culture of poverty idea. The *culture of poverty* argument is basically the notion that in industrial societies, urban female-headed households have socialized their children into fatalistic, live-for-the-moment attitudes, which keep them from attempting to get more education and better jobs. Hence, it is the fault of their families and subcultures, according to this view.

Both versions of the human capital argument within the neoclassical economic model agree that the market functions in an impersonal way to pay the worker for what is produced. The equilibrium wage rate is presumed to be set where labor supply and demand curves intersect. The short-run demand curve for labor is established according to the marginal revenue product of the last person hired (Flanagan, Smith, and Ehrenberg 1984:Chapters 2, 3). The underlying assumption is that there is little wrong with how the labor market functions; it is fair and impartial. Problems for workers in gaining entrance to better jobs and higher wages are basically problems these workers will have to solve for themselves, perhaps with the help of educators and social workers. These workers are going to have to raise their marginal productivity by investing in their own human capital.

Note that this neoclassical economic view of the world fits nicely in many respects with the functionalist view of social stratification—that the people at the top of the social hierarchy are accorded more status and income because they have produced more for society and are filling jobs that are functionally important (Davis and Moore 1966; Tumin 1966). People at the bottom are being paid according to their productivity, their worth in production. This discussion continues in Chapter 8 in the section on social stratification theories.

Institutional Discrimination

The second opinion on earnings and job status inequality comes from an *institutional discrimination* or macro/structural conflict view. Under conflict theory assumptions, wages are established by the "relative power (resources) of employers to give as little possible, and employees to obtain as much as possible" (Tausky 1984:77).

Each of the several revisions to the preceeding human capital, neoclassical economic explanation moves toward a more macro institutional discrimination approach. Becker (1964) noted that employers do not always hire according to productivity alone. They frequently exercise certain tastes for some workers over others—for example, for younger, white male workers over minorities, women, or older workers—on characteristics that have little to do with contribution to production. Thurow (1975:170–177) refers to employers' hiring on the basis of "statistical discrimination" (read "stereotyping")—or what the employer thinks someone from that group will be capable of producing.

Another important factor in the wage gap is the amount of on-the-job training women receive. Here the opinions of people above them in management become vital; they may think training will be wasted on women workers. Even though on-the-job training is seen as an individual human capital factor in the first view, people looking at structural factors see that part of the problem may be this kind of discrimination, which has become traditional in society.

Neoinstitutionalists of the 1940s and 1950s, building on the earlier ideas of Thorstein Veblen, Wesley C. Mitchell, and John R. Commons, criticized the perfect competition assumptions of the orthodox neoclassical economic model by noting barriers to the free flow of labor—large organizations with internal labor markets, unions that exclude some groups, and other divisive or Balkanizing processes that negate the existence of one large labor queue* from which employers choose on ability alone (Dunlop 1957; Kerr 1954). Other writers have critiqued the culture

---

*Neoclassical economists use the term *labor queue* to mean a pool of labor arranged (or queued up) in a line according to ability from which employers choose.

of poverty argument—that poor people socialize their children into fatalistic, reckless, live-for-today subcultural attitudes and behaviors, which then keep them from achieving in the marketplace and gaining upward social mobility (Valentine 1968; Ford 1973, 1977). We return to some of the institutional arguments in Chapter 5 in the discussion of dual, internal, and split labor markets and their effects on minorities and women. (For a succinct summary of all of these views on women in the labor market, see Blau and Jusenius 1977).

These are a few of the theoretical arguments, but fortunately there are empirical studies that test these theories. Social scientists have used multiple regression and other statistical techniques to calculate the effects on earnings for such human capital variables as formal education, age, vocational and on-the-job training, job tenure, hours worked per week, marital and parental status (for the effect on earnings of having family responsibilities), and so forth. Even though the findings in studies vary somewhat with the variables in the equation, the manner in which they are measured, the sample (whether individual establishment or aggregate data, etc.) the results are fairly predictable on one point (See Treiman and Hartmann 1981 for review of these studies). That one point is that human capital definitely does *not* account for at least half of the wage gap. In these empirical studies, human capital usually contributes from 20 to 50 percent of the earnings gap (Corcoran and Duncan 1979:3–20; Norwood 1984:2; Shack-Marquez 1984:14–16). The other 50 percent or more of the gap must be attributed to other unknown factors—such as discrimination in some form.

Much of the total wage gap between men and women seems to be due to the nature of the jobs 70 percent of women workers hold—traditional women's underpaid jobs, including clerk-secretaries, bookkeepers, cashiers, salesworkers, typists, librarians, registered nurses, elementary school teachers, dieticians, hairdressers, cooks, waitresses, and nurses' aides (Norwood 1984:2; Berryman and Waite 1985). Bureau of Labor Statistics economist Janice Shack-Marquez (1984:14) summarizes the importance of differences in jobs held:

> The earnings gap may also arise from the types of jobs men and women hold. A number of studies have supplemented data on individual characteristics with data on occupation, industry, and type of employer (for example, government versus private, or large versus small firm). These studies have been able to explain a substantially larger portion (as much as 88 percent) of the earnings gap than those using only individual characteristics. [Note: Individual characteristics means human capital.]

From this statement we can see the importance of the comparable worth argument. Comparable worth differs from equal pay for men and women who hold jobs with substantially the same work content. This latter type of discrimination is less debatable and is considered illegal under the Equal Pay Act of 1983. Comparable worth, however, is addressing the point that traditional women's jobs are underpaid compared to men's when all jobs are analyzed, with points being given for the amount of education and skills, mental effort, responsibility, and working conditions required on the job. Jobs ranking equally on the overall point scale should, presumably, be paid close to the same amount. They never are, however, if one job is traditionally male and the other traditionally female. In all cases in which these evaluations have been done on jobs in the United States, the ones women usually hold are underpaid. Other industrial nations, such as Australia and Sweden, have comparable worth laws and are gradually increasing wages in undervalued jobs. This issue is addressed again in Chapter 7 with regard to how some unions are dealing with the problem of women's wages, both in the courts and at the bargaining table.

SUMMARY

Some of the main points covered in the chapter are:

1. Since 1800 the United States has shifted from predominantly agriculture to predominantly services, and heavy manufacturing has been slowly declining since the 1950s in its percentage of the work force. This trend also can be seen in other mature industrial countries.

2. There have been some shifts in occupations among minorities since World War II, but basically minorities are still in low-skill and/or low-paying jobs.

3. Labor force participation rates for males have declined somewhat overall in this century, particularly those of black males since the 1960s. The participation rates for females have been increasing rather dramatically since World War II and are expected to continue to rise.

4. Structural unemployment has been increasing since the 1970s, and perhaps earlier for black males, due to automation and computerization and capital flight/plant shutdowns. Unemployment for minorities is consistently more than twice as high for blacks and one and a half times as high for Hispanics as for whites. Employment of discouraged workers in the underground economy may account for part of the declining participation rates of some social categories. Unemployment rates differ among the mature industrial nations, due in part to variations in policies regarding the importance of full employment.

5. Education in terms of years of attainment has increased remarkably in this century. Many workers are finding themselves underemployed by being overskilled for their jobs. Median years of education for minorities in the labor force are almost identical to those of whites. The type and/or quality of education for minorities and women should be considered.

6. The earnings gap between males and females (females earned 64.7 percent of male wages for full-time, year-round work in 1983) has been shown to be more the result of the nature of pay for traditional women's jobs (70 percent of employed women) than of human capital factors of education, tenure on the job, and so forth. Lack of access to on-the-job training for advancement and other forms of discrimination are also seen as structural problems that affect the individual's chances for enhancing human capital. In addition, women workers in the United States are next to the bottom among mature industrial societies in percentage of men's pay.

BIBLIOGRAPHY

Becker, Gary S. 1964. *Human capital.* New York: National Bureau for Economic Research.
Berg, Ivar. 1970. *Education and jobs: The great training robbery.* New York: Praeger.
Berryman, Sue, and Linda J. Waite. 1985. *Women in nontraditional occupations: Choice and turnover.* Santa Monica, Calif.: Rand.
Blau, Francine D., and Carol L. Jusenius. 1977. "Sex segregation in the labor market." In *Woman in a man-made world: A socioeconomic handbook,* 2nd ed., edited by Nona Glazer and Helen Youngelson Waehrer, 194–207. Boston: Houghton Mifflin.
Bluestone, Barry, and Bennett Harrison. 1987. The grim truth about the job "miracle:" A low wage explosion. *New York Times,* Forum Section 15 (February 1).
Blumenthal, Karen. 1986. Room at the top: U.S. industry, despite some advances, remains mostly devoid of women in senior posts. *Austin NOW Times* 14, 6:1–3 (June).
Bowles, Samuel S., and Herbert Gintis. 1975. The problem with human capital theory—a Marxist critique. *American Economic Review* 65, 2:74–82 (May).
———. 1976. *Schooling in capitalist America: Educational reform and the contradictions of economic life.* New York: Basic Books.
Corcoran, Mary, and George J. Duncan. 1979. Work history, labor force attachment, and earnings differences between the races and sexes. *Journal of Human Resources* 14, 1:3–20 (Winter).
Council on Interracial Books for Children. 1982. *Fact sheets on institutional sexism.* New York: The Council.

Davis, Kingsley, and Wilbert E. Moore. 1966. "Some principles of stratification." In *Class, status, and power: Social stratification in comparative perspective,* 2nd ed., edited by Reinhard Bendix and Seymour Martin Lipset, 47–52. New York: Free Press.

Dunlop, John. 1957. "The task of contemporary wage theory." In *New concepts in wage discrimination,* edited by George W. Taylor and Frank C. Pierson, 117–139. New York: McGraw-Hill.

Ehrenreich, Barbara. 1985. America's illiteracy program. *Mother Jones* 10, 3:54 (April).

Feagin, Joe R., and Clairece B. Feagin. 1978. *Discrimination American style: Institutional sexism and racism.* Englewood Cliffs, N.J.: Prentice-Hall.

Flanagan, Robert J., Robert S. Smith, and Ronald G. Ehrenberg. 1984. *Labor economics and labor relations.* Glenview, Ill.: Scott, Foresman.

Ford, Arthur M. 1973. *Political economics of rural poverty in the South.* Cambridge Mass.: Ballinger.

———. 1977. Social and cultural issues in poverty models. *Journal of Cultural Economics* 1, 2:13–24 (December).

Guzzardi, Walter, Jr. 1976. The uncertain passage from college to job. *Fortune* 93, 1:126–129, 168–172 (January).

Hewlett, Sylvia Ann. 1986. *A lesser life: The myth of women's liberation in America.* New York: William Morrow.

Kerr, Clark. 1954. "The Balkanization of labor markets." In *Labor Mobility and Economic Opportunity,* E. Wight Bakke et al., pp. 43–109. Cambridge, Mass.: MIT and Wiley.

King, Michael. 1985. Why the hewers of wood can't read. *The Texas Observer* 77, 7:18–21 (August 30).

Kutscher, Ronald E., and Valerie A. Personick. 1986. Deindustrialization and the shift to services. *Monthly Labor Review* 109, 6:3–13 (June).

Large gap separates work place, family. 1986. *Austin NOW Times* 14, 4:3–4 (April).

Lengermann, Patricia Madoo, and Ruth A. Wallace. 1985. *Gender in America: Social control and social change.* Englewood Cliffs, N.J.: Prentice-Hall.

Mann, Judy. 1986. The new nonmajority. *Washington Post,* 109th year, no. III: c3 (March 26).

McMahon, Patrick J., and John H. Tschetter. 1986. The declining middle class: A further analysis. *Monthly Labor Review* 109, 9:22–27 (September).

Mellor, Earl F. 1986. Weekly earnings in 1985: A look at more than 200 occupations. *Monthly Labor Review* 109, 9:28–32 (September).

Morgan, Robin 1984. *Sisterhood is global: The international women's movement anthology.* Garden City, N.Y.: Anchor/Doubleday.

Newton, Ed. 1987. Careers and opportunities, 1987. *Black Enterprise* 17, 7:75–78, 128 (February).

Norwood, Janet L. 1984. *Working women and public policy.* Washington, D.C.: U.S. Department of Labor, Bureau of Labor Statistics (August).

O'Kelly, Charlotte G., and Larry S. Carney. 1986. *Women and men in society,* 2nd ed. Belmont, Calif.: Wadsworth.

Ritzer, George, and David Walczak. 1986. *Working: Conflict and change.* Englewood Cliffs, N.J.: Prentice-Hall.

Roos, Patricia A. 1985. *Gender and work: A comparative analysis of industrial societies.* Albany: State University of New York Press.

Rudolph, Barbara. 1986. Singing the shutdown blues. *Time* 127, 25:58–60 (June 23).

Scott, Hilda. 1984. *Working your way to the bottom: The feminization of poverty.* London: Pandora Press/Routledge & Kegan Paul.

Shack-Marquez, Janice. 1984. Earnings differences between men and women: An introductory note. *Monthly Labor Review* 107, 6:14–16 (June).

Strautmanis, Maris. 1987. Lies, damned lies, and unemployment statistics. *In These Times* 11, 8:5 (January 14–20).

Tausky, Curt. 1984. *Work and society: An introduction to industrial sociology.* Itasca, Ill.: F. E. Peacock.

Thurow, Lester C. 1975. *Generating inequality: Mechanisms of distribution in the U.S. economy.* New York: Basic Books.

Treiman, Donald J., and Heidi I. Hartmann, eds. 1981. *Women, work and wages: Equal pay for jobs of equal value.* Washington, D.C.: National Academy Press.

Tumin, Melvin M. 1966. "Some principles of stratification: A critical analysis." In *Class, status, and power: Social stratification in comparative perspective,* 2nd ed., edited by Reinhard Bendix and Seymour Lipset, pp. 53–58. New York: Free Press.

U.S. Bureau of the Census. 1975. *Historical statistics of the United States: Colonial times to 1970,* Part I. Washington, D.C.: GPO.

——.1984. *Statistical abstract of the United States: 1985.* Washington, D.C.: GPO.

——. 1985. *Statistical abstract of the United States: 1986.* Washington, D.C.: GPO.

U.S. Bureau of Labor Statistics. 1982. *News* (August 12).

——. 1983. *Handbook of labor Statistics.* Washington, D.C: GPO.

——. 1984. *Educational attainment of workers, 1982–83* (Bulletin 2191). Washington D.C.: GPO.

Valentine, Charles A. 1968. *Culture and poverty.* Chicago: University of Chicago Press.

World Almanac. 1985. *World almanac and book of facts: 1986.* New York: Newspaper Enterprise Association.

4

Theories of Human
Motivation and Management

INTRODUCTION

The following four points should be kept in mind while reading this chapter:

1. Management theories grow out of the experiences of people in a particular historical time and social space. Management theories, like any other ideology or belief system, can change with changing conditions. They contain assumptions (often unrecognized) and ideas that become popular and are taken for granted, rather than examined. They are political as well as economic in nature in that they deal with the distribution of power and may serve as justifications for that power distribution.

2. Management practices in an industrial society affect both economic survival and the quality of life of the society.

3. Management theories, as ideologies, are verbal expressions; the actual practices of management may differ. We subsequently note that democracy and worker participation in decision making, and even the less revolutionary human relations view of treating workers as though they are real people, may get more verbal agreement than actual use.

4. Rear Admiral Grace Hooper, U.S. Naval Reserve (Ret.), has pointed out that one "manages" things and "leads" people (CBS 1986:9). Whether or not we quibble over specific use of the terms *management* and *leadership*, this point might cause you to think about what people should be managed or led to. Does this statement mean that the person "in charge" must tell others what to do all of the time, or does it imply that one might "lead" people to come up with new ways of doing things and new ideas on what should be done (a facilitator manager)? Perhaps this is the most important question we have addressed. These manage-

ment and leadership styles are quite different. One calls for the ideas to come from the top and for subordinates to be led to agree; the other approach calls for ideas to come from wherever the source may lie. Each management theory we consider takes a definite stand on these views (except for the fourth one, which can include both views, according to the theorist or the manager proposing it) as each theory depends on the view of human nature and motivation the theory accepts.

The rest of the chapter reviews four management (leadership) theories in their chronological order of appearance: (1) scientific management/Taylorism, (2) human relations, (3) human resources, and (4) structural contingencies theories. We see some of the social forces, events, and beliefs that helped shape each view. Each new wave of thinking did not supplant the earlier school but was usually added to the practices of the first scientific management ideas of Frederick Winslow Taylor and his followers. Scientific management still remains the bedrock of management practice, both in the United States and in much of the rest of the industrial world that adopted the practices.

The third school of thinking discussed—human resources—takes a different approach to human motivation and how work should be organized, but, although this view gets much lip service and much press, few companies in the United States have really implemented it as theorists and some management consultants propose. Chapter 11 again discusses some alternatives in workplace organization and management based on this third school of thought.

First, let us recall from Chapter 2 the two opposing assumptions about work and human motivation that underlie the various management theories.

TWO OPPOSING WESTERN VIEWS OF THE NATURE OF HUMAN BEINGS AND MOTIVATION TO WORK: THE PROTESTANT ETHIC AND THE RENAISSANCE VIEWS

Views of Work in Other Societies

Chapter 2 relates the wide variety of views different societies have held regarding the nature of human beings and their motivation. This variety makes us aware that these views are truly "socially defined" concepts, growing out of the interactions peculiar to that time and place (Mills 1951: 215–223; U.S. Dept. of Health . . . 1973: 1–2; Tilgher 1930). We noted, for example, that hunting and gathering societies scarcely distinguish between work and leisure. Perhaps the lack of divisions of labor and social stratification makes tasks seem appropriate things for that gender or age group to do without further labeling. The activities themselves are integrated into the daily life as opportunity and necessity dictate. Since not much surplus can be stored, there is little incentive to do more than fill the group's immediate needs.

Western ideology, based on Judeo-Christian roots, initially took a dim view of human nature and motivation. The Hebrews, with their frequently angry God, saw work as a punishment for human frailty. It was said that people who went to Heaven would live in blissful idleness, having atoned for their sins by earthly toil. The Greeks, with slaves to do their bidding, saw manual work as demeaning, brutalizing to the mind, and making one unfit for higher virtues. Even though this is also a negative view of work, it encompasses the idea that the citizen should be using the head, not the hands. The early Church Fathers suppressed these pagan thoughts along with other Greek ideas.

The Christians, by the time of St. Augustine (354–430 A.D.), saw work as obligatory. Work was humbling and the monasteries had plenty of work that needed doing. People must work to keep away the devil and to keep down the sins of the flesh. This interpretation did not include rising out of one's station in life where God had put him or her.

The Protestant Ethic

During the Reformation, Martin Luther elevated work to man's first duty. Working hard in the position into which you had been born was a way of serving God. This interpretation added only a slightly more positive tone than did medieval Church doctrine. By the time Calvinists reinterpreted work, however, it became more than a duty; prospering from work was an indication that one was predestined to be among the chosen of God. The doctrine of predestination says that you were born already destined to be among either the chosen or the damned; but prospering in life indicated you were undoubtedly among the former. In the Calvinist view, salvation was the extrinsic reward to be sought, but making money was now respectable and a sign of grace. If you were not prospering in the position into which you had been born, then you needed to find a better occupation (Tawney 1958:2–3). This interpretation put the burden for prospering squarely on the individual's own initiative. It differentiates the new social order from what had gone before in an important way (Weber 1958).

In the latter part of the nineteenth century the Calvinist view, or Protestant ethic as it was called, was thriving in the industrializing United States. It still held that one must fulfill a duty to God by working as hard as possible on one's "calling." One must also live frugally and invest and thereby prosper. The Protestant ethic became enmeshed with Herbert Spencer's social Darwinism. This doctrine held that the fittest in society would prosper and rise to the top. (Social Darwinism followed the popularization of Charles Darwin's ideas concerning the adaptation of species to their environment and subsequent survival. As sometimes happens, people attempt to transfer so-called natural laws to laws governing human society.) This ideology suited the needs of the emerging industrial society in the United States with its urge for diligent labor and capital accumulation. People had replaced the extrinsic reward of salvation with the extrinsic reward of money and had lost sight of the goal of ultimate salvation. They did not consider the intrinsic reward—the content of the job.

The prevalence of the Horatio Alger myth also encouraged people to believe that anyone could rise from rags-to-riches or log cabin to the presidency if one worked hard enough. All the major social institutions—the economic, political, family, education, and media systems—supported this optimistic view of the efficacy of individual effort in an industrial society. Journalists, churchmen, and college presidents expounded on the virtues of businessmen and the good example they set. Even a few social scientists, such as sociologist William Graham Sumner, supported the social Darwin ideas (Bendix 1974:258). The implication was that people who did not prosper and rise in the social system lacked either talent or motivation to work. In this view the poor are at fault for their condition, because the social system was thought to provide opportunity for all people who really tried.

The Protestant ethic does not concern itself with conflict of interest between workers and owners, or workers' goals and goals of the organization. It also does not consider the power and interests of various strata of society since the analysis is at the individual, micro level. If employees work hard they will prosper along with their organization. Competition among workers within a firm and among businesses within an industry will make a stronger economy from which everyone will eventually gain. Adam Smith's "invisible hand"—each person's pursuing individual interest in the marketplace will improve the good of the whole—is an underlying assumption. Max Weber (1958, original 1904–1905) argued that it was necessary for the Protestant ethic to arise to throw out the traditional ideas of "just price" and "just wage" and to give positive reinforcement to self-interest and acquisitive activities before modern industrialism could emerge.

The Renaissance View

The Protestant ethic with its "economic rational" man motivated by the extrinsic reward of money was not the only view in Western society, although it was decidedly the predominant one. The Renaissance view of man, as we have discussed, developed during that time of exuberance in Southern Europe in which creative effort was thought to be one of the best reasons for living. In the nineteenth century such men as Tolstoy, Ruskin, Carlyle, William Morris, and Marx and Engels were revolted by what they felt classical economic theory and the organization of modern industry were doing to the average worker. They agreed with the Renaissance view that human beings were by nature *homo faber*, tool users, creators, craftspersons who developed themselves through the planning and execution of their labor. This was a head-and-hand approach that John Dewey tried to implement in the U.S. school system, with some results he did not intend.

Some of these critics of the system looked back to preindustrial days to a romanticized view of the medieval artisan as a model. Other critics had less fear of modern technology and criticized, instead, how the productive process and the economic system were organized—not the technology but the skewed distribution of ownership and control and the abysmal work conditions. Repetitive work created mindless workers, rather than persons who developed all-around personalities to the full of their human potential. The joy of work, which has the proper content to develop the worker both mentally and physically, is the intrinsic reward that motivates, according to the Renaissance view. Work would thus have to be reorganized if this intrinsic enjoyment and human development were to be fulfilled.

Both of these views of man, work, and motivation have the Western ideas that people should want to work and that nature exists to be used and exploited or reworked by human effort. As we have discussed, not all societies view work so positively. By the same token, not all societies hold an active mastery view of the natural environment. Many cultures, for example, the original American Indian societies, felt that people should live symbiotically with nature but not rework it.

Given the cultural ideas of the Protestant ethic, social Darwinism, and rags-to-riches prevalent in U.S. popular media, in education, and in the churches, plus the great respect for any idea appearing scientific and rational, it is not surprising that the first—and quite enduring—management theory is scientific management, which legitimates and consolidates the authority of the people already in power (Bendix 1974). Actually, many factors were involved in the development of this theory.

FOUR THEORIES OF MANAGEMENT

Scientific Management

Scientific management theory places the decision making for what will be produced, how it will be done, and who will do it directly in the hands of management. Managers, together with their staff, study the overall production process, break each job down to its smallest parts, do time-and-motion studies to determine how each task can be done efficiently, and instruct the worker on how to do it. The theory, seemingly simple in its top-down approach, had a complex beginning.

In addition to the cultural setting of the late nineteenth century, other factors encouraged the shape of management ideas around the turn of the century. The factors on which we comment include growth in size of both companies (often through mergers) and individual plants owned by the company and shifting of management from personal supervision of the individual entrepreneur and his few supervisors to foremen and supervisors who might not be in contact with distant owners and managers. Absentee owners were now financial capitalists who knew little about production. The supervisors were notoriously harsh and arbitrary. These conditions made control of the work force difficult.

The wider society experienced a rise of militance among workers, socialist parties, unions, and middle-class reformers who opposed growing monopolies and the often scandalous working conditions during the Progressive era. Introduction of new technologies further deskilled craftsworkers' jobs, adding to workers' objections. Increased immigration of workers with different languages, customs, and work habits also contributed to problems for both unions and management. Managers of large companies found themselves characterized in the media as both heroes and robber barons. They faced workers who resented both treatment on the job and their low wages. Strikes were no longer local matters between managers and workers; mass marketing by the monopolies/oligopolies brought in consumers from all over who could pressure the government to keep the industrial peace. For example, in 1902, when a dispute arose between workers and owners in the coal fields, Roosevelt intervened to keep the mines running for the East Coast with winter coming.

Management of the emerging large corporations wanted three basic things: (1) a tighter control over the work force, (2) bureaucratization and rationalization of the work process for efficiency, (3) increased public acceptance for whatever the companies were doing.

Two Social Factors—Size of Organizations and the New Industrial Work Force

The years between 1880 and 1920 saw a surge in industrial growth in the United States. The industrial work force tripled in size with increasing immigration (Hill 1981:24). Firms also increased in size, both at the company level and at the individual plant site. In the 1870s one of the largest plants was Cyrus McCormick's farm implement plant in Chicago, with 400 to 500 workers. Most companies, however, were still shop size, employing a few dozen people (Hill 1981:19–20; Nelson 1975:4). With the wave of mergers at the turn of the century, monopolies and oligopolies were created in steel (U.S. Steel), petroleum (Standard Oil), agricultural equipment (International Harvester), electrical equipment (General Electric and Westinghouse), tobacco (American Tobacco), and even cookies (National Biscuit), bananas (United Fruit), sugar (American Sugar), chewing gum (Wrigley's), meat (Swift and Armour), paper (International Paper), typewriters (Union), bicycles (American Bicycle), photographic supplies (Eastman Kodak), and sewing machines (Singer) (Edwards 1979:43–44). In 1902 U.S. Steel had 168,000 workers in their various plants, each of which had a great deal of autonomy (Edwards 1979:52–55). By 1920 the largest plants in the United States had more than 10,000 employees (Hill 1981:24). The primary/core industries discussed in Chapter 5 were being created.

The growth in size of these organizations led to increasing bureaucracy and functional rationality. The new management philosophy spurred this trend at the turn of the century. Max Weber described this bureaucracy in the second decade of the twentieth century, seeing both its good and bad features. He foresaw problems for individual freedom inherent in increased division of labor, hierarchy of authority, and set rules and procedures. We again discuss bureaucracy in Chapter 10; for now we see its occurrence as a factor in the management process of the period, away from personal management control of individual entrepreneurs to a bureaucratic, hierarchical form.

The new industrial workers were primarily first-generation factory workers, coming from the farm in the United States or joining the swelling ranks of immigrants who were often from peasantlike conditions in Europe (Gutman 1977:69). Many workers were not pleased with factory conditions (as we note in Chapter 7), and the turnover rate at some companies was sometimes 100 percent or more per year (Goldman and Van Houten 1981:210). Most of these new workers were not craftsmen. Management saw them as needing a great deal of organization and guidance.

Advancing technology appeared to make the craftsman less necessary. On some occasions new machinery was introduced in order to reduce the need for skilled craftsmen, who repeatedly organized unions to keep their wages up and maintain some control over their work situation (Goldman and Van Houten 1981). In the new factories of the nineteenth century some of these craftsmen, acting as foremen, had been given some control over less skilled workers and the production process. Particularly in the metal trades (steel, heavy machinery), foremen subcontracted jobs within the factory—hiring, firing, paying their own workers, handling the paperwork, and organizing production to some extent. The managers had trouble controlling the foremen (outside of firing them), and the workers had many grievances about the arbitrary cruelty of many foremen (Edwards 1979:30–34). The new management practices thus were to eliminate this foreman autonomy.

Engineering New Management Techniques

In this climate, managers, who were occasionally the entrepreneurs but increasingly persons hired by absentee owners in the joint stock companies, grew in numbers and in functions. As the organization became more complex and the new positions of hired manager increased in number, professional preparation for the position became important. The first business school to train management for the expanding industrial society was the Wharton School, established at the University of Pennsylvania in 1881. In 1898 the University of California and University of Chicago created business schools, soon followed by many more. New employers' associations also were formed, and business and technical journals appeared.

Many managers were active in the newly organized American Society of Mechanical Engineers (Chandler 1977: 272–281). In 1886 Henry R. Towne, the senior executive and major stockholder of Yale and Towne Lock Company, chose the theme of organization and management improvement for the annual meeting. Papers on cost accounting and capital accounting were given by such persons as Captain Henry Metcalfe, who had served as superintendent of several federal arsenals. His report on modifications of the account system first adopted by Springfield Armory brought agreements, discussion, and suggestions from Frederick W. Taylor of Midvale Steel and from other managers. This report suggested that the voucher accounting system be taken out of the hands of the foremen acting as internal contractors and placed in centralized clerical hands. A gain-sharing plan could be substituted for internal contracting that would be acceptable to foremen in return for the loss of their former control. As they reorganized, companies could also introduce new machinery that workers had often resisted.

Frederick Winslow Taylor (1911, 1947) delivered his first paper in 1895 on what he soon called "scientific management." He stated that the gains of the new gain-sharing plans should be based not on past experience but on new scientific studies of time and motion to set the standard or base line. Anyone working above the set rate would receive a higher piece rate. This system called for both managers and workers to accept the nonarbitrary dictates of consultants, something management was wary of, as it turned out.

The new scientific management practices Taylor proposed worked in this manner: (1) managers or the planning department would have to learn the entire production process from the skilled workers (an indication of how far from the production process management had come in the large companies); (2) the process of production would then be analyzed and divided into its smallest tasks; (3) time-and-motion studies would be conducted on each task to see how it could be performed most routinely and efficiently; and (4) workers would be hired and trained for one task, according to the worker's aptitudes. Taylor's studies in the steel industry indicate how high his base was for the piece rates.

One particularly well known study was accomplished with a Dutchman named Schmidt, whom Taylor described as "the type of the ox" and whom he taught to load 47.5 tons of pig iron per day with a shovel (in 92-pound scoops). Taylor himself admitted that only one man in eight could meet Schmidt's achievements (Braverman 1974:102–108). This high standard and the fact that jobs were reclassified at a lower rate under scientific management practices (according to economist Robert F. Hoxie's 1915 report to the U.S. Commission on Industrial Relations) appear to be why the productivity gains actually made were not shared with the workers (Braverman 1974:107–108). Economists Paul Douglas and Harold Faulkner (quoted in Goldman and Van Houten 1981:198–199; Edwards 1979:62, 229) noted that real wages in industry between 1890 and 1926 showed fluctuations but no real gains before World War I and that income was not adequate to support most working-class families decently.

Taylor's view was not so much that he thought all workers were stupid (although he does make occasional reference to management's being "better fitted" to make decisions than are workmen), but that he thought workers were "soldiering," not producing what they could if they worked at their top pace all day long. No doubt he was partly right in that most workers might not produce willingly and at top speed under the conditions that prevailed. Documentation abounds on the physical and mental stress and the high industrial accident and death rate during this period as fast-paced scientific management was put in place (Goldman and Van Houten 1981:196; Gersuny 1981).

A planning department was needed to carry out this reorganization of tasks, and later (especially from 1910 into the 1920s) companies added personnel departments to handle the increased functions of screening and hiring the right people for the right job. Hopefully, workers would be employees who had no leanings toward unions, which management did not want and which Taylor said were unnecessary now that wages were scientifically determined.

In the early part of the twentieth century many larger companies were beginning to take on the organizational structure we recognize as common practice today. This structure included the *line* (production) and *staff* (support functions, such as planning, personnel, finance, and bookkeeping) divisions. This increase in layers of bureaucracy on the administrative side emphasized distinct differences between blue- and white-collar jobs. A workman could no longer expect to enter into an apprenticeship and rise to manage his own shop, as in previous times.

The effects of these ideas when practiced in varying degrees of rigidity were (1) to increase worker efficiency and cut the cost of labor per unit produced, (2) to reduce the power of foremen and workers, (3) to cheapen and de-skill labor (particularly for the skilled craftsman) since each task could be easily taught and workers could be substituted for each other, (4) to place decision making, planning, and worker control firmly at higher management levels, (5) to expand the layers of white-collar jobs and bureaucracy, and (6) to reinforce the idea that people work only for pay incentives. In addition to the craftsmen's loss of self-esteem and job control were increased boredom and stress for the worker. High job turnover rates were to continue, except in times of economic recession and high unemployment.

Taylor and his fellow consultants applied their scientific management principles to about 250 U.S. firms between 1900 and 1925. The ideas soon caught on with other firms, which adapted the plans to suit their individual situations.

Germany and even the Soviet Union followed suit. Lenin, impressed with the efficiency and control over workers offered by scientific management, introduced it into the USSR in the 1920s (Braverman 1974:12–14). Britain followed more slowly. Management there was criticized for being old fashioned. British trade unions fought, often violently, against giving up their traditional occupational controls (Hill 1981: 32). Scientific management was not widely adopted in Great Britain until after World War II.

Human Relations School of Management

Human relations management theory, in a way a reaction to the harshness of scientific management, posited that workers were people and had social needs. The informal work groups they invariably formed could be used to the company's advantage. This theory was shaped in the following way.

Just as the principles of scientific management became almost universally accepted in some form in the 1920s, the Hawthorne studies at the Hawthorne plant of Western Electric (a profitable wholly owned subsidiary of AT&T) near Chicago were begun by management in 1924. These studies gave scientific support to what many people were already saying.

In this period the work of Freud was becoming more widely known. Industrial psychologists in the new personnel departments (using the new IQ tests developed during World War I and new personality tests) and other people writing in the business literature of the teens and twenties were talking about human engineering, the necessity of managers' becoming leaders of men, not just manipulators of production processes, and the possible effects of worker attitudes on productivity (Bendix 1974: 287–340). The groundwork for the adaptable organization man in a bureaucracy was being laid. Individualism and competitive spirit of the entrepreneur in the social Darwinist theory were giving way to the image of the communicator and the human relations expert who led people to cooperate. The general public was reading Dale Carnegie's first popular work, *Public Speaking and Influencing Men in Business* (1926), which expressed his ideas on how to get ahead by influencing people. This all built on the ideas of the New Thought movement at the turn of the century, regarding positive thinking and charisma and growing rich by using these assets to control the people around you.

The original purpose of the Hawthorne studies was to test the scientific management ideas that the physical surroundings of the worker, the worker's own physical abilities, and pay incentives all affected productivity. The company found their experiments so puzzling, Elton Mayo (1945, 1960) from Harvard Business School was called in to head an academic and business research team comprised of academicians and business people. The team included industrial psychologist F. J. Roethlisberger and Western Electric manager W. J. Dickson, who later wrote an exhaustive account of the studies (1939). They experimented with lighting, wall color, pay plans, and rest periods. In most experiments productivity rose regardless of what the change was—a new wall color, more light or less light, or changes in work break schedules.

By the end of the studies in 1932 the findings had led the researchers to conclude that the attention paid to the workers by management and researchers and the sociability developed among the workers in the experiment groups were the human "social needs" factors that affected productivity. The workers were happier, found work more pleasant, and produced more.

The Hawthorne effect of sparking increased effort through increased attention to and interest in the worker is firmly part of the vocabulary.

The conclusions of the studies have been questioned on serious grounds (Carey 1967; Macarov 1982; Rice 1982; Bramel and Friend 1981). For example, in the Relay Assembly experimental group of six women who wired telephone relay equipment, two workers who continued to talk and slow down group production were replaced by more cooperative workers, one of whom needed money desperately. The workers were paid according to their output as a group, and the new worker spurred the others on. In another experimental group paid by their effort as a group and given immediate feedback on performance, productivity went up. When their pay system was changed back to the output of the entire department, their productivity fell. Aside from the methodological error of deliberately changing workers to get rid of less motivated workers, the researchers did not emphasize that pay was apparently a very important factor in productivity in these groups.

In a men's experimental group (the Bank Wiring Room, where banks of equipment were wired) group pay incentives did not work as they had in the women's groups. The men set a quota and let workers who overproduced know their displeasure (the soldiering of which Taylor had become aware as a foreman at Midland Steel), sometimes by "binging" them painfully on the arm. Eventually the rate busters would slow their production. Output records were falsified "to retaliate against supervisors and inspectors who played favorites, to cover up for certain workers, and to discipline others" (Perrow 1986a:81). In addition to trying to maintain some control over their work situation, the men perhaps felt their quotas would be raised or a worker would be laid off if superiors discovered they could produce more. The Depression was deepening as this study was done and job security could have been a potent factor. The team, however, insisted on interpreting the behavior as "nonrational group sentiments."

Despite these later critiques of methodology and of the interpretation of results, the finding of the Hawthorne studies continue to have an impact on management thinking. Workers' social needs and their informal work groups need to be considered. Managers try to convince workers through human relations that the company cares for them, and they try to influence the norms set by informal groups to cooperate with company goals, rather than to resist them. To this end, counseling services were expanded in the personnel departments so workers could express both personal problems and work-related grievances. Suggestion boxes, company ball teams, picnics, service awards, sensitivity training groups for management and supervisors, and more studies on the impact of human relations on productivity were initiated. The findings of these studies have been inconclusive and inconsistent (Perrow 1986a:85−96).

The Mayo research team may also have overlooked another factor. Sociologist Paul Blumberg (1968) suggests that it was not just the attention paid to workers that satisfied their social needs, but also the amount of their participation in decision making about their own working conditions that increased their satisfaction and productivity. Many of the seventeen studies Blumberg cites were inspired by this conclusion that later researchers had drawn from the Hawthorne studies.

An example of the research prompted by such questions is the well-known 1939 study by Lippit and White (1958) and Lewin (1958). These researchers examined the effects of three leadership styles—authoritarian, democratic, and laissez faire. They recorded the reactions of four groups of eleven-year-old boys. Each group was exposed to two types of leadership during the observations. Under supervised authoritarian and democratic leadership the boys performed their activities, but when the authoritarian leader left the room activities stopped. When the democratic leader left the room, the boys continued the activities they had discussed and decided on. The laissez faire group, who were allowed to do as they pleased, spent so much time discussing that they seldom got around to the activities. The groups preferred the democratic leadership format. Having a voice in deciding what was to be done appeared to affect both satisfaction and motivation positively.

Other studies (Coch and French 1947: 512–532; Goldsmidt and Wilson 1980) summarizing teaching effectiveness in numerous situations indicate that participation in group discussion and decision making motivate people to act on the policies more frequently than does being told what to do by an authority figure. Apparently, people can learn content equally well from a lecture as from discussion. People are more readily motivated to act, however, if they have had a voice in arriving at the policies and procedures they are to follow. These conclusions bring us to some of the assumptions underlying the human resources theories discussed next.

Whether the human relations view was a well-intentioned effort to improve working conditions or a capitalist trick to get the workers to produce more without giving them a real voice in decision making (Bramel and Friend 1981) is moot. That it did bring about some minimal reforms by encouraging management to try to appear to treat workers as human beings rather than as robots must be viewed as an improvement. Corporations began talking a great deal about "our team" and "our company family."

On the other hand, the movement did not appear to change many managers' minds concerning the lack of capabilities of their workers and the subsequent need for managers to make all the decisions. Some researchers (Herzberg et al. 1959: 185–192; Braverman 1974: 37–39) feel that the human relations emphasis on sensitivity training for managers to learn to handle their workers in less irritating ways is a facade for manipulation and a handy public relations hype. It treats the symptoms of employee dissatisfaction but does not reach the underlying problem of the authority structure that prevents meaningful worker participation in decision making.

Human Resources

Human resources management theory, coming from the Renaissance view of workers as being creative and needing an opportunity to develop, emphasizes worker participation in decision making in varying degrees, depending on the inclination of the theorist.

Chapter 3 discusses some remarkable changes taking place in the United States in the post–World War II period: (1) the country had its longest period of prosperity in history; (2) educational levels had risen to new highs; (3) unemployment was low, for the most part, freeing many people to worry about other things besides subsistence; (4) minorities, including women, were pushing for civil rights, including better jobs; and (5) countercultures in the 1960s urged the worth of individuals, personal creativity, and individuality, and the alienation inherent in routinized, industrialized societies. *Alienation* and *liberation* became common words in the language. The media talked about worker dissatisfactions—"blue-collar blues" and "white-collar woes." People pointed to signs of dissatisfaction—absenteeism, turnover, poor work quality, drug use, and occasional sabotage. It was said that workers also wanted freedom to make decisions and more social equality.

Social psychologists and other people imbued with the humanistic spirit of the 1960s began to support a Renaissance view of people closer to Marx's *homo faber* than to the economic man view of scientific management or the social man view of the human relations school of management. The Renaissance view stressed that people have a need to self-actualize or to develop themselves to the best of their potential. This view fit well into the humanistic flavor of the times. Important theorists, such as Maslow, Argyris, Herzberg, Dubin, McGregor, and Likert contended that workplace organization under previous schools of thought left workers at the immature stage of obedient, dependent children and did not develop mature, responsible, creative powers. These theorists felt that the content of the job must be improved if workers are to gain intrinsic rewards. Their views on motivation have been called content theories of motivation.

Alienation

To understand what attracted social psychologists to study in this area, it is necessary to consider the concept of alienation. *Alienation* means being separated or estranged from something; the connotation is that people are made unhappy by this separation. In *Das Kapital* (1867) Marx noted that under the new mode of organization in industrial Great Britain, the worker's loss of ownership and control produced alienation and lack of job satisfaction in the following manner:

1. Loss of control over product: Alienation from recognition that what the workers have created is theirs in the sense that their skills in planning and shaping the product have made it what it is—it has been appropriated by other people who then have control over it.

2. Loss of control over the production process: The workers sell their labor as a commodity and all their efforts are directed by the commands of other people.
3. Alienation from other people: Social relations become market relations and people are judged by their position in the market rather than by their human qualities; hence, their job status and income determine their esteem and worth in the eyes of other people and this translates into one's degree of self-esteem.
4. Alienation from the worker's human nature or his or her species being: The worker's labor has become a commodity, and the worker has no opportunity to develop personal potential as a human being; the worker cannot self-actualize.

Stated in slightly different ways, these four basic points are supported by theorists who take the human resources approach.

Maslow

Abraham H. Maslow (1954: 80–98) contends that human beings are motivated by a hierarchy of needs. When people's lower needs are relatively satisfied, they usually strive to fill a higher need. Maslow's hierarchy of needs includes:

1. Physiological (hunger, thirst, sex, sleep).
2. Safety and security (protection of the physical self and life-style).
3. Belongingness and love (affection, companionship, being a part of a group).
4. Self-esteem, esteem by other people (self-approval, approval by other people for one's accomplishments, power, prestige).
5. Self-actualization (the desire to become what one is potentially, to become more and more what one is capable of becoming).

Maslow recognized that not only would people operate at varying need levels, but that one might be trying to fulfill needs on various levels at the same time and that some people might seek higher needs without seeking to fulfill lower needs. Personality and cultural environment keep the hierarchy from complete rigidity and predictability.

Argyris

Christopher Argyris's personality theory (1960) emphasizes that modern hierarchically structured organizations force workers back to immature stages of blind obedience and dependency. Workers' qualities of activity, independence and autonomy, interest in work for its own sake, long-term perspective, self-esteem, and self-control either atrophy or never get a chance to develop at work. Organizations need to restructure authority and jobs to foster this human growth, if individual satisfaction and motivation and organizational productivity and adaptability are to flourish. For its own good the organization must be restructured to meet the development needs of its employees.

Herzberg

Frederick Herzberg (Herzberg, Mausner, and Snyderman 1959) attempted to find out what satisfied and dissatisfied people in the workplace by asking: "Think of a time when you felt exceptionally good or exceptionally bad about your present job or any other job you have had. Tell me what happened." This question was followed in the interview with fourteen questions concerning each of the two events described. Herzberg found that he had two separate lists instead of a continuum from satisfaction to dissatisfaction on the same variables. The satisfiers or motivators are in the area of job content—the task itself, achievement, recognition for achievement, autonomy, advancement, and acquisition of new skills. Items that caused dissatisfaction were related to job environment, which Herzberg calls hygiene factors—salary; security; company policies and administration; working conditions; relationships with superiors, peers, and subordinates; status of the job; and personal life. A person could be pleased with the job environment without necessarily being satisfied with the job; one was just less dissatisfied. By the same token, one could be satisfied with the job content and at the same time dissatisfied with the job environment. Satisfactions from the intrinsic rewards of job content seem to last longer. Herzberg goes on to present a more elaborate scheme of people who look only for extrinsic rewards and people who are motivated by intrinsic rewards by placing each variable on separate scales of mental health.

Many studies have replicated Herzberg's work. Herzberg discusses nine of them in detail (1966), all of which confirm his major findings with only minor departures. Another review (Kaplan, Tausky, and Bolaria 1969) found thirty-nine studies dealing in some way with Herzberg's theory. Nineteen confirmed the importance of self-actualization; twenty did not. Leaving aside methodological differences in the studies, Tausky (1978: 58–59) estimates that half the workers were interested in self-actualization and half were not.

Who has the satisfiers/motivators? Is it only the college-educated or white-collar workers? Herzberg says:

From a survey of industrial research efforts reported in my book *Job Attitudes: Research and Opinion*, which encompassed almost a half-century of

effort on the part of industrial psychologists, I have documented this difference between the blue-collar workers and their more fortunate white-
collar brothers. But the reader will recall that contrary to this established
belief, the samples of blue-collar workers and women in the replications of
the motivation-hygiene study appeared to be no different in their job attitudes from engineers, scientists and managers. Such differences as did occur were clearly attributed to the way in which these workers were used
on the job. (1966: 191)

The not-too-surprising finding is that people with dull, routine jobs
turn to pay and other hygiene factors for their satisfaction (or, more
appropriately, less dissatisfaction) criteria. People with more challenging
jobs that offer some measure of intrinsic reward, whether blue-collar or
white-collar, express more satisfaction with this type of reward. Expectations are, in large part, learned on the job—people who have never had
a challenging job are less likely to complain of what they are missing
and, instead, complain about the pay and working conditions. As Maslow (1973:29) says in commenting on the level in the hierarchy of needs
at which someone is functioning:

> There are various ways of judging the motivational level of life. For in-
> stance, one can judge the level at which people live by the kind of humor
> that they laugh at . . . . In the same way it was my thought that the level
> of complaints—which is to say, the level of what one needs and craves and
> wishes for—can be an indicator of the motivational level at which the
> person is living; and if the level of complaints is studied in the industrial
> situation, it can be used also as a measure of the level of health of the
> whole organization, especially if one has a large enough sampling.

Maslow (1973:30) suggests that people operating on the self-
actualization level will not complain about the pay or the washroom
facilities but about barriers in communication, not getting all the facts,
injustice when virtue is not rewarded, inefficiency, and, it might be added, lack of opportunity for growth.

Another comment on Herzberg's work regards his claim that his
studies demonstrate that workers who are satisfied by intrinsic job content rewards are harder workers or more productive, in general. He finds
that these workers tend to be "overachievers," whereas workers who are
seeking only extrinsic hygiene rewards, if they do achieve on the job, do
so because of talent rather than any special effort (Herzberg 1966:90).
Professor of social work David Macarov (1982) questions this connection between satisfaction and increased productivity. We return to the
question of worker aspirations in the section on internal labor markets
in Chapter 10 and to a discussion of the satisfaction-productivity
connection in Chapter 11.

Herzberg's solution to the dilemmas of job satisfaction and, if he is correct, increased productivity is job enrichment. Job enrichment does not mean only job rotation or job enlargement—which give the worker more tasks but not necessarily more stimulating ones. Job enrichment means eliminating the task simplification aspect of scientific management, because morale problems have become too expensive. It also means organizing jobs around more complexity and responsibility, an opportunity for growth in skills, and a chance for creativity and interesting content that will make the job seem worthwhile (1966: 177–178). Jenkins (1974: 170) complains that in his consulting work Herzberg settled for less than job enrichment. Instead of letting the workers themselves participate in restructuring the job, the consultants and management usually do it and the result of the restructuring often became a case of job enlargement.

Herzberg himself recognized the problem of restructuring the organization into more flexible job enrichment that fully uses its human resources/personnel. One major barrier is that managers are fearful and "not prepared to meet the challenge of managing adults" (Herzberg 1966: 189–190). These inadequate managers justify their failure to restructure in terms of short-run economic necessity while ignoring the long-run costs of fossilization of the organization and loss of creativity and productivity on the part of all levels of employees.

Dubin

Related to this discussion of which workers are motivated by the contents of the job itself are the findings of studies on central life interest. Dubin and other researchers (Dubin and Champoux 1975; Dubin, Champoux, and Porter 1975; Dubin 1956) sought to determine what areas of their lives workers considered most important and in which situations would they prefer to be involved. Job orientation was the important area for 48 percent of white-collar employees in industrial organizations, for 45 percent of white-collar workers in nonindustrial organizations, for 25 percent of blue-collar workers in industrial settings, and for only 12 percent of blue-collar workers in nonindustrial organizations. Even though these percentages are lower than those for people reported to be oriented to intrinsic job content, there is a close correlation in another way between the two sets of figures. More challenging jobs are found more frequently in the white-collar area, particularly among professionals and managers. Wherever challenging jobs are found, it might be expected that they would positively influence job orientation as a central life interest.

Tausky (1978: 60) sees the lower job-orientation percentages as a criticism of self-actualization as being an effective work motivator. If a person is not interested in work, how can restructuring job content be of value? This begs the question of causal direction in the work and interest relationship. If having challenging work increases the motivation for self-actualization on the job, as it appears to do, then would this increased enthusiasm not cause a person to become more work-oriented—perhaps even cause work to become a central life interest? This sounds plausible, but the issue remains unresolved. The alternative would be to assume that old experiences on and off the job are so deeply ingrained that people will not or cannot change. In Chapter 12 we return to the question of whether people should be job oriented in the discussion of what might lie in the future for U.S. society.

McGregor.

Douglas McGregor (1957) describes two opposing styles of organization and management based on differing assumptions about the nature of human motivation.

Theory X, fairly typical of U.S. organizations, is described as bureaucratically structured, with managers deciding and workers being persuaded to follow orders through rewards or punishments. The underlying assumptions of Theory X are that workers are inherently lazy, uninterested in the goals of the organization, work only for monetary rewards, and not very intelligent. *Theory Y* organizations structure the workplace so workers can assume responsibility, have input on their own jobs, and actively pursue their own goals while promoting those of the organization. The view of human motivation in this theory is that workers have abilities and will want to develop their human capabilities if given the opportunity. Theory Y assumes that people are not naturally passive or inherently opposed to the goals of organizations, but that their work experiences may have made them that way.

Likert.

Rensis Likert's (1967) studies come to similar conclusions. He categorizes organizations into four types. System 1, "exploitative authoritative," uses threats, punishment, and rewards to encourage worker activity. System 2, "benevolent authoritative," uses economic rewards and human relations techniques to placate the worker. System 3, "consultative," still offers basically economic rewards but allows a modicum of worker involvement—a Scanlon plan might be an example. System 4, "participative group," offers both economic rewards and active participation in decision making for workers.

Likert suggests that System 4 organizations may use a *linking pin* form of overlapping problem-solving groups throughout the company. The leader of each group (similar to quality circles on the shop floor, discussed in Chapter 11) participates in the discussions of higher level groups, passing on information from his or her own work group and gaining information for this group from the higher level. Likert suggests that this form of organization should produce new ideas, ego involvement, higher productivity, greater worker satisfaction, and less turnover. Experiments based on his plan have not always supported these contentions, however, leaving one to speculate whether Likert was incorrect in his contentions or whether the plan was incorrectly implemented (Tausky 1978: 52). From the evidence of the success or failure of quality circles and other worker participation plans, one might suspect that implementation is a key factor in the success of any worker participation plan (see Chapter 11).

Japan's Theory Z

One cannot complete a discussion of human resources theories without noting the impact of Japanese management methods on U.S. management thinking. By the late 1960s lagging U.S. productivity and problems with product quality were being compared to Japanese high productivity and high quality control. Japanese management practices came under scrutiny. Quality circles were adopted by companies in the United States. Ouchi (1981) suggests that U.S. companies need to incorporate some of their ideas into a *Theory Z,* which includes long-term and less specialized careers, consensual decision-making, more individual responsibility, and increased communications and cooperation. Use of human resources is a key factor. We continue the comments on Japan and quality circles in Chapter 11.

Summary of Studies on Human Resources Approaches

What can be said about the results of experiments with worker participation in decision making? Many researchers (Berman 1967; Frieden 1980; Ford 1983; Conte, Tannenbaum, and McCulloch 1981; New York Stock Exchange 1982; Thomas and Logan 1982; Zwerdling 1980) investigating the impact of different forms of participation report a positive connection between worker participation in decision making and gain-sharing and productivity. Others (Tausky 1978: 60–61; Hellriegel, Slocum, and Woodman 1983) find these claims inconclusive since one can cite cases in which participation did not appear to work. The structural contingency theories, discussed in the next section, find human resources theorists are relying too heavily on one best way of organizing and are unrealistic in their assumption of the ability of most people to rise to a content theory of motivation, that is, to the need for self-actualization.

Structural Contingencies Theories

A fourth dimension added to management theory is discussed here under the rubric of structural contingencies theories, although various writers have labeled their approaches with such terms as *resource dependency theory, dependence exchange,* and *political economy model.* These terms are not synonymous, but they all imply interdependence of either the organization with its external environment or of the units within the organization.

Structural contingency theorists are concerned with (1) organizational structure (technology process and nature of the product, departmental function and structure, departmental interdependency); (2) the environment in which the organization finds itself (nature and degree of uncertainty in material supply, political/legal factors, international and domestic competition and markets); (3) how the organization operates in this environment (there is always more than one way an organization can deal with uncertainty); and (4) reward system set up to encourage the workers to increase their effort (given that departments may be structured differently and people's needs are different).

In the complex environment of the 1970s, U.S. businesses found themselves being outcompeted many times on the world market, and government and other service agencies in the domestic scene found conflicting and increasing demands on them. Instant communications were creating more regional and global interdependence for many if not all organizations. Organizational theorists, political economists, and sociologists had been studying the effects of technology and the organization in the wider environment during the postwar period. It seems reasonable that management theories should begin to incorporate environmental features and information from as many disciplines as possible in order to deal with the complexities of their situation. The results have been varied and eclectic—taking ideas from many sources. With this growing complexity and cross-disciplinary approach, a certain amount of pragmatism seems apparent in structural contingency theories, in general. This flurry of activity and production of ideas, articles, and consulting is interesting to compare to hundred years ago or so when two papers and a keynote address at a newly formed association of engineer/managers and a few earlier works were all the formal management theory materials available.

Since much of the work done by structural contingency theorists is covered elsewhere in this text, this section only highlights the contributions of a few people and summarizes some general ideas. Chapter 5 looks at political economy and resource dependency work dealing with organizations trying to control uncertain environments. Chapter 10 returns to the writings on technology processes and products and departmental functions and interdependencies within organizations.

The External Environment

Most organizations are *open systems*—they receive inputs from the environment (such as raw materials) and must deal with the environment to distribute their output (such as sales and marketing). With departments that act as buffers to the outside world (procurement, personnel, marketing and sales, legal, and public relations), the organization tries to operate, as best it can, as a closed system in the production department. This is true whether the organization is producing autos or social services. Closed systems are predictable; open systems are not. The boundary buffer positions (see Figure 10.1 in Chapter 10) try to reduce uncertainty and keep internal production as level as possible by whatever mechanisms can be mustered (Domhoff 1970; Mills 1956; Tausky 1978: 64–67). For example, organizations have the following six options.

1. Materials can be stockpiled or a supplier or distributor can be purchased in vertical integration. One example of this is in the Florida citrus industry, where five corporations dominate the industry. While their business initially was processing, to stabilize input and output these companies now control the orange from the field to the truck that distributes the frozen and canned juice to the retailer. Some conglomerates in other fields have even purchased retail chains to assure that what they process has a guaranteed retailer. A corporation that owned a meat packing company purchased the Hickory Farms retail chain to assure that their sausages had a place to go.

2. Through their associations (the American Dairy Association, the American Medical Association, and the National Association of Manufacturers, for example) or through their power as giant corporations, industries try to make sure that national and state laws and regulations are favorable. This can be accomplished through their lobbies, campaign contributions, staffing regulatory boards and government agencies with personnel from the industry, and financial support of foundations and policy-making associations that influence public policy (for example, the Committee on Economic Development, the Foreign Policy Association, and the Brookings Institution.

3. Horizontal mergers (buying out companies in the same industry) help reduce competition for market shares. Interlocking directorates help reduce uncertainty though information sharing or by gaining privileged channels of credit. Interlocks can be either direct, by a corporation placing its representative on another company's board, or indirect, by having persons from each company on the board of a third company. Every corporation wants to be interlocked to a bank and/or an insurance company to assure credit at favorable terms when needed.

4. Advertising and special offers to encourage consumer buying during slack times help smooth some of the peaks and valleys in demand in order to keep production stable. Marketing departments try to make sales more predictable through their forecasts, working hand-in-hand with research and development departments as new products are suggested.

5. Personnel departments attempt to hire employees they feel will fit in and be good company workers. Since workers also have problems with their outside environments, many personnel departments offer employee-assistance programs (EAPs) that provide counseling and other services to help the workers solve personal problems (family and drug abuse, for example).

6. Public relations and the legal department may even have to handle outputs that the public does not want—such as toxic wastes, unsafe products, and occupational disease.

Buffer departments that deal with these uncertainties or contingencies in the outside environment must be organized flexibly for more communications. Rigid rules and procedures can hamper dealing with new or uncertain situations. Research and development departments are a prime example of the need for flexibility and communications among themselves, with other departments, and with the outside world (such as consumers or the scientific community) to foster creativity and problem solving.

Technology, Product and Interdependencies within the Organization

As discussed, *technology*, as used in this book and by structural contingency theorists, is not limited only to machinery or computers. Rather, technology is used here in its generic sense, which also includes the study of techniques or tasks (Perrow 1986a: 141). Structural contingency notes that the internal production unit of the organization is affected by both the nature of its technology and the nature of the product. One well-known early example of categories of technology and product is Joan Woodward's (1965). She classified the following three types of units produced that seem to call for different forms of technology organization: (1) large-batch and mass production of the same or similar units, often on assembly lines; (2) continuous process production, such as the production of gases or liquids that pass through stages of production in pipes handled only by gauges; and (3) unit and small-batch production of a limited number of units according to the specifications of a customer—custom production.

Small-batch production, like buffer departments dealing with the outside world, need more flexibility. Worker participation in a more craftsperson manner and frequent communications between workers and managers are necessry to solve the problems of new products. Large-batch production can run on ready-made rules and semiskilled operators, instead of craftspersons. In continuous process operations the workers who handle the gauges must be skilled in case something goes amiss. In such a crisis the worker must understand the whole process and act quickly to forestall damage. The problems at the Three Mile Island nuclear power plant are a memorable example of what happens if equipment malfunctions, the system design is faulty, and operators are not completely knowledgeable about the situation due to poor instruction about what can happen when several things go wrong at once. One organizational theorist suggests that as our industrial processes become more complex and risky, it is normal for system, equipment, and operator failures to occur together. Because of all the permutations of causes and effects and contingencies, he argues that it is impossible for anyone to be adequately trained (Perrow 1984, 1986b).

James Thompson (1967: 14–19) uses another typology of technologies. This typology focuses on how departments within an organization function and interact with one another. In mediating technology, interdependent elements are linked when necessary in a standardized manner, such as in banking, the postal service, departments of a university; each unit contributes its discrete service to the whole. In long-linked technology, the output of one group or department becomes the input for another in a standardized manner, such as a routine assembly-line. Intensive technology is the custom-made technology with no predictable sequence and in which various groups are called on as needed, such as custom production, research units, hospital emergency units, social work, and maintenance and operating units of airlines. Each unit is dependent on the others but in no particular sequence. As you may surmise from understanding Woodward's categories, intensive technology calls for a great deal of flexibility and communications among units for maximum efficiency. Long-linked technology allows a more rigid structure of rules and less responsibility for lower-level decision making. Mediating technology can operate with overall policy coordination, with some flexibility within each unit.

Charles Perrow (1970, 1986a) is a contingency theorist who analyzes organizational technology in terms of the amount of discretion workers must have for efficient operation. His fourfold typology is based on two independent dimensions—the degree of variability in process and product and the degree of uncertainty and complexity in search procedures for production problem solving.

1. In a routine situation, rules and policies can be made at the top, and lower-level workers have little to decide.
2. In an engineering technology, plans are made centrally, but discretionary judgments are made at the middle-managerial level.
3. In craft technology, schedules are made at the administrative level, but workers on the shop floor have discretionary judgment.
4. In nonroutine technology, interdependence among units and management calls for much communication and frequent discretionary judgments by mutual agreement.

Perrow (1986a:43) later expanded his typology to include other "clusters" of technological types. He notes that most organizations are more centralized in decision making than they need to be, according to the various factors involved in the model. This overcentralization occurs because of tradition, rather than necessity (Perrow 1986a: 149–152).

We have been talking here about degrees of uncertainty in the environment for organizations and their units, differing technologies they use due to both product and uncertainty of the environment, and different discretionary judgment levels. One study tried to see the simultaneous effects of all these factors.

Lawrence and Lorsch (1967) studied three industries that have different levels of uncertainty and different degrees of diversity or homogeneity in their environments. *Diversity* here means that not all departments face certainty or uncertainty uniformly. *Homogeneity* here means that the environment was uniformly either certain or uncertain for all departments—such as sales, production, and design. The plastics industry was found to have a highly uncertain environment with diverse uncertainty for departments. The food-processing industry had a moderately uncertain environment with moderately diverse impact on departments. The standard-container industry had a relatively certain environment with a fairly homogeneous impact on all departments.

These external features strongly affected how departments were organized with regard to (1) time orientation—short- or long-range planning; (2) interpersonal orientation of managers—whether they were task oriented or had a more congenial facilitator leadership style; and (3) formality of structure—whether departments ran by rigid rules or were more flexible. The economically more successful firms had developed structures adapted to their environments. Again, from previous discussion, we can surmise what these adaptations will look like. The more uncertain and diverse the environment, then the more differentiation there will be in style among organizational units (plastics, in this case). The more certain and homogeneous the environment, the more similarly organized the units (standard containers) will be.

In addition, the successful companies had managed to integrate their organizations with appropriate communications—very difficult for plastics with diversely organized units. The standard-container companies could get by with memos between departments, the food-processing companies had to have temporary cross-departmental teams to work out problems, and the plastics firms had permanent cross-departmental, cross-functional teams. Frequent problem solving and intense communications were extremely important in an uncertain environment with departments organized quite differently to meet their varying degrees of uncertainty.

Jay Galbraith (1973) continues this line of study on how organizations must be structured to cope with the different problems arising from differing degrees of certainty and uncertainty. Uncertainty, calling for increased communications and frequent decision making, can be done by work teams (people from varying departments working on the problem together), rapid communications (computers collecting instant information from all departments so that management makes decisions with all data at their finger tips), or decentralized decision making (decisions made at the level where the information is). It is interesting to note that in the teams, liaison individuals, task forces, or matrix design (where individuals from several departments report to a higher project manager for the duration of the project), Galbraith seems to be talking about managers at the lower and middle levels participating, not the line workers.

Motivation in Contingency Theories

According to contingency theorists, how are people motivated to perform? If organizational structures are somewhat determined by contingent environmental conditions (certainty and uncertainty) and by the technology required for the product and the environment, how are people to be rewarded in such differently structured departments and organizations? We have noted that some contingency theorists criticize human resource people for relying on one best way. Contingency theorists often emphasize that a variety of rewards are needed, although some theorists emphasize human resources (intrinsic) motivation whenever possible. Recall, for example, Perrow's comment that most organizations are much more centralized than their operations call for. These organizations would benefit, he feels, from some decentralization of decision making.

Contingency theory implies that some organizations may not need worker involvement, in the sense of self-actualizing, if the environment and technology are certain and routine. Taking this view, of course, would ignore the needs and possible contributions of the worker. If the worker's motivations are not to be self-actualization and job content, what does elicit worker effort in these cases? The answer given is that a variety of types of rewards must be available. Even though process motivation theories recognize that intrinsic rewards (human resources argument) do give more and longer lasting job satisfaction, they also often emphasize the extrinsic rewards of pay and status. The basis is behaviorism of the B. F. Skinner operant conditioning (stimulus-response) variety, positive reinforcement of performance through the rewards people want.

What operant conditioning means in this context is that a person must be able to expect that good performance will elicit a certain reward. The implication for managers, then, is that they must first know what rewards their workers seek and how intensely they desire the rewards. Second, managers must clearly spell out what constitutes good performance in each case and what reward can be expected for this achievement. Third, workers must be encouraged to believe that they can actually achieve high performance (the criteria for this performance must be realistic). Fourth, the actual reward must be high enough to be worth the effort and must be delivered promptly if high performance is to be reinforced. Above all, employees must have the perception of fairness, or equity, in their situation. Process theories of motivation have been variously called exchange theory, instrumentality-valence (valence refers to the intensity with which one seeks the reward), instrumentality theory, expectancy, and equity theory. Each theory emphasizes some aspect of the expectations–performance–reward process.

QUESTIONS FOR THOUGHT

Many questions arise from considering the evolution of management thought and practices in the twentieth century. The overall questions are: Are our ideas and our goals being unduly limited by our past experiences, or by our perceptions of what those experiences were? Are there more workable choices than we are allowing ourselves to consider?

How much bureaucratic rationalization and social control—legacies from scientific management—are really necessary in the United States today? How much environmental and technological determinism is desirable or allowable? Is there only one way of organizing large-batch operations, such as automobile assembly lines? One might want to consider the work team approach of Volvo and Saab-Scania and its advantages and disadvantages.

Should workers be encouraged to seek self-actualization and intrinsic rewards in their work through job redesign and authority restructuring, or should only their current perceptions of their needs be fostered if they work only for extrinsic rewards? How much do individuals and organizations stand to gain or lose by not promoting worker decision-making at all levels? Is this even possible? Are worker and organizational goals truly compatible or can they be made so if they are not? Charles Perrow (1986a: 98–99) provides a lengthy list of questionable business practices and asks us to ponder if it is "mature" and "self-actualizing" and "participating in meaningful work" for workers to agree to go along with them—false advertising, cover-ups of unjustified expenses in government contracts, price-fixing, inadequately tested drugs, and developing chemical warfare materials, for example. Can organizations rethink their goals to include rewarding self-actualizing whistle-blowers? Surely this step calls for a major reordering of priorities in society at large.

Again, recourse to worker participation plans already in existence, more information on the structure of the political economy, more labor history, and more information on the types of worker satisfaction are important for considering these questions. Later chapters examine a little on each of these areas. The "moral judgments" Perrow asks us to think about are somewhat beyond the purview of this book, but information concerning some of the behind-the-scenes practices of which he spoke is provided in a consideration of power and its use in Chapters 5, 6, and 7.

SUMMARY

All of the management views discussed here have added something to our knowledge. Seen in chronological order, each view has been a reaction to or an addition to what has gone before—shaped by the time period out of which it grew.

1. Each view incorporates an ideology of how people either are or ought to be—the Protestant ethic view, which emphasizes that people

work for extrinsic rewards, and the Renaissance view, which claims that the real motivators are intrinsic rewards.

2. Scientific management appeared in a time of rapidly growing organizational size, technological innovation, immigration, and labor/management conflict. Both for rationalization and social control purposes, decision making was centralized in the hands of management. Scientific management does not emphasize the capabilities of the average worker. The entire work process is analyzed and subdivided into tasks. Each task in the process is studied to determine the most efficient manner in which it is to be performed. Extrinsic rewards (pay, benefits, etc.) are emphasized.

3. Human relations, coming after Freud's writings and the works of communications people such as Dale Carnegie were becoming well-known, emphasized the worker's social needs. The manager was urged to treat workers as human beings rather than as machines and to try influencing their informal groups' goals to support organizational goals. To the extrinsic rewards of pay and benefits, the employer must add recognition of workers' achievements.

4. Human resources, blossoming in the humanistic liberation period of the 1960s, sought autonomy and self-actualization in the workplace befitting a society that calls itself democratic. This view stressed reorganizing the workplace to allow for more worker participation in decision making on the shop-floor or higher levels. Intrinsic rewards of job content were emphasized.

5. In the period of the 1970s, with its increasing economic and interdependency problems, theorists turned to what they considered a pragmatic, realistic approach, emphasizing that numerous factors within and outside of the organization must be considered, including technology and product, material supply, political and legal factors, and department interaction. Along with this, clear-cut performance standards and the delivery of various types of rewards to fit varying needs of workers also must be available. Contingency theories call for an exceptionally flexible style of leadership ready to cope with numerous uncertainties. .

6. Studying the history of various management theories seems to call forth consideration of future directions, which include serious questions of our values and priorities in our society.

BIBLIOGRAPHY

Argyris, Christopher. 1960. *Understanding organizational behavior.* Homewood, Ill.: Dorsey.
Bendix, Reinhard. 1974. *Work and authority in industry: Ideologies of manage-*

ment in the course of industrialization. Berkeley: University of California Press. Originally published 1956.

Berman, Katrina. 1967. *Worker-owner plywood companies: An economic analysis.* Pullman: Washington State University Press.

Blumberg, Paul. 1968. *Industrial democracy: The sociology of participation.* New York: Schocken.

Bramel, Dana, and Ronald Friend. 1981. Hawthorne, the myth of the docile worker and class bias in psychology. *American Psychologist* 36:867–878 (August).

Braverman, Harry. 1974. *Labor and monopoly capital: The degradation of work in the twentieth century.* New York: Monthly Review Press.

CBS. 1986. The captain is a lady, (transcript). *60 Minutes,* 18, 50:6–11 (August 24).

Carey, Alex. 1967. The Hawthorne studies: A radical criticism. *American Sociological Review* 3:403–416 (June).

Carnegie, Dale. 1926. *Public speaking and influencing men in business.* New York: W. W. Norton.

Chandler, Alfred D., Jr. 1977. *The visible hand: The managerial revolution in American business.* Cambridge, Mass.: Belknap Press of Harvard University Press.

Coch, Lester, and John R. P. French, Jr. 1947. Overcoming resistance to change. *Human Relations* 1:512–532.

Conte, Michael A., Arnold S. Tannenbaum, and Donna McCulloch. 1981. *Employee ownership.* Ann Arbor: Institute for Social Research, University of Michigan.

Domhoff, G. William. 1970. *The higher circles: The governing class in America.* New York: Random.

Dubin, Robert. 1956. Industrial workers' worlds: A study of the 'central life interests' of industrial workers. *Social Problems* 3, 1–4:131–142.

———, and Joseph E. Champoux. 1975. Workers' central life interests and personality characteristics. *Journal of Vocational Behavior* 6, 2:165–174.

———, Joseph E. Champoux, and Lyman W. Porter. 1975. Central life interests and organizational commitment of blue-collar workers. *Administrative Science Quarterly* 20:411–421.

Edwards, Richard. 1979. *Contested terrain: The transformation of the workplace in the twentieth century.* New York: Harper & Row (Torchbooks).

Ford, Ramona. 1983. Case study: Phillips Paper Products. *Employee Ownership* 3, 2:8 (June).

Frieden, Karl. 1980. *Workplace democracy and productivity.* Washington, D.C.: National Center for Economic Alternatives.

Galbraith, Jay. 1973. *Designing complex organizations.* Reading, Mass.: Addison-Wesley.

Gersuny, Carl. 1981. *Work hazards and industrial conflict.* Hanover, N.H.: University Press of New England for the University of Rhode Island.

Goldman, Paul, and Donald R. Van Houten. 1981. "Bureaucracy and domination: Managerial strategy in turn-of-the-century American industry." In *Complex Organizations: Critical Perspectives,* edited by Mary Zey-Ferrell and Michael Aiken, 189–216. Glenview, Ill.: Scott, Foresman.

Goldsmidt, Charles A., and Everett K. Wilson. 1980. *Passing on sociology: The teaching of a discipline.* Belmont, Calif.: Wadsworth.

Gutman, Herbert G. 1977. *Work, culture and society in industrializing America.* New York: Oxford.

Hellriegel, Don, John W. Slocum, Jr., and Richard W. Woodman. 1983. *Organizational behavior.* 3rd ed. St. Paul, Minn.: West.

Herzberg, Frederick. 1966. *Work and the nature of man.* Cleveland: World.

————, Bernard Mausner, and Barbara Bloch Snyderman. 1959. *The motivation to work.* New York: John Wiley.

Hill, Stephen. 1981. *Competition and control at work: The new industrial sociology.* Cambridge, Mass.: MIT Press.

Jenkins, David. 1974. *Job power: Blue and white collar democracy.* New York: Penguin Books.

Kaplan, H. Roy, Curt Tausky, and Bhopinder Bolaria. 1969. Job enrichment. *Personnel Journal* 48:791–798.

Lawrence, Paul R., and Jay W. Lorsch. 1967. *Organization and environment: Managing differentiation and integration.* Boston: Graduate School of Business Administration, Harvard University Press.

Lewin, Kurt. 1958. "Group decision and social change." In *Readings in social psychology,* 3rd ed., edited by Eleanor E. Maccoby, Theodore M. Newcomb, and Eugene L. Hartley, 197–211. New York: Holt.

Likert, Rensis. 1967. *The human organization.* New York: McGraw-Hill.

Lippit, Ronald, and Ralph K. White. 1958. "An experimental study of leadership and group life." In *Readings in social psychology,* 3rd ed., edited by Eleanor E. Maccoby, Theodore M. Newcomb, and Eugene L. Hartley, 496–511. New York: Holt.

Macarov, David. 1982. *Worker productivity: Myths and reality.* Beverly Hills, Calif,: Sage.

Marx, Karl. 1867. *Das Kapital.* Vol. 1. 1958. Hamburg: Otto Meissner.

Maslow, Abraham H. 1954. *Motivation and personality.* New York: Harper Brothers.

————. 1973. "A theory of human motivation: The goals of work." In *The future of work,* edited by Fred Best, 17–31. Englewood Cliffs, N.J.: Prentice-Hall (Spectrum).

Mayo, Elton. 1945. *The social problems of an industrial society.* Cambridge, Mass.: Harvard University Press.

————. 1960. *The human problems of an industrial society.* New York: Viking Press. Reprint of 1933 edition.

McGregor, Douglas, 1957. The human side of enterprise. *The Management Review* 46:22–28, 88–92.

Mills, C. Wright. 1951. *White collar: The American middle classes.* New York: Oxford.

————. 1956. *The power elite.* New York: Oxford.

Nelson, Daniel. 1975. *Managers and workers: Origins of the new factory system in the United States, 1880–1920.* Madison: University of Wisconsin Press.

New York Stock Exchange. 1982. *People and productivity: A challenge to corporate America.* New York: Office of Economic Research, New York Stock Exchange.

Ouchi, William G. 1981. *Theory Z: How American business can meet the Japanese challenge.* Reading, Mass.: Addison-Wesley.

Perrow, Charles. 1970. *Organizational analysis: A sociological view.* Belmont, Calif.: Wadsworth.

———. 1984. "Normal accident at Three Mile Island." In *Critical studies in organization and bureaucracy,* edited by Frank Fischer and Carmen Sirianni, 287–305. Philadelphia: Temple University Press.

———. 1986a. *Complex organizations: A critical essay.* 3rd ed., New York: Random.

———. 1986b. The habit of courting disaster. *The Nation* 243, 11:329, 347–356 (October 11).

Rice, Berkeley. 1982. The Hawthorne defect: Persistence of a flawed theory. *Psychology Today* 2:70–74 (February).

Roethlisberger, F. J., and William J. Dickson. 1939. *Management and the worker: Technical versus social organization in an industrial plant.* Cambridge, Mass.: Harvard University Press.

Tausky, Curt. 1978. *Work organizations: Major theoretical perspectives.* 2nd ed., Itasca, Ill.: F. E. Peacock.

Tawney, R. H. 1958. "Foreword." In *The Protestant ethic and the spirit of capitalism,* Max Weber, 1(a–e)–11, New York: Charles Scribner's Sons.

Taylor, Frederick Winslow. 1911. *The principles of scientific management.* New York: Norton.

———. 1947. *Scientific management.* New York: Harper and Row.

Thomas, Henk, and Chris Logan. 1982. *Mondragon: An economic analysis.* London: George Allen & Unwin.

Thompson, James D. 1967. *Organizations in action.* New York: McGraw-Hill.

Tilgher, Adriano. 1930. *Work: What it has meant to men through the ages.* New York: Harcourt Brace.

U.S. Department of Health, Education and Welfare, Special Task Force. 1973. *Work in America.* Cambridge, Mass.: MIT Press.

Weber, Max. 1958. *The Protestant ethic and the spirit of capitalism.* New York: Charles Scribner's Sons. Originally published 1904–1905.

Woodward, Joan. 1965. *Industrial organization: Theory and practice.* New York: Oxford.

Zwerdling, Daniel. 1980. *Workplace democracy: A guide to workplace ownership, participation, and self-management experiments in the United States and Europe.* New York: Harper Colophon Books.

Where Power Lies

5

Political and Economic
Power in the United States
Today: Alternative Views

INTRODUCTION

Who has the power to shape public policy today in the United States? Is it the voting public whose elected representatives pass the laws and administer policy according to the wishes the voters seem to express? Is it interest groups whose conflicting interests balance each other to arrive at compromise? Is it the policy of powerful elites—wealthy families, corporate management, or financiers—who fund political campaigns? Is there any consensus among individuals in the corporate sector, or are there sharp differences of opinion among them that counterbalance each other behind the scenes, away from the eyes of the voting public? Are there other mechanisms besides the power of the ballot box and campaign contributions that might strongly influence the formation of public policy?

Public school textbooks are fairly uniform in answering these questions by describing our political and economic systems as operating with countervailing powers—individuals, corporations, and interest groups competing with each other, making compromises, arriving at public policy for the good of society in the manner described by the power pluralists. The mass media, although in general supporting this view, daily bombard us with tantalizing information perhaps implying that public policy is often shaped behind the scenes, with the public's being the last to know. The press's hints that the world may not be operating as textbooks say it should do not give us an adequate framework within which to understand how power relationships might be working.

For some decades social scientists have been developing theoretical frameworks and testing them empirically on the subject of power relationships in the United States (See Berg and Zald 1978 for a review of some of the literature on these relationships.) This chapter considers power—both political and economic—in the light of some of this theorizing and research. The topic is divided into eight subsections.

1. General definitions of economic and political systems, since the definitions offer rough guidelines as to where power *might* reside in each type of system.
2. Two major opposing views on how power is distributed in the United States.
3. Empirical evidence of economic concentration in various industries and centralization of economic power in conglomerates in several industries.
4. Interlocks across sectors and the formation of business cliques or networks.
5. Opposing theories and evidence about who controls or is in a strategic position to influence corporations—management, financial institutions, or wealthy individuals or families.
6. Profiles of the kinds of individuals who fill the top leadership positions in the United States.
7. Ways in which the economic system interacts with the political sphere to shape public policy.
8. How differences in economic concentration and power in the dual economic sectors have negatively affected minority workers over the years.

Even though one chapter does not have enough time and space to develop each topic in depth, it does allow us room to integrate some parts into a skeletal framework. Actually, two competing frameworks emerge. On these frameworks can be hung the bits and pieces of subsequent information both in this book and from the media and other sources. Chapter 6 extends this complicated question of concentration of power by examining how multinationals affect U.S. workers through plant shutdowns, capital flight, and off-shore sourcing. We also consider what this concentration of power might mean to the Third World nations to which these corporations flee.

DEFINITIONS OF ECONOMIC AND POLITICAL SYSTEMS

There is a great deal of vagueness in the way people talk about existing economic and political systems. Frequently heard are such statements as "The United States has creeping socialism;" "Communism is dictatorship;" "Sweden and Great Britain have socialist economies;" "Capitalism means the people decide through representative democracy." Such statements indicate a confusion of policial with economic systems, which muddles our thinking about what our real world systems are in actual operations and what possibilities are theoretically available to choose from. This confusion is not surprising in that political parties who say they prefer some form of economic system obtain office and then preside over another form of economy. Hence, we have socialist party governments presiding over capitalist economic systems. Further, ideologies and their rhetoric are used to convince people on an emotional rather than an analytical basis. Hence, *communism* becomes synonymous with *dictatorship*, and *capitalism* becomes the same as *representative democracy* in our minds.

In modern industrial (*Gesellschaft*) societies it seems particularly important to understand definitions of political systems and economic systems in terms of ideal types or categories before we consider some ways these systems interact and operate in the real world. First, then, a few definitions of ideal types of political and economic systems are in order.

Ideal Types and Models

When we speak of defining *ideal types* of political and economic systems, we are not referring to something that should ideally exist because we prefer it, but to a mental construct that social scientists use to help them understand what goes on in a world they cannot manipulate deliberately in an experiment. An *ideal type*, then, is a list of characteristics that a particular social phenomenon would have *if* it were ever found in the real world. It is a generalization about how such a social phenomenon might look if it were to exist. One can then compare empirical observations of the social world to the ideal type. German sociologist Max Weber, for example, used ideal types to categorize the bases of authority to help social scientists think about real societies and how they differed.

A *model* is a more complicated mental construct for thinking about the social world. In a model, relationships are specified between characteristics listed in ideal types. Propositions are formulated—"If this happens to this characteristic, then another characteristic will change in a certain manner." The classic example of model building is the pure competition model of classical economics. At the point of intersection between supply and demand curves, price is established in the model. Hence, one can predict, "If supply increases and demand does not change, then price is lowered to this point." Because relationships among factors are specified in a model, one factor can be "wiggled" and the changes in the system can be hypothesized or predicted. If the prediction does not hold in the real world observations, then one can examine where the conditions specified in the model did not agree with those observed in the real world system; and if this examination does not delineate differences, then the model may need to be changed. In the area of mental constructs, models are inherently more useful to the social scientist than are ideal types. Ideal types can, however, differentiate social phenomena into simple typologies/classifications/categories to help us in our thinking. Let us now describe some economic and political systems in their simple, very basic definitions.

Economic Systems

Economic ideal types can be characterized (1) by who owns the means of production, (2) by who does the planning for the economy, and (3) for what goal. First, in a *capitalist economy*, ownership is private and the goal is profit. The planning is presumably, therefore, in the hands of the management or owners of individual firms. Consumers are said to vote with their dollars when they purchase, and the supply and demand of the marketplace allocates resources and establishes prices. Government enters the picture in the ideal type only to ensure that competition is fair and the public interest is protected. In this sense the state is supposed to be the independent arbitrator among competing groups. Since the days of John Maynard Keynes, governments also use fiscal and monetary policies to speed up or slow down the economy in an attempt to avoid depressions. The means used are regulation and *fiscal* (budgetary—spending and taxing) and *monetary* (influencing the flow of money and credit) policies.

Second, a *socialist economy* requires that the basic industry (producing materials that go into the production of almost everything else) and the infrastructure (such as communications, banking, transportation, and perhaps utilities) be in public hands. Public may be either state-owned or virtually nonowned, as in the case of some industry in Yugoslavia. Under Marshall Tito, Yugoslavia was determined to take a different path from the state-owned economic system of the Soviet Union. The basic Yugoslavian industries were set up by government but then turned over to the workers to run, and the state does not maintain ownership. National planning for the economy includes planning investment and production for public-owned enterprises and some suggestive or indicative goals for private firms in the nonbasic sectors. The goal in such an economy is not merely profit; it also includes some aim toward equity and social justice.

Third, under a *communist economy*, which is difficult to locate in the real world, all major enterprises and industrial sectors are publicly owned. Planning for the overall economy is detailed. Who produces what, for whom, and for what price are carefully calculated in extensive plans that may cover five or ten years ahead. The marketplace does not allocate resources or set prices. In the ideal type the goal is not profit, but an attempt to allocate from each according to his or her ability, to each according to his or her need.

The fourth category of economies is a *mixed economy*. In this system ownership usually begins as private but the state may buy out companies that are important and are about to fail. In this way, the state becomes owner of large corporations, but not necessarily of basic industries, more by default than by design. Occasionally government takeover can be by design, as when a socialist government takes office in a capitalist economy and begins to nationalize an industry. An example of this is the beginning of nationalization of banking in France in the early 1980s by the socialist Mitterand government. Even though Great Britain has had Labour Party governments that have been called socialist, most state-owned companies were acquired by default. Planning under such a mixed system may be indicative. Under *indicative planning* the government can urge various sectors to meet particular goals but cannot force the private companies to cooperate. Sweden is an example of successful indicative planning. Sweden's economy is 85 percent privately owned, but these capitalist firms attempt to meet goals established by a tripartite national planning commission made up of representatives of management, labor, and government (Short 1984:116–122). Because of this economic planning and the various social services offered by the state, Sweden has often erroneously been called a socialist economy. Some economists prefer the term "welfare capitalism" to describe Sweden or other mixed economies with indicative planning.

Political Systems

Simple ideal types of political systems are even more straightforward. Each type, in our simple classification system, can be characterized by how many people make the decisions. First, in an *autocracy* (*auto*-means self, -*cracy* and -*archy* mean rule of) is the rule of one person. Under this rubric fall the dictatorship, the absolute monarchy, and the charismatic ruler whom people follow because they believe in him or her. Second, under the *oligarchy* (*olig*- means a few) are hereditary landed aristocracies, plutocracies of wealth, meritocracies of people who have achieved, committees of top party leaders in states with only one political party, top religious leaders in a theocracy, and juntas who have taken over through military strength. The third category includes *de-*

mocracies (demo- means the people), such as these ideal types: (1) pure
or classical, in which all voting adults meet face-to-face to set policies;
(2) representative, in which people elect other people to represent their
opinions in decision making; and (3) democratic elitism, in which the
people get their choice of representatives who will actually represent an
elite behind the scenes. This third type may appear to be a representative democracy, but in reality the people elected represent some elite
and not the voters who elected them (Pateman 1970; Bachrach 1967).

Theoretically, ideal types of political and economic systems can be
mixed and matched with regard to what kinds of political system an
economy can have, or what kinds of economy a political system can
have. One can begin to understand this eclecticism by thinking of various combinations currently or historically in real societies. A modern
Brazil may have a capitalist system ruled by a military junta for many
years. In Nazi Germany the capitalist economy was dominated by the
elite of the political party (which called itself socialist) and might qualify as a dictatorship. In this case, too, the government did a lot of economic planning for the privately owned economy.

Japan and the United States have capitalist economies dominated by
some form of democracy, either representative or democratic elitism depending on the perception of the person doing the analysis. Socialist
economies also run the gamut from some form of democracy, to oligarchy, to autocracy in some smaller developing nations. The Union of
Socialist Soviet Republics (USSR), which calls itself a communist economy but is called a socialist economy by some western economists, has
a political system dominated by the party oligarchy. Great Britain has
been called a mixed economy, since it has picked up a few industries
that were failing, although more than 82 percent of the economy is private capital. It has a form of democracy—a constitutional monarchy (although the constitution is unwritten) with a titular head.

In addition to these mix-and-match political and economic types is
the consideration of how these systems interact and have evolved in
each country, given its particular history and culture. We examine this
to some extent for the United States in this chapter and also in Chapters
3, 4, and 7 and for Japan in Chapter 11. Neither country's economy quite
fits the neoclassical characteristics given in our ideal type.

Varying degrees of public ownership also fall within the range of
capitalism, mixed economy, and socialism. A study done by the International Monetary Fund using 1978 to 1982 data indicated that only 4.4
percent of the capital formed in the United States came from publicly
owned enterprises. West Germany had 10.8 percent in publicly owned
firms; Japan had 11.2 percent for this period; Sweden had 15.3 percent;
Britain had 17.1 percent in 1982—a decline from 22.4 percent in the
mid-1950s; Norway has a rising rate of 22.2 percent. For the period from
1974 to 1977 the world average was 13.4 percent and the industrial

countries averaged 11.1 percent. Some of the highest rates of state capital formation were in the Third World nations. Algeria had 67.6 percent; Zambia, 61.2 percent; Burma, 60.6 percent in public ownership (Short 1984:116–122). Where to draw the line between capitalism and mixed economies and mixed economies and socialism can be difficult to decide.

POWER PLURALISM VERSUS POWER ELITE VIEWS OF THE UNITED STATES

There is an ongoing debate over how political and economic power is actually distributed in the United States. (See Domhoff and Ballard 1968 for articles from both views.) The power pluralists are on one end of a continuum and the power elitists are at the other end, with some writers falling in between but usually leaning toward one end or the other. Presumably if one could stand in the center of the spectrum, one could assume there is no social structure, that everything happens by chance or fate, and hence that power means nothing.

Power Pluralism View

The *power pluralists*, who may include much of the public and some influential political scientists, argue that power is widely dispersed in our society. Power pluralists usually contend that the United States has a form of capitalism in which enterprises compete individually in the marketplace—or at least groups compete against each other. If some businesses are powerful, they will be countered by other groups (see the polyarchy argument below). An element of neoclassical economic competition is in the power pluralism thesis—there must be some kind of competition, vetoing, and blocking action in the economic sector.

Looking at the political structure, power pluralists hold that the United States is a representative democracy, the people elected serve the interests of their constituents, who elected them—or at least a variety of groups are represented. Representative democracy is an essential belief in the power pluralism view. Most important is the polyarchy of many competing interest groups who balance each other and are concerned with their own sphere, not overlapping in enough areas to form a national policy-making elite (Riesman 1953; Dahl 1957, 1958, 1967; Polsby 1963; Rose 1967). The five major points of the pluralist view of political power are as follows:

1. There are too many conflicting interest groups for any to become predominant with regard to major national decision-making on policy; these groups compete with and veto each other.

2. Countervailing powers spring up to keep large organizations in check; for example, big business is said to be countered by big unions.
3. The government checks the power of groups that might coalesce to obtain undue influence for their interest; its mission is to protect the public interest.
4. The media keep the public(s) informed as to public issues and what is happening in society.
5. The public(s) can then discuss issues, form opinions, and influence their representatives or join an interest group or political party to make known their wishes on policy—and can "throw the rascals out" if elected officials misuse their power.

Figure 5.1 represents the power pluralism and power elite views in a summary sketch. Note that in the pluralist view the publics on various issues can influence policy through their membership in various groups and through their votes. This mechanism is weak or missing in the power elite view, and the competing groups in the middle lack influence on the elite, who make the major national policy decisions. In fact, the influence is in the opposite direction. The power pluralism view does not see an elite.

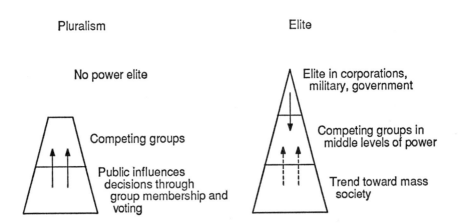

Figure 5.1 Diagrams of the Power Pluralism and Power Elite Views of Power Distribution in the United States

Power Elite View

An opposing view of how power is currently distributed in the United States is held by the *power elite* theorists. They feel the system does not work in the check-and-balances manner indicated in the polyarchy view portrayed in public school textbooks. They argue that oligopolies and conglomerates in the corporate sector have been able to use their enormous resources and, together with the top personnel in the government and military, influence the national agenda and important policy decisions in ways suitable to their own interests (Mills 1956; Domhoff 1970; Dye 1983a, 1983b). Less important policy decisions and some details of how the major policies are carried out are made at the middle levels of power, that is, by Congress, state governments, unions, the courts, and other pressure groups and organizations. At the middle levels these organizations or groups conflict and balance each other in a more pluralistic manner. The general public plays little part in any important national decisions. After the policy has been decided, the public is convinced by the media that the decision was appropriate and reached through the democratic process. This is the mass society toward which Mills feared the United States was headed. At election time the public gets to vote for its choice of representatives of the elites—democratic elitism.

This is not put forward as a conspiracy of evil people, but as how the political and economic systems have come to operate over time. The structural contingency/resource dependency people explain such occurrences as attempts by giant organizations to reduce environmental uncertainty (Aldrich and Pfeffer 1976; Pfeffer and Salancik 1978).

According to the power elite theorists, the power elite use the following seven mechanisms to coordinate their interests and influence policy.

1. Interlocking directorates, both direct and indirect, connect corporate boards and facilitate information sharing and coordination in planning.

2. Corporate personnel and corporation lawyers serve on advisory boards and committees in the executive branch—for example, representatives of agribusiness in the Department of Agriculture.

3. Businesspeople from the industries concerned serve on government regulatory boards—for example, people from the transportation industry staff the Interstate Commerce Commission and the communications industry provides staff for the Federal Communications Commission.

4. Top corporations hire retired military men because a large part of

the federal budget—more than 29 percent in 1985—is related to military spending and the top 100 corporations get 75 percent of the defense contracts, of which only 10 percent are put out for competitive bidding (Sinzinger 1985:3; The military spending debate 1984). Retiring top officers have invaluable connections to the Pentagon, where the contracts for military equipment, provisions, and research are let.

   5. Big business and wealthy individuals and families fund and staff policy-making associations, such as the Committee on Economic Development (CED), the Council on Foreign Relations (CFR), the Business Roundtable, the Brookings Institution, American Assembly, Foreign Policy Association (FPA), and the Trilateral Commission at the international level. These bodies commission research and reports on issues in public policy and sometimes write legislation to be presented by congresspersons.

   6. Big business and the wealthy fund and staff foundations that also produce influential position papers. These foundations include the Carnegie Corporation, Ford Foundation, Rockefeller Foundation, Russell Sage Foundation, and Heritage Foundation.

   7. Big business far outspends other interest groups in campaign contributions and lobbying (political action committees [PACs] are discussed later in this chapter).

   We thus can see that people who hold the power pluralism view are likely to share the order/consensus view of the world discussed in Chapter 1. This view sees equilibrium, checks and balances, and a fairly smoothly operating system of social institutions. The power elite view is related to the power/conflict view of the world, which sees the social institutions as dominated by people with more power and as being used to further the interests of the dominant groups.

   The following sections discuss both data and opposing arguments regarding where power and influence might lie in U.S. society.

ECONOMIC CONCENTRATION, CENTRALIZATION OF ECONOMIC POWER, AND PENETRATION OF THE POLITICAL SPHERE

How much economic concentration is there in the major industries in the United States today? How much centralization of economic power is there across industries? Who owns, controls, and/or influences corporations in the United States and have these positions changed during the century? How much opportunity for cooperation among corporations is there? What influence do large corporations or the groups they form have on government? Let us first clarify a few terms used in these questions.

A distinction exists between *economic concentration* and the broader term, *centralization of economic power.* Economic concentration, as used by many economists, refers to the amount of concentration in a particular industry. The government measures economic concentration ratios by looking at the share of the market held by the top four firms in any specific industry, *specific* meaning the four-digit Standard Industrial Classification (SIC) number. The various regulatory agencies and the Department of Justice watch concentration ratios for signs of the possibility of price-fixing or antitrust law violations in mergers (Bluestone and Harrison 1982:119–120; Spruill 1982:8–9, 94). Other writers watch the ratios, not just for possible monopolistic pricing and restricted output, but also for possibilities of political influence and centralized control in other areas, such as capital location (Bluestone and Harrison 1982:121).

Economic concentration and its continuing growth in many important industries are not difficult to describe in terms of numbers. Obviously, economic concentration affects pricing, wages, and for workers in these firms, as we see in the discussion of dual economic sectors. However, in terms of overall power, economic concentration in specific industries is only the beginning of the story.

Real *centralization of economic power* comes from being broader than one industry. This centralization occurs through the corporate giants forming conglomerates with influence in a number of industries and through the networks these corporations form with each other. This chapter looks at some means of identifying this centralization of economic power: mergers and acquisitions, interlocking directorates, business cliques (networks), and membership in policy-making associations and foundations. In trying to approach the subject of centralization of economic power and its possible effects on public policy, some of these mechanisms, which the power pluralists and power elite theorists cite, are examined in the light of recent research. The matter of international concentration of economic power through supranational joint ventures with foreign firms is further addressed in the following chapter on multinational corporations.

Economic Concentration and the Centralization of Economic Power

Concentration and Centralization Before World War II

At the turn of the century there was a great deal of talk about growing economic concentration in some of the major industries and of the need for trust-busting. The post–Civil War period and particularly the years between 1890 and 1905 saw *horizontal integration*—the buying up of competing firms—which formed virtual *monopolies* in which one firm controlled more than half the industry's market. U.S. Steel, American Tobacco, International Harvester, and General Electric had practically eliminated their competition. The Sherman Antitrust Act (1890) was passed with an eye to breaking up monopolies and limiting monopolistic practices. In the Supreme Court case *U.S. versus Standard Oil* (1911) the giant Rockefeller-owned company was divided into separate corporations often called the seven sisters: Exxon, Atlantic Richfield, Standard Oil of California, Standard Oil of Indiana, Standard Oil of Ohio, Mobil Oil, and Marathon. Because of the "rule of reason" part of this decision, apparently allowing for monopolies that acted with more finesse than did Standard Oil, the Clayton Antitrust Act (1914) was passed to strengthen the law (see Chapter 7 for the formation of the monopoly-controlled National Civic Federation, which Rockefeller refused to join). Competing corporations were forbidden to interlock directly with each other by placing representatives on each other's boards of directors or by both being held by a third holding company.

Of particular concern in the legislation was the possible dominance of financial institutions, such as the powerful J. P. Morgan trust. When Congress investigated J. P. Morgan and Company in 1912, it found that the partners of the company and the directors of its two affiliated banks, First National Bank of New York and National City Bank, held 341 directorships in 112 of the largest U.S. corporations (Allen 1978:598). In the J. P. Morgan holdings were elements of both economic concentration in specific industries and centralization of economic power, as an early kind of conglomerate holding firms in many industries.

From the mid-1920s to the early 1930s, *vertical integration* was more the vogue, with companies buying up their suppliers and distributors, backed by the leading financial houses (Bluestone and Harrison 1982:123). Among the corporations growing in this manner were Kennecott Copper, B. F. Goodrich, General Foods, and the petroleum companies that were now in the business from drilling to retail sales.

Post-World War II Merger Mania

Later legislation and court cases did not slow the pace of economic concentration and centralization of power, which have been increasing steadily, especially since World War II. During this time the growth was largely by conglomerate diversification. Before the Depression conglomerate-type mergers were less than 20 percent of corporate mergers and acquisitions. By the late-1960s this type of merger accounted for more than 80 percent of the total (Bluestone and Harrison 1982:124). The Cellar-Kefauver amendment to Section 7 of the Clayton Antitrust Act in 1950 tried to cut off this loophole by forbidding the purchasing of assets of competitive firms, not just the stock, as outlawed in the Clayton Act. This change spurred diversified acquisition and perhaps slowed concentration in specific industries in favor of centralization of economic power in the hands of conglomerates (Spruill 1982:7–8).

> In short, this handful of giant firms has used the corporate merger device to capture the high ground of the American economy, the commanding market shares in the highly concentrated, highly differentiated oligopolies where the largest profits are regularly earned. (Willard Mueller, quoted in Spruill 1982:8)

Why has conglomeration come to the fore with more clout than mere concentration in an industry? Size of the firm, no matter how scattered its diversification, has an effect. *High ground* in this quotation equals the large and powerful. Market power in a particular industry helps, but economic power by size of assets and resources in the total economy helps more. This power translates into such factors as advertising, threats of legal pursuit, political power, reciprocity buying agreements, and sheer intimidation by size. The urge to merge of the 1960s and the mid-1970s through the mid-1980s is addressed below.

Meanwhile, some of the handful of giant firms "capturing the high ground" are of interest. Table 5.1 indicates the size by sales of the top twenty U.S. industrials in 1985. *Industrial* here is used in the narrow sense of manufacturing. Earlier, political scientist Thomas Dye (1983b: 20) noted that the proportion of all industrial assets in the United States controlled by the top 100 corporations had grown from 39.8 percent in 1950 to 55 percent in 1980. His description of economic concentration as of 1980 is worth quoting at length (Dye 1983b:20).

> There are about 200,000 *industrial corporations* in the United States with total assets in 1980 of about $1.2 trillion. The 100 corporations . . . control 55.0 percent ($683 billion) of all assets. Industrial corporations—Exxon (formerly Standard Oil of New Jersey), General Motors, Mobil, IBM, and Ford—control 13 percent of all industrial assets.

Dye (1983b:20) continues with concentration in other sectors of the economy:

> Concentration in *transportation, communications,* and *utilities* is even greater than in industry. Fifty corporations . . . out of 67,000 in these fields,

Table 5.1 The Twenty Largest Industrial Corporations in the United States in
1985, Ranked by Sales

Company (Headquarters)	Sales $ thousands	Assets $ thousands	Net Income $ thousands
General Motors (Detroit)	96,371,700	63,832,800	3,999,000
Exxon (NY)	86,673,000	69,160,000	4,870,000
Mobil (NY)	55,960,000	41,752,000	1,040,000
Ford (Dearborn, MI)	52,774,400	31,603,600	2,515,400
IBM (Armonk, NY)	50,056,000	52,634,000	6,555,000
Texaco (Harrison, NY)	46,297,000	37,703,000	1,233,000
Chevron (San Francisco)	41,741,905	38,899,492	1,547,360
AT&T (NY)	34,909,500	40,462,500	1,556,800
duPont (Wilmington, DE)	29,483,000	25,140,000	1,118,000
General Electric (Fairfield, CT)	28,285,000	26,432,000	2,336,000
Amoco (Chicago)	27,215,000	25,198,000	1,953,000
Atlanta Richfield (L.A.)	22,357,000	20,279,000	(202,000)
Chrysler (Highland Park, MI)	21,255,500	12,605,300	1,635,200
Shell Oil (Houston)	20,309,000	26,528,000	1,650,000
U.S. Steel (Pittsburgh)	18,429,000	18,446,000	409,000
United Technologies (Hartford)	15,748,674	10,528,105	312,724
Phillips Pet. (Bartlesville, OK)	15,676,000	14,045,000	418,000
Tenneco (Houston)	15,400,000	20,437,000	172,000
Occidental Petroleum (L.A.)	14,534,400	11,585,900	696,000
Sun (Radnor, PA)	13,769,000	12,923,000	527,000

Source: "The 500 Largest U.S. Industrial Corporations, Ranked by Sales," *Fortune*, p. 182.

control over two-thirds of the nation's assets in airlines and railroads, communications, and electricity and gas. This sector of the nation's economy is dominated by the American Telephone and Telegraph Company (AT&T)—the single largest private corporation in the world. AT&T has over 100 billion dollars in assets, 70 million customers, and a work force larger than the U.S. Army—over one million employees. Although AT&T is now divesting itself of 22 subsidiary Bell companies, this giant utility company will remain [one of] America's largest corporation[s].

The financial world is equally concentrated. The 50 largest *banks* . . . out of 17,700 banks serving the nation, control 61.3 percent of all banking assets. Three banks (Bank America, Citicorp, and Chase Manhattan) control 19.4 percent of all banking assets.

In the *insurance* field, 50 companies . . . out of 1,890 control over 75 percent of all insurance assets. Two companies (Prudential and Metropolitan) control nearly one quarter of all insurance assets.

Elsewhere, Dye (1983b:269–270) notes that

50 *foundations* control 40 percent of all foundation assets; 25 *universities* control 50 percent of all private endowment funds in higher education; 3 *network broadcasting* companies control 90 percent of the television news; and 10 *newspaper* chains account for one-third of the nation's daily newspaper circulation. It is highly probable that 30 Wall Street and Washington *law firms* exercise comparable dominance in the legal field; that 15 Wall Street *investment firms* dominate decision-making in securities; and that a dozen *cultural and civic organizations* dominate music, drama, the arts, and civic affairs.*

Because the power pluralism view relies on the ability of the mass media to keep the public informed, it might be useful to pursue concentration here more specifically. Dye noted that in 1980 ten newspaper chains controlled one-third of the daily readership. The three largest chains, Knight-Ridder, Newhouse & Sons, and Gannett, alone had 88 dailies and 3.8 million readers in more than thirty states in 1983. Twenty firms controlled more than half the readership. Only 2 percent of all cities with daily papers had two or more published by different owners. Some cities appear to have competing dailies, but they are owned by the same company. Of large U.S. cities, only New York, Baltimore, and Los Angeles had three separate papers. One might note that London has eleven dailies, Paris has fourteen, and Tokyo readers can choose from among seventeen papers *(Media Monotony* 1984:6). In 1981 more than half of the $12 billion in revenues made by 11,000 magazines was made by twenty companies. The three top corporations in magazines in 1981 were Time, Inc., Triangle Publications, and the Hearst Corporation.

Nor is this the end of concentration in the media. There is also a growing centralization of economic power. Conglomerates that are in many other fields are also big owners in the media. Seven of the largest twenty newspaper chains are owned by conglomerates, as are eight of the top twenty magazine companies *(Media Monotony* 1984:7). There is only one major independent book publisher left. A single conglomerate may own two or three different publishing houses. Media critic Ben Bagdikian (1983:xv) of the University of California Graduate School of Journalism describes the situation this way:

Source: Thomas R. Dye, *Who's Running America? The Reagan* Years, 3/C, © 1983. Reprinted by permission of Prentice-Hall, Inc., Englewood Cliffs, New Jersey.

By the 1980s, the majority of all major American media—newspapers, magazines, radio, television, books, and movies—were controlled by fifty giant corporations. These corporations were interlocked in common financial interest with other massive industries and with a few dominant international banks.

Some people fear "the arrogance of corporate power" and state that "the major media speak with clarity and persistence about the sins of the powerless, but they do not speak with clarity and persistence about the sins of private power" (Bagdikian 1983:238). The deliberate and systematic distortions in the media produced by "the ideological and economic conditions under which the media operate" have been documented elsewhere (Parenti 1986:ix). Other people look at the situation from the power pluralist view that the media is controlled "by tens of thousands of stockholders, as well as by public opinion" (Compaine 1982:494). A disagreement is ongoing between the two sides of the power argument about who is the shaper and who is being shaped.

Centralization of economic power cannot be discussed without mentioning the recent wave of mergers and acquisitions. What this absorption of other companies by companies that already were giants means is that 1 in 8 workers works for one of the top 500 corporations. Fewer than 9 percent of workers are self-employed in the United States today. In a mature industrial society, workers can expect to be employees of some company, and the chances of being employed by one of the major corporations at some point in one's work life are very good. Through mergers and acquisitions, most of these companies are now conglomerates—owning subsidiaries in lines of business other than that of the parent company. For example, ITT owns more than 400 separate companies. Fifty percent of ITT's domestic income is from defense and space contracts; the corporation is also in finance, life insurance, investment funds, small loans, car rentals, baking (until the recent divesture of Continental Baking), and book publishing. U.S. Steel (now USX) is scarcely in the steel business anymore—only 25 percent of its investments are in the steel industry.

Companies are still expanding their vertical integration—buying up suppliers or distributors for the company's original product. For example, the citrus industries of Florida now control the oranges from the field, through processing, through distribution. A food processor may buy up a distribution chain to have a guaranteed place for its produce to go. Agribusiness, which raises bananas in Central America, may go into shipping to control transportation back to the metropolitan countries in which the bananas will be sold, in addition to making the boxes in which to ship them. Occasionally companies still buy out their smaller competitors in horizontal mergers, especially companies that have come up with new processes or products. American International Group (AIG) controls more than 200 insurance companies. AIG's parent is the holding company C. V. Starr.

Mergers hit their peak in the late 1960s, when many of today's conglomerates were formed. The record year was 1969, with more than 6,000 mergers.

Restructuring in the 1980s

The trend toward mergers increased again in the favorable anti-antitrust climate of the 1980s, when the dollar values were much higher. The value of mergers and acquisitions jumped from less than $40 billion in 1980 to around $170 billion in 1986 (The raiding game 1987:13). In 1985, for example, there were 3,165 completed mergers, which were valued at $1 million or more, of which one party was a U.S. corporation (1985 profile 1986:45). Only 6.5 percent were transactions in which foreign firms bought a U.S. company; in 5.5 percent of the cases a U.S. firm bought a foreign company overseas. Royal Dutch/Shell spent the most money in buying out the publicly held stock of Shell Oil for $5.7 billion, and Philip Morris purchased General Foods for $5.63 billion (optimistic outlook for M&A 1986:5). The most active purchaser was Merrill Lynch & Co., which bought fourteen firms (1985 profile 1986:45). Banks were the most active industry with 236 acquisitions, but the oil industry spent more than twice as much, $15.277 billion, on their 113 purchases (1985 profile 1986:46). No industry was exempt from mergers within its own industry and from buying into other lines of business.

Interestingly, as the pace of acquisition has quickened, there may be a modest decline in centralization at the very top. The top twenty-five nonfinancials saw a drop from 17 percent of all nonfinancial assets in 1970 to 13 percent in 1984 (The raiding game 1987:15). Many of the largest corporations have had to restructure to fend off hostile takeovers by corporate raiders (sharks).

Why has this happened? As economic growth slowed, demand decreased, and international overcapacity to produce occurred in many basic industries in the 1980s, mergers and acquisitions took on a new importance for profit making. The introduction of the junk bond in 1983 by Wall Street investment house Drexel Burnham Lambert allowed corporate raiders, such as T. Boone Pickens, Sid Bass, Sir James Goldsmith, Irwin L. Jacobs, Saul Steinberg, and Carl Icahn, to finance takeovers of giant corporations. Junk bonds are bonds with no collateral behind them, but yielding higher than the going interest rate. Junk bonds accounted for one-third of all new corporate bonds issued in 1986 (The raiding game 1987:15). To preserve themselves corporate management must come up with quick capital to buy the shares already held by the raider (greenmail) or shares held by other stockholders—to keep the stock from being bought by the raider. All of these purchases are made at inflated stock prices. To do this subsidiaries may be sold, jobs in middle management and the work force eliminated, and wage concessions sought. The corporation emerges leaner with fewer subsidiaries, fewer workers, and enormous debt. If raiders are successful in their takeover bid, they do the same things to pay for their debt incurred in the takeover.

Some of the pros and cons of mergers and acquisitions are discussed in Chapter 10, when we discuss what constitutes real productivity and economic growth. For now, we note its importance for economic concentration in industry and centralization of economic power across the economy.

Granted that there is concentration at the top of the various industries (industrials, transportation, communications, utilities, banks, insurance, the media) and that conglomerates own subsidiaries in other industries; are there any other connections between major corporations across the different industries? The next section discusses interlocking boards of directors among some of the major financial and nonfinancial corporations and the business cliques or networks they form.

Interlocking Boards of Directors

Whether one sees interlocking directorates as a means of control by other major corporations in the same interlocking group, by wealthy individuals or families, by financial institutions, or as a purely social event (managerial view that the management of each corporation is autonomous), it is clear that this mechanism allows companies to share information and coordinate action (Glasberg and Schwartz 1983:316). *Direct interlocks* occur when one company places a representative on the board of directors of another company. An *indirect interlock* occurs when two companies each place representatives on the board of a third company. In some cases the same individual may serve on the boards of several companies, providing another means of indirectly linking companies. Computer analysis has greatly aided researchers in tracking interlocks on boards of directors across industries.

In their report on a number of studies of interlocking directorates, sociologists Glasberg and Schwartz find little data for simple industrial groupings, that is, groups containing only companies in a particular industry, such as the auto industry or the food industry. Rather, "interlock studies have consistently found that banks and insurance firms are the most central corporations in the network and that firms from the same region are heavily tied to each other" (Glasberg and Schwartz 1983:323). Looking at interlocks of 1,000 companies, Mintz and Schwartz (1981:862) found financial institutions (predominantly banks) were the hub in 15 of the top 20 groups in both 1962 and 1966. In other words, their interlocks were more numerous and tied the group together. An example of regional groupings in which the centrality of financial institutions is apparent, taken from another study on 1970 data, is shown in Table 5.2.

Regional groups with financial hubs do not tell the whole story, either. Companies from one region may have multiple interlocks to firms in other regional groups. Not only are the nonfinancial corporations frequently linked with other groups, but the financials are also. In fact, the major banks and other financials are heavily interlocked with each other and also often sit on the same boards of third companies (Mintz and Schwartz 1981:863–865). The larger the company, the more interlocks it is likely to have, and the largest New York money market firms have the most ties of all. Regional groupings may stand out by the density of their mutual interlocks, but what really emerges from patient analysis is a pattern of overlapping ties binding major companies together in a loosely integrated whole, with Eastern financial corporations in a central position. We return to these interlocks in a later section on financial control.

The media also are involved in interlocks. Ads placed by companies are exceedingly important to media (newspapers get about 60 to 80 percent of their revenues from ads, and magazines average 40 percent of income from them), but interlocks may also be of some importance. For example, in 1979 the Gannett newspaper chain shared directors with such corporations as Merrill Lynch, Kerr-McGee, McDonnell-Douglas Aircraft, Eastern Airlines, and Kellogg. Knight-Ridder and corporations owning *The New York Times* and the *Washington Post* are "similarly well connected" (*Media Monotony* 1984:15).

Although interlocks of major corporations with financial institutions and financial institutions with each other are now well documented, the importance of this for companies, for the economy, and for public information and policy is still under debate by people with differing views of the use of power in the United States. In subsequent parts of this chapter we return to implications for public policy, and in Chapter 6 extend the discussion to foreign policy. Direct interventions in the management of companies by financial institutions seem to be frequent but of short duration. This fact casts some doubt on bank control theories, but it does not resolve the question of long-run influence. The next section continues to examine the three alternative views on who controls or influences corporate policy with more evidence from research.

Table 5.2   Ten Principal Interlock Groups, 1970

	IC	Location	PCS	TI	GI
Group I					
Chemical New York	B	New York	5.3	41	12
New York Life	L	New York	5.0	32	8
Consolidated Edison	U	New York	5.0	22	11
Southern Pacific	T	San Francisco	2.8	24	4
Equitable Life Assurance	L	New York	2.7	41	6
Borden	I	New York	2.5	12	5
Group II					
Continental Illinois	B	Chicago	5.2	29	15
International Harvester	I	Chicago	4.8	22	11
Commonwealth Edison	U	Chicago	4.0	12	10
First Chicago Corp.	B	Chicago	3.5	25	11
Sears Roebuck	R	Chicago	2.8	18	5
Standard Oil (Indiana)	I	Chicago	2.6	11	6
Inland Steel	I	Chicago	2.6	10	6
Illinois Central, Inc.	I	Chicago	2.6	18	5
Borg-Warner	I	Chicago	2.1	10	5
Group III					
Mellon National Bank	B	Pittsburgh	5.6	30	15
Gulf Oil	I	Pittsburgh	5.4	11	10
Aluminum Co. of America	I	Pittsburgh	4.3	10	6
Pittsburgh Plate Glass, Inc.	I	Pittsburgh	3.4	7	6
Westinghouse Electric	I	Pittsburgh	2.5	19	4
Group IV					
Morgan Guaranty Bank	B	New York	5.1	38	11
General Electric	I	New York	3.2	26	7
General Motors	I	Detroit	2.8	27	5
Continental Oil	I	New York	2.5	20	4
Scott Paper	I	Philadelphia	2.5	12	4
U.S. Steel	I	New York	2.0	27	3
Procter & Gamble	I	Cincinnati	2.0	18	4
Group V					
Citicorp	B	New York	4.6	51	11
Monsanto	I	St. Louis	2.6	13	6
National Cash Register	I	Cleveland	2.6	17	5
Westinghouse Electric	I	Pittsburgh	2.4	19	3
Kimberly-Clark	I	Milwaukee	2.2	7	5
Pan-American World Airways	T	New York	2.1	22	4
AT&T	U	New York	2.0	33	2
Group VI					
Republic Steel	I	Cleveland	5.2	21	13
Avco	I	Greenwich	4.1	13	10
Metropolitan Life	L	New York	2.8	39	7

	IC	Location	PCS	TI	GI
Standard Oil (Ohio)	I	Cleveland	2.7	9	4
Chemical New York	B	New York	2.6	47	7
International Business Machines	I	Armonk	2.2	25	7
Illinois Central, Inc.	I	Chicago	2.1	18	6
Olin	I	Stamford	2.0	9	6
Group VII					
Chase Manhattan	B	New York	4.8	37	9
General Foods	I	New York	2.8	20	5
Metropolitan Life	L	New York	2.6	39	5
International Paper	I	New York	2.1	15	5
AT&T	U	New York	2.	33	4
Group VIII					
Western Bancorporation	B	Los Angeles	4.1	19	6
Southern California Edison	U	Los Angeles	3.4	11	9
Union Oil of California	I	Los Angeles	3.2	18	6
BankAmerica	B	San Francisco	2.8	17	5
North American Rockwell	I	Los Angeles	2.7	13	6
Security Pacific National Bank	B	Los Angeles	2.5	13	5
Getty Oil	I	Los Angeles	2.0	14	5
Group IX					
Pennsylvania Mutual	L	Philadelphia	5.1	21	12
First Pennsylvania	B	Philadelphia	4.1	11	7
Girard	B	Philadelphia	3.2	8	6
Philadelphia Electric	U	Philadelphia	3.2	10	8
Philadelphia National Bank	B	Philadelphia	2.6	7	5
Atlantic Richfield	I	New York	2.4	15	4
Group X					
National Bank of Detriot	B	Detroit	4.7	21	10
Burroughs	I	Detroit	2.8	8	6
Detroit Edison	U	Detroit	2.8	10	4
National Steel	I	Detroit	2.5	10	4
Bendix	I	Detroit	2.2	7	4
S.S. Kresge	R	Detroit	2.2	7	4

Source: Michael Patrick Allen, "Economic Interest Groups and the Corporate Elite Structure" *Social Science Quarterly*, 4, March, 1978, pp. 608–609. Reprinted by permission of the author and the University of Texas Press.

Legend: IC = Industry Code   U = Utility
        PCS = Principal Component Score T = Transportation
        TI = Total Interlocks   R = Retailing
        GI = Group Interlocks   B = Banking
        I = Industrial   L = Life Insurance

Competing Ideas on Ownership, Control, and Influence

In two preceding sections we noted a picture emerging from the studies of social scientists. The main outlines include (1) economic concentraton in many important industries, (2) a centralization of economic power across industries by giant conglomerates, (3) a network of interlocking boards of directors, and (4) a seeming centrality of financial institutions in terms of interlocks. The question of who actually controls major corporations, however, has not been settled among either social scientists or the general public. Several views on how ownership, control, or influence operates have been offered and lend support to one or the other of the two competing theories of how economic and political power is distributed in the United States today—power pluralism and power elite.

Managerialism

Initially, the *managerialism* view was put forth by economists Berle and Means in 1932, followed in the 1950s and 1960s by other writers speaking about the "managerial revolution" (Burnham 1941). This argument states that with the dispersion of common voting stock to a large, passive group of stockholders, control over the individual firm shifted from the entrepreneur or the financial trust to the managers of the firm who held the stockholders' proxies or to the technical staff of the firm who controlled the new scientific knowledge. The key point of this view is that the autonomy of management frees them from outside influences and from the "profit nexus" emphasized by owners when they manage corporations.

In the early twentieth century powerful individuals, such as J. P. Morgan, John D. Rockefeller, and Edward H. Harriman, each owned several corporations. By World War I many of these men had died or retired and this interconnection appeared to decline. Along with this trend, other writers (Parsons 1953, 1970; Dahrendorf 1959; Bell 1960) saw the breakup of the ruling class and a dissolution of the top "Sixty Families." "The captain of industry no longer runs business" and, therefore, "no longer runs politics" (Riesman 1953:242).

Largely independent of external influence or control, the large corporations were said to have become powerful, autonomous institutions shaping and controlling their own environments. People who take the managerialism view also argue that the goals of the corporations, without pressure from the stockholders, turned from profit maximization to an emphasis on growth, sales, public relations, and even charitable and cultural concerns. The corporation became just another bureaucracy among the many. The individual firm is taken as the unit of analysis since it is cut off from outside influences. This makes a unified business elite impossible. Political power is pluralistic, and social stratification depends more on occupational status and education than on wealth and ownership (Mizruchi 1982:15–21).

In 1932 Berle and Means reported that more than 40 percent of the large corporations they studied were dominated by management. A more conservative analysis of the same data base they used found 20 percent of those companies to be management controlled (Zeitlin 1974:1081). More recent studies of the control of the largest firms disagree on Berle and Means's findings. In a review of these studies, sociologist Michael Useem (1980:47) estimates "at least one-fifth but no more than one half of the largest corporations are apparently under the control of their own managers." Whether this is an increasing or decreasing phenomenon cannot be decided from the conflicting reports. As we discuss, there is also a question as to how autonomous the managers can be in their control, in whatever percent of companies are management-dominated.

One aspect of the managerialism view has been successfully challenged in recent years—the supposed supplanting of the capitalist profit motive. Studies on the motivation of management—from their speeches, private conversations, and actions—do not find a relaxation of the profit motive or that their interests differ in any significant way from those of owners (Useem 1980:47–51; Zeitlin 1976:901–902). Indeed, management compensation and tenure are directly linked to company profit. Even on a quarterly basis the price/earnings (P/E) ratio must be healthy if a manager is to keep a job. Reviewing thirteen studies comparing profit rate in owner-managed and manager-managed firms in various industries, Useem (1980:50–51) reported that nine found no significant differences.

Another reason for this similarity of behavior and attitude between owners and managers may be that management is not completely autonomous and free from the constraints of other environmental pressures, as the structural contingency/resource dependency people remind us (Glasberg and Schwartz 1983). These external pressures might be such interest groups as cliques of corporations, financial institutions that control needed capital, shareholders who own strategic blocks of voting common stock, interlocking boards of directors, or a combination of these. If these external influences impede management's autonomy in the 20 to 50 percent of firms that may have management control, then the managerialism view must be qualified and the wider network must be taken as a unit of analysis. This brings us to a second view of control or influence.

Financial control or hegemony

The second view of control or influence sees financial institutions—banks, insurance companies, investment firms—behind the scenes influencing (*hegemony* means dominance or strong influence) and/or controlling corporations. In this view, the unit of analysis cannot be limited just to the corporation; it must be the network of ownership and the social relationships within the network (Mizruchi 1982:26). The means through which financials gain this control are by investing their portfolios in corporations, placing their representatives on the boards of directors of those firms, and controlling outside sources of capital those corporations need. With regard to the last two points, from 1965 to 1974 financial institutions alone accounted for as much as 30 percent of corporate funding. In addition, they are much more likely than other kinds of corporations to place their officers on boards of directors (Useem 1980:51–52; Eitzen, Purdy, and Jung 1985:45).

The control by or hegemony of banks and other financial institutions relies, just like managerialism, on widely dispersed stock ownership so that the institutions' influence on the self-perpetuating board of directors through ownership of a strategic block of voting stock becomes an easier task. Many researchers seem to feel that the ownership of 4 to 5 percent of stock (or even less in some cases) in a block is enough to allow some direct control, if ownership of the rest of the stock is dispersed (Glasberg and Schwartz 1983:320). Berle and Means (1968) felt this meant control reverted to the officers of the company, but an alternative scenario could be that of a dominating board controlled by financial interests. This becomes a particularly important question if one accepts the possibility that as much as 70 percent of the stock traded may be in the hands of institutional investors (Glasberg and Schwartz 1983:320; Moberg 1986:5). There is some debate on whether this means that the institutional holders of these funds have complete control over them. The ultimate owners of the stock may want to be more actively involved.

When the J. P. Morgan trust, so visible at the turn of the century, seemed to decline, writers began to ignore this possible control or influence by banks and other financial institutions interlocking with other corporations. Sociologist Mark Mizruchi (1982:24) notes that the "belief in the declining power of banks was so pervasive among Amerian social scientists in the 1930–1970 period" that there was a virtual absence of discussion of the possibility of bank control. In the mid-1960s, however, the information Wright Patman's House Committee on Banking and Currency obtained on the stockholdings of bank trust departments indicated that in 147 of the top 500 industrials a bank owned 5 percent or more of the common voting stock. To the Patman Committee this suggested the possibility of bank control (U.S. Congress 1968). Using the 5 percent and a director on the board criteria, economist David Kotz (1978) studied the leading 200 nonfinancial corporations between 1967 and 1969 and found 40 percent could be considered as bank controlled. Sociologist Michael Allen (1978:611), however, felt that financial interest group ties were less cohesive in 1970 than in 1935. Some of his data on the 1970 interlocks appear in Table 5.2

Other researchers disagree with this view of declining cohesiveness among financial institutions (Mariolis 1983; Sonquist and Koenig 1975). As stated, Mintz and Schwartz (1981) have found dense and ongoing connections among the boards of directors of financial institutions. A second intriguing piece of information, which seems to suggest more cohesion than competition on interbank affairs, is the interlocking ownership among the nation's leading banks.

Examining the mutual ownership of common stock among 18 of the top 20 banks, a recent study reports an impressive amount of interaction (Eitzen, Purdy, and Jung 1985). In other words, the major banks themselves form a network through their ownership of strategic voting blocks in each other's corporations. As a background of the power of the top 20 banks in 1978 (when the study was done), they held 25 percent of all assets of the more than 14,000 banks in the United States and more than 70 percent of all bank trust departments' common stocks. Two of the leading 20 banks, Charter of New York and Marine Midland, were omitted from the study because their stock was so widely dispersed that no strategic block appeared. Among the other 18, however, 12 banks (two-thirds) had 5 percent or more of their stock owned by other banks in the group. Interlocking ownership was frequent, as 14 of the banks (78 percent) had an interest in one-third or more of the others. In looking at who the top shareholders were in terms of voting rights, even though they sometimes held less than 5 percent of the stock, in 78 percent of the cases the number one controller of these stock voting rights was another bank within the group of 18. Again the ties were thick as 11 of the banks had at least two of their largest five stockholders from within the group. Seven banks had as many as four fellow-bank owners among the top 10 stockvoters. Morgan Guaranty was the central member of the cluster—the number one stockholder in five banks in the group and the number two stockholder in two others. Regional subclusters emerged with BankAmerica and Security Pacific dominating the West, Continental Illinois and First Chicago leading in the Midwest, and Morgan Guaranty and Citicorp influencing the Eastern banks.

In addition Morgan Guaranty has been identified as among the top five shareholders in 56 of the nation's leading 122 corporations. It was the major stockholder in 27 of them. Citibank is among the leading five stockholders in 25 corporations and the major stockholder in seven. As noted in the section on economic concentration, banks continue to be the leaders in mergers and acquisitions.

In sum, three aspects of the structure of the U.S. economy in recent times suggest the importance of financial institutions in the control of, or as a dominant influence on, the major corporations. These three aspects are (1) the ability of financial institutions to control important sources of capital; (2) their centrality in the interlocking regional and national board of directors network(s); and (3) ownership of common stock in other major corporations and in each other. Perhaps more important, the interlocking of the major banks themselves indicates the strong possibility of commonality of interest and cooperation, rather than competition, in both the activity of banks and their view of social reality. This lack of competition and this common view of reality, in turn, may be widely shared among nonfinancial corporations through these links. This commonality of policy and view of reality may have ramifications for national policy, as we discuss shortly, as well as for the individual corporation and the economy. As one study put it:

> We interpret these results as suggesting that New York is the base of a national network of corporate interlocks, uniting regional clusters into a loosely integrated whole. . . . The overall shape of the network is consistent with the findings of Domhoff (1970, 1978), Ratcliff (1979–1980, 1980), Useem (1978, 1979), Whitt (1982), and others that the corporate community is capable of coordinated economic decision making and united political action. (Mintz and Schwartz 1981:864,866).

In Chapter 11 we see that the Japanese economy is also organized around bank-centered groups (*zaibatsu*), which are reported to maintain fierce competition with competitors in other groups. A final point, touched on in Chapter 6, is that this view of the world and conservative financial behavior is passed on to nations of the Third World, which are heavily in debt to these same multinational banks and must sometimes trim their economic sails to the winds from the North. The network spreads rather widely.

Individual, family, and/or class control

A third view of ownership, control, or influence is that of wealthy individual or family control, stated as a ruling class argument by some researchers. Such control can be at the level of either the individual or the family-controlled corporation or in a wider network of corporations in which the family has an interest. The family holdings may also include an interest in a financial institution, which, in turn, controls other firms. Sociologist Maurice Zeitlin (1976:899) states his view rather plainly that "large banks are units in, and instrumentalities of, the system of propertied interests controlled by principal capitalist families." This view also brings forth the possibility that some companies that are largely family owned may have to share some control with banks they do not own, through the ownership of blocks of stock by the bank and their membership of the board of directors of the company. This is one of the most difficult areas to research, since ultimate ownership is often well disguised from the government as well as the public, including the inquiring social scientist.

In 1932 Berle and Means (1968) found that 34 percent of the top 200 corporations were family controlled. Larner (1966) estimated only 14 percent of the 200 largest nonfinancial companies were dominated by a family. Sheehan (1967) cited 11 percent of the top 100 and 17 percent of the top 200 as family controlled. Philip Burch (1972:77), not content to rely just on stock ownership data from the Securities and Exchange Commission, searched business periodicals and business directories for ownership information on the top 500 industrials from 1950 to 1971. He found 60 percent of the 300 largest were "probably or possibly" family controlled.

Reminding us that directors, lenders, and managers may share power with people who own blocks of common stock and that being in a position of influence does not guarantee it will be used, Dye (1983a) uses the findings of the Corporate Data Exchange (*CDE Stock Ownership Directory* 1981) to locate strategic ownership in the Fortune 500 corporations. He identified 2,156 such holdings. These holdings represented about 21.4 percent of the total value of common stock, or $170 billion in 1981. The other 78.6 percent was in "smaller, diffused, nonstrategic blocks" (Dye 1983a:865). Bank trusts held 486 blocks worth $36 billion. It was not possible to track the ultimate owners of some of these trusts. Other investment firms held 860 strategic blocks, although employee stock ownership plans, pension funds, and industrial corporations themselves were ultimate owners of most of these shares and could presumably retain some control over them and how heir shares were voted. Foreign ownership accounted for 63 valuable positions.

Family and individual holdings represented 424 blocks (19.7 percent of strategic positions). At $48.6 billion these family-held shares represented 28.5 percent of the total value of all strategic positions and were more valuable than any other type of holding—banks, financial firms, employee stock plans, insurance companies, pension funds, or foreign owners (Dye 1983a:868). The duPonts led with 24 strategic blocks worth $5 billion in Fortune 500 industrials (35 percent of DuPont, 7 percent of General Motors, 3.6 percent of ITT, and so forth). The Fords were second, with more than 40 percent of Ford Motors, plus the rest of their holdings.

It is not easy to say that this means in terms of specific influence and control. It is obvious that wealthy family influence has not disappeared, according to the statistics available. And this may not be the complete picture by any means. Not only can they vote their stock and maybe run, or strongly influence, their family-dominated corporations, but they can also place family members and their trusted employees in positions of importance. (See the debate on management elite versus old family elite importance in the ruling class between Zeitlin 1974, 1976 and Allen 1976, 1978.) We now turn to the area of leadership to try to identify the backgrounds and other demographic characteristics of people in high places and to attempt to sort out which places might be higher than others.

Leadership and Key Positions

The top organizations in business, education, the media, civic and cultural areas, government, and military provided 7,314 leadership positions in 1980. These positions were filled by 5,778 persons, since some individuals held more than one top position (Dye 1983b:171). The questions then become: Do the people in these positions see common interests, and are women and other minorities and lower socioeconomic groups gaining a foothold in elite positions, or are these positions recruited from a more narrow background? Are there patterns of interlocks among organizations through these people, so that interest groups are formed? Does the public influence major national policy or are there means by which some or all of the elites interlock and interact to shape policy? If little overlap or logrolling seems to occur among these elites in terms of policy making, this supports the view of the power pluralists. If there seems to be concerted effort and effect on national policy, however, then there is some support for the power elite view.

Not all top positions in government, on boards of directors in big business, arts, and education are equivalent. From analyzing these positions, tracing the backgrounds of the incumbents, examining individual and corporate interlocks, and digging into the origins of specific national policies, Dye gives convincing evidence for what he terms an *oligarchic model*. He explains the power of large corporations and wealth to shape national policy in the following manner:

> Pluralist scholars focus their attention on the activities of "the proximate policy-makers"—the President, Congress, and the courts. They observe competition, bargaining, and compromise among and within these public bodies over specific policies and programs. They observe the role of parties, interest groups, and constituents in shaping the decision-making behavior

of these proximate policy-makers. But it is quite possible that the activities of the proximate policy-makers are merely the final phase of a much more complex structure of national policy formation.

Our "oligarchic model" of national policy-making attempts to trace elite interaction in determining the major direction of national policy. It portrays the role of the proximate policy-makers as one of implementing through law, the policies that have been formulated by a network of elite-financed and elite-directed policy-planning groups, foundations, and universities. The proximate policy-makers act only after the agenda for policy-making has already been set, the major directions of policy changes have been decided, and all that remains is the determination of programmatic specifics.

The initial resources for research, study, planning, and formulation of policy come from donations of corporate and personal wealth. These resources are channeled into foundations, universities, and policy-planning groups. Moreover, top corporate elites also sit on the governing boards of these institutions to help determine how their money will be spent. The policy-planning groups—such as the Council on Foreign Relations, the Committee for Economic Development, and The Brookings Institution—play a central role in bringing together individuals at the top of the corporate and governmental worlds, the foundations, the law firms, and the mass media, in which to reach a consensus about policy direction. The mass media, in addition to participating in policy formulation, play a vital role in preparing public opinion for policy change. Special presidential commissions, governmental study groups, or citizens' councils can also be employed to mobilize support for new policies. (Dye 1983b:264)

In other words, Dye's research on the activities of the people in the top positions supports the power elite view. While we are busy watching the middle levels and the people out front, the national policy agenda has already been shaped behind the scenes by the network of elites who fund and direct the policy-making associations and foundations. The media then prepare the public to accept the policies as right and necessary.

Who are these decision makers in the policy-making associations and foundations? As of 1980, Dye (1983b) tells us:

95 percent were members of corporation boards
50 percent have also had some governmental experience
68 percent were on university boards of directors
They averaged five posts each in civic and cultural organizations (97 percent had some position)
Ivy League colleges produced 75 percent
20 percent were lawyers

50 percent had advanced degrees and 66 percent were in private social clubs for the rich and powerful

3 percent were women and one percent black (these two categories
appeared in the 1970s).

In sum, 96 percent are white males from upper-middle- and upper-
class backgrounds—well educated in largely Ivy League schools, belonging to the same clubs, and serving as directors of the nation's largest
corporations.

Does this conclusion imply complete consensus on the part of these
elites, particularly the corporate elites whose agendas become public
policy, according to Dye? The answer appears to be no. As far back as
1956 sociologist C. Wright Mills had identified a split among the elites.
Old line wealth and the top executives of large corporations tended to be
somewhat more liberal, or moderately conservative, in that they projected a noblesse oblige view that government intervention should be
forthcoming to support social programs and Keynesian demand-side government pump-priming. On the other hand, the heads of smaller corporations and businesses, represented by the National Association of Manufacturers (NAM) and the National Chamber of Commerce (CofC),
sought an ultraconservative program of tax incentives and accelerated
write-offs for business, less government intervention, and a laissez faire,
free enterprise climate.

In recent years, however, there seems to be some evidence of at least
temporary agreement on some aspects of national policy among these
leadership groups. The next section discusses the formation of national
social policy in the recent past.

Some Evidence on National Policy Making

The data above suggest how policy might be shaped by elites. The question arises as to whether this power has been used in the past to shape
policy. Is there evidence to support this question?

Domhoff (1970) documented the power of the liberal big business
agenda in the New Deal programs of the 1930s. These programs not
only helped people caught in the decline of the economy, but, the policy
makers thought, would also preserve the capitalist economic system.
Ferguson and Rogers (1986; Scialabba 1986) outline the New Deal coalition as consisting of capital-intensive industries, investment banks, and
multinational commerical banks. Firms in this group include, for example, General Electric, IBM, Pan Am, R. J. Reynolds, Standard Oil of New
Jersey, Standard Oil of California, Cities Service, Shell, BankAmerica,
Chase Manhattan, Brown Brothers Harriman, Goldman Sachs, Lehman
Brothers, and Dillon Reed. These corporations wanted free trade and so-

cial welfare policies that would keep workers at home satisfied. In opposition were the labor-intensive domestic industries, which formed the base of the Republican party.

Dye (1983a, 1983b) continues this line of research for the 1960s and early 1970s. He describes where national policy was shaped by these old-line liberal (yankee) policy-making associations with regard to these issues: entering and leaving the Vietnam War; the Great Society social programs; international human rights under President Carter; loans to Third World governments; and even population control in Third World countries, which defused ideas of redistribution of resources in favor of blaming population explosion for lack of development. Women's rights groups may have helped spread the idea of prochoice, but, according to Dye, the Rockefeller Foundation wanted population control and was acting on it before it became a widely known public issue, in the belief that it would improve the quality of life without altering the social relations of production.

In the mid-1970s and 1980s liberal policy-making associations became increasingly discouraged with some aspects of government intervention in the social sector—due to the failure of the Vietnam War, the downturn of the economy, stagflation, and the failure of Great Society programs to stem poverty. Long-term economic decline moved the old-line liberals toward cutting wages and social welfare programs, bringing the liberals into conflict with labor. As domestic capital and bank loans of petrodollars began to move to the Third World, there was an increased interest in a military buildup to "enhance America's capacity for intervention" there (Scialabba 1986: 9).

Another factor that may have contributed to the galvanization of the business community to begin to act more as a class—from the chief executive officers (CEOs) of major corporations in the Business Roundtable to the National Association of Manufacturers and Chamber of Commerce—was the formation of government agencies that affected firms across industries (Edsall 1984:128–136). The Environmental Protection Agency (EPA) and the Occupational Health and Safety Administration (OSHA) are examples. A Consumer Protection Agency appeared to be in the offing, which added incentive to collective business action to defeat it. A minor Labor Law Reform bill provoked tremendous business lobbying activity.

The old-line liberals' gradually more conservative policies were bolstered on the far right by the establishment of a new wing of support for the NAM and CofC policies, which had not been able to gain ground earlier. The new wealth of the so-called sunbelt cowboys supported supply-side economics, a tightened federal budget, tax breaks for business, and fewer social programs. The new money joining the smaller corporations and businesses came from oil, gas, real estate, aerospace, computer technology, discount retailing, fast foods, construction giants, and low-cost insurance companies—mostly in the South and Southwest. They founded new think tanks such as the Heritage Foundation, the American Enterprise Institute, the Center for the Study of American Business at Washington University in St. Louis, the American Council for Capital Formation, and the American Security Council. They also influenced other, older foundations and policy-making bodies such as the National Bureau of Economic Research and the Hoover Institution on War, Revolution, and Peace at Stanford.

Among these groups, the Heritage Foundation has been particularly notable as a think tank for the new ultraconservative views. Edsall (1984:117–118) describes its backers in the following manner:

> Created in 1973, the Heritage Foundation in Washington has seen its budget grow by 40 percent per year: in the 1976–77 fiscal year, its budget was $1,008,557; by 1980–81, it had expanded to $5.2 million and by 1981–82 to $7.1 million. Major supporters of the Heritage Foundation include Joseph Coors, President of the Adolph Coors Company; Richard Mellon Scaife, heir to the Mellon banking, oil, and industrial fortune and the Sarah Mellon Scaife Foundation; the John M. Olin Fund, established by the Chairman of the board of the Olin Mathieson Chemical Corporation, a foundation chaired by former Treasury Secretary William Simon; the Noble Foundation, established by Edward E. Noble, an Oklahoma oil and gas company president; the Reader's Digest Association, Inc.; Mobil Oil Corp.; Dow Chemical Co.; Fluor Corp.; Gulf Oil Corp.; Sears Roebuck; and Dart and Kraft. Many of these corporate backers have become integral parts of that nexus of interests uniting a major segment of the business community, the ideological right wing, and the Republican party.

In the Reagan years these think tanks have begun to supply policy papers and bills for congresspersons along with the Council on Foreign Relations, Committee on Economic Development, Brookings Institution, and other old yankee groups. The combination of the old-line NAM conservatives and the new sunbelt think tanks has led to the current agenda of cutting social welfare, anti-abortion, anti-affirmative action, deregulating of environment and health and safety, opposing busing to gain desegregation, and furthering the aforementioned business tax-breaks for capital formation. In addition, it has provided a climate for union busting (discussed in Chapter 7) and increased military spending, foregoing earlier conservative isolationism.

Assisting further in the direction public policy takes are the political action committee (PAC) contributions to people running for election. In 1974 there were 608 PACs, which donated a total of $12.5 million to congressional candidates. In 1984 there were 4,009 PACs, which contributed more than $100 million to congressional campaigns. By 1987 there were about 4,400 PACs, and Congress had spent $286 million on campaigns the year before, much of it from PACs (Dockser 1987:24).

People who take a power pluralism view see PACs as another system of checks and balances, but there do appear to be more checks than balance (*Special interest snipers* 1985:A34; Adamany 1986:20–23). As mentioned in Chapter 7, business PACs outspend labor by a margin of more than four to one (Rehmus 1984:43; Adamany 1986:21). Common Cause and other groups interested in lessening this overwhelming influence have been attempting to limit the amount candidates can receive from PACs and the amount they can spend in any campaign. As Senator Barry Goldwater (R–AZ) stated in defending the Boren-Goldwater Amendment to cap PACs in December 1985:

> As far as the general public is concerned, it is no longer 'we the people,' but PACs and the special interests they represent, who set the country's political agenda and control nearly every candidate's position on the important issues of the day. (Notable comments . . . 1987:1).

"In short, corporate personal wealth provided both the financial resources and the overall direction of the policy research, planning, and development" (Dye 1983b:239). Even though voting is free, "the setting of the agenda is enormously expensive" (Scialabba 1986:8). The nature of the national agenda seems to be shaped in part by (1) whether the policy-influencing groups were new or old wealth and (2) the state of the national economy at the time—boom or bust—and how various business elites view action to bolster investor confidence (Dye 1983b:273–274; Scialabba 1986:8). In the economic uncertainty of the 1980s, it was the conservative agenda of new money.

Again, how objective are the popular media in keeping the public informed? The media usually report different points of view as the opinions of authorities and experts. The press has often been active in scrutinizing and doing some investigative reporting on a few government activities. Attention has focused on those out-front—Dye's "proximate policy-makers" (Dye 1983:264). When something goes amiss these individuals are seen as the culprits who have strayed from the narrow path of checks and balances. Harry Truman was right when he said "the buck stops here"—meaning in the Oval Office of the president. Power elite research reminds us, however, that the real story—the ultimate responsibility for policy/"the buck"—lies in the wider fellowship behind the scenes and away from the public eye and most reporting. As discussed in the previous section on economic concentration and centralization of power, some media critics think that the points of view most likely to be omitted and the area most likely to be neglected in investigative reporting are those critical of the private corporate sector (Bagdikian 1983; Parenti 1986). The system of economic and political power continues unscathed.

LABOR MARKET SEGMENTATION: DUAL ECONOMIC SECTORS, THE INTERNAL AND SPLIT LABOR MARKETS

In addition to the shaping of major U.S. policy, the concentration of power has had other effects on the average citizen—depending on where one is employed. Earlier in this chapter we saw economic concentration in major industries, then an expansion of this concentration into a centralization of economic power across industries and a broader concentration of power across the political economy. This section focuses on the nature of the firms at either end of a continuum in the private economy (excluding the government sector and employment there) and what this means for people employed in either sector.

At one end of the continuum lie the large, oligopolistic, capital-intensive firms that have developed internal labor markets and the strongest unions. At the other end are the small, competitive, labor-intensive firms. In between are varying degrees of competitiveness. For example, somewhere in the middle are the retain chains of varying size whose franchises compete with local small firms, but who have many more resources behind them. After examining the general characteristics of these two groups on either end of the spectrum, we will have a basic understanding of how the structure of economic sectors affects people in the labor market, particularly minority workers who frequently have found themselves the victims of the split labor market.

Dual Economic Sectors (Dual Labor Market Labor Markets) and the Internal Labor Market

Neoinstitutionalists had been noting for some time that the economy was a long way from the pure competition model of neoclassical economic theory (Dunlop 1957). Giant corporations rose to control their markets. Bureaucratization of large organizations and unions had created internal labor markets insulated from competition from the outside. (See Edwards, Reich, and Gordon 1975 for an historical account of labor market segmentation.)

Basically, however, the dual labor market, or dual economic sectors, perspective developed out of studies of ghetto employment in Boston, Chicago, Detroit, and Harlem (Doeringer and Piore 1971: Baron and

Hymer 1968; Bluestone 1970; Bluestone, Murphy, and Stevenson 1973; Wachtel 1975; Vietorisz and Harrison 1970; see also comments on earlier critiques in Dunlop 1957; Kerr 1954; Chamberlain 1969). The ideas of Piore (1968, 1969, 1970) and Averitt (1968) have also been seminal. What the various studies agree on is that the organization of the economic sectors makes a difference in the nature of the labor markets available to the labor force. The power elite theorists would, of course, recognize the corporations of the primary/core sector of the dual sectors research as the major corporate influence on important national policy.

The *primary* or *core* sector consists of the larger firms in *oligopolistic industries* (in which three to seven firms are able to control more than half of their industry's market). Occasionally, this sector may include smaller firms that, as subsidiaries of conglomerates, have adopted some practices of the parent corporation, and may be able to take advantage of the clout offered by the size of the parent (Bluestone and Harrison 1980; Moberg 1979). Primary sector firms are able to administer prices to some degree and to compete with each other mainly in advertising, but not in price (unless competition comes from foreign firms, as currently in autos, steel, and electronics). These firms use high technology and are capital intensive (have heavy investments in automation and other equipment).

The companies have a fairly stable employment situation, high profits, and high productivity per labor input—due in part to on-the-job training that firms can afford in stable employment and in part to the capital intensive nature of the industry. The gradations in work allowed by technology and size permit the formation of internal labor markets and career ladders. One can be trained on-the-job for the next step up without outside competition for those better jobs. Blue-collar workers in the primary sector are able to develop strong unions, which can ask for and get good wages and benefits for their workers from the high profits of the company. In a noncompetitive, administered price situation, the company can pass along increased labor costs to the consumer.

Because of the nature of oligopolies these firms are able to avoid some curbs of government monetary policy through some internal financing and privileged channels of credit through interlocking boards of directors with financial institutions. As we have seen, they are able to affect fiscal policy and regulations through their influence on regulatory boards, campaign contributions (PACs), lobbying, advisory boards and cabinet positions, employment of influential retired military in the defense industries, and policy-making associations and foundations (Mills 1956; Domhoff 1970, 1975; Parenti 1980). The advantages to the labor force in this primary sector are that the workers have better pay and benefits, on-the-job training, job stability, promotion possibilities, and representation of their interests by unions.

In contrast, firms in the *secondary* or *periphery* sector at the other end of the continuum are likely to be marginal in profits, labor intensive, low in capital input or have antiquated capital and low technology. Also, they must compete because they are too small and there are too many firms in their industry for a few to influence their market. Their workers are usually low-skilled, or at least most of the jobs in this sector call for a low range of skills. Wages are lower, and work is often unstable, fluctuating with the season or the market and subject to the high risk of company failure. Unions are weak or nonexistent. Jobs do not offer training for higher-skilled positions and are often dead end; that is, workers do not increase in skill or get started up a promotional ladder from such jobs. In fact, there is a lack of internal labor market or job mobility chains in the secondary sector. When the secondary or periphery worker moves from one job to another, it is usually to take another dead-end job without increase in skill, status, or pay. Credentials and human capital are less important, generally, in this sector. These jobs usually require just "warm bodies" (Gordon 1972; Beck, Horan, and Tolbert 1978, 1980). Table 5.3 outlines the two sectors.

The growth of internal labor markets in the primary sector of the economy can be told in terms of the necessities of growth in the size of organizations, the state of technology that requires an hierarchical divi-

Table 5.3 Summary of Dual Economic Sectors

Primary/Core Sector	Secondary/Periphery Sector
Larger capital intensive oligopolistic manufacturing and extractive firms —administers prices, unless foreign competition —access to internal financing, privileged channels of credit	Smaller, less powerful, more competitve firms —lower profit margins —more antiquated capital, less automation, often labor intensive —more subject to government monetary controls
Job Security	Low job security
More on-the-job training, some chance for promotion (internal labor market)	Low skilled work, dead-end jobs
High productivity per labor input due to high capital investment in automation, research & development (often government supported)	Low productivity per labor unit— need casual labor with high turnover, part-time, less disciplined
Large unions—better wages and benefits	Less powerful unions, if any
Examples: chemical, electronic, steel, auto, rubber, petroleum, minerals, etc. industries	Examples: laundry and cleaning, eating and drinking places, gas stations, small retail stores, light manufacturing, etc.

sion of labor. This division and stratification of labor can also be viewed critically from the power/conflict perspective. Individuals taking this perspective explain the rise of this labor market segmentation not just in terms of necessity, but also in terms of class interest. Internal divisions of job titles, job descriptions, different credentials, statuses, even office furnishings, kept the labor force from seeing that they might be in a common position (Edwards, Reich, and Gordon 1975; Gordon 1972; Beck, Horan, and Tolbert 1978). Unionization was a growing threat during the period of transition from smaller entrepreneurial firms to large corporations. It was easier to separate the white-collar workers from the unionizing blue collars, but it was also useful to separate the blue- and white-collar groups internally through job stratification.

All of this growing bureaucratization had the effect of making the worker feel that he or she was being dealt with impersonally, less arbitrarily, and that his or her job was different from the jobs of other workers. Power was less visible, and the structure and its rules were legitimated—especially when unions acquiesed to or helped establish some of the procedures. The lower-tier or blue-collar workers of the primary sector had their own job mobility chains, and the upper-tier white-collar workers had theirs—except for the unfortunate workers who somehow became stuck in entry-level positions in each tier (Piore 1975; see Chapter 10 for some ways in which the internal labor market affects worker attitudes and behaviors).

Split Labor Market

Sociologist Edna Bonacich (1972, 1975, 1976) defines a *split labor market* as one in which there is a large differential in the price of labor between two or more groups of workers, holding constant their efficiency and productivity. The split occurs between the privileged and the less privileged and is shaped, in part, by the conditions of initial contact between the incoming group and the labor market. Historically, incoming groups had less knowledge of the market, less power, fewer skills, low socioeconomic backgrounds, and were willing to take low paying, noncareer type jobs. They were hired into secondary labor market jobs. In other words, they lacked some of the human capital we have been discussing; but there is more to their situation than that, in terms of what the initial placement in the secondary labor market means today for some groups.

Identifiable minorities, such as blacks, Mexican Americans, American Indians, and women, found themselves more or less permanently placed as groups into this economic sector, or stuck in entry-level positions in the primary sector in corporations that already were hiring minorities when they were organized by industrial unions. Unions of white males in blue-collar jobs in the primary sector did their part to eliminate this cheap competition by supporting immigration laws and through union tactics, such as hiring halls, apprenticeship programs, and influence on promotion practices within firms in the primary sector (Kalleberg and Sorensen 1979:370). Fear of economic competition is a powerful force. Race, ethnicity, religion, gender, and regional negative stereotyping of groups offering cheap competition (such as the Anglo Okies immigrating to the Southwest in the 1930s) have been handy devices used to keep these groups out of better jobs. The prejudice more likely follows the fear of economic competition than the other way around. This job discrimination has been particularly long-term for visible minorities.

Affirmative action laws have attempted to limit some of these discriminatory practices by employers and unions. However, some empirical data indicate that they have not yet affected the vast majority in these categories, as we saw in Chapter 3.

More recently, the so-called Cambridge Controversy, from the Cambridge School of Economics, has elaborated on the institutionalists' critiques of neoclassical economic theory and ties in our ideas from Bonacich's historical split labor market data. Along with the free flow of other factors, neoclassical economists had assumed a free flow of workers and a single labor queue (Ford 1973:70–76). In this view employers would hire from workers lined up, figuratively speaking, according to attainment in human capital—education, skills, work habits, and so forth. It did not consider discriminatory policies on the part of employers or labor unions that might exclude some groups from an opportunity to obtain entry-level jobs in a privileged sector or on-the-job training to advance thereafter. There is not a single labor market queue, but perhaps several—each for types of persons traditionally hired for certain jobs. Internal labor markets were also not foreseen, that is, training on-the-job and promotion from within to skilled blue-collar positions, rather than hiring from an outside labor queue. Because of these factors, and other factors in the arguments made by the Cambridge economists, neoclassical marginal productivity does not explain income distribution and low-wage poverty in the real world.

SUMMARY

This chapter briefly touched on many subjects related to the overall rubric of concentration of power in the economic and political spheres. Hopefully, a pattern or framework has emerged. In essence, we have seen that:

1. Political and economic system definitions need to be formalized to avoid confusion when constructing ideal types or models in the mind to compare with evidence, sometimes conflicting, of the real world. We briefly defined *economic systems* (capitalism, socialism, communism, and mixed economies) according to who owns the means of production, who does the economic planning, and for what goals. We defined *political systems* (autocracy, oligopoly, and democracy—pure/classical, representative, and democratic elitism) according to how many peopel made the major political decisions.

2. The power pluralism and power elite views are the two polar opposite theories of how political and economic power are distributed in the United States. Each view puts forth mechanisms proporting to describe how social institutions operate in our society. Some limited empirical evidence is presented on both sides, particularly from the power elite view since it is least available in the popular media or the educational system.

3. Economic concentration exists in the basic industries in the United States and there also is centralization of economic power across industries. Centralization of power is achieved by means of conglomerates and financial institutions owning/controlling strategic shares of voting stock and interlocking their boards of directors and/or controlling channels of credit. The rate of acquisitions and mergers indicates that this trend in centralization of economic power through conglomeration will continue, although at the very top there has been some restructuring toward fewer subsidiaries, to fend off corporate raiding in recent years.

4. Key positions in society, in terms of setting the national agenda, are found in large corporations and in national policy-making associations and foundations. The research done by these policy-making bodies is funded by large corporations and wealthy individuals and families whose interests may frequently be served. The demographics of the incumbents of these key positions are reviewed. Some differences of opinion exist on some issues between conservative and old-line liberal elites, who have somewhat different regional and wealth bases. In any case, national policy can be documented historically to have been ultimately directed toward propertied interests. Through the penetration of the political sphere by centralized economic power, we have some indication of the concentration of power across the political economy.

5. Looking at the shape of the economy from the dual economic sectors point of view, we see how oligopolies in the basic industries fostered the growth of privileged blue-collar work group. An internal

labor market within these industries advanced acceptable workers from entry-level jobs through on-the-job training and promotion. These workers attempted to protect their higher-skilled and higher-paid jobs from encroachments of minority/marginal workers through union tactics described in the split labor market. Minorities, disadvantaged in knowledge of the market and discriminated against by both employers and unions, became relegated to secondary labor market jobs, or to entry-level jobs only, if they were able to get into the primary sector.

BIBLIOGRAPHY

Adamany, David. 1986. The new faces of American politics. *Annals of the American Academy of Political and Social Science* 486:12–33 (July).
Aldrich, H. E., and J. Pfeffer. 1976. Environments of organizations. *Annual Review of Sociology* 2:79–105.
Allen, Michael Patrick. 1976. Management control in the large corporation: Comment on Zeitlin. *American Journal of Sociology* 81, 4:885–894 (January).
———. 1978. Economic interest groups and the corporate elite structure. *Social Science Quarterly* 58, 4:597–615 (March).
Averitt, R. T. 1968. *The dual economy: The dynamics of American industry structure.* New York: Norton.
Bachrach, Peter. 1967. *The theory of democratic elitism: A critique.* Boston: Little, Brown.
Bagdikian, Ben H. 1983. *The media monopoly.* Boston: Beacon.
Baron, Harold, and Bennett Hymer. 1968. "The Negro in the Chicago labor market." In *The Negro and the American labor movement,* edited by Julius Jabobson, 232–285. New York: Doubleday (Anchor).
Beck, E. M., Patrick M. Horan, and Charles M. Tolbert II. 1978. Stratification in a dual economy: A sectoral model of earnings determination. *American Sociological Review* 43, 5:704–720 (October).
———. 1980. Industrial segmentation and labor market discrimination. *Social Problems* 28, 2:113–130 (December).
Bell, Daniel. 1960. *The end of ideology.* New York: Collier.
Berg, Ivar, and M. N. Zald. 1978. Business and society. *Annual Review of Sociology* 4:115–143.
Berle, Adolf A., and Gardiner C. Means. 1968. *The modern corporation and private property.* New York: Harcourt Brace and Jovanovich. (Originally published in 1932.)
Bluestone, Barry. 1970. The tripartite economy: Labor markets and the working poor. *Poverty and Human Resources* 5:15–35 (July–August).
Bluestone, Barry, and Bennett Harrison. 1982. *The deindustrialization of America: Plant closings, community abandonment, and the dismantling of basic industry.* New York: Basic Books.
Bluestone, Barry, W. M. Murphy, and M. Stevenson. 1973. *Low wages and the*

working poor. Ann Arbor: Institute of Labor and Industrial Relations, University of Michigan and Wayne State University.

Bonacich, Edna. 1972. A theory of ethnic antagonism: The split labor market. *American Sociological Review* 37, 5:547–559 (October).

———. 1975. Abolition, the extension of slavery and the position of blacks: A study of the split labor markets in the United States, 1830–1836. *American Journal of Sociology* 81, 3:601–628 (November).

———. 1976. Advanced capitalism and black/white relations in the United States: A split labor market interpretation. *American Sociological Review* 41, 1:34–51 (February).

Burch, Philip H., Jr. 1972 *The managerial revolution reassessed: Family control in America's largest corporations*. Lexington, Mass.: D.C. Heath.

Burnham, James. 1941. *The managerial revolution*. New York: John Day.

CDE stock ownership directory. 1981. New York: Corporate Data Exchange, Inc.

Chamberlain, Neil W. 1969. "Some further thoughts on the concept of human capital." In *Cost-benefit analysis of manpower policies*, edited by G. C. Somers and W. D. Wood, 230–248. Madison: Industrial Relations Research Institute, University of Wisconsin.

Compaine, Benjamin M., ed. 1982. *Who owns the media?: Concentration of ownership in the mass communications industry*, 2nd ed. White Plains, N.Y.: Knowledge Industry Publications.

Dahl, Robert A. 1957. The concept of power. *Behavioral Science* 2:201–215.

———. 1958. Critique of the ruling elite model. *American Political Science Review* 52, 2:463–469 (June).

———. 1967. *Pluralist democracy in the United States*. Chicago: Rand McNally.

Dahrendorf, Ralf. 1959. *Class and class conflict in industrial society*. Stanford, Calif.: Stanford University Press.

Dockser, Amy. 1987. Nice PAC you've got here. . . . A pity if anything should happen to it. *Washington Monthly* 18, 12:21–24 (January).

Doeringer, Peter B., and Michael J. Piore. 1971. *Internal labor markets and manpower analysis*. Lexington, Mass.: D. C. Heath.

Domhoff, G. William. 1970. *The higher circles*. New York: Random House.

———. 1975. New directions in power structure research. *The Insurgent Sociologist* 5 (Spring) (Special issue).

———. 1978. *The powers that be: Processes of ruling class domination in America*. New York: Random (Vintage).

Domhoff, G. William, and Hoyt B. Ballard, compilers. 1968. *C. Wright Mills and the power elite*. Boston: Beacon.

Dunlop, John. 1957. "The task of contemporary wage theory." In *New concepts in wage discrimination*, edited by George W. Taylor and Frank C. Pierson, 117–139. New York: McGraw-Hill.

Dye, Thomas R. 1983a. Who owns America; Strategic ownership positions in industrial corporations. *Social Science Quarterly* 64, 4:862–870 (December).

———. 1983b. *Who's running America? The Reagan years*, 3rd ed. Englewood Cliffs, N.J.: Prentice-Hall.

Edsall, Thomas Byrne. 1984. *The new politics of inequality*. New York: W. W. Norton.

Edwards, Richard C. 1975. "The social relations of production in the firm and labor market structure." In *Labor market segmentation*, edited by R. C. Edwards, M. Reich, and D. M. Gordon, 3–26. Lexington, Mass.: D. C. Heath.

Eitzen, D. Stanley, Dean A. Purdy, and Maureen Jung. 1985. Interlocking ownership among the major banks. *The Insurgent Sociologist* 4:45–50 (Winter).

Ferguson, Thomas, and Joel Rogers. 1986. *Right turn: The decline of the Democrats and the future of American politics*. New York: Hill and Wang.

The 500 largest U.S. industrial corporations, ranked by sales. 1986. *Fortune* 113, 9:182–183 (April 28).

Ford, Arthur Morton. 1973. *Political economics of rural poverty in the South*. Cambridge, Mass.: Ballinger (Lippincott).

Glasberg, Davita Silfen, and Michael Schwartz. 1983. Ownership and control of corporations. *Annual Review of Sociology* 9:311–332.

Gordon, David M. 1972. *Theories of poverty and underemployment*. Lexington, Mass.: D. C. Heath.

Kalleberg, Arne L., and Aage Sorensen. 1979. The sociology of labor markets. *Annual Review of Sociology* 5:351–379.

Kerr, Clark. 1954. "The Balkanization of labor markets." In *Labor mobility and economic opportunity*, edited by E. Wight Bakke et al. 93–109. Cambridge, Mass.: MIT and John Wiley.

Kotz, David M. 1978. *Bank control of large corporations in the United States*. Berkeley: University of California Press.

Larner, Robert J. 1966. Ownership and control of the 200 largest nonfinancial corporations. *American Economic Review* 56, 4:777–787 (September).

Mariolis, Peter. 1983. Interlocking directorates and financial groups: A peak analysis. *Sociological Spectrum* 3, 3–4:237–252 (July–December).

Media Monotony: Corporate media support status quo. 1984. *Dollars & Sense* 101:6–7 (November).

The military-spending debate. 1984. *The Washington Spectator* 7:1–4 (April 15).

Mills, C. Wright. 1956. *The power elite*. New York: Oxford.

Mintz, Beth, and Michael Schwartz. 1981. Interlocking directorates and interest group formation. *American Sociologist Review* 46, 6:851–869 (December).

Mizruchi, Mark S. 1982. *The American corporate network: 1904–1974*. Beverly Hills, Calif.: Sage.

Moberg, David. 1986. The biting problem of corporate control. *In These Times* 11, 6:5 (December 17–23).

1985 profile: Almanac. 1986. *Mergers & Acquisitions* 20, 5:45–53 (May/June).

Notable comments from members of Congress about the abuses of our current congressional campaign financing system. 1987. Washington, D.C.: Common Cause.

Optimistic outlook for M&A: Review/preview. 1986. *Mergers & Acquisitions* 5:5–6 (May/June).

Parenti, Michael. 1980. *Democracy for the few*, 3rd ed. New York: St. Martin's Press.

————. 1986. *Inventing reality: The politics of the mass media.* New York: St. Martin's Press.

Parsons, Talcott. 1953. "A revised analytical approach to the theory of stratification." In *Class, Status, and Power*, edited by R. Bendix and S. M. Lipset, 92–128. New York: Free Press.

————. 1970. Equality and inequality in modern society, or social stratification revisited. *Sociological Inquiry* 40:13–72.

Pateman, Carole. 1970. *Participation and democratic theory.* Cambridge, England: University of Cambridge Press.

Pfeffer, Jeffrey, and Gerald R. Salancik. 1978. *The external control of organizations: A resource dependency perspective.* New York: Harper & Row.

Piore, Michael J. 1968. The impact of the labor market upon the design and selection of production techniques within the manufacturing plant. *Quarterly Journal of Economics* 82:602–620 (November).

————. 1969. "On-the-job training in the dual labor market." In *Public private manpower policies*, edited by A. R. Weber, R. Cassell, and W. L. Ginsberg, 101–132. Madison: Industrial Relations Research Association, University of Wisconsin.

————. 1970. "Jobs and training." In *The state and the poor*, edited by S. H. Beer and R. E. Barringer, 53–83. Cambridge, Mass.: Winthrop.

————. 1975. "Notes for a theory of labor market stratification." In *Labor market segmentation*, edited by Richard C. Edwards, Michael Reich, and David M. Gordon, pp. 125–150. Lexington, Mass.: Lexington Books.

Polsby, Nelson. 1963. *Community power and political theory.* New Haven, Conn.: Yale University Press.

The raiding game, 1987. *Dollars and Sense* 124: 13–15, 21 (March).

Ratcliff, Richard. 1979–1980. Capitalist class structure and the decline of older industrial cities. *Insurgent Sociologist* 2–3:60–74.

————. 1980. "Banks and the command of capital flows: An analysis of capitalist class structure and mortgage disinvestment in a metropolitan area." In *Classes, class conflict and the state*, edited by Maurice Zeitlin, 107–132. Boston: Little Brown.

Rehmus, Charles M. 1984. Labor and politics in the 1980s. *Annals of the American Academy of Political and Social Sciences* 473:40–51 (May).

Riesman, David. 1953. *The lonely crowd.* Garden City, N.Y.: Doubleday (Anchor).

Rose, Arnold M. 1967. *The power structure.* New York: Oxford.

Scialabba, George. 1986. The political monopoly. *The Texas Observer* 78, 25:8–11 (December 19).

Sheehan, Robert. 1967. Proprietors in the world of big business. *Fortune* 15:178–183, 242 (June).

Short, R. P. 1984. "The role of public enterprises: An international comparison." In *Public enterprise in mixed economies: Some macroeconomic aspects*, edited by Robert H. Floyd, Clive S. Gray, and R. P. Short, 110–194. Washington, D. C.: International Monetary Fund.

Sinzinger, Keith A. 1985. Uncovering the real defense share. *In These Times* 9, 13:3 (February 20–26).

Sonquist, John A., and Thomas Koenig. 1975. Interlocking directorates in the top U.S. corporations: A graph theory approach. *The Insurgent Sociologist* 3:196–229 (Spring).

Special interest snipers. 1985. *New York Times* 135, #46,600:A34 (November 21).

Spruill, Charles R. 1982. *Conglomerates and the evolution of capitalism.* Carbondale: Southern Illinois University Press.

U.S. Congress. 1968. Commerical banks and their trust activities: Emerging influence on the American economy. House Banking and Currency Committee, Subcommittee on Domestic Finance, 90th Congress, 2nd Session. Washington, D. C.: G.P.O.

Useem, Michael. 1978. The inner group of the American capitalist class. *Social Problems* 25, 3:225–240 (February).

———. 1979. The social organization of the American business class. *American Sociological Review* 44, 4:553–571 (August).

———. 1980. Corporations and the corporate elite. *Annual Review of Sociology* 6:41–77.

———. 1983. *The inner circle: Large corporations and business politics in the United States and the United Kingdom.* New York: Oxford.

Vietorisz, Thomas, and Bennett Harrison. 1970. *The economic development of Harlem.* New York: Praeger.

Wachtel, Howard M. 1975. "Class consciousness and stratification in the labor process." *Labor market segmentation,* edited by Richard C. Edwards, Michael Reich, and David M. Gordon, 95–122. Lexington, Mass.: D. C. Heath.

Whitt, J. Allen. 1982. *Means of motion.* Princeton, N.J.: Princeton University Press.

Zeitlin, Maurice. 1974. Corporate ownership and control: The large corporation and the capitalist class. *American Journal of Sociology* 79, 5:1073–1119 (March).

———. 1976. On class theory of the large corporation: Response to Allen. *American Journal of Sociology* 81, 4:894–903 (January).

6

Multinational
Corporations

In the previous chapter we saw the concentration of economic power in the United States—how the top corporations and financial institutions are interlocked through their boards of directors and through owning strategic blocks of stock in each other's companies and particularly how financial corporations are interlocked to each other. We also saw some outcomes for public policy through the interaction of the economic and political sectors and the historical effect of the dual structure of the economy on minority workers. In this chapter we look at large U.S. corporations that operate in foreign countries; thus, the reference to *multinational corporations* (MNCs); some writers use the term *transnational corporations* (TNCs).

As might be expected, there are differing opinions on the effects that large multinational corporations, together with the assistance of U.S. government policy, have on the less industrially developed countries (LDCs) or Third World societies. Some writers differentiate between less technologically developed societies that have some industrial development, which they term *Third World* or the *semiperiphery*, and the almost nonindustrial societies, which they term *Fourth World* or *periphery*. We use *Three Worlds*, but you may want to keep in mind that there is a continuum of industrial development. Some evidence on their activities and what this might mean for development are considered, particularly in the case of Central America and parts of the Caribbean in which the U.S. MNCs are increasingly involved. We next turn to the stated purposes of the Trilateral Commission and some commentary on joint ventures between U.S. and foreign MNCs. Finally, the effects of plant shutdowns and off-shore sourcing on U.S. workers and their communities are discussed, along with worker and community and grassroot organization reactions to this capital flight.

THE BACKGROUND AND SIZE OF THE SITUATION

We should note early on that not all MNCs are U.S. based. Table 6.1 shows the fifteen largest world MNCs and their country of origin. Commercial banks and other lending agencies also operate abroad and have an extremely strong influence on what happens in Third World countries. Table 6.2 indicates the size of the twenty largest multinational banks in the industrially developed world.

If major corporations seem large in the United States and powerful enough to influence governments, including the national government at home, their power in other countries is even more decided. The individual *assets* of Exxon, Texaco, IBM, or DuPont are larger than the combined gross national products (GNPs) of all seven Central American countries (Barry, Wood, and Preusch 1983:9). In fact the assets of Exxon or General Motors are larger than the GNPs of all but twenty countries of the world.

In 1977 the assets of all U.S. overseas branches (not the parent companies and not including the foreign subsidiaries of financial institutions) were worth $490 billion; by 1983 they were valued at $761 billion and employed 6.5 million workers, two-thirds of whom were in manufacturing (Belli 1986:24, 29). Only about one-third of these assets and one-third of the workers were in less developed countries, $234.6 billion

Table 6.1 Fifteen Largest Industrial Companies in the World in 1985, Ranked by Sales

Company	Headquarters	Industry	Sales $000	Net Income $000
General Motors	Detroit	Motor vehicles	96,471,700	3,999,000
Exxon	New York	Petroleum	86,673,000	4,870,000
Royal Dutch/Shell	The Hague/London	Petroleum	81,743,514	3,928,208
Mobil	New York	Petroleum	55,960,000	1,040,000
British Petroleum	London	Petroleum	53,100,765	866,745
Ford Motor	Dearborn	Motor vehicles	52,774,400	2,515,400
IBM	Armonk, NY	Computers	50,056,000	6,555,000
Texaco	Harrison, NY	Petroleum	46,297,000	1,233,000
Chevron	San Francisco	Petroleum	41,741,905	1,547,360
AT&T	New York	Electronics	34,909,500	1,556,800
DuPont	Wilmington, DE	Chemicals	29,483,000	1,118,000
General Electric	Fairfield, CT	Electronics	28,285,000	2,336,000
Standard Oil (IN)	Chicago	Petroleum	27,215,000	1,953,000
IRI	Rome	Metals	26,758,000	(664,000)
Toyota Motor	Toyota City (Japan)	Motor vehicles	26,040,288	1,624,184

Source: Adapted from Farnham and Gottlieb, "The World's Largest Industrial Corporations," *Fortune*, pp. 170–171.

Table 6.2 The Top Twenty Commercial Banks in the World in 1984, by Size
of Deposit

Bank, Country	Deposits (millions U.S.$)
Dai-Ichi Kangyo Ltd., Tokyo, Japan	$95,096
Fuji Bank Ltd., Tokyo, Japan	90,304
Sumitomo Bank Lts., Osaka, Japan	88,873
Bank of America, San Francisco, U.S.A.	88,167
Mitsubishi Bank Ltd., Tokyo, Japan	87,324
Credit Agricole Mutuel, Paris, France	84,828
Banque Nationale de Paris, France	82,832
Sanwa Bank Ltd., Osaka, Japan	80,928
Citibank, New York, U.S.A.	79,551
Credit Lyonnais, Paris, France	77,525
Société Generale, Paris, France	75,822
Barclays, London, U.K.	73,715
Norinchukin, Tokyo, Japan	73,311
National Westminster Bank, London, U.K.	73,266
Industrial Bank of Japan Ltd., Tokyo, Japan	71,222
Deutsche Bank, Frankfurt, West Germany	67,310
Midland Bank, London, U.K.	65,427
Tokai Bank Ltd., Nagoya, Japan	65,038
Mitsui Bank Ltd., Tokyo, Japan	60,037
Chase Manhattan, New York, U.S.A.	59,400

Source: World Almanac, *World Almanac and Book of Facts: 1986*, pp. 111–112.

and 2,119 million workers respectively in 1983. The impact on the
Third World, however, is more important in terms of its effects on popu-
lations than is the larger investment in industrially developed nations.

The Commerce Department defines foreign *direct investment* as
control of 10 percent or more of a foreign company. Total direct foreign
investment in 1984 stood at $233.4 billion (World Almanac 1985:101).
Direct investment in developed countries accounted for $174.1 billion,
LDCs received $53.9 billion, and other international investments were
$5.4 billion. In 1960, 1969, and 1984 direct investment just in off-shore
manufacturing (not including trade, financial, and services) by U.S.
firms in LDCs was $11.1 billion, $29.5 billion, $20.1 billion (Fuentes
and Ehrenreich 1983:8; World Almanac 1985:101). Only about one-
fourth of direct investment is specifically in LDCs.

Why would U.S. corporations leave the comforts of home to operate
abroad, especially in Third World countries? Perhaps because corporations find that with only one-third of their assets located outside the
United States they obtain half of their reported profits from foreign investment; in other words, rates of return are higher abroad than in the

United States ("Controlling Interest" 1978). Further, the average profit rate is higher in LDCs than in developed areas. Cavanagh and Broad (1982:8) calculate an 18.7 percent profit for companies investing in the developed world, compared to a 24.6 percent rate in LDCs.

The profit rate also varies by region in the Third World; returns were 45.2 percent in Asia, 39.8 percent in Africa, and 19.4 percent in Latin America as of 1980. Profit rates are highest where wage rates are lowest, although wages are not the total reason (Cavanagh and Broad 1982:8). Also, it appears that direct investment dollars generate more assets in LDCs than in developed countries, as indicated in the preceeding paragraphs. These ratios of investment to assets in developed countries and LDCs have held fairly constant for two decades. The U.S. Department of Commerce has noted that for every dollar U.S. MNCs invest in Latin America, an estimated three dollars comes back to the United States in some form (Barry, Wood, and Preusch 1983:9). It is no surprise, then, that 70 of the top 100 corporations in the United States have investments in Central America and the Caribbean and that more than 1,400 MNCs operate in Central America and more than 1,000 in the Caribbean, with a book value of $4.2 billion in Central America and $15.7 billion (mostly oil) in the Caribbean (Barry, Wood, and Preusch 1983:8–9; Armstrong 1985:1).

We have noted that Third World nations receive only about 25 percent of U.S. MNC direct foreign investment, although it brings the corporations one-third of their foreign assets and higher profits. If the payback is better in the Third World, why would MNCs invest so much in developed countries? There are several explanations. One important reason for investing in European nations is to get plants inside of the European Economic Community tariff barriers. Europe is a large market for goods and services, including banking, retailing, and fast foods.

Joint ventures with local corporations are also very attractive in developed nations, since the local business can provide connections and expertise on the culture and marketing. Since about 75 percent of the money invested by MNCs abroad is raised in the foreign country itself, savings rates in Europe may account for some of the pull to that area (Cavanagh and Broad 1982). They have more savings to invest. Probably the most frequently cited reason is the political stability of European nations, compared to LDCs. This concern with stability becomes an important aspect of MNC operations and U.S. government foreign policy in Third World nations.

Before looking at some pros and cons of MNCs and how they operate, it might be useful to consider the general social structure of most Third World developing nations in which they operate. Both theory and empirical study have noted the importance of social structure in the host country for understanding the nature of the operations of MNCs.

The following section looks at such a general model of social structure that is common in many Latin American countries. Merle Kling provides a model applicable to many Latin American social structures.

THE KLING MODEL OF LATIN AMERICAN SOCIAL STRUCTURES

Even though it is difficult to make generalizations that fit all Third World societies, political scientist Merle Kling (1968) briefly outlined a social structure that seems to fit most Latin American countries even today. His analysis of social strata helps explain the stability of the underlying social and economic structure, despite the many palace coups in Latin America that change the personnel in government but foster little in the way of real social change. Most Latin American societies have a fairly feudal agrarian base with an old landed aristocracy, a military establishment, a small middle class, and the majority of the population as peasants working for the landed elite or as small freeholders. Into this structure come foreign investors. The resulting social structure Kling characterizes in the following manner (some examples from the 1980s have been added for illustrative purposes).

1. *Landowning aristocracy*: Sets cultural pattern for rest of society; cooperation with industrial/extractive sector to ensure political and economic stability since they do not want land reforms that might take away their estates; in Central America 59 percent of the population is rural, and of this 59 percent, 40 to 70 percent is landless and works on the estates of the aristocracy or for foreign-owned agribusiness (only Belize and Costa Rica have escaped a large landed indigenous aristocracy, although they have much foreign land ownership); overall in Central America 3 percent of the total population has 50 percent of the income and the bottom 20 percent has 3 to 4 percent of the income (Barry, Wood, and Preusch 1983:4, 6, 112).

2. *Industrial/extractive sector*: Relatively small sector, basically foreign owned with the profits accruing to the foreign owners and often taken back to the home country of the MNC; some domestic ownership, usually in joint ventures with foreign owners and subject to terms of trade and markets set by industrial countries and to loan terms established by foreign banks and lending agencies. This sector fears social change because it might lead to nationalization of industry. It protects the landed aristocracy from land reform—a possible first step toward industrial or extractive company expropriation (nationalization of the assets of the MNC by the host country). Extractive industries in Cen-

tral America include such MNCs as United Brands (formerly United Fruit), Castle and Cooke, Exxon, and R. J. Reynolds.

3. *Government sector*: Provides upward social mobility for a small number of the middle class.

4. *Military sector*: Another limited avenue of social mobility available to the middle class; usually U.S.-trained and -equipped in Central America; jockeys for position with the governmental sector providing the many so-called *palace coups* in Latin America that offer a change in governmental personnel but no particular change, in most cases, in the stable economic and social base, that is, ownership by the landed aristocracy and the industrial/extractive sectors.

5. *Middle class*: A small, but growing in Central America, privileged (relative to the majority of landless or unemployed) sector that works for the industrial/extractive sector or government—usually supporting economic stability and modernization theories of development; looking to both the local aristocracy and middle classes of the developed nations as cultural reference groups. Sullivan (1983:207) cites several studies that refer to this *comprador* class as the "local arm of foreign business whose interests they serve."

6. *Urban poor*: Unemployed, underemployed in the service sector, expanding rapidly in some countries as estates mechanize or small farms are bought out, and often restless; may be 30 percent or more of the population in Central America as a whole.

7. *Peasants*: Approximately 50 percent of the population in most countries of Latin America, except countries such as Argentina and Panama, which have a more industrial base or more agricultural mechanization. See Table 6.3 for work force employed in agriculture and indus-

Table 6.3 Employment Percentages by Sector in Central America, 1960 and 1980

| | 1960 | | 1980 | |
	Industry	Agriculture	Industry	Agriculture
Belize	22.0	39.0	16.5	37.1
Costa Rica	18.5	51.2	23.0	29.0
El Salvador	17.1	61.7	22.4	50.5
Guatemala	14.4	66.7	20.5	55.0
Honduras	10.6	70.2	14.6	62.6
Nicaragua	16.0	62.3	19.9	42.6
Panama	13.7	50.9	18.1	27.3

Source: World Bank, *World Tables*, Vol. II: *Social Data*, 3rd ed.

try in Central America in 1960 and 1980. Note that this is an undercount of total population depending on agriculture, since it counts only workers.

CONFLICTING VIEWS ON MULTINATIONAL OPERATIONS IN THE THIRD WORLD

Modernization Theory

When individuals in government development and assistance agencies and those in multinational corporations speak of the effects of developed nations doing business in the Third World nations trying to develop, they use some form of modernization theory, or what has been called the *Fortune* magazine view of the situation. This view sees the Third World as benefiting from foreign investment, technology, job creation and training for industrialization, and modernization in terms of increasing education, changing individual attitudes toward the Protestant ethic, and building infrastructure. Further, when business among countries is well established it will raise the gross national product of the host country, increase the standard of living for workers, and promote the peaceful political and economic climate so necessary for trade by keeping down discontent and the threat of communism. More recently, the argument that this foreign investment allows U.S. corporations to compete with other industrial countries has been added. In sum, the pro argument includes the following six points:

1. Pax Americana (keeps peace and economic and political stability)
2. Saves the Third World from communism
3. MNCs are more efficient than are smaller firms already operating within Third World countries
4. Provides jobs and training for people in less developed countries
5. Promotes Third World economic development by increasing their GNP, transfering technology, and building infrastructure
6. Allows U.S. firms to compete and make higher profits and stay alive in a highly competitive world market.

Dependency Theory

An opposing view is based on the premise that the developed nations of the world and their multinational corporations are hindering, not helping, developing countries. In fact, according to this view the policies of the developed world helped create and maintain underdevelopment. The value of goods, resources, and labor of Third World peoples are siphoned off to the developed or metropolitan countries.

André Gunder Frank (1972) and others who take this dependency theory, or world-systems (Wallerstein 1974, 1976), approach point out that this is an extension of the old colonial system practiced by European nations on the Third World societies in Africa, Southeast Asia, and Latin America since at least the sixteenth century. Under old style colonialism the dominant metropolitan countries of Europe exploited their colonies for (1) land and resources, (2) cheap labor, and (3) terms of trade favorable to the developed nation. In the latter instance, the colony gave up its raw materials and labor for a fraction of what they were worth and bought back expensive manufactured goods from the mother country, which had the power to set these terms of trade.

As colonies gained their political independence in the twentieth century, however, the exploitation did not usually end. Political colonialism was replaced by economic colonialism or neocolonialism. Pressures from the governments of developed countries in support of powerful multinational corporations continued. Terms of trade were still set by developed nations for exports from the less developed countries (LDCs) and imports into LDCs. MNCs have used cheap labor within these countries in increasing numbers since the 1970s. In addition, the LDCs are now deeply in debt to lending agencies of developed nations.

Brenner (1977) modifies dependency theory by pointing out that even under these unequal conditions some progress toward development can be made by the periphery country if there is not too unequal a division within the social class system in that country. Of course, less developed countries usually have a polarized class structure with a few people at the top and the mass as peasants below, as noted in the Kling model (Agee 1975:565). The metropole can usually make the system even more unequal by working through indigenous elites and by creating a few individuals who become elites through the support of the foreign powers, a system similar to the indirect rule practiced by Great Britain in the days of old-style political colonialism.

Other writers (Barnet and Mueller 1974a; Sklar 1980, 1986; Klare 1981; Klare and Arnson 1981; *Multinational Monitor* 1980-date; Barry, Wood, and Preusch 1983) have documented nine ways that, in their opinion, MNCs and U.S. government policy have carried out the exploitation alluded to in dependency theory. This policy:

1. Stops social reforms needed for real internal growth and development
2. Increases social inequality and poverty
3. Avoids taxes to both the United States and the host LDC through creative bookkeeping, transfer pricing, and free trade zone agreements with local governments

4. Promotes government corruption, militarism, and repression
5. Emphasizes production for export and for luxury goods, often decreasing local food supply for local consumption
6. Introduces health and environmental hazards, both in the workplace and for the general population
7. Does not provide the number of jobs promised, and the jobs provided are often dead-end jobs filled by women; drives out home-owned, labor-intensive industries (Green Revolution has flushed peasants and small landholders into urban areas, increasing unemployment and unrest)
8. Creates larger imbalances between imports and exports and public debt of host nations
9. Creates plant shutdowns, unemployment, problems for communities and for labor, in general, in the developed nations.

SOME EVIDENCE OF MNC OPERATIONS AND THE EFFECTS ON DEVELOPMENT

Public Coffers, Private Bookkeeping

First, we can substantiate that the *Fortune* magazine view that foreign investment increases GNP in Third World countries is undoubtedly correct in most instances. Brazil's GNP tripled in the first few years after the 1964 military coup encouraged investors from abroad. The amount of exports also increases. Unfortunately, counter effects also are at work. The balance between imports and exports tips in favor of the developed nations as MNCs require materials and overpriced capital equipment from the mother country and the middle and upper classes require more imported luxury items from abroad. In addition, there is the matter of increasing public debt for Third World nations.

Why should this debt increase? In the 1970s U.S. banks and multilateral lending agencies, such as the World Bank and the International Monetary Fund (IMF) and private multinational bank consortia, had many dollars to invest. The Middle Eastern petrodollars were pouring in, and banks and lending agencies were anxious to lend them at steadily increasing rates of interest—so-called *third window* lending. Third World nations were competing for MNC investment and promised foreign companies many things, including infrastructure, such as new industrial parks in free trade zones, roads from the resources to the processing area, and power plants. All of these promises meant public borrowing to build these facilities. An unknown amount seems to have evaporated into the hands of government officials in some countries. Table 6.4 indicates the indebtedness of some Third World nations by

Table 6.4 Dept Incurred by Several Third World Countries, 1985

Country	Debt $100,000	Country	Debt $000,000
Brazil	$107.3	Yugoslavia	$19.6
Mexico	99.0	Nigeria	19.3
Argentina	50.8	Morocco	14.0
Venezuela	33.6	Peru	13.4
Philippines	24.8	Colombia	11.3
Chile	21.0	Ecuador	8.5

Source: *World Almanac and Book of Facts: 1987,* p. 119. (Data obtained from World Bank.)

mid-1985. (See Moffitt 1983:93–132 for an analysis of Third World indebtedness.)

All the public debt owed to foreign lending agencies has allowed another mechanism for influencing the internal economic affairs of developing countries. The IMF acts as a lender of last resort to Third World nations who are about to default on loans from developed nations. They lend to the LDCs to repay at least the interest on the loans, if the countries will agree to their terms. The IMF terms promote MNC interests—make severe cuts in public spending for social services, freeze wages, liberalize exchange rates, allow unrestricted currency convertibility to facilitate easy flow of capital, eliminate price ceilings on commodities, grant incentives for new foreign investment, and promote export-led growth.

These are good conditions for foreign investment; but for the poor and working people they mean lower wages, higher prices, and fewer social services (Barry, Wood, and Preusch 1983:54). Why would multilateral lending agencies such as the World Bank and the IMF follow these lines? The number of votes granted to the United Nations countries involved in these agencies depends on the amount of money each country contributed. The United States is the largest contributor. The president of the United States appoints the head of the World Bank. Donald Regan, then U.S. Treasury Secretary, has noted that the U.S. gets back two dollars for every one it puts into the World Bank (Barry, Wood, and Preusch 1983:55).

Public borrowing, in the Keynesian economic tradition, is acceptable if it generates public income at the same time. The idea in modernization theory was that the new investment would create new taxes, new export and import duties, and new jobs that would generate both taxes and consumer demand for local products. The free trade zones and other agreements to which Third World nations agreed in order to attract foreign investment often granted foreign companies exemption from taxes or low tax rates for ten to fifteen years, granted freedom from import duties on the equipment and materials they needed, and gave breaks on export duties. These tax breaks do not generate income for the host country. In addition the consumer demand generated was often for imported products. This demand further exacerbated the balance of payments problem with import and export trade. Taxes elicited from the new industries were too small to cover costs. As the GNP increased, the fiscal crises also increased.

A major part of this loss of foreign exchange may be traced to the so-called *creative bookkeeping* possible between a home office and its foreign subsidiary. Transfer pricing overcharges the foreign subsidiary for materials purchased from the parent company in the United States. Items leaving the United States at low cost (hence, low export duty from the United States) are shipped through a free port in Panama or the Bahamas and suddenly become much higher in value to the subsidiary who must import them. Remember, the import duties are low or nil to attract the foreign investor, so the importing country does not gain much in duties but does lose foreign exchange in the balance of payments. If the products are to be sold to consumers in the Third World country, they are buying at inflated prices. A study of import overpricing in Colombia by Constantine Vaitsos (1974), former chief economist for the Andean Pact nations, documented overpricing of 155 percent in pharmaceuticals, 40 percent in rubber, and 16 to 60 percent in electronics (Barnet and Mueller 1974b:90). The subsidiary sells its products back to the parent company at bargain basement prices, lowering the value of exports and negatively affecting the balance of payments. These transfer prices may have little relation to their actual market value. This is a new "triangular trade pattern," as some writers call it (Barnet and Mueller 1974:158).

This double accounting also keeps governments from being aware of actual profits these corporations make. Vaitsos examined fifteen U.S.-owned pharmaceuticals in Colombia for 1968, figuring on overpricing of imports and underpricing of exports. His data showed an annual profit rate from a low of 38 percent to a high of 962 percent, with an average of 136 percent (Barnet and Mueller 1974b:94). The companies had reported a profit rate to tax authorities of 6.7 percent. Pharmaceuticals may be an extreme case, but they are not unique in the methods used. The tax savings in both the United States and in the host country are obvious.

One important point in modernization theory is that the developed countries will be sharing technology with LDCs. What is actually shared is a last generation, outmoded technology, overpriced to the subsidiary, and sometimes including used equipment from a shutdown in the United States. This action extends the life of antiquated capital equipment already depreciated for its full value in the developed nation, but it certainly is not transfering state-of-the-art technology. Further, possibly 80 percent of the contracts with foreign subsidiaries restrict their ability to re-export it to neighboring countries. Local research and development are discouraged by not sharing the technological training necessary to understand this complicated equipment—even if it is outdated (Barnet and Mueller 1974b:98–99). Dumont (cited in Barnet and Mueller 1974a:165) argues that this is the wrong technology, at any rate. Developing countries do not yet need capital-intensive, labor-saving equipment. They need labor-intensive technology that will absorb the unemployed people.

Job Creation

Another major argument of modernization theory is that foreign investment will create jobs that were not there before. This has sometimes been true, especially since the mid-1970s, when labor-intensive assembly work was transfered to the Third World. In these newer assembly jobs, the work force is about 80 percent female. Even though their wages average one-eighth of their counterparts' in the United States, the situation can be viewed as better than having no job. These jobs are generally dead-end jobs not offering training for advancement. In addition, in some industries, such as electronics, the women are fired after a few years service when seniority would build up their wages. Some industries have health hazards (see comments in following section). This employment situation also does not solve the problem of unemployment among male workers (Fuentes and Ehrenreich 1983; Nash and Fernandez-Kelly 1983).

In some cases MNCs actually made the unemployment situation worse. Brazil and Mexico lost industrial jobs after MNCs entered (Newfarmer 1980). Local firms were bought up or run out of business. Automation replaced labor-intensive industries. One International Labor Organization study indicated that global corporations in Latin America use less than half the number of workers per $10,000 of sales compared to local companies. "From 1925 to 1970 the percentage of the Latin American work force employed in the manufacturing sector actually decreased" (Barnet and Mueller 1974b:104). However, between 1960 and 1980 industrial employment increased in Central America, from about 5 percent to an average of approximately 20 percent of the workforce in all countries except Belize, which declined (World Bank 1983:9, 24, 29, 36, 40, 67, 71). Look back at Table 6.3.

In agriculture, in which the majority are employed, the situation is very serious. The Green Revolution, put in place in the Third World by MNCs and international development agencies in the 1960s, introduced mechanization, petrochemical pesticides and fertilizers, and hybrid

seeds for export crops. The effect was to displace peasants from traditional estates and from estates owned by foreign agribusiness. In addition, small farmers were displaced from their holdings as land became
more valuable and they were bought out or could not compete in the
new capital-intensive production. (Note: The Green Revolution did not
displace small freeholders in Japan, Taiwan, and South Korea, where associations of small farmers were already in existence and could supply
credit and other infrastructure requirements.) These former agricultural
workers were forced into urban areas, where they swelled the ranks of
the unemployed and underemployed (Barry, Wood, and Preusch
1983:23). There is also the draw of the city lights, which may pull some
people toward urban areas with exaggerated ideas gained from the media
as to their chances of participating in the modern consumer society (Evans and Timberlake 1980:533).

Social Inequality

In terms of social inequality, then, the income distribution has become
more skewed in the Third World since the influx of foreign investment.
Since aggregate cross-national data are becoming available from an increasing number of data collection agencies, a number of empirical
studies have documented this inequality and have tried to account for
its causes—the intervening mechanisms by which increased foreign investment appears to affect inequality (Evans 1981). The top 5 percent are
better off, whereas the bottom 40 to 60 percent (80 percent in Brazil) are
worse off (Barnet and Mueller 1974b; Chase-Dunn 1975; "Controlling
Interest" 1978; Bornschier 1980; Evans and Timberlake 1980; Sullivan
1983; UN Economic Commission for Latin America quoted in Agee
1975:565).

Whether pushed or pulled to urban areas, rural migrants find themselves in urban slums unemployed or underemployed in the bottom end
of the tertiary (service) sector, rather than in the more skilled secondary
sector (manufacturing and construction) where they hoped to be (Evans
and Timberlake 1980). In a study of about fifty LDCs with 1960 and
1970 data, Evans and Timberlake (1980) found that investment dependence on MNCs was associated with the rapid growth of the tertiary
sectors; this was the intervening variable associated with the growth in
income inequality in these Third World nations.

Health and Environmental Hazards

Whether rural or urban poor, being in the lower 40 to 60 percent of
those in a declining economic position has serious effects. Malnutrition
now accounts for half the deaths in many parts of Latin America; it also

accounts for mental retardation in people who do not die. In 1978 the Inter-American Development Bank reported that 75 percent of the children of El Salvador, Guatemala, and Honduras were malnourished; the Policy Alternatives in the Caribbean and Central America report (PACCA 1984:18) states that the situation has become worse since then. Infant mortality is decidedly on the increase in some areas of Latin America (Barnet and Mueller 1974b:10, 12, 14), including El Salvador, Honduras, Panama, and Nicaragua (Barry, Wood, and Preusch 1983:112). The problems are aggravated by a decline in per capita food production for local consumption in Central America, raising the prices to people who have even less with which to pay.

Another criticism made by the dependency theorists is that the MNCs introduce new health and environmental hazards. Toxic chemicals, pesticides, fertilizers, and defoliants are products frequently mentioned. Products banned for use in the United States or not properly tested are dumped on Third World nations. Five days before leaving office in 1980 President Carter signed Executive Order 12264 banning the export of hazardous substances; 34 days later President Reagan in one of his first official acts rescinded the order. Information on these kinds of products can be found in various sources (Silverman, Lee, and Lydecker 1982; Scherr 1982; Anderson 1986b).

Agribusiness has been actively destroying tropical forests around the world to create pasture for cattle. Since 1950 nearly two-thirds of the Central American forests have been cleared or severely degraded (Skinner 1985:25). Defoliants being used along with the bulldozers to clear Central American forests contain ingredients such as 2,4,5T with dioxins—the basic ingredient of Agent Orange (Barry, Wood, and Preusch 1983:24–25; Skinner 1985:29). In addition to poisoning the plant and animal life, defoliation itself will make these delicate lands unusable within twenty years, according to environmentalists. Further, the rapid loss of tropical forests, which support half the species of the world's living things and two-thirds of the world's genetic resources, means an estimated loss of at least one species a day and possible genetic calamity in terms of disease resistance and the possibilities for developing new hybrids (Skinner 1985:30).

Other types of products shipped to Third World nations are consumer products, such as outdated food and drugs donated as tax write-offs to charities serving the LDCs (Anderson 1981). Sometimes these products may be useful, but sometimes they are spoiled, harmful, or, at the least in the case of drugs, ineffective, before they reach their destination to people who need them in Third World countries. Further, drugs and other untested goods or goods that are dangerous when used improperly (the literacy rate is generally low in LDCs) are pushed by modern marketing in Third World countries. The range of these kinds of consumer products run from Tris-treated infants' wear, to Nestlé infant formula, to dangerous contraceptives, to untested drugs (Export of hazards 1984:1−23).

In addition to endangering public health, the industrial health and safety record of some but not all MNCs has not been good. During its economic miracle of industrial expansion after 1964, Brazil had the highest rate of industrial accidents of any nation in the world ("Controlling Interest" 1978). Other developing countries also share high health and safety hazards because they usually do not have the manpower or the will to police the standards of the workplace. The incidence of brown lung in textile and clothing factories, of asbestosis, and of toxic chemical burns and eye problems in electronics have been well documented (Fuentes and Ehrenrich 1983; Nash and Fernandez-Kelly 1983; Export of hazards 1984). In some Central American agribusinesses the accident rate in the fields runs to one injury per worker a year (Barry, Wood, and Preusch 1983:3). In many cases the workers are not protected by such fringe benefits as medical insurance (Fuentes and Ehrenreich 1983).

Third World Governments, Corruption, and the Military

In 1977 the Foreign Corrupt Practices Act was passed in an attempt to stem bribery of foreign governments by MNCs. Attempts since then have tried to dismiss the idea that bribes are corruption and to consider them as a "legitimate business expense in foreign countries" (Anderson 1986a:4; *Corrupt Practices Act* 1982). A Justice Department investigation of fifty-four cases of "alleged bribery" in 1981−82 found thirty-five cases in which the competition could be ascertained. In 40 percent of the thiry-five cases the only competition was from other U.S. firms. Five of the alleged fifty-four bribes went to a president or prime minister, or to a member of a royal family. Most of the other payments went to cabinet ministers and agency directors or their deputies. Payment size ranged from a low of $5,000 to a high of approximately $2.0 million per payment. The highest total aggregate payment was about $35 million; the range as percent of total contract sought ran from 2 to 10 percent (Bribery 1982).

The sixty-one big companies that have formed the Emergency Committee for American Trade backing legislation to gut the Foreign Corrupt Practices Act argue that not bribing hurts the U.S. balance of trade. A study by John Graham, professor of business at the University of Southern California, refutes this argument. In the three years after the Act was passed, "U.S. trade with 'bribe-prone' countries was actually outpaced by trade with 'non-bribe-prone' countries" (Anderson 1986a:4).

The harshest indictment made by the dependency theorists is, perhaps, the allegation that MNCs draw in the U.S. government to assist in their interests and thereby stop social reform, support repressive dictators, and advance militarism in the Third World. As evidence, they present the following cases, which also point out that U.S. MNC investment is not an entirely new phenomenon (Barry, Wood, and Preusch 1983:251–255; PACCA 1984). Between 1856 and 1865 the U.S. militarily invaded Panama five times to secure it for the Panama Railroad Company, a private U.S. firm providing access to California gold and the Oregon Territory. In the late 1800s the forerunner of United Brands (United Fruit) was already operating plantations in the so-called banana republics of Central America. In the 1890s U.S. military intervened in Nicaragua four times "to protect U.S. interests" (PACCA 1984:19, quoting from U.S. State Department documents).

In the first thirty years of this century the United States sent troops on twenty-eight separate occasions to Central America and the Caribbean (PACCA 1984:18). In 1903 the United States invaded Honduras, as the U.S. State Department put it, "during a period of revolutionary activity." During the same year the U.S. Marines landed in Panama again to free it from Colombia, which had refused to allow U.S. companies to build a canal (See Barry, Wood, and Preusch 1983:251–255 for the following examples). From 1908 to 1918 U.S. troops landed in Panama four more times to protect the canal the United States was building.

In 1911 the United States placed Nicaragua under a customs receivership and controlled the country's trade revenues for the next thirty-eight years to assure that loans to U.S. banks were repaid. The U.S. Marines' occupation of Nicaragua ended in 1933, when the dictator Somoza Garcia was installed in power; this was after six years of resistance led by Augusto Cesar Sandino. In 1931 new dictators Jorge Ubico of Guatemala, Maximiliano Hernandez of El Salvador, and Carias Andino of Honduras promised favorable treatment of U.S. agribusiness corporation in their countries.

In the post–World War II period these overt activities have not ceased, and covert activities have also been employed (Agee 1975, 1981; Barry, Wood, and Preusch 1983:251–255). The 1948 Costa Rican anti-communist revolution was led by dictator Jose Figueres, with CIA assistance, he says. In 1954 the CIA's Operation Success coup against reformist Arbenz in Guatemala restored the plantations of United Fruit (now United Brands) that had been nationalized. In 1961 United Fruit provided two ships for the Bay of Pigs invasion of Cuba in an attempt to restore business as usual on that island. The invading troops had been trained at U.S. bases in Guatemala and Nicaragua. In 1965 20,000 U.S. troops invaded the Dominican Republic to avoid reinstatement of the 1963 Constitution and reformer Juan Bosch to power.

The CIA's 1976–77 Operation Werewolf against Jamaican Prime

Minister Michael Manley, who wanted gradually to nationalize the U.S.-owned bauxite industry, failed when its activities were exposed by former CIA agent James Agee (Agee 1976; Wheaton 1980:412; see Agee 1975, 1981 for other CIA activities in Latin America). The islanders were very upset with the killings, injuries, and burned-out homes during this operation and re-elected Manley.

One reason given for the 1983 invasion of Granada was to rid the Caribbean of any reformist governments that might be making U.S. investors too nervous to take advantage of the President's new Caribbean Basin Initiative, which had been signed a few months before the invasion (Clark 1986:604–605). Grenada, according to World Bank and IMF reports, had been doing well during the four years of the People's Revolutionary Government, its 3 percent growth rate per year made it one of the few countries in the western hemisphere that was growing during the period (Rescuing Grenada 1985:9). Functional literacy rose from 70 to 90 percent during the period. Unemployment had dropped from 49 to 14 percent in three years. Lawyers were drafting a new constitution, and people were acting to raise women's pay and legal status. None of these improvements were reported in the U.S. media. "U.S. Marines and the 82nd Airborne Division were portrayed as rescuers and helpers, while Cuban teachers, doctors, and construction workers were seen as agents of terriorism" (Parenti 1986:184). Grenada's economy has declined since the invasion (Rescuing Grenada 1985).

Military training and aid to indigenous armed forces also have their roles in counterinsurgency. Whether one takes the modernization/ *Fortune* magazine view that such aid is to fight communism or the dependency theory view that it is to keep down nationalist social reform movements, one must conclude that the military presence is prevasive. U.S. military training, assistance, and arms sales to military and police forces around the world have been well documented by Klare and Arnson and others (Klare 1981; Klare and Arnson 1981; Sklar 1986).

From 1964 to 1979 the Central American Council for Defense (CONDECA) was supported and supplied by the United States. When Nicaragua pulled out in 1979, the Central American Democratic Community (CDC)—El Salvador, Costa Rica, Honduras, and Guatemala— continued joint military exercises, common training, and philosophical indoctrination to fight the common enemy (alleged communist-inspired internal subversion), with U.S. training and equipment (Barry, Wood, and Preusch 1983:65–81).

The International Military Education and Training (IMET) trained more than 22,000 Central Americans from 1962 to 1982. The U.S. Southern Command (SOUTHCOM) based in Panama has jurisdiction over fourteen military bases and is the home of the Eighth Special Forces (Green Berets) and, until the mid-1980s, the School of the Americas training facility, in addition to sending people to training camps in the United States and training on site in Central American countries (Barry, Wood, and Preusch 1983:69–70). Military installations in Central America are "small potatoes" among the 359 installations outside the United States in forty foreign countries and territories, according to Sklar (1986:15).

In 1985 a reported $27 million in military aid went to the contras harassing Nicaragua, in addition to the covert aid. Another $500 million in military assistance was spent in El Salvador, despite opposition from some members of Congress and the general public to supporting this repressive regime, which has allegedly been responsible for the deaths of more than 37,000 civilians in the last four years (Klare 1981:95–97; PACCA 1984:26–27, 66–67; Sklar 1986:66–67). In all, a total of $2.3 billion in security assistance was sent to Central America between 1980 and 1984 (Sklar 1986:48). A defense lobby, The American League for Exports and Security Assistance (ALESA), composed of thirty-one U.S. defense contractors and four unions, was set in motion in 1983 to help convince Congress of the necessity for foreign military support.

In sum, the U.S. military and CIA presence in Central America, together with military assistance and training, have been invaluable over the years in maintaining elites in power and protecting the interests of U.S. corporations. This aid does not count the growing number of private U.S. organizations providing military aid and personnel to right-wing governments or contras, in the case of Nicaraugua. (See Barry and Preusch 1986:97–102, for a list of twenty-three such organizations, their activities, their principal leadership, and their business connections.)

Regional Banks and Other International Agencies

U.S. policy has included not just apparent covert and overt military action, but agencies and organizations also have been established with U.S. backing to further MNC policies. In the 1950s the U.N. Economic Commission for Latin America (ECLA) urged Central America to set up a common market. The ECLA had suggested a program of locally controlled business that would produce for the local markets and provide import substitution. This program was designed for internal economic growth. In 1961 the Kennedy administration announced a counter program, the Alliance for Progress, combining development assistance, U.S. investment, and counterinsurgency training for Latin American nations.

The Central American Bank for Economic Integration (BCIE), controlled by the United States, was set up the same year to lend to MNCs in the area. In 1959 the Inter-American Development Bank (IDB) had been established by U.S. financial institutions to handle multilateral grants and loans to governments the United States favored, for projects of MNC and military value.

Later, in 1971, the Overseas Private Investment Corporation (OPIC) was established as a U.S. government agency to insure MNCs against nationalization and other unwanted actions in their foreign investments. The Pentagon guarantees loans taken out by Third World nations to buy military hardware—to insure U.S. defense contractors will be paid.

On the labor front the American Institute of Free Labor Development (AIFLD) was established in 1961–1962 to train Central American workers in the principles of free enterprise; more than 90,000 had been trained by the early 1980s. This organization is reported to be operated by the CIA with U.S. Agency for International Development (AID) money (Agee 1981:2; Barry, Wood, and Preusch 1983:103–110).

Postscript on Development from the Dependency View

Does the investment of MNCs assist in Third World development and modernization? The mass media usually tell us that it does, and that without it Third World nations, particularly those in our backyard, would go communist. Woodrow Wilson once said that "I am going to teach South American republics to elect good men" (quoted in Williams 1976:146). Statements of this kind imply that with continued U.S. political and economic assistance Latin America should prosper.

Dependency theorists argue that the history of U.S. intervention in Central America has been harmful to social reform and development. For example, when reformers are elected to try to rid the social system of extreme poverty and repression, they can expect the United States to object. Reform leaders might nationalize U.S. property or at least limit the laissez faire business climate. U.S. interventionism cannot be blamed for all the social problems of Latin America, but a case might be made that something is amiss with the current U.S. approach to development.

We do not know all about the effects of MNCs on LDCs. Evans (1981) makes a good case for more historical studies of individual companies and industries and how they have operated within the world system to create inequality, not only within individual LDCs, which is already being studied to some degree, but also between the developed and Third World countries. He hypothesizes that "MNCs affect inequality through global reinforcement of the bargaining power of capital vis-a-vis labor, resulting in a general increase in within-nation inequality throughout the system" (Evans 1981:218). One advantage of power, of course, is of secrecy in many aspects of operations. Evans is handing historians and other writers a challenge.

MULTILATERALS: MERGING AT THE
SUPRANATIONAL LEVEL

Joint Ventures, Licensing, and Lending Abroad

By 1970 the United States realized it was sharing leadership in the global economy with other nations. In 1959 the United States accounted for 111 of the world's 156 largest MNCs (71 percent); by 1976 just 68 of the largest 156 (43 percent) were from the United States (Bluestone and Harrison 1982:142). This change may have surprised many people in the United States, but it surely was not entirely surprising to many people in MNC industrial and banking circles. During the 1950s and 1960s the companies of Japan and West Germany, freed by the agreements after World War II from military expenditures, were returning most of their domestic savings to research and development, new plants, and production.

In fact, U.S. corporations were actively helping to build this future competition by granting licenses to foreign companies to enter an industry using technologies developed in the United States for a royalty fee. Bluestone and Harrison (1982:142–147) report the following examples. G.E. had such licensing arrangements with more than 60 Japanese companies. In joint production ventures U.S. firms sometimes constructed turnkey plants in foreign countries, complete with technology, that would eventually revert to the host country owners. In 1973 there were about 600 such co-production agreements between Western MNCs and socialist countries, and such agreements have been increasing rapidly since, under MNCs' favorite conditions—no expropriation and no labor unrest (Girvan 1980:448, 450). Presumably competing firms—Goodyear, Michelin (French), and Bridgestone (Japanese)—co-produce synthetic rubber and share technology. Direct investment by U.S. companies continued, as well. Westinghouse continued its long association with Mitsubishi (since 1923) and was its principal stockholder by 1970.

Foreign countries often demanded offset agreements, promising to deal with U.S. firms if they, in turn, would guarantee U.S. markets for other products from the bargaining nation. Such an agreement with Belgium secured the NATO F-16 contract for General Dynamics.

A South African Story

A peculiar story of international cooperation between U.S. and foreign MNCs and banks emerged during the 1970s. While complaining of foreign dumping of cheap steel on the U.S. market and the lack of capital to up-date plants at home, U.S. Steel was investing in four mining and mineral processing businesses in the South Africa (holding from 20 to 49 percent of the stock in these firms). These processing companies were working with the state-owned South African Iron and Steel Corporation (ISCOR), which was exporting iron to Japanese steelmakers, who were exporting steel to the United States. By 1979 ISCOR was itself the fifth largest exporter of processed iron and steel to the United States, having benefited not only from U.S. Steel money and technology, but also from investments by ARMCO, Phelps Dodge, Allegheny Ludlum, and Standard Pressed Steel.

Also heavily involved were U.S. banks and investment houses. In the mid-1970s U.S. banks were withdrawing support from Lykes Corporation, which claimed it could not borrow to upgrade its subsidiary Youngstown Sheet and Tube. At this same time, between 1972 and 1978, ISCOR received about $538 million in loans from these U.S. banks. Ninety percent of these loans were from Chase Manhattan and Citicorp; Continental Illinois, Kidder Peabody, First Boston, Merrill Lynch, Smith Barney, Manufacturers Hanover, and Morgan Guarantee Trust were also investing. While workers were being laid off from U.S. Steel's Southworks plant in Chicago, the city's new state building was being built with South African steel beams, and Continental Illinois, a Chicago area bank, was extending loans to ISCOR.

Where did Japanese steel get an important part of its financing? Between 1975 and 1977, Citibank increased its loans to Japanese steel from $59 million to $230 million; Chase Manhattan, from $59 million to $204 million; and Chemical Bank of New York from $15 million to more than $82 million (Bluestone and Harrison 1982:145−147; Haas 1985:20−21). Investing abroad seemed more appealing to large financial institutions than did investing at home, as long as the climate was right. When the climate changed, as in the mid-1980s with civil unrest in South Africa, corporations began pulling out.

Trilateral Commission and the Uncertainties Leading to Its Creation

In addition to the decline in global economic hegemony, the U.S. faced other problems in the early 1970s. One problem was the so-called crisis of democracy. In the late 1960s in Western Europe, the United States, and Japan, workers, students, and minorities protested social injustice and the lack of accountability of governments. Western governments seemed to have lost credibility and the ability to control their own people. One result of this public demand (discussed in the previous chapter) was the government's attempt to regulate corporations in broad areas, such as environmental protection and occupational safety and health.

Another problem facing MNCs became apparent in 1971 with the two Nixon shocks, as they became called. First, Nixon unilaterally revoked the Bretton Woods world economic system. This post-World War II agreement had tied all foreign currencies to the U.S. dollar, thus forcing Third World nations to buy U.S. dollars. This arrangement helped MNCs by attaching the measuring rod of world currency to the U.S.'s lower inflation rate and by providing them with Third World currency to invest in those countries.

The second shock was the protectionism of Nixon's New Economic Policy. Protectionism caused concern among MNC free traders, who wanted no barriers to the flow of financial capital, goods, and services among countries, including OPEC money channeled through their lending agencies to the Third World. MNCs also are free traders with regard to export and import duties on goods—and here is where they sometimes differ from corporations primarily limited to production in the United States for domestic markets who ask for protectionism. As early as 1973 the U.S. Senate Committee on Finance pointed out that U.S. MNCs are responsible for 62 percent of the exports and 35 percent of the imports of manufactured goods of the country—most of it between parent and subsidiary in another country. Domestically, they account for at least one-third of U.S. economic activity (U.S. Senate 1973). MNCs justifiably fear retaliation of high tariff barriers from other developed nations. Such barriers would create problems, whether the MNCs were shipping from the United States or from a foreign branch.

In this climate of economic and political uncertainty, the Trilateral Commission was founded in 1973 by David Rockefeller of Chase Manhattan Bank, Zbigniew Brzezinski, Carter's national security advisor, and 200 other people from international business and banking, government, academia, media, and conservative labor (Sklar 1980:1–2). Political scientist Holly Sklar (1980:90–131) lists the 300 members from Japan, the United States and Canada, and Western Europe (the three sides of trilateralism) as of 1979, together with their affiliations to corporations, universities, foundations, and policy-making associations.

The Trilateral Commission is a private international policy-making organization whose avowed purpose is to manage in a consensual manner the global affairs of Western capitalism and cut down on the political and economic uncertainties so that all developed nations may benefit without resorting to fierce competition. According to its Constitution, its areas of interest include (1) economic matters, (2) political and defense matters, (3) developing countries, and (4) Communist countries. The Commission will operate "to foster understanding and support of Commission recommendations both in governmental and private sectors in the three regions" (Sklar 1980:84). Without the Bretton Woods system, a carefully coordinated policy for the World Bank, IMF, and MNC banking consortia would have to be agreed to. The Second World—China, Eastern Bloc, and even the Soviet Union—should be enticed to join the world economy, whose rules will be decided in the First World capitalist group. Detente, especially with China, began during the 1970s.

In addition to coordinating economic activities, the Commission is interested in the political affairs of their own countries. Democracies must be made governable to discourage the militancy of the 1960s.

The Crisis of Democracy: Report on the Governability of Democracies to the Trilateral Commission, written by social scientists Crozier, Huntington, and Watanuki (1975), is one of the many reports prepared for the Commission as possible policy positions. The boldness of its statements on a wide range of topics affronted some of the more liberal members, but the report was not repudiated and was stoutly defended by many other members. In the report, Huntington warned trilateral governments that "some of the problems of governance in the United States today stem from an excess of democracy. . . . Needed, instead, is a greater degree of moderation in democracy" (quoted in Sklar 1980:37). Crozier said essentially the same thing about European governments. The developed nations were warned that government officials were shaking the investors' confidence by too many social service programs, running up a budget deficit. They might have added that attempts to do something about the social costs that businesses pass on to the public, such as environmental problems, also make investors nervous.

Although much of the communications industry is owned by big business, the media are revealing too much.

> There is also the need to assure government the right to withhold information at the source. . . . Journalists should develop their own standards of professionalism and create new mechanisms, such as press councils, for enforcing these standards on themselves. The alternative could well be regulation by government. (Crozier, Huntington, and Watanuki 1975:182, quoted in Sklar 1980:40)

From such concerns, a reader might conclude that the press should have avoided this crisis in legitimation and censored itself on *The Pentagon Papers* and the Watergate scandal, although on the latter issue the Trilateral Commission could not have viewed Nixon's departure with much regret.

In the modern governable society, many people must lower their career aspirations and aim for vocational schools. Rising expectations that are not being fulfilled are a threat to the status quo, as some social scientists have known for some time (Davies 1962). Both government and the media could help people curb their aspirations and expectations. In essence, there must be closer cooperation among business leaders; union leaders of the business union type, who have some control their own membership; and government—in the Japanese and Western European style with more planning at the top. Further, "a government which lacks authority and which is committed to substantial domestic programs will have little ability, short of cataclysmic crisis, to impose on its people the sacrifices which may be necessary to deal with foreign policy problems and defense" (Crozier, Huntington, and Watanuki 1975:105; Sklar 1980). This last quote brings us full circle to MNCs and LDCs—a tight grip on their home political scenes will allow trilateral nations to operate effectively abroad, namely, in the Third World.

Related to the arguments that a government must control its people, the Commission's report emphasizes that for democracy to work, it needs a relatively passive constituency. Passive, consumerist, formal (as opposed to active, participatory) democracy is possible only in a climate of economic success. The Trilateralists are stressing what many old-line liberals and conservatives usually denied—that the political and economic spheres are not autonomous but inextricably intertwined. The strong political leadership called for should share mutual learning experiences with supranational agencies of cooperation, such as the Trilateral Commission.

The importance of the Trilateral Commission is that is provides a formal mechanism through which people at the peak of concentrated power in each industrial nation can attempt to shape the direction of the global economy and the political agendas of capitalist nations, as well as the smaller nations under their sphere of influence. Whether this international concentration of power is seen as a threat or a promise depends on the beholder's worldview. People with the power/conflict view of the world fear such control and the possibility of further declines in democracy as outlined in *The Crisis of Democracy* report.

Joint Ventures in the United States

In addition to the joint ventures between MNCs from different home countries mentioned in the beginning of this section, many current joint ventures undertaken by U.S. and other MNCs have their plants in the United States and thus have received much national publicity. Joint ventures and direct investments made earlier were usually placed in other countries (hence, the public was frequently unaware of their existence) and from a power position for U.S. companies. The more recent genre (type) may appear to the public to be in the nature of bailouts for troubled U.S. auto giants. Dual economic sector theorists might see this as a move to re-form oligopolies at the supranational level when local national oligopolies cannot maintain their share of the home market because of foreign competition. General Motors and Toyota, Ford and Nissan, Ford and Mazda, Chrysler and Mitsubishi, Chrysler and Maserati (Italy) are currently the best known examples, although Japanese and other foreign direct investment and joint ventures in the United States are in many fields. Real estate development (shopping centers, for example), chemicals, steel, and financial institutions are quite popular for either joint ventures or direct investment. It appears that much direct investment in the United States, as opposed to joint ventures between corporations, is currently coming from OPEC nations and Hong Kong, as capital leaves Hong Kong anticipating the take over by the Chinese mainland in 1997.

PLANT SHUTDOWNS AND CAPITAL FLIGHT

The preceeding section commented on some activities of MNCs and their possible effects on Third World developing nations, particularly nations closest to the United States in the western hemisphere. Since the late 1960s we have been noticing two effects of MNCs within the United States itself: plant shutdowns and capital flight. First, many companies fled the more unionized Northeastern and North Central states to the Sunbelt, and then on to the Third World countries, such as Hong Kong, Taiwan, South Korea, Mexico, Singapore, Malaysia, and eventually to the Philippines, Thailand, Central America, and the Caribbean Basin.

If the trend continues, blue-collar work, which, as we saw in Chapter 3, has been more than 30 percent of the work force in the United States since the industrial revolution—with a high of 41 percent in 1950 while the United States was rebuilding Europe and Japan and filling consumer needs at home after World War II—will continue to shrink. The 1984 figure for blue-collar workers (including manufacturing, transportation, and nonfarm labor) stands at about 28.5 percent of civilian employment. Actually, only 22 percent were engaged in manufacturing (Haas 1985:29). During the same year the service sector accounted for 68 percent of employment, and the Bureau of Labor Statistics projects that this sector will supply perhaps 90 percent of the new jobs between now and 1995.

Looking at this trend, some people fear a worst-case scenario. This would mean that eventually only local companies, governments (local, state, and federal), and professional and other services (teaching, health, welfare, retailing, etc.) would be left. Presumably also remaining would be engineering, management, and design jobs in large corporations to direct the efforts of the foreign work force (Bluestone and Harrison 1980). Blue-collar workers in large corporations that do stay might be replaced by robotics.

Even white-collar workers are beginning to find that some of their jobs can be exported. In 1983 American Airlines moved most of its data processing operations to Barbados, as did National Demographics, Kline & Company, New American Library, and The William Byrd Press. The satellite communications technology available now allows computer operators in distant places, at $2.20 an hour, to bounce their data instantly back to the home office on the mainland (Long-distance typists 1984:9). By 1986 about 15,000 jobs in the area of computer data processing were estimated to be abroad in such places as the People's Republic of China, Jamaica, and Ireland, where key punch operators and programmers and computer engineers are employed at one-third the salary of their U.S. equivalents (Rudolph 1986:60).

Plant shutdowns have become so common in industry that some writers have referred to them as the deindustrialization of the U.S. economy (Bluestone and Harrison 1982; Deindustrialization and restructuring the economy 1984; Staudohar and Brown 1987). Economists Bluestone and Harrison (1982:26 and 35; Bluestone, Harrison, and Baker 1981), extrapolating from available Dun and Bradstreet data, estimate "conservatively," they say, that in the decade of the 1970s 38 million jobs were lost in the United States because of plant shutdowns. This figure includes contractions in nonmanufacturing sectors due to shutdowns, as well as the manufacturing jobs lost directly. The U.S. Chamber of Commerce estimates that for every three jobs lost in manufacturing, two jobs also are lost in the service sector (Bluestone and Harrison 1982:69). Between 1978 and 1982 6.8 million manufacturing jobs were lost, or one-third of all manufacturing jobs (Hass 1985:12). Some of these jobs were replaced in growth industries, but they were in different localities and required different skills (Harris, 1984:15).

As jobs and income are lost, workers also lose pensions, seniority, and medical care. There is an increase in alcoholism, suicide, divorce, child abuse, thefts, bad checks, and less tangible psychological costs (Briar 1978; Moberg 1979:6; Cobb and Kasl 1977; "Business of America" 1983).

The communities also lose. They lose supporting business and a tax base with which to provide social services that are needed even more with high unemployment and underemployment. In communities that relied on one major industry, this situation can be a disaster. Workers who live in these communities cannot sell their houses to escape to other areas that might offer some kind of employment. (See Zipp 1984 for a brief citation of the literature on the effects on workers and the community.)

What happens to these workers in the job market? Ideally they would be retrained and hired in new industries in the vicinity or, not so agreeable, moved to other areas. However, the Bureau of Labor Statistics reported that of people who lost their jobs in the plant closures and layoffs from 1979 to 1984, only 60 percent had been rehired and 45 percent of those who found jobs were earning less money. They were likely to be in the lower paid trade and services in which the jobs are expanding (Haas 1985:9). Among workers fifty-five to sixty-four years old, 41 percent were able to find new jobs of some kind. The Hull House and U.S. Steelworkers study (Haas 1985:29—30) conducted in 1984 found that "the average income of workers laid off . . . in the last five years has been cut almost in half. . . . The laid-off workers, whose household income averaged $22,000 a year in 1979 had a median household income of about $12,500 in 1983."

While looking at actual plant closures, we must not overlook the climate of fear they have produced in management-employee-community relations. Companies can now use the threat of plant shutdowns to demand concessions and givebacks in wages and benefits from workers. At the same time corporations can threaten the community with shutdowns if the community does not provide a new plant, tax cuts, acreage, and other items. The well-documented story of Poletown, in which the city of Detroit destroyed a neighborhood through eminent domain to build General Motors a new plant and cut GM's taxes by 50 percent, is a case in point (Haas 1985:24; "Poletown Lives" 1980).

Urban planner Robert Goodman (1979) describes the scramble of state and local governments to offer publicly subsidized loans, tax forgiveness, free job training, lax environmental controls, and antilabor procedures to outbid each other for runaway plants to settle in their communities, much in the same manner that Third World nations vie with each other for MNCs. The new Chrysler-Mitsubishi 50-50 joint venture plant in central Illinois will cost the state an estimated $200 million in tax incentives and education and training assistance, for example (Levin 1985:2). The point is that in this new business climate of threats and concessions, workers, their unions, and communities have no chips when corporations have the whole world in which to go.

This discussion has shown the serious effects of capital flight on workers and their communities. To understand the situation more completely in order to develop remedial policies, it is useful to understand the causes of capital flight. Observers often disagree about the importance of the various factors involved.

THE ARGUMENT OVER CAUSES OF CAPITAL FLIGHTS

What has caused this capital flight to other countries? The answer usually given by management, the media, and the public is that unions and government regulations are keeping U.S. corporations from being able to compete with less fettered foreign competition. For example, wages are said to be lower in other industrial countries and union work rules are more flexible. Foreign companies use new technologies and more robots. Foreign competition is said to be unfair; their governments sometimes subsidize research and development or sponsor the dumping of cheap goods on the U.S. market. It is said foreign competitors do not have such impediments as the Environmental Protection Agency (EPA), the Occupational Safety and Health Administration (OSHA), antitrust laws, or other government regulations. The tax burden is reported to be less in foreign countries, allowing companies to retain profits to reinvest in their operations. Unions and government hinderance are said to be at fault. In summary, the U.S. imbalance of trade forces corporations to find cheaper places in which to operate, free from heavy wage bills and regulations.

No one can argue that wages and taxes are not lower in LDCs and that there are fewer restrictions on companies there. For these reasons MNCs from other countries also began to do some off-shore sourcing and capital flight of their own in the 1970s, although some countries have restrictions on how this is done. What is interesting is to compare the corporate situation of the United States with that of other MNCs in the rest of the industrial world, since they are outperforming the United States in many cases.

Wages

Is it true that high wages of blue-collar workers in the United States are the main problem? It is true that after World War II, U.S. blue-collar manufacturing workers were among the highest paid, if not the highest, in the world. Table 6.5 presents the situation before the devaluation of the U.S. dollar took place beginning in 1985. Wages in the other industrialized countries had already begun to catch up by then. In 1980 U.S. manufacturing workers made less than comparable workers in West Germany, Norway, Luxembourg, Sweden, the Netherlands, Belgium, Denmark, and Switzerland, although by 1982 U.S. workers temporarily regained their edge in monetary terms. The recent devaluation of the U.S. dollar can be expected to have lowered the U.S. wage by comparison to European currencies.

For example, when Japanese auto workers' bonuses and overtime, subsidized housing, health insurance, and job security are taken into account, they make more than a U.S. auto worker (Haas 1985:13). A 1982 study reported the following average gross earnings (not including fringes) of nonmanagement workers in the following Japanese auto companies and General Motors (Haas 1985:14):

Toyota $21,855
Nissan $21,647
Honda $20,010
General Motors $22,000 to $24,000.

Comparing the top thirty-four Toyota executives who made $43.90 an hour with the top fifty-five General Motors executives who averaged $236.54 an hour, we do find a substantial difference. More recently, however, a Japanese study indicates that the rise in the yen against the U.S. dollar has made the average Japanese factory wage 12 percent higher than the average U.S. factory wage (Kristol 1986:B1) (see Table 6.5).

In terms of standard of living, however, a 1983 survey put the United States in ninth place, tied with Belgium, behind Sweden, Norway, Denmark, France, Iceland, West Germany, Australia, and Finland (Sivard 1983). Standard of living includes not only wages but also fringe benefits and social services, such as health care, from the government. In another quality of life survey, Magaziner and Reich (1983) compared the industrial nations of Western Europe, the United States, and Japan; they found the United States was:

Most unequal in distribution of wealth
Last in social welfare expenditures as a percentage of gross national product
Last in workers' average paid vacations
The only country without national health insurance
Highest in infant mortality rate
Last in percentage of unemployed workers covered by unemployment insurance and in unemployment benefits as a percentage of average earnings
Worst in air pollution
Highest in homicide rate
The least unionized.

Low wages have definitely been an inducement to move to LDCs, but by the 1980s the problem of not being able to compete was not low wages in other industrial nations. What other factors might be involved?

Environmental and Occupational Safety Regulations

Perhaps the expense of meeting environmental and safety regulations has kept the United States from competing. Chapter 9 briefly discusses the nature and effect of the Occupational Safety and Health Administration (OSHA). Here, for our purposes of looking for causes of capital

Table 6.5 Average Hourly Compensation in U.S. Dollars of Production Workers in Manufacturing in Thirty-Four Countries, 1975–1982[a]

Country	1975	1978	1960	1981	1982
United States[b]	$6.35	$ 8.30	$ 9.91	$10.96	$11.79
Canada[b]	6.11	7.69	8.98	9.87	10.77
Brazil	1.13	1.67	1.70	2.15	2.43
Mexico	1.92	2.04	2.95	3.62	1.97
Venezuela	2.02	2.47	3.42	3.88	na
Australia[b]	5.02	6.09	7.37	8.87	9.11
Hong Kong	.72	1.13	1.44	1.48	1.55
India	.19	.35	na	na	na
Israel[b]	2.25	2.57	3.79	4.18	4.67
Japan[b]	3.05	5.54	5.61	6.18	5.82
Korea	.36	.86	1.08	1.15	1.22
New Zealand[b]	3.07	3.97	5.11	5.46	na
Pakistan	.21	.36	na	na	na
Singapore	.83	1.05	1.47	1.77	na
Sri Lanka	.28	.26	.22	.21	na
Taiwan	.48	.80	1.27	151	1.57
Austria[b]	4.06	6.22	7.88	6.93	6.89
Belgium[b]	6.54	10.39	13.18	11.10	8.81
Denmark[b]	6.28	8.79	10.54	9.12	8.64
Finland[b]	4.58	5.80	8.21	7.94	7.83
France[b]	4.58	6.54	9.24	8.32	8.15
Germany (F.R.)[b]	6.19	9.65	12.30	10.54	10.43
Greece	1.40	2.36	3.12	3.06	3.45
Ireland[b]	3.01	3.87	5.81	5.40	5.29
Italy	4.60	6.09	8.17	7.58	7.39
Luxembourg[b]	6.34	9.81	11.86	9.65	8.09
Netherlands[b]	6.56	9.98	12.15	10.02	9.93
Norway[b]	6.76	9.56	11.68	11.08	10.95
Portugal	1.58	1.63	2.03	1.98	na
Spain	2.60	3.90	5.96	5.60	4.99
Sweden[b]	7.18	9.65	12.51	11.80	10.33
Switzerland[b]	6.07	9.60	11.15	10.22	10.47
Turkey	.70	1.05	na	na	na
United Kingdom[b]	3.26	4.28	6.29	7.12	6.67

Source: U.S. Bureau of Labor Statistics, *Handbook of Labor Statistics*, p. 435.

[a] Total compensation includes all direct payments made to the worker (pay for time worked; pay for vacations, holidays, and other leave; all bonuses and other special payments; and pay in kind) before payroll deductions of any kind, plus employer expenditures for legally required insurance programs and contractural and private plans for the benefit of employees. In addition, compensation includes other significant taxes on payrolls or employment that are regarded as labor costs. For consistency, compensation is measured per hour worked for every country.

[b] Industrial country

flight, it is enough to recognize that other industrial countries are also controlling pollution and doing something about safety in the workplace.

Japan's steel industry, for example, spent more on pollution control both in absolute dollars and as a percentage of total investment than did the U.S. steel industry (Magaziner and Reich 1983:165). The GAF Corporation, which had acquired the Vermont Asbestos Group (VAG) in an earlier merger, planned a shutdown of the mines on the grounds that to comply with the Environmental Protection Agency's pollution standards would put them out of business. To save their jobs the employees and community bought out the company, complied with safety standards, operated more profitably than previously, and sold part of the company back to the public to make an enormous profit on the stock (Zwerdling 1980:53–63).

Anecdotal cases such as this are supported by aggregate data. A Data Resources, Inc., study found that in 1979 pollution control added only two-tenths of 1 percent to consumer prices (Haas 1985:17). Sweden and other industrial European nations have put much more into worker health and safety than has the United States, as we discuss in Chapter 9).

Corporate Taxes

Perhaps the tax burden of which corporations complain is the answer to inability to compete. In the 1950s the corporate share of total federal tax revenues was about 28 percent. By 1980 this figure had dropped to 12 percent, and many of the largest companies paid no tax or earned tax credits, including such firms as Bankers Trust, Chase Manhattan, Citicorp, Manufacturers Hanover, Hercules, Monsanto, Olin, Southern California Edison, Squibb, Richardson Merrill, and ITT, according to a nonprofit research group, Tax Analysts (Taxes 1982:6). The study found that by industry the largest commercial banks average a tax rate of 2.2 percent, large oil companies paid 15.1 percent, chemicals paid 7.7 percent, big steel paid 14.5 percent, regulated utilities paid 7.9 percent, drug companies, 35.5 percent, and for all major non-oil industries the rate was 27.7 percent. This is on reported profits and does not take creative bookkeeping into account.

In 1981 came an even bigger boost for corporate tax loopholes/incentives under the Economic Recovery Tax Act. By 1982 the corporate share of the national tax burden fell to 7.5 percent and by 1983, to 6 percent. Taxing corporations at the same rate as individuals would add another $100 billion to the federal coffers (Welfare for corporations 1984:16; Kosterlitz 1981:24–29). A Ralph Nader group, Public Citizen Congress Watch, reported the investment tax credit alone would cost the Treasury more than $38 billion in 1986 (Nader group says . . .

1985:Fl). "Japan—with an economy one-third the size of ours—now collects more in corporate income taxes than the U.S. does" (Center on Budget and Policy Priorities 1984:11, 17), although Japan provides only minimal social services for its tax bite. The European countries tax their corporations to support the better social services they provide.

Given that corporations in the United States are not paying what some people consider a normal share of taxes, other people think differently. The idea of supply-side economics and the 1981 tax recovery act was that tax breaks would stimulate investment in new plant and equipment and make our business competitive with foreign firms. How has this succeeded? A Citizens for Tax Justice study of corporate annual reports and Securities and Exchange Commission data on 250 of the Fortune 500 companies from 1981 through 1983 found that (McIntyre, 1984:3–10):

The companies paid an overall federal income tax rate of 14.1 percent on domestic profits totalling $291.4 billion—circumventing the 46 percent corporate tax rate by means of loopholes/incentives and thus adding $91.4 billion to the federal deficit

Seventeen companies with $14.90 billion in profits paid no federal income taxes at all during the three years and claimed benefits totalling $1.2 billion through rebates of taxes paid before Reagan took office or from the sale of excess tax credits to other companies (five of these companies—GE, Boeing, General Dynamics, Lockheed, and Grumman—were major defense contractors)

Sixty-five companies with $49.5 billion in pretax profits paid an average of zero or less (meaning rebates) in all three of the years, receiving outright tax subsidies that brought their after-tax profits to $3.2 billion more than they made before taxes—a negative 6.5 tax rate

One hundred eight companies paid zero or less in taxes in at least one of the three years, claiming an additional $5.7 billion in tax benefits on top of the $578.1 billion pretax profits they earned in their no-tax years.

Did these tax breaks lead to increased investment in their own industries? The fifty lowest-taxed nonfinancials in the study, with an average tax rate of minus 8.4 percent, reduced their investment by 21.6 percent. Overall, the firms in the study reduced their investment by 15.5 percent, while in the entire U.S. economy plant and equipment spending fell by 8.8 percent in constant dollars over the same period. However, the fifty corporations with the highest tax rates, averaging 31.1 percent of their profits in federal income tax, increased their investment during the same period by 4.3 percent. In other words, investment was in inverse relation to tax incentives.

What did these corporations do with the money they saved on taxes? They raised dividends by an average of 17 percent; companies also added to their cash reserves and spent $209 billion on mergers and acquisitions during the 1981–1983 period and another $100 plus billion in 1984 (McIntyre 1984; Judis 1985). McIntyre notes that investment decisions are largely unrelated to tax policy and depend, rather, on demand-side market foces. The up-turn in the economy in 1984 was apparently not a product of the 1981 tax policy on corporations, but rather on comsumer tax cuts and Federal Reserve policy, which loosened the money supply—in other words, things that produced consumer demand (Judis 1985).

Subsidiaries and Their Parents

Corporations say that plants that are shut down are unprofitable, but critics point to other factors for shutdowns. Often subsidiaries of conglomerates have been mismanaged by the parent corporation. Many times subsidiaries have been cash cows milked of their profits by the parent company and have not received any reinvestment in new plant and equipment. Because of how tax laws have been written, the parent company can write off old plants as a loss and receive tax credits to invest overseas. Some plants that have been shut down showed a profit, but not the 20 or more percent hurdle rate the corporation wants and can get elsewhere.

Examples of this milking, mismanagement, or shutting down from lack of high enough profits have been well-documented (see Zwerdling 1980:71–79; Bluestone and Harrison 1980; Moberg 1979 for details on the following cases). Saratoga Knitting Mills (Van Raalte brand underwear) was seriously mismarketed by its new parent, Cluett Peabody, who wanted to dump it when profits then fell. Herkimer Library Bureau was not making the 22 percent return on investment required by its conglomerate parent, Sperry Rand. Similarly, Chicopee Manufacturing Company of Massachusetts, which generated a steady 12 percent rate of return on apparel products, was threatened with shutdown by parent Johnson & Johnson because it did not meet the required rate of return. The Esmark conglomerate cost Peabody tannery in Massachusetts $500,000 a year in overhead to the parent company, before it dumped the subsidiary.

Colonial Press was charged $900,000 a year in overhead by parent Sheller-Globe, a maker of auto parts, school buses, and ambulances. The conglomerate parent changed Colonial's manner of customer service and flexibility, which lost the company its customers. Then the corporation dropped the press. The Lykes conglomerate (in the African steel story cited earlier) used the profits of Youngstown Sheet and Tube (that they could not afford to up-date) to pay off the debt acquired for its purchase and to purchase other types of companies before abandoning it eight years later. Most of the companies in these examples were subsequently purchasd by the employees or employee/community buyouts, but most shutdowns have not been so fortunate, as the number of jobs lost indicates. Employee and community buyouts are discussed further in Chapter 11.

In essence, many subsidiaries have been shut down, not because they are inherently unprofitable, but because they have been made so by their parent corporation or because their regular profits are too low for the company's hurdle rate.

Risk Avoidance and the Short-run View

Even though higher union wages and government regulations were initially a problem for corporate management, again critics argue that the basic problem lies elsewhere. Until the late 1960s oligopolistic industries in the United States did not have much competition, foreign or otherwise—as dual economic sectors economists suggested in the preceeding chapter. In the post-World War II period a new style of management in large corporations was also appearing. The management of financial assets to show the best profit on the quarterly statement became the norm—through merging and acquiring new firms in diversified fields (sometimes deliberately milking their new subsidiaries' profits, as noted) and from accelerated depreciation, foreign investment credits, and other tax breaks. Instead of attention to higher quality, new products, new processes, and new markets, companies turned their attention to making a profit through less risky and more short-run means. This phenomenon has been called *paper entrepreneurship.* Chapter 10 returns to these arguments concerning asset rearrangement versus what real economic growth might be. In addition, we see a historical example of how the structure of the primary sector in the United States gave rise to the noncompetitive stance observed since the late 1960s in a case study entitled U.S. Steel: *From Monopoly, Oligopoly, to Conglomerate.*

Another theory argues that concentrating on military production so heavily for the last forty years has lessened the ability of the United States to compete in the consumer market. With 30 percent of its engineers and scientists involved in the defense industry, the United States has fewer resources to devote to cost-saving improvements and new technologies of production in other areas. Despite the spin off argument of how R&D in defense has fostered new ideas for the consumer market, the use of these resources can still be a real loss to the overall economy in terms of competition with foreign producers (Dumas and Gordon 1986:11).

In a roundabout way, two of the common complaints explaining inability to compete and subsequent plant shutdowns—union work rules and foreign government assistance to their major corporations (at least with regard to Japan)—may have some validity here. Union work rules, an attempt by workers to maintain some control over their jobs, can limit flexibility and increase production costs.

Economists Bluestone and Harrison (1982:214–240) and other writers have noted the different orientation of the Japanese manager in taking a long-run view of corporate growth, including risks. If most workers (including management) in Japan's large corporations are with that company for life and if the government, through the Ministry of International Trade and Industry (MITI), is willing to fund R&D and sunrise industries for long-run investments, then management can attend to things other than the quarterly price/earnings ratio. The economy and management practices of Japan are summarized in Chapter 11.

The U.S. government does fund some research, but most of it is in the defense sector. In addition, the Export-Import Bank gives assistance to U.S. companies producing for export, but not as great as the more direct investment of MITI in Japan. In this chapter, however, the concern is more with the current plant shutdown situation, its homemade causes and possible remedies.

In summary, what has been said so far about the possible causes of shutdowns is that U.S. basic industry, which is oligopolistic, enjoyed a comfortable position in the United States until the late 1960s. During this earlier period before foreign competition surfaced, large corporations did not have to be very concerned about competition. They did not have to innovate in products and processes unless they chose to. They could pass on the demands of unions for a cut of the profits in increased prices. Suddenly (or so it may have seemed to some corporations that were not paying attention to the competition) they were being outsold by West Germany, Japan, and even Third World countries in terms of quality, price, and new products.

Apparently, feeling that long-run investments in R&D would not be acceptable to the stockholders, corporate executives relied heavily (but not entirely) on the political/legal side of the ledger and turned to paper entrepreneurship in rearranging assets and manipulating tax write-offs on the books. This also meant that costs would have to be cut and, since new processes, products, and marketing ideas were not in place, wages appeared to be the obvious place. Hence, corporate flight to areas with cheaper, more tractable workers was appealing and also offered more opportunity for tax breaks. In retrospect, such moves seem understandable. In prospect, they beg the question of whether this is viable for the long-run economic health of all people concerned.

RESPONSES TO SHUTDOWNS

The most immediate response to plant shutdowns was, in some communities, an attempt to buy out the plant and operate it on an employee- or community-owned basis. After more than seventy successful buyouts and a number of attempts to purchase that fell through, usually from a lack of time to organize and gain financing, people interested in saving local industries learned five key points. With regard to the short notice, *Business Week* in 1983 reported a study indicating that 54 percent of shutdowns gave workers less than a week's notice (Haas 1985:36).

Point One

In any industry, especially industries that have already experienced plant relocation, workers should organize an early warning committee composed of representatives in key departments to watch for the following occurrences: lack of maintenance of plant and equipment; cut backs in spare parts; plants that duplicate production being set up in low-cost areas elsewhere; movement of key personnel to other plants; cutbacks on research and development; cuts in ads for your product and pushes for alternative products produced elsewhere; increased productivity standards followed by firing of older workers who cannot meet them; management's not settling grievances and pushing every point to arbitration; forecast for a general decline in the industry in the business press; and/or indication of a shift in operations appearing in the company's annual reports (Haas 1985:36-37).

Point Two

Any community that has had a plant closure should form coalitions with workers to investigate the items listed above for companies still in the community. In addition, the coalition of community groups and workers should contact existing groups that can offer information, such as legal advice, where to obtain funding and backing for buyouts, where to have feasibility studies done, how to get media coverage of the community's problem with a company, and whether local laws allow communities to declare eminent domain over a company, for example (Luria and Russell 1981; Kelly and Webb 1979).

Point Three

Communities and employee groups should be alerted as to possible shutdowns from the signals just cited or from more overt threats of closure and demands for concessions in employee wages or community taxes. Some companies have demanded that the community build a new plant, for example. The workers and community should have the information in Point Two and be ready with a plan of their own, including ideas for economic conversion—new products that the old plant could be retooled to produce profitably.

Lucas Aerospace, Great Britain's largest military contractor, set the pace for other companies to consider this possibility. After a loss of more than 5,000 jobs due to new technology, in 1976 workers produced a 1,200-page Alternative Corporate Plan that included more than 150 new nonmilitary products in such areas as transportation, energy, and medical equipment and a number of new production reorganization proposals with an eye both to retaining jobs and to producing something socially useful (Haas 1985:45–46; Moberg 1979:18–19). Even though Lucas formally refused to accept the workers' plan, the company later produced some of the products suggested, indicating the viability of the workers' ideas (Moberg 1979).

Since then, Italy, West Germany, and Sweden have used union conversion plans to save jobs in several industries (Dumas and Gordon 1986:11). Some unions in the United States have produced conversion plans and are training the rank and file in engineering skills to assist in planning future possibilities, notably the Oil, Chemical, and Atomic Workers Union (OCAW), the International Association of Machinists & Aerospace Workers (IAM), and the United Electrical Workers (UE). In the United States and Canada the Center for Economic Conversion provides a clearinghouse and organizing assistance to groups considering conversion.

Point Four

Federal legislation is needed in several areas to deal with capital flight and plant shutdowns.

(1) One of the most obvious areas is tax reform, which would make it less profitable for companies to divest and run. Tax loopholes/incentives such as the accelerated depreciation allowance and the Domestic International Sales Corporations (DISCs) could be eliminated (Forgive and forget 1984:17).

(2) Plant closure legislation, similar to the Vredling proposal of the European Economic Community and to laws already on the books of individual European nations, has been proposed in Congress but not yet

passed (Rothschild 1982:18–19). One such bill presented by William Ford (Michigan) provides for a closing notice of six months to two years, depending on company size; the Secretary of Labor is to investigate alternatives for keeping the plant open, such as new products, technical aid, and loans; severance pay and benefits to be provided to employees for one year; payment of 85 percent of lost community taxes and 300 percent of lost federal tax, if moved to another country; worker retraining; and assistance to groups trying to buy out a plant (Haas 1985:49). States that have passed such laws, usually in a weaker form, include Ohio, Connecticut, Maine, Massachusetts, South Carolina, and Wisconsin. Other states are considering such laws (New Jersey, New York, Rhode Island, Pennsylvania, Oregon, and California) (Moberg 1979:21; Peck 1985:34).

Point Five

Workers need to cooperate nationally and internationally to improve their conditions. Obviously, unions in the heavy industry being shut down most frequently have a vested interest in sharing information and support. Some unions are sharing information on corporate activities; local, state, and federal laws; how to avoid concessions; and how to plan for conversion to other products. University research and other groups are producing case studies and theory; notable in this field are the Midwest Center for Labor Research in Chicago and Cornell's New York State School of Industrial and Labor Relations. Associations are forming to assist workers and communities in buyouts; updated lists appear frequently in *Employee Ownership* (1980–date) published by the National Center for Employee Ownership, Arlington, Virginia, and Oakland, California.

However, because the problem of runaway shops pits workers in industrial countries against workers in less industrial countries, it can be seen as international from the workers' point of view, as well as from managements' global economy view. The International Economic Conversion Conference (IECC) held its first meeting in Boston in 1984 with 700 people from 41 states and 13 countries attending. The IECC met to discuss conversion to alternative products, peace, economic security, and social justice (Haas 1985:51). Peaceniks and defense industry workers, and First and Third World workers were discussing economic development and jobs.

The Transnational Information Exchange (TIE), headquartered in Europe since 1978, collects information on specific companies and industries and brings together worker representatives from companies, such as Philips, or industries, such as automobiles, from plants around the world (Haas 1985:52). The United Farmworkers have taken a more direct approach by funding development projects in villages in Mexico, where many undocumented workers in the United States are from. These projects increase village productivity and enable workers to find employment at home.

Religious groups have been active in protesting shutdowns in the United States (for example, the Ecumenical Coalition of the Mahoning Valley) and corporate activities in the Third World, and in formulating plans for international grassroots development. After years of not questioning the power structure, from the late 1960s on, local Latin American Catholic clergy and their supporters have produced the liberation theology so disliked by the Church hierarchy in Rome (PACCA 1984:23).

Protestant groups in North America have also protested shutdowns. Statements by these religious bodies have been issued, such as the 1982 Pastoral Letter by the U.S. Episcopal Urban Bishops Coalition, the earlier letter from the Bishops of Brazil, and the National Conference of Catholic Bishops' "Pastoral Letter on Catholic Social Teaching and the U.S. Economy" ("Controlling Interest" 1978; Haas 1985:55). The latter document, four years in the making, emphasized the U.S. government's responsibility to divert resources away from militarism, to create jobs, and to allow foreign workers to organize for better wages and working conditions and for other social reforms without fear of U.S. intervention (Haas 1985:56). The letter from Brazil stressed the impoverishment of the bottom 80 percent of society there since MNCs had begun to invest heavily, using crop land for exports and cutting wages ("Controlling Interest" 1978). The Sanctuary Movement in the United States is backed by many religious groups, as well as other people, who protest the exclusion of alleged political refugees running from repressive regimes in Central America, which they say the United States wrongly supports.

From an idealistic stance, these organizations feature the common interest of opposing what they see as the exploitation of the Third World workers, the U.S. contribution to the lack of development of these countries, and plant shutdowns and long-run growth problems for the United States, which may be created under the current system as it has come to operate.

Opponents disagree with some or all of these positions. Some economists argue that the sunset industries in which some, but not all, of the shutdowns occur should be allowed to go. Workers will be re-employed in the sunrise high-technology sector. As to effects on the Third World, they argue that it takes time to trickle down, and they expect modernization through foreign investment to work.

They expect Brazil, for example, to be a developed nation sometime in the early twenty-first century. Rudiger Dornbusch of the Massachusetts Institute of Technology (MIT) is quoted as saying, "So everybody

knows the only way to keep the peace politically is high growth that
trickles down and because everybody knows the country will grow, people will invest and hire new workers—it all feeds on itself" (Lee and
Pouschine 1986:111).

Brazil, the fifth largest nation in the world, had a growth rate of
about 7 percent a year between 1950 and 1980. This rate is very impressive in macroeconomic terms. Except for the period from 1956 to 1964,
military strongmen have presided over this economic miracle. Currently, however, Brazil is in a severe recession, and the country's foreign
debt was more than $107 billion in 1985, the largest in the world (World
Almanac 1986:119). This may, of course, be only a temporary setback,
but maldistribution of income and land policies will have to be
addressed if internal consumption and political stability are to be gained
in the truly developed society they predict.

Another issue does not emphasize development of Third World
countries as much as health and environmental issues that involve the
entire planet, as we saw in the section on health and environmental
hazards. These concerns have brought scientists and health care professionals into the protest of U.S. activities in LDCs. The special issue of
Multinational Monitor (Export of hazards 1984), "Export of hazards,"
lists a few of the complaints, the U.S. companies and products involved,
and an excellent bibliography for further reading.

Scientific groups also fear the loss of tropical forests' influence on
the atmosphere and the loss of types of seeds from the world's gene
pools by deforestation and imported hybrids under Green Revolution
programs, which promote the use of similar crops around the world to
the exclusion and loss of others that might be resistant to certain diseases. Scientists argue that it is not just animal life (which includes
human beings) endangered by pesticides and herbicides that should be of
concern. The basic genetic structures of plant life on the planet are endangered by the current political/economic/technological course of de-
pleting the equatorial seed beds of the plant life on which human life
depends.

In the previous section on the Trilateral Commission we saw corporate recognition of the global economy and how people at the top of the
MNCs would like to share their mutual learning experiences with governments of the industrially developed world. In this section we see reactions from unions and workers, civil rights, environmental, and religious groups and their attempts to empower workers and communities
(which includes Third World countries) to recognize the interdependence of their situations and gain some control over their own destinies.
Even though the struggle does not appear to be an equal one in terms of
the power distribution, still the debate and, in some places, the fight go
on.

SUMMARY

This chapter briefly looked at multinational corporations and the effects of some of their activities on developing nations of the Third World and on workers and communities in the United States. The following major points were covered:

1. MNCs, which include most of the largest corporations in the United States as well as many small companies, enjoy very favorable rates of return from their foreign operations, especially those in the LDCs of the Third World.

2. The reasons for this are many: lower wages and worker benefits, tax breaks from the United States and the LDCs, little regulation with regard to environmental and worker protection, opportunities for creative bookkeeping, for example.

3. The social structure of many LDCs (we looked at the Kling model of Latin American social structure) allows the foreign investor a great deal of latitude in operations, and it also seems to encourage further maldistribution of income in those countries when foreign investment is introduced.

4. There are two opposing views on the effects on MNC investment on LDC development. The modernization view sees MNCs as aiding development; the dependency view sees them as detrimental to those societies and future well-being.

5. U.S. MNCs have found it necessary to join with MNCs from other developed nations in joint ventures and other organizations, including multilateral banking and a supranational policy-making association, the Trilateral Commission.

6. Shutdowns and capital flight by U.S. MNCs have caused serious problems for U.S. workers, their unions, and their communities. Often workers and their friends have attempted to fight back through buy outs of shutdowns, proposed legislation, early warning systems, planning ahead for economic conversion, and networking with other groups, for example.

7. Other groups in the United States and abroad have protested the activities of the United States and other industrially developed countries in the Third World on issues ranging from various human rights, development, and workplace health, to the environment. These groups

include religious, pacifist, civil liberties, health care, and environmental and scientific organizations.

BIBLIOGRAPHY

Agee, James. 1975. *Inside the company: CIA diary*. New York: Stonehill.
———. 1976. CIA and local gunmen plan Jamaica coup. *Counterspy* 3, 2:36. (December).
———. 1981. *White paper whitewash*, edited by Warner Poelschau. New York: Deep Cover Books.
Anderson, Jack. 1981. Business foists spoiled goods upon the needy. *Washington Post*. 104th year, no. 330, p. E45 (October 31).
———. 1986a. Heinz would ease Corrupt Practices Act. *Washington Post*, 109th year, no. 208, p. E9 (July 1).
———. 1986b. U.S. bends pesticide ban for growers. *Washington Post*, 109th year, no. 84, p. DC15 (February 27).
Armstrong, Robert. 1985. "Dollars and Doctrines: U.S. Economic and Political Interests in the Caribbean Basin." Paper presented at Policy Alternatives for the Caribbean and Central America (PACCA), Austin, Texas, October 1985. (Available from Central American Resource Center, Austin, Texas.)
Barnet, Richard J., and Ronald E. Mueller. 1974a. *Global reach: The power of the multinational corporations*. New York: Simon & Schuster.
Barnet, Richard J., and Ronald E. Mueller. 1974b. A reporter at large: Global reach, Part 1. *New Yorker* 50, 1:53–128 (December 2).
Barry, Tom, and Deb Preusch. 1986. *The Central American fact book*. New York: Grove Press.
Barry, Tom, Beth Wood, and Deb Preusch. 1983. *Dollars and dictators: A guide to Central America*. New York: Grove Press.
Belli, R. David. 1986. U.S. multinational companies: Operations in 1983. *Survey of Current Business* 66, 1:23–35 (January).
Bluestone, Barry, and Bennett Harrison. 1980. Why corporations close profitable plants. *Working Papers for a New Society* 7, 3:15–23 (May/June).
———. 1982. *The deindustrialization of America: Plant closings, community abandonment, and the dismantling of basic industry*. New York: Basic Books.
——— and Lawrence Baker. 1981. *Corporate flight: The causes and consequences of economic dislocation*. Washington, D.C.: The Progressive Alliance.
Bornschier, Volker. 1980. Multinational corporations, economic policy and national development. *International Social Science* 32:158–171.
Brenner, R. 1977. Capitalist development: A critique of neo-Smithian Marxism. *New Left Review* 104:25–92.
Briar, Katherine H. 1978. *The effect of long-term unemployment on workers and their families*. San Francisco: R&E Associates.
Bribery: U. S. companies outbribe each other overseas. 1982. *Multinational Monitor* 3, 1:4 (January).

"Business of America." 1983. (film) San Francisco: California Newsreel.

Cavanagh, John, and Robin Broad. 1982. U.S. investment around the world—latest figures. *Multinational Monitor* 3, 3:8 (March).

Center on Budget and Policy Priorities. 1984. *End results: The impact of federal policies since 1980 on low income Americans*. Washington, D.C.: Interfaith Action for Social Justice.

Chase-Dunn, Christopher. 1975. The effects of international economic dependence on development and inequality. *American Sociological Review* 40:720–739 (December).

Clark, Ramsey. 1986. Libya, Grenada and Reagan. *The Nation* 242, 17:604–605 (May 3).

Cobb, Sidney, and Stanislaw Kasl. 1977. *Termination: The consequences of job loss*. Washington, D.C.: U.S. Department of Health, Education and Welfare, Public Health Service, National Institute for Occupational Safety and Health (June).

"Controlling Interest." 1978. (film) San Francisco: California Newsreel.

Corrupt Practices Act: Bribery by another name is no longer bribery. 1982. *Multinational Monitor* 3, 1:4 (January).

Crozier, Michael, Samuel P. Huntington, and Joji Watanuki. 1975. *The crisis of democracy: Report on the governability of democracies to the Trilateral Commission* (Triangle Paper 8). New York: New York University Press.

Davies, James Chowning. 1962. Toward a theory of revolution. *American Sociological Review* 27, 1:5–19 (February).

Deindustrialization and restructuring the economy. 1984. *Annals of the American Academy of Political and Social Sciences* 476:1–229 (September).

Dumas, Lloyd J., and Suzanne Gordon. 1986. Representation of conversion ideas. *In These Times* 10, 13:11 (February 19–25).

Employee Ownership. 1980-date. Vol. 1-date. Alexandria, Va.: National Center for Employee Ownership.

Evans, Peter B. 1981. Recent research on multinational corporations. *Annual Review of Sociology* 7:199–223.

Evans, Peter B., and Michael Timberlake. 1980. Dependence, inequality and the growth of the tertiary: A comparative analysis of less developed countries. *American Sociological Review* 45, 4:531–552 (August).

Export of hazards. Special issue. 1984. *Multinational Monitor* 5, 9:1–23 (September).

Farnham, Alan, and Carrie Gottlieb. 1986. The world's largest industrial corporations. *Fortune* 114, 3:170–171 (August 4).

Forgive and forget: Multinationals' DISC taxes. 1984. *Multinational Monitor* 5, 8:17 (August).

Frank, André Gunder. 1972. *Lumpen-bourgeoisie, lumpen-development: Dependence, class, and politics in Latin America*. New York: Monthly Review Press.

Fuentes, Annette, and Barbara Ehrenreich. 1983. *Women in the global factory*. Boston: South End Press.

Girvan, Norman. 1980. "Economic nationalism vs. multinational corporations: Revolutionary or evolutionary change?" In *Trilateralism: The Trilateral*

Commission and elite planning for world management, edited by Holly Sklar, 437–467. Boston: South End Press.

Goodman, Robert. 1979. *The last entrepreneurs: America's regional wars for jobs and dollars.* New York: Simon & Schuster.

Haas, Gilda. 1985. *Plant closures: Myths, realities, and responses.* Boston: South End Press.

Harris, Candee S. 1984. The magnitude of job loss from plant closings and the generation of replacement jobs: Some recent evidence. *Annals of the American Academy of Political and Social Sciences* 475:15–27 (September).

Judis, John B. 1985. Corporate tax reductions are undermining economic upsurge. *In These Times* 9, 12:5 (February 13–19).

Kelly, Ed, and Lee Webb, editors. 1979. *Plant closings: Resources for public officials, trade unionists and community leaders.* Washington, D.C.: Conference on Alternative State and Local Policies.

Klare, Michael T. 1981. *Beyond the 'Vietnam syndrome': U.S. interventionism in the 1980s.* Washington, D.C.: Institute for Policy Studies.

Klare, Michael T., and Cynthia Arnson. 1981. *Supplying repression: U.S. support for authoritarian regimes abroad.* Washington, D.C.: Institute for Policy Studies.

Kling, Merle. 1968. "Toward a theory of power and political stability in Latin America." In *State and society,* edited by Reinhard Bendix, 489–502. Berkeley: University of California Press.

Kosterlitz, Julie. 1981. Double-talk: When the private sector tells government 'hands off!' why does it have its hands out? *Common Cause* pp. 24–29 (August).

Kristol, Nicholas D. 1986. Japanese increase stake in America. *Austin (TX) American-Statesman* pp. B1, 12 (August 11).

Lee, Susan, and Tatiana Pouschine. 1986. The rising stars. *Forbes* 137, 10: 106–112 (May 5).

Levin, Doran P. 1985. Chrysler Corp., Mitsubishi set site for plant. *Wall Street Journal* 206, 70:2 (October 8).

Long-distance typists. 1984. *Multinational Monitor* 5, 5:9 (May).

Luria, Dan, and Jack Russell. 1981. *Rational reindustrialization: An economic development agenda for Detroit.* Detroit: Widgetripper Press.

Magaziner, Ira, and Robert Reich. 1983. *Minding America's business.* New York: Random (Vintage).

McIntyre, Robert S. 1984. The failure of corporate tax incentives. *Multinational Monitor* 5, 10/11:3–10 (October/November).

Moberg, David. 1979. *Shutdown.* Chicago: In These Times.

Moffitt, Michael. 1983. *The world's money: International banking from Bretton Woods to the brink of insolvency.* New York: Simon & Schuster.

Multinational Monitor. 1980-date. Vol. 1-date. Washington, D.C.: Essential Information, Inc.

Nader group says "breaks" cost billions. 1985. *Austin (TX) American-Statesman* p. F1 (March 15).

Nash, June, and Maria Patricia Fernandez-Kelly, editors. 1983. *Women, men, and the international division of labor.* Albany: State University of New York Press.

Newfarmer, R. J. 1980. *Transnational conglomerates and the economics of dependent development*. Greenwich, Conn.: JAI Press.

Parenti, Michael. 1986. *Inventing realilty: The politics of the mass media*. New York: St. Martin's Press.

Peck, Keenen. 1985. How the states handle shutdowns. *The Progressive* 49, 10:34 (October).

"Poletown Lives." 1980. (film) San Francisco: California Newsreel.

Policy Alternatives for the Caribbean and Central America (PACCA). 1984. *Changing course: Blueprint for peace in Central America and the Caribbean*. Washington, D.C.: Institute for Policy Studies.

Rescuing Grenada: AID conceals new economic failures. 1985. *Dollars & Sense*. 103:9 (January/February).

Rothschild, Matthew. 1982. Europe's unions gaining say over corporate shutdown decisions. *Multinational Monitor* 3, 8:18–19 (August).

Rudolph, Barbara. 1986. Singing the shutdown blues. *Time* 127, 25:58–60 (June 23).

Scherr, S. Jacob. 1982. New hazards policy in the offing: Reagan to U.S. exporters, 'Dump away.' *Multinational Monitor* 3, 7:9–12 (July).

Silverman, Milton, Philip R. Lee, and Mia Lydecker. 1982. *Prescriptions for death: The drugging of the Third World*. Berkeley: University of California Press.

Sivard, Ruth Leger. 1983. *World military and social expenditures 1983*. Washington, D.C.: World Priorities.

Skinner, Joseph K. 1985. Big Mac and the tropical forests. *Monthly Review* 37, 7:25–32 (December).

Sklar, Holly, editor. 1980. *Trilateralism: The Trilateral Commission and elite planning for world management*. Boston: South End Press.

———. 1986. *Reagan, trilateralism and the neoliberals: Containment and intervention in the 1980s*. Boston: South End Press.

Staudohar, Paul D., and Holly E. Brown, eds. 1987. *Deindustrialization and plant closure*. Lexington, Mass.: Lexington Books.

Sullivan, Gerard. 1983. Uneven development and national income inequality in Third World countries: A cross-national study of the effects of external economic dependency. *Sociological Perspectives* (formerly *Pacific Sociological Review*) 26, 2:201–231 (April).

Taxes: Report says many corporate giants paid none in 1980. 1982. *Multinational Monitor* 3, 1:6 (January).

U.S. Bureau of Labor Statistics. 1983. *Handbook of labor statistics*. Washington, D.C.: G.P.O.

U.S. Senate. Committee on Finance. 1973. *The multinational corporation and the world economy*. Washington, D.C.: G.P.O.

Vaitsos, Constantine. 1974. *Intercountry income distribution and transnational enterprises*. Oxford, England: Clarendon Press.

Wallerstein, Immanuel. 1974. *The modern world system: Capitalist agriculture and the origins of the European world economy in the sixteenth century*. New York: Academic Press.

———. 1976. Semi-peripheral countries and the contemporary world-crisis. *Theoretical Sociology* 3:461–484.

Welfare for corporations. 1984. *Parade Magazine* p. 16 (April 8).

Wheaton, Philip. 1980. "Trilateralism and the Caribbean: Tying up 'loose strings' in the Western Hemisphere." In *Trilateralism: The Trilateral Commission and elite planning for world management*, edited by Holly Sklar, 403–434. Boston: South End Press.

Williams, William Appleman. 1976. *America confronts a revolutionary world: 1776–1976*. New York: William Morrow.

The world almanac and book of facts: 1986. 1985. New York: Newspaper Enterprise Association.

The world almanac and book of facts: 1987. 1986. New York: World Almanac.

World Bank. 1983. *World tables*, Vol. II: *Social data*, 3rd ed. Baltimore: Johns Hopkins University Press.

Zipp, John F. 1984. "Plant closings and the conflict between capital and labor." In *Research in Social Movements, Conflict and Change*, Richard E. Ratcliff and Louis Kriesberg, 225–247. Greenwich, Conn.: JAI Press.

Zwerdling, Daniel. 1980. *Workplace democracy: A guide to workplace ownership, participation, and self-management experiments in the United States and Europe.* New York: Harper & Row (Colophon).

How Workers Are Affected by the Social Structure

7

Labor Unions

Looking at the history of the labor movement in the United States presents an opportunity to go beyond the great-man approach to the study of history—memorizing the dates and deeds of political leaders and generals and their wars. Instead, labor history is based on the aspirations, organizations, struggles, and achievements of average working people, including the native-born, the new immigrants, women, and other minorities. Labor historians Herbert Gutman (1976) and Stanley Aronowitz (1973) are researchers who have described the reactions of U.S. workers to their situations, as has E. P. Thompson (1963) for the making of the English working class. Oral historians Studs Terkel (1974) and Barbara Garson (1975) have added more detail by describing the thoughts of more recent workers. Our understanding of social forces in political and economic history (such as economic growth and recessions, immigration waves, and wars) is richer for knowing how people conducted their lives and occasionally organized to fight for their dreams. This historical insight will better enable us to examine the current situation and the problems labor faces and also to consider future possibilities that affect the quality of workers' lives.

A brief outline of labor history cannot cover all important social factors shaping the labor movement, but it can shed some light on recurring questions. This chapter examines the following questions:

1. Why do U.S. unions and the labor movement in general seem to be less political than European labor, especially with regard to not forming labor-backed political parties or establishing platforms calling for major changes in the social system? Is this seeming lack of politial unity and class consciousness due to differences in ethnic backgrounds of immigrant workers, the geographic mobility of labor, a belief in the American ideology of rags-to-riches, a better economic and social situation than their European counterparts (including an earlier right to vote, pub-

lic education for the children of workers, a less obvious stratification system due to the absence of a traditional aristocracy, the availability of frontier land in earlier history), the differing ability/power to mobilize resources among workers and employers, or to some combination of these factors? (Dubofsky 1975:11−12; Gutman 1976:3−78; Pelling 1960:15, 222).

2. Why has the United States had "the bloodiest and most violent labor history of any industrial nation in the world" (Taft and Ross 1969:270)? No union called for violence in its platform, if one accepts the IWW calls for sabotage as merely work stoppage, as some members claimed.

3. What have been the effects of technology, growth in the size of organizations, workers' tactics to secure gains and employers' to resist them, depressions or recessions (as in 1819−22, 1829−33, 1837, 1854, 1857, 1873−78, 1883−85, 1893−97, 1913−14, 1929−39, 1957, 1979−83), wars, government policies, and immigration? The effects of the more recent plant shutdowns and capital flight are discussed in Chapter 6.

COLONIAL PERIOD TO CIVIL WAR

The period from Colonial times to the Civil War was marked by working people's constant struggle or to obtain economic and political rights. Initially workers and many merchants, farmers, and professionals worked together to resist the limits put on them by British rule. These restrictions included limits on exports, requirements that British goods be imported and be brought in on British ships, limits on the number of apprentices craftsmen could employ, and, of course, taxation without representation. Even after the American Revolution, Great Britain and France placed U.S. shipping under an embargo, which was resisted by almost all classes in the United States.

In addition to this more or less unified resistance to the British, U.S. workers resisted the limits put on them from the propertied classes in the United States. The merchants, large landowners, and professionals controlled the legislatures and the courts. A few local craft unions were formed in the 1790s, among them the skilled carpenters, shoemarkers, and printers of Boston, Philadelphia, and New York. The right to organize was denied, however, in the Philadelphia Cordwainers (shoemakers) case in 1806. The decision in the case was based on English common law conspiracy doctrine. The shoemakers, found "guilty of a combination to raise wages," were ordered to pay a fine and disband (Foner 1947:78−81). Nevertheless, strikes and attempts to form unions continued, with the courts' continuing to disband them as conspiracies or with recessions causing unions to fail. The conspiracy argument was somewhat altered in 1842 in the case of *Commonwealth (Mass.) v. Hunt*, when unions were declared not conspiracies if lawful means were used to organize. Thereafter it was left to the usually unfriendly courts to decide on the lawfulness of union means.

Working men in this early period were also attempting to gain universal manhood suffrage. In the eighteenth century all of the colonies, with the exception of Pennsylvania, had denied the vote to the propertyless. Despite the fact that mechanics, laborers, carpenters, joiners, printers, shipwrights, smiths, caulkers, rope makers, seamen, masons, and other members of the urban working class had joined the Sons of Liberty and fought in the American Revolution, they were denied the vote if they did not meet the property qualifications (Foner 1947:34; Pelling 1960:18).

After the War of 1812, Connecticut, New York, Massachusetts, and other states followed the earlier lead of Maryland and South Carolina and dropped their property qualifications for voting (Foner 1947:95). Many workers thought their needs would now be met by legislatures and courts, with the power of the vote in the hands of the working class. The propertied classes feared this also and complained that "the dregs had come to the top" and "mechanics and country clowns" saw themselves as fit to discuss any political issue (Foner 1947:39).

From the 1820s through the 1850s, workers tried to gain power to further their interests by forming their own workingmen's parties and by forming larger union aggregates. The platforms of the labor parties contained a number of social justice issues, such as free public education, no more imprisonment for debt, mechanics lien laws so workers in failed businesses could be paid along with other creditors, cessation of chartered monopolies such as Biddle's National Bank, reform of tax laws, and greater democracy for the propertyless (Foner 1947:123–126). These labor parties were short-lived as the Whigs and Democrats wooed away workers on various local issues. Labor party members from the working class also fell out with their middle-class utopian leaders, who were more interested in changing the monopoly-capitalist economic system than in promoting the workers' more immediate concerns for higher wages and shorter working hours.

These political efforts were not without some fruit, however. In the 1850s the political parties and some middle-class reformers picked up the 10-hour work day issue for which men, women, and children working in the mills and mines had been striking. By 1860 the average work day had decreased to 11 hours from the 12.5 hours of 1830, but most skilled mechanics had a 10-hour work day (Foner 1947:218). Women and children operatives continued to work the same long hours. Women and children, after all, could not vote.

The attempts to form larger aggregate unions also were not very successful, due to the opposition of business and the courts and to frequent recessions and depressions that cause unions to fail. In twelve cities in the 1830s and 1850s, workers formed citywide unions of several crafts, and five crafts formed national unions. From 1834 to 1837 the National Trades' Union affiliated several trades into one national union. The union succumbed to the depression along with many individual unions.

From the American Revolution to the Civil War technology and transportation were changing rapidly and creating new conditions for U.S. workers. U.S. inventors had been busy, averaging 77 patents a year since 1790. Sam Slater, a mechanic from England, brought with him the plans of the Arkwright machine for spinning thread. He had David Wilkinson, A Pawtucket, Rhode Island, blacksmith, build the machine, and Slater set up a spinning mill to make cotton yarn. Slater's Pawtucket mill was not a full-fledged factory. The weaving was still done by local craftspersons in their homes. The first modern factory in the United States was opened in 1815 by Francis Cabot Lowell, who had copied the English process for bringing all cloth-making production under one roof (Foner 1947:54).

Standardization of parts, possibly introduced by Eli Whitney in the manufacture of small arms, was applied to agricultural implements, time pieces, locks, and sewing machines (Pelling 1960:25). Slowly the use of machinery and mass production advanced in the textile, iron and steel, coal, railroad, and boot and shoe industries.

As canals and then railroads expanded, mass marketing of standardized products became possible. In the post–American Revolution period, standardization took place in the individual craftshops. Merchant capitalists, who could obtain financing, would place orders for a large number of standard products from the craftsman and supply him with the raw materials. The craftsman, in turn, could divide the production process for standardized items into small low-skilled tasks and hire women and children at low wages to perform the work (Gitlow 1963:30–31; Foner 1947:67–68). This deskilling process continued in the factories as they began to appear in the second decade of the nineteenth century. Women usually performed at least 50 percent of the operative jobs in the textile mills; children comprised about 25 percent of the operatives; the rest of the workers were men mechanics who kept the machines functioning.

As factories grew in size and capital needs, joint stock corporations increased, although individual and partnership ownership of companies were still the most common forms of ownership on the eve of the Civil War. The number of monopolies was also increasing. Even though capital investment was growing, the actual numbers of establishments in these industries were declining. Between 1800 and 1860, when the gen eral population grew from 5.3 million to 31.4 million, there were more and more workers working for fewer and fewer owners.

The rapid expansion of the population in this period was aided by waves of immigration. More than four million immigrants arrived between 1840 and 1860; they came to escape potato famines in Ireland, to avoid political strife in Germany, or to seek their fortunes in the gold fields. Between the effects of wage leveling by the flood of newcomers and the inflation caused by the Gold Rush, the workers' standard of living declined. The result of this decline was often worker opposition to immigration. Workers joined other citizens with nativist ideas about the possible decline of U.S. civilization due to the influx of non-Anglo Saxon and often non-Protestant foreigners. The anti-Catholic, anti-foreigner Know-Nothing Party (1852 to 1856) was formed to limit immigration. Some unions, however, welcomed the newcomers in order to educate them not to undercut union wages.

By the time of the Civil War the working class exhibited a variety of cultural backgrounds. Even though each group of workers celebrated different religious and ritual holidays and sometimes spoke different languages, they were similar in one respect. They expected to be free from the tyrannies of feudal barons and other powerful, entrenched groups. What they found in the urban United States, however, was the tyranny of the capitalist owners and factory routine. Nothing in their nonindustrial backgrounds had prepared them for this (Gutman 1976:3–117).

FROM THE CIVIL WAR TO 1930

The Civil War and immediate postwar years were relatively peaceful for the labor movement. Unions generally favored the cause of the North, where 85 percent of the manufacturing was located. Labor won the 1860 election for the Republicans both to stop seccession and to keep the western lands from becoming slave states. Many northerners felt the latter would give the southern aristocracy the balance of political power to carry out policies unfriendly to northern industry (Foner 1947:276–393).

During the decade of the 1860s the Civil War stimulated industry, and labor unions expanded their memberships in both old and new fields. By the end of the decade, thirteen unions had followed the lead of the printers (1850) and organized on the national level (Gitlow 1963:52–53). The Daughters of St. Crispin (women shoebinders) had 40 lodges from Lynn, Massachusetts, to San Francisco.

In 1866 the National Labor Union (NLU) attempted a loose federation of local and national unions. In addition to collective bargaining, the NLU sponsored producers' cooperatives and established the National Reform and Labor Party. The disasterous defeat in its first election in 1872 and the death in 1869 of William Sylvis, its dynamic founder, led to the NLU's downfall. The importance of the NLU is that it tried to be an umbrella organization and unite various unions, much as the AFL-CIO is today. The difference was that the NLU was also political in that it espoused overall system reforms, unlike today's business unionism. *Business unionism* now accepts the system as legitimate and deals basically with bread-and-butter issues of wages, benefits, and working conditions.

The Civil War years did contain problems for workers. Inflation outstripped wages, and real earning power did not to reach prewar levels until ten years after the war. Class differences in military conscription led to a three-day workers' riot in New York City. Middle-class men could buy their way out of serving in the Army for $300. Workers also objected to competing with convict labor, being forced to buy goods at company stores, and the huge sections of the best western lands being granted to railroads and other corporations.

The Setting for Violence

In the last four decades of the nineteenth century and the first three decades of the twentieth, the social history of the United States became a complex fabric of frustration, violence, apathy, and hope. Immigration continued until World War I, including more southern and eastern Europeans by the turn of the century. Depressions occurred on fairly regular ten-year cycles—1873–1878, 1883–1885, 1893–1897, 1908–1909, 1913–1914, 1929–1939—with major depressions about every twenty years, bringing unemployment and often wage cuts for people who remained employed. Even though receiving wages in U.S. industries was better than being a peasant in Europe, the standard of living was low for much of the urban working class. In an early statistical study of poverty, Robert Hunter estimated that at the turn of the century, after decades of struggle by labor to improve their lot, 20 percent of the population in industrial states was in poverty, basically because of frequent unemployment as well as low wages for the average worker (Dubofsky 1975:22).

The period from 1879 to 1908 was the most violent in terms of loss of civilian human life of any period in U.S. history, due largely to workers' efforts to organize and employers' to resist (Levy 1969:84; Taft and Ross 1969). As we discussed in Chapter 4, companies were increasing in size, and the personal relationships with the capitalist entrepreneur were no longer possible in the larger plants. Bureaucracy and new technology were deskilling the craftsman, dividing jobs into ever smaller, lesser skilled tasks. Workers resisted these things. When local law enforcement refused to go against their striking neighbors, state and federal troops were brought in or private goon squads, such as the Pinkerton Detective Agency, were hired by corporations. These detectives were used as spies in the union ranks and as private armed guards to remove strikers forcibly from company property.

As corporations merged even more rapidly during the late nineteenth century, they had the economic and political resources to achieve their goals. In addition to armed force, management used the *blacklist* (barring fired union activists from employment elsewhere), the *yellow-dog contract* (making the worker promise as a condition of employment that he or she would not join a union), strikebreakers or scabs (often blacks from the South or recent immigrants, which did not improve ethnic relations), court injunctions against union activities, trials (frequently on trumped up charges) and hanging of union leaders, and company spies. Further, employers could break a union by locking workers out until they came to terms or by shifting production from a striking plant to a plant in another area.

The Molly Maguires, 1870s.

By the 1880s the general public, because of publicity by the powerful corporate associations and the federal government, associated unions with anarchism, socialism, or terrorism. Especially effective in alienating the general public from unions were the notorious trials of the so-called Molly Maguires in the mid-1870s, government intervention on the side of employers in a number of strikes, the Haymarket Square incident of 1886, and the dynamiting of the Los Angeles Times Building in 1910.

The story of the Molly Maguires demonstrates how one powerful person could use the court system, the media, and public fear to damage an entire movement. Franklin B. Gowan, mine owner and president of the Reading Railroad, sought to discipline workers and eliminate their union, the Workingmen's Benevolent Association, in the anthracite coal region of northeastern Pennsylvania.

After the boom years of the Civil War had come the bust of the 1873 depression. Social disorganization and crimes of violence were rampant. The region's mineowners and superintendents were Protestant Scots-Irish, Welsh, and English. The miners were more recent Catholic Irish immigrants. Gowan found the community receptive to the tale of an Irish conspiracy among members of an Irish secret society, the Ancient Order of Hibernians. He called its alleged inner circle the *Molly Maguires*. This group was supposed to be carrying out the illegal activities and violence in the community while sometimes dressed in women's clothes, hence the name *Mollies*. Later research revealed that the mine owners may have paid some individuals to terrorize the neighborhood, although the unemployed miners also did some of the damage when they had imbibed too much (Foner 1947:461).

A spy named James McParland, who had infiltrated into the Hibernians, provided testimony in the trials of 1875–1876, in which Gowan was prosecuting attorney. Twenty Mollies were convicted and hanged. Individuals who testified for the miners were accused of perjury and given jail terms; those who testified for the prosecution were well rewarded financially (Foner 1947:461). Even though McParland, on whose word much of the prosecution's case rested, was subsequently proved to be a Pinkerton detective, an agent provocateur, and a perjurer, this union and unions in general were forever linked with terrorism in the minds of many people (Dubofsky 1975:34–38).

Railroad Strikes and Federal Troops

The public also became used to the idea that their government would use its power and prestige on the side of business owners. This fact is understandable when you realize that government leaders were frequently stockholders, members of boards of directors, and socially acquainted with the industrialists. Under President Rutherford B. Hayes, the federal government sent in troops in the 1877 railroad strike against wage cuts and layoffs in West Virginia, Pennsylvania, and Maryland. The troops killed dozens of workers, women, and children. The media called the union leaders "communists" (Foner 1947:464).

In 1894 President Grover Cleveland, at the behest of Attorney General Richard Olney, who was on the board of several railroad companies, sent federal troops against Eugene V. Debs's American Railway Union (ARU) to end the Pullman boycott. The ARU presented a threat to the railway owners because it was trying to unite both skilled and unskilled rail workers into one large union, whereas other rail unions organized basically one occupation. Debs was arrested and jailed for defying the blanket injunction to end the boycott. Debs, who later became a socialist, perhaps because of this experience with capitalist influence on government, was accused in the press of being an anarchist (Dubofsky 1975:46–48).

Haymarket Square, 1886

The Chicago Haymarket Square incident, May 4, 1886, occurred at a rally called by anarchist, labor organizer, and publisher of the *Arbeiter Zeitung* (German language labor paper) August Spies to protest the shooting of strikers at the McCormick reaper plant. The police attacked the crowd, and someone threw a bomb, killing some policemen. In the following melee policemen killed each other and some spectators. Four unionists, including Spies and Albert Parsons (a member of the Knights of Labor), were hanged for organizing the rally, since the bomb thrower was never found. This occurred even though Parsons and his wife and children had already left the rally to join friends in a celebration at a pub. Another organizer committed suicide, and three others sentenced to be hanged were eventually pardoned in 1894 by German-born Illinois Governor John Peter Altgeld, who said the trial had been a farce.

The trial took place amidst a frenzy of fear of German anarchy in Chicago, fanned by city officials, police, newspapers, and clergy. The convictions were based on flimsy and questionable evidence before a biased judge and a handpicked rather than randomly selected jury. One juror was related to a slain policeman, and the others said they were sure the accused were guilty before being sworn in. The media accusations and the trial outcome, however, were enough to convince many, if not most, people that unionists were anarchists led by foreign agents.

Knights of Labor

The Noble and Holy Order of the Knights of Labor, is an exception to the usually nonpolitical nature of unions in the United States. The order was organized in 1869 by Uriah S. Stephens. The Knights' program called for an inclusive union—without regard to ethnicity, sex, skill, or trade status. Sixty-thousand blacks rushed to join, as did immigrants, and women led by Leonora Barry (Boyer and Morais 1971:89). The union became nationally known with its first general assembly in 1878 and was led thereafter by Terence V. Powderly. The Knights' populist and egalitarian sentiments made it a prime target of the authorities after the Haymarket Square incident, and its membership, which peaked at 700,000 in 1886, dropped by more than half by 1887 after the Haymarket incident. Gitlow (1963:55–56) ascribes the Union's decline to internal strife and the pullout of the strong craft unions to join the American Federation of Labor (AFL).

We should note that the AFL began with a membership of 138,000 in 1886 and took twelve years to almost double but even then had considerably fewer members than the 350,000 members lost by the Knights in 1886–87. This fact questions the contention that the demise of the Knights was due entirely to the pullout of the craft unions to form the AFL. An alternative explanation is that workers saw it could be personally dangerous to push for major political changes. The Knights of Labor was reduced to about 200,000 members by the turn of the century, by which time the AFL membership stood at about 1.4 million. (Table 7.1, featured later in this chapter, shows more details of union membership from 1897 to 1984.)

American Federation of Labor

The decline of the Knights, however, signaled the birth of the American Federation of Labor in 1886, led by Samuel Gompers and Adolph Strasser, both from the Cigar Makers' Union. From Dutch-Jewish ancestry, Gompers was apparently disillusioned from the socialism of his youth by observing socialist parties in the United States. The AFL loosely joined together the autonomous skilled craft unions. Rather than a more politically oriented position, the AFL opted for a business-unionism (a push for wage increases and fringe benefits) and also recognized the right of capitalists to ownership and control over most matters.

On the theory that labor organizations should be large to fight large companies and their trade associations, Gompers tried to get the unions to admit blacks. When locals refused, he chartered separate "colored federations" (Pelling 1960:84). He also favored, at least initially, bringing less skilled workers into industrial-type unions. The skilled locals resisted. It was not until the 1930s that today's *industrial unions* were formed to admit both the skilled and unskilled workers in an industry.

In addition to the problems that the loose federation and lack of central executive power gave him, Gompers had difficulty achieving solidarity because of the heterogeneity of the work force. Ethnic rivalries were underlined by occupations dominated by a particular national group in some urban areas.

The most highly skilled workers—railroad engineers and printers for instance—tend to be predominantly American-born. The older immigrants, Irish and German, dominated the building trades, and the Germans were well established in cigar-making, brewing, and furniture work. The lake seamen of Chicago were Scandinavian, the apartment janitors Flemish. The humbler and less well-paid jobs necessarily went to the most recent immigrants, many of whom in the 1890's came from eastern and southern Europe, one-third to one-half of them being illiterate and very few of them having any industrial skills. The Jews tended to concentrate in the clothing trades, in which they had been established in Europe, and worked in "sweated" conditions for miserable wages. Being both more educated and more radical than the other new immigrants they soon developed an interest in labor organization, but they formed their separate Jewish unions, which in New York were united in a body called the United Hebrew Trades. The Czechs, the Poles, and the Italians also crowded into the big cities and were available for all types of unskilled work. Because they found it difficult to communicate with earlier immigrants or with the native Americans [i.e., American-born], they could readily be used as strikebreakers. (Pelling 1960:87–88)

Gompers was successful in keeping out of the AFL unions affiliated with the Socialist Labor Party, whose leader Daniel DeLeon he found too strident and doctrinaire. Given this fact, it seems ironic that Gompers gave European socialist and communist parties one of their more aggressive and militant holidays. He planned to force the eight-hour-day issue by having a larger union affiliated with the AFL go on strike each year. The first strike was on May 1, 1890; it was successful. The second year the weaker mineworkers union's strike fizzled, and the annual strike idea was scrapped. European unionists were impressed, however, with the organized show of worker militancy and began celebrating their own May Day show of strength and solidarity.

Turn-of-the-Century Radical Criticism in the Progressive Era

The Socialist Labor Party (SLP) and Socialist Party of America (SPA), which had split off from the SLP in the 1890s and reorganized in 1900 as the SPA, were openly critical of AFL's business unionism. Under Daniel DeLeon the SLP founded its own union in the 1890s, the Socialist Trade and Labor Alliance, thereby dividing labor further. The two parties were briefly involved with the Industrial Workers of the World (IWW, or Wobblies) from its founding in 1905, by William W. "Big Bill" Haywood, Eugene Debs, Lucy Gonzales Parsons (Texas-born widow of Albert Parsons and a labor organizer and labor journalist in her own right), and other individuals, until 1908, when the IWW ousted DeLeon and the SLP.

The IWW's structure was more centralized than the AFL's. It consisted of thirteen departments organized by industry, taking in skilled and unskilled regardless of ethnicity, color, creed, or gender.

The IWW spent much time in early years infighting over tactics and goals. Its dislike of Gompers's business unionism seems to have been about the members' only common idea. The IWW unionists were more in favor of syndicalism—the workers' control of production without intervention from either state or political parties, which they basically distrusted as too willing to collaborate with the Establishment in order to stay on the ballot and gain "respectability" (Dubofsky 1975:101–106; Renshaw 1967:55, 72; Boyer and Morais 1971:164–177).

From 1905 to 1924 the IWW issued about a million membership cards for its One Big Union. Membership included 100,000 blacks, many women and other minorities, the skilled and unskilled, and was drawn from mining, agriculture, lumbering, and textiles (Boyer and Morais 1971:146–191; Renshaw 1967:140). These successes, plus the IWW's opposition to World War I, led the government to allow companies and vigilante groups a free hand in eliminating the local organizers by any means necessary. In 1917, after a raid on IWW headquarters, 200 top officials were indicted for espionage and sedition. The union declined as its energies and funds were expended in legal battles (Dubofsky 1975:124–125).

The idealism of its equality, frontier style of independent militancy, and stirring songs by Joe Hill made the IWW a part of American folklore (Pelling 1960:114; see Renshaw 1967 for a more complete history).

The efforts of politically oriented labor unions, opposed and defeated as they were by industry and government, were not without some fruit. In 1868 Congress enacted a law for an eight-hour work day for federal employees, and in 1884 it established the U.S. Bureau of Labor (forerunner of the Bureau of Labor Statistics)—advocated by the National Labor Union. In 1842 in *Commonwealth v. Hunt* the view of unions as illegal conspiracies had been overturned. From that time on, only the unions' intents and methods were questioned.

> The universal adoption by the federal and state courts of the "ends" and "means" tests allowed ample room for condemning concerted activities by labor organizations based upon disapproval of either their objectives or methods. Consequently, peaceful strikes conducted for the purpose of union security or for the reinstatement of discharged employees have been enjoined while strikes for higher wages and shorter hours were interdicted because of pick-line violence or simply because there was picketing. Needless to say, the boycott in its various forms was outlawed. (Ross, 1963:76)

The radicalism of some workers and some of the general public also had other effects. During the so-called Progressive era (from the 1890s to World War I) some conditions of the urban working class were exposed by middle-class social reformers, muckraking journalists, and populist trust busters. Local, state, and even a few federal laws were passed to deal with workmen's compensation, limits on working hours, working conditions of women and children, minimum wage, and corporate trusts. These laws were often declared unconstitutional by conservative state and federal supreme courts or reinterpreted to permit evasion (Auerbach 1969:123, 203, 210). The AFL under Gompers was opposed to national health and unemployment insurance and to minimum-wage laws, apparently fearful that such laws would usurp some of the unions' functions.

Some of the larger companies, notably U.S. Steel, International Harvester, Pullman, and General Electric, fearful of the hue and cry over trusts and monopolies, wanted to gain the loyalty of their workers. They introduced what they called welfare capitalism.

The National Civic Federation (NCF) was launched to expound on big business's concern for the worker. The NCF's first president was "Dollar Mark" Hanna, wealthy banker and mineowner, U.S. senator, and in 1896 the manager of William McKinley's successful Republican presidential campaign against populist William Jennings Bryan (Berman 1978:16). Of all the monopolies of the period, only the Rockefeller interests did not support the NCF (Berman 1978:16).

These experimental welfare programs offered workers some fringe benefits in the form of company clinics, recreational facilities, company housing (including clauses in the lease that the family must vacate if the worker went on strike), stock purchase plans, apprenticeship training, Americanization classes for immigrants, and pension plans (which could be revoked if the worker joined a union or went on strike) (Edwards 1979:91–97). The numerous limitations, eligibility clauses, and restrictions kept most workers from benefiting from these programs (Edwards 1979:92). The companies considered the programs strictly voluntary on their part and could withhold benefits at will. Nevertheless, thousands of workers did receive some kinds of benefits over the years, and Congress and the media were apparently impressed that these good monopolies had the interests of their workers at heart. At the peak of the popularity of these programs in the mid-1920s, 80 percent of the largest corporations had some form of plan at an average annual welfare benefit of about $27 per worker (Edwards 1979:95).

The plans may have forestalled some trust-busting and earned some good will, but they did not stop union organizing and strikes. Strikes at International Harvester, General Electric, and U.S. Steel were particularly violent. At U.S. Steel the workers were trying to rebuild their union broken in the 1892 Homestead battle and totally wiped out in the U.S. Steel strike of 1901. The company's benefit packages were nice, but peripheral. They did not address the problems of hours, wages, and particularly the dangerous and demeaning working conditions. In other words, the plans did not deal with power relationships (Edwards 1979:97). By the late 1920s, realizing that welfare capitalism programs were not going to control workers, the companies began dismantling these plans.

The high rate of poverty in industrial states at the turn of the century has already been noted. In 1910, a large gulf in pay existed between the skilled and the less skilled, even after years of strikes; labor marches (such as the uprising of the twenty thousand seamstresses in New York City in 1909); the Triangle Shirtwaist fire in which 145 women died (underlining sweatshop conditions); the wars in the mines, forests, and wheatfields of the West; and consciousness raising journalism and social reform laws. Skilled workers in the AFL and railway unions were making $1,500 to $2,000 a year, whereas the less skilled industrial workers, usually unorganized and representing one-fourth to one-third of all industrial workers, often made less than $500 a year.

The minimum standard an urban family could subsist on was judged to be $700 a year. It thus is not surprising that as many as 20 percent of urban children were said to be noticeably undernourished (Pelling 1960:119–120). The less skilled and unorganized also worked longer hours for their pay.

During this period the AFL found itself pressured not only by business, but also by the remnants of the Knights, the militant IWW, and the demonstration of more political effectiveness of British labor when the Labour Party was formed in 1906. The AFL found that it needed to enter the political arena. Despite the fact that Republican President Theodore Roosevelt had, for the first time in history, refused to provide federal troops to strikebreak, but had threatened instead to send in the Army to take over the mines when owners refused to arbitrate with representatives of the striking mine workers in 1902, the AFL supported the Democrat Party. Many union Catholics and immigrants had already found the Democrat Party more supportive than the Republicans. In 1912 the AFL failed to support Roosevelt's Progressive (Bull Moose) Party, whose platform contained more social and labor reform than either the Democrat's or Republican's.

Antitrust Laws, the Courts, and Unions

Newly elected, President Wilson acknowledged his debt to labor support in several ways. In 1913, as the depression worsened, the Department of Labor was established. In 1914 the Clayton Antitrust Act was passed, presumably to undo the damage to unions caused by court interpretations of the Sherman Antitrust Act of 1890. The Sherman Act had termed unlawful "any combination or conspiracy in restraint of trade between states." The original intent was for use against the monopolies that had arisen since the Civil War. It had been used occasionally against big business, especially in the well-known case of making an oligopoly out of Rockefeller's Standard Oil monopoly. This act became a favored tool to use against union activists.

The Supreme Court decision in the Danbury Hatters case (*Loewe v. Lawler*) in 1908 upheld the use of the Sherman Act to outlaw union boycotts. The Bucks Stove and Range decision supported the use of injunctions against unions. In the latter case the AFL had published the name of Bucks Stove in its list of corporations with "unfair labor practices" in its journal, *The American Federationist*, after a court injunction not to do so (Pelling 1960:107; Auerbach 1979:123, 203, 210).

Gompers hailed the Clayton Act as the Magna Carta of labor, but injunctions continued and the Supreme Court was to permit its continued use against unions in 1921 (*Duplex v. Deering*). The 1915 LaFollette Seamen's Act was one of the few federal laws of the period that apparently worked for labor in the manner intended. It was successful in ameliorating the working conditions of this group of workers who had previously had almost no rights while on shipboard.

World War I and Organized Labor

World War I pulled the economy out of the 1913–1914 depression and saw the appointment of union officials to national boards, such as the Mediation Commission, National Council of Defense, Labor Adjustment Commission, and the National War Labor Board. The AFL, in turn, helped President Wilson by convincing workers that the war was in their interest to save the world for democracy. Many workers initially saw the war in Europe as a squabble among foreign interest groups and of no concern to the United States. A labor delegation was sent to Europe to encourage the workes in allied countries. Gompers and his group persisted in denouncing socialism, an idea not well received by most European labor groups who were themselves socialist. A delegation of union officials was even sent to the Russian Soviet Republic (now the USSR) after the revolution to urge the Bolsheviks to stay in the war against Germany. Anyone who opposed the war for any reason was deemed un-American and probably in the pay of the German government.

The war had positive effects on some segments of the working class. Between 200,000 and 400,000 blacks moved to the North for better jobs that had opened up because of the war (Pelling 1960:135). Mexican Americans and women also took advantage of the new opportunities.

The war did not stop strikes, however. As wartime inflation shrunk the value of the dollar, union strikers were joined by nonunion workers to press for higher wages. At the end of the war real earnings were estimated to be 6 percent higher for workers than in the prewar depression year of 1914 (Pelling 1960:129). Union membership jumped from 2.8 million in 1916 to more than 4 million in 1919—three-fourths in AFL unions—and to 5 million in 1920. This number represented 12 percent of the people gainfully employed.

The Not-So-Roaring Twenties

In general, the AFL failed to use its advantageous wartime position to organize the less skilled or to better the condition of the mass of the urban industrial working class. Part of the AFL's lack of innovation can be traced to the leadership policies of Gompers, whose ideas had evolved to emphasize that the skilled elite in labor should gain respectability in the eyes of employers. Hence, the illiterate, the unskilled, the poor, and most immigrants would not be useful to the movement. This position was a long way from his socialist youth.

Also, in the late 1890s Gompers had decided that labor should work with the corporations. He hunted and dined with and received investment tips from corporate executives and even became vice-president of the business-founded National Civic Federation (NCF) (Berman 1978:16–17). Gompers, who was seventy in 1920, was described as looking austere, grim, respectable, and always in impeccable black. He denounced anything that was not laissez-faire capitalism and called for a program of voluntarism, which eschewed unemployment insurance or any form of welfare.

The 1920s are depicted as an antiunion period in which the post-Russian Revolution Red Scare turned the public away from labor organizations. The American plan of the period called for *open shops*, in which workers are not required to join a union even if one is representing all the workers in the shop. This plan made it difficult for unions to gain members. Some companies refused to recognize unions already in their plants. Strikebreaking, spies, yellow-dog contracts, injunctions, and company unions were effective in further reducing union membership and strength (Gitlow 1963:61).

The 1920–1921 postwar deflation left 4.5 million people unemployed. These workers were reabsorbed slowly during the decade as the spread of new technology and new scientific management techniques made the workplace more efficient. New industries—automobiles, electrical appliances, and aircraft, for example—were growing at a lively pace. Consumer products, building, and services (including motion pictures) increased, spurred by expansion of credit. These industries helped employ and entertain more workers. Real wages increased by 26 percent during the decade, due more to increased productivity and markets rather than to redistribution of income.

Feeble efforts to organize textiles and other new industries in the South and automobiles in the North were not well supported by either autonomous unions or the AFL. William Green, the new AFL head in 1925, was not militant. He hoped to reason with employers to accept unions voluntarily by using facts, figures, and friendly persuasion.

Unions appeared to have arrived at a new stage in the cycle of organizations—they were larger, more prosperous, somewhat less democratic, and bureaucratic at the national level. Union officials had more power and were busy setting up investment trusts, occasionally receiving a little graft on the side; organizing was too much of a bother.

In discussing the 1920s, we should comment on the progress of workmen's compensation. A beginning was made with the National Civic Federation's espousal of private health programs in the big companies. Safety and health programs remained in the hands of private industry, and states controlled workers' compensation until the late 1960s (Berman 1978:22). Little attention was paid to occupational disease. Between 1911 (after the disasterous Triangle Shirtwaist fire in New York) and 1948, all states eventually passed some form of workmen's compensation. The general ideas of these laws were to cover part of the wages lost by people injured at work and to defray medical costs. The no-fault plan was similar to the model passed in Germany in 1884 and Britain in 1897; that is, the company did not admit negligence (Gersuny 1981:99).

Previously, to collect such compensation the worker had to take the employer to court; the burden of proof of employer negligence was on the worker. Such proof was often difficult because (1) it was assumed that the worker accepted risks when taking the job; (2) it required testimony of the unsafe conditions from workers still employed and, in cases of worker death, fellow workers were all the family had to rely on; (3) the laissez-faire ideology led many employers and the courts (which struck down the first two compensation laws passed) to regard such worker protection as a socialistic fad; (4) the employers had more legal power than the worker could afford and could usually hold up the case until the worker became desperate and settled for a small sum out of court; and (5) employers assumed that accidents were caused by employee carelessness (Gersuny 1981:99). Under this liability system 85 percent of workers received no compensation (Gersuny 1981:104). After the peak injury year of 1905, however, juries became more sympathetic to workers' claims and business began to see the no-fault system as possibly being cheaper than the liability system (Gersuny 981:100–105). Compensation plans in the late 1920s cost about 1 percent of payroll.

Workmen's compensation did not end litigation, however. In the 1920s industrial psychologists tried to determine what made workers so psychologically accident prone. If a chain broke and dumped a load of steel on a worker, why had he been under it? Studies initially undertaken during World War I by the British Industrial Fatigue Research Board yielded such categories as "impulsive character" and "anxiety reaction" (people who have accidents), "compulsive personality" (people who moonlight at second jobs), "depressive reaction" (people who have trouble breathing after working at the plant for a while), "psychological cycles" (for women), and "paranoid personality" (people who file grievances) (Berman 1978:23, from a 1966 article in *American Handbook of Psychiatry*, is still useful for psychiatrists to consider).

Before the 1930s the public sympathies were seldom captured by labor's problems except for certain issues, such as, national immigration policy. The Chinese Exclusion Act of 1882, the Gentlemen's Agreement of 1907–1908 (excluding Japanese immigrants), and the immigration quota acts beginning in the 1920s were labor's successful attempts to keep out cheap labor competition from abroad. Stereotypes of non-European peoples were quickly picked up by the popular media, which focused public attention on the evils inherent in other cultures (Foner 1947:488–493; Pelling 1960:101–102).

FUNCTIONS UNIONS CAME TO FULFILL

This discrimination against minorities is understandable given the functions that unions in the United States had come to fulfill:

1. Collective bargaining for better wages and working conditions
2. Solidarity and personal relationships in the impersonal work setting, hence, the term *brotherhood* in many union names
3. Limination of entrance to occupation
4. The more latent function of disciplining the labor force for management—an agreement with union officials meant it was up to the union to make its members conform to the terms without wildcat strikes.

THE 1930s: A NEW DEAL FOR LABOR

Favorable Laws

The 1930s saw a radical departure from the previous antiunion stance of the populace and federal government. At this time, with almost one-third of the work force unemployed and some people questioning the capitalist economic system itself, the New Deal era took a fresh look at labor. The National Industrial Recovery Act (NIRA) of 1933, Section 7(a), recognized the right of workers to organize and bargain collectively through a union of their choice. This act followed the 1926 Railway Labor Act, which had outlawed yellow-dog contracts in the railways, and the 1932 Norris-LaGuardia Act, which had declared that yellow-dog contracts should not be enforced through federal courts.

Even though the NIRA was declared unconstitutional in 1934 (*Schecter Corporation v. U.S.*) Section 7(a), recognizing workers' rights to organize, was preserved in the National Labor Relations Act of 1935. This act became the cornerstone of U.S. labor law. When enforced, it became the Magna Carta Gompers had been looking for. The NLRA, or Wagner Act, further forbade company unions and established the National Labor Relations Board (NLRB) to supervise elections certifying unions and to handle worker grievances covered under the Act. The Act was declared constitutional in *Jones-Laughlin Steel v. NLRB*, 1937.

Several other pieces of legislation important to the working person were passed during this period, with or without the help of organized labor. Union membership had dropped from 3.6 million in 1930 to 2.1 million in 1933 and, in the face of the decline in jobs, the AFL decided to support unemployment insurance. In 1935 the federal government passed the Social Security Act, but the AFL had no research staff to help and not much interest in Social Security. States were passing laws regarding minimum wages and maximum work hours for women and children, pressured by the Women's Trade Union League and the National Consumers League and assisted by Roosevelt's Secretary of Labor, Frances Perkins (Pelling 1960:162). In 1938 the Fair Labor Standards Act set minimum wage and maximum work weeks for most workers, but the law was opposed by the AFL, which must have seen this as an intrusion into its bargaining territory.

The CIO

In addition to the boost from the federal government during the decade of the 1930s, labor itself was attempting to expand by accepting more unskilled workers in an industry. The Congress of Industrial Organizations (CIO) developed out of an AFL caucus group, initially formed in 1935 and called the Committee for Industrial Organization. When the ten national unions in the Committee were suspended from the AFL, nine of them founded the Congress for Industrial Organization in November 1938, with John L. Lewis of the United Mine Workers (UMW) as its head.

Lewis himself is one of the most interesting people in labor union history. Legend has it that his wife taught him to read as an adult, using the Bible and Shakespeare as texts. With a head like a shaggy lion, he held his audiences rapt with his oratory. He thundered his ponderous and powerful phrases, punctuated with expressions a miner could be expected to use and appreciate. Despite his seeming to favor Nazi Germany in the 1930s, his redeeming feature was that he would do anything for his men. The UMW pushed the companies for new technology and safety regulations. He lived frugally and above the suspicion of making anything extra from his position. His men returned the favor with undying loyalty.

The CIO unions had a great deal of success in organizing industrial unions in automobiles, rubber, and steel, industries in which the AFL had tried and not done well. The CIO's campaign efforts were well-financed and flamboyant. Sit-down strikes were used effectively until declared illegal by the Supreme Court. The competition from the militant CIO actually helped the AFL organize. The AFL became more enthusiastic at recruiting and employers signed up with the AFL to avoid dealing with tougher CIO people. This last statement should not be taken to mean that management was ready to accept unions, however. The Pinkerton Detective Agency reported that it had 1,228 spies planted in almost every union in the country between January 1, 1933, through April 1937 and that many of the spies had become officials in the unions at the national or local level (Wolf 1968:117–122).

In 1938 almost 9 million workers belonged to unions—1 million in independent unions and 4 million each in the AFL and CIO. The organized labor movement came out of the decade on a better footing both in legal terms and membership than it had entered it. Unions were to make further gains in the coming war, as we have seen to be true of past wars.

WORLD WAR II AND AFTER

World War II and Labor

With World War II on the horizon labor was represented on a number of national boards and unions grew steadily. The U.S. government created the Office of Production Management in January 1941 with Sidney Hillman, president of the Amalgamated Clothing Workers of America (CIO), and William S. Knudsen, president of General Motors, sharing its leadership. The War Production Board was set up after Pearl Harbor, and under its auspices labor-management committees were established in many plants to stimulate production. The National War Labor Board, consisting of representatives from labor, management, and the general public, was responsible for settling grievances affecting the war industries. Even though goverment policies stabilized wages, workers made gains in fringe benefits.

During the war black workers also made gains, thanks to the efforts of A. Phillip Randolph of the Sleeping Car Porters and his influence on President Roosevelt. The Fair Employment Practices Committee was set up in 1941 to help minorities obtain an opportunity in war work contract industries. Women were also hired for better jobs. Despite the popularity of Rosie the Riveter jokes, women took seriously their new opportunities and wages and were to remain in the work force in increasing numbers after a brief temporary decline in the postwar period.

The Image Dims: Red-Scare, Taft-Hartley, and Hoffa

Union membership did not decline in the postwar McCarthy era, but the public image of unions did. The Labor-Management Relations (Taft-

Hartley) Act, passed in 1947, stipulated that every important union official must sign an affidavit annually that he or she was not a member of the Communist Party. It was estimated that less than 1 percent of the CIO were Communist Party members (Pelling 1960:192). The act outlawed secondary boycotts and jurisdictional strikes as unfair labor practices for unions. It allowed court injunctions for sixty-day cooling off periods and forbade closed shops, in which employers must hire from among workers who are already union members.

One major provision of the law permitted states to pass right-to-work laws. *Right-to-work* is a euphemism for "never-have-to-join-a-union." In essence, this law does away with *union shops*, where a worker must join a union after employment. This law makes it more difficult for unions to recruit members, since a worker will be represented by the union without paying dues. (Note that closed shops are occasionally found in the trucking and construction trades, indicating that Taft-Hartley has not always been enforced [Tausky 1984:128].) Supervisory personnel were excluded from NLRB protection under the act, putting these workers in jeopardy if they spoke up for the workers.

In 1949 the CIO ousted the last of the communist-dominated unions (communists had been very useful as labor organizers of some industrial unions in the 1930s). This act cleared the way for the merger of the AFL and CIO in December 1955 under the joint leadership of George Meany and Walter Reuther. (Since the days of Gompers the AFL had taken a nonpolitical, business-unionism, antisocialist stance and would not affiliate with any group that contained socialists or communists.) Hopes ran high for union sympathizers as the merger agreement supported the autonomy of the affiliated unions, guaranteed each union its historical jurisdiction and the settling of jurisdictional disputes by agreement, and eschewed corruption, communism, and discrimination with regard to race, creed, color, or national origin. Other less optimistic people saw the merger as a last-ditch effort to preserve unions, which were now organizing in a hostile environment.

The Welfare and Pension Plans Disclosure Act of 1958, amended in 1962, attempted to correct abuses in the handling of rapidly growing union pension funds, which had been exposed by the Douglas Committee in the Senate.

In 1957 the Senate's McClellan committee and its chief counsel Robert F. Kennedy began exposing corruption and underworld links in the most notorious union, the Teamsters. Even after the Teamsters Union was expelled for corruption in the same year, it continued to grow outside the AFL-CIO, first under Dave Beck, then Jimmy Hoffa, Frank Fitzsimmons, Roy Williams, and Jackie Presser. Their image tainted other unions, and the public seldom heard of the struggles by honest, hard-working union persons at the local level who kept racketeers out and provided important services to their members (Pelling 1960:209).

The Labor-Management Reporting and Disclosure (Landrum-Griffin) Act of 1959—often called the Hoffa Act because Jimmy Hoffa's attitudes and behaviors strongly convinced Congress of the necessity for the act— was intended to counter the corrupt or undemocratic practices uncovered by the McClellan Committee. The law and its bill of rights and responsibilities for union members and officials provided some impetus for counter groups in some unions to work toward extending union democracy (see all issues of *Union Democracy Review 1979-date* and of *Labor Notes 1979-date*).

Despite the merger of the AFL-CIO, active recruitment and union organizing did not occur. Jurisdictional disputes continued. Discrimination, corruption, and undemocratic practices in a few unions did not disappear. Racial discrimination and other questionable practices continued in some unions, buttressed by individual and local union autonomy. The media coverage of racketeering, featherbedding, and postwar strikes rekindled the negative public image, abetted by the antiunion propaganda of the National Association of Manufacturers and the International Chamber of Commerce, whose lawyers had written the Taft-Hartley Act. Unions were viewed as fat, powerful, corrupt, self-seeking, and also as being for lower class people, whereas most people preferred to think of themselves as part of a higher middle-class. In 1956 white-collar jobs in industry outnumbered blue-collar jobs and farmers continued to decline in numbers. Professionals who had organized for some of the same purposes as unions were always careful to call their groups *associations*, such as the American Medical Association and the National Education Association, in an effort to distance themselves from manual workers.

CURRENT UNION SITUATION AND PROBLEMS

Union Membership: The United States and Other Industrialized Countries

Today, union membership stands at less than 19 percent of the nonagricultural workforce in the United States, down from a high of more than 30 percent from 1945 to the mid-1950s. Table 7.1 shows membership in U.S. unions since 1897. The United States, France, and Japan have the lowest rates of union membership among the industrialized nations. The United States is the only industrial nation that has a declining union membership. See Table 7.2 for percentage of workers in unions in twelve industrial countries.

Table 7.1   Union Membership in the United States, 1897 to 1984

Year	Membership (000s)	Percentage of Nonagricultural Workers
1897	440	na
1898	467	na
1899	550	na
1900	791	3.0
1910	2,116	8.2
1920	5,034	12.0
1930	3,632	11.7
1940	8,944	27.2
1950	14,267	31.5
1960	18,117	31.5
1970	19,381	27.3
1980	22,811	25.2
1984	17,300	18.8

Sources: Compiled from: U.S. Bureau of Census, *Historical statistics of the United States, Colonial Times to 1957*, 97–98; U.S. Bureau of Census, *Statistical abstract of the United States: 1984*, 439; U.S. Bureau of Census, *Statistical abstract of the United States: 1986*, 424.

Table 7.2   Percentage Unionized in Twelve Industrial Countries, 1977 or after

Country	Percentage of Workers
Belgium	68%
Canada	31
Denmark	64
France	25*
Germany	32
Italy	60*
Japan	24
Netherlands	42*
Norway	66
Sweden	80
United Kingdom	53*
United States	19

Sources: Compiled from: Hill, *Competition and control at work: The new industrial sociology*, 130; Hewlett, *A lesser life*, 361–362.

*Hewlett data from *Social Europe*, Luxembourg: Commission of the European Community, May 1984, p. 120.

Union Problems

External Structural Problems

Some background for current union problems of the 1960s, 1970s, and 1980s has already been discussed in other chapters: the slowdown of economic growth; foreign competition with certain U.S. industries; larger structural unemployment than the previously acceptable frictional unemployment rate; inflation, which keeps the pressure on for increasing wages and/or benefits; deregulation, which forces old unionized companies to compete with new nonunion firms; capital flight and plant shutdowns; a shrinking of the proportion of workers in the more heavily unionized manufacturing industries and new job growth in the less unionized white-collar and service areas; the lack of enthusiasm by many government agencies in enforcing regulations on health and safety and unfair labor practices; and the introduction of robotics and other labor-displacing technology. In addition, the courts and NLRB in recent years have allowed management a great deal of latitude in opposing union organizing under the free speech provision of the Taft-Hartley Act.

Explanations for the decline of unions in the United States that focus on changes in occupational structure or work force composition, however, are found wanting. First, these changes have been taking place in other industrial countries while their unions have grown, including in Canada, where many of the same companies and unions operate. In these countries unions have maintained their membership in the older unionized industries and gone on to organize the increasing number of white-collar and service workers. Second, women in the United States today are as likely to vote for a union as are men, and nonwhites are more likely than all other people to vote a union in (Freeman and Medoff 1984:227). The idea that these workers cannot be organized is fallacious today. We must look elsewhere for answers about the decline. One place to look is within the unions themselves.

Internal Problems

In addition to these above problems, which are external to unions and not of union making, there are some problems internal to unions, or at least more under union control (AFL-CIO Committee 1985). First is the lack of a good public image, due in part to what has been manipulated into a new traditional antiunion ideology in the United States and in part to the well-publicized undemocratic practices of a few unions. Second, the labor movement in general has failed to develop a stand on social issues of interest to the rank-and-file and backed some social reforms in the 1960s with which much of the membership did not agree—mandatory school busing, for example.

Third, for many decades top union leaders have lacked charismatic leadership abilities and organizational impetus (Schwartz and Hoyman 1984). In constant dollars, union organizing expenditures per nonunion member declined 30 percent between 1953 and 1974. This decline may account for as much as one-quarter of the lost NLRB elections (Freeman and Medoff 1984:228–230). Fourth, the unions' political power in relation to that of big business has declined since the 1940s, not just in being outspent by business, but also in being able to deliver the union vote at the polls.

These internal problems and the somewhat sluggish nature of union leadership in general still does not explain the major part of the decline in unionism in the United States. After examining the major studies on NLRB elections, Freeman and Medoff (1984:233) concluded:

> Despite considerable differences among studies [in methodology], virtually all tell the same story: managerial opposition to unionism, and illegal campaign tactics in particular, are a major, if not the major, determinant of NLRB election results.

Managerial Opposition: Union-busting Today

Managerial opposition, both legal and illegal, has been increasing apparently since the mid-1950s. Some of the most serious types of opposition in practice today include threats of shutdowns, concessions and give-backs, Chapter 11 bankruptcy filings, use of union-busting consultants, an antiunion NLRB, unfavorable court decisions, new pseudoparticipation management programs, and labor-displacing technology.

Since about 1970 unions have been encountering plant shutdowns or threats of shutdowns and Chapter 11 bankruptcy filings by their companies. By these means employers can break union contracts or wring concessions or give-backs from unions. The 1984 Supreme Court Bildisco ruling made *Chapter 11* easy to use—no immediate collapse need be demonstrated, but only a company statement that the union contract was "burdensome" (Rosenstiel and Weinstein 1984:A7; Serrin 1984:D25). This ruling, of course, makes union organizing more difficult as workers note that unionized industries are the first to flee the country or file Chapter 11, unless the company is using the latter to avoid lawsuits, as in the Johns Manville Asbestos case. Workers say they do not need to pay union dues in order to make concessions and that unions cannot guarantee job security.

Union-busting consultants do a multimillion-dollar-a-year business;

in 1983 1,500 such consulting firms had 10,000 employees (Georgine 1980:91; Union busting today 1983:8; AFL-CIO Committee 1985:10). These consultants teach management and particularly supervisors how to keep unions out or how to gain decertification through an NLRB election. In *decertification* elections, workers can vote a union out of the company. The consultants train the supervisors in techniques for intimidating workers, not always within NLRA Section 8(a) (2) legal limits. They also have prepared leaflets and films of allegedly possible union atrocities to which employees will be exposed if they join. They help management screen employees for potential union sympathies and offer advice on pseudoparticipation and paternalistic practices, interspersed with threats, to win over hesitant employees (Chernow 1981; Askin 1983; Hauser 1979; Howard, 1982; Bankrupt but not broke 1983; Union busting today 1983; Kisler 1984:103; Wilson and Askin 1981; Lagerfeld 1981). Modern Management (MM—formerly Modern Management Methods, 3M) is the most well known consulting firm using these methods.

Are these tactics effective? MM claims to win more than 90 percent of its campaigns. Apparently it is worth the $200 an hour its consultants receive (Union busting today 1983:8). In 1970 unions won 55 percent of representation elections. By 1981 they won only 30 percent of certification elections and were decertified in 74.9 percent of decertification elections (Anderson et al. 1983:52). These statistics are similar to findings from a study on elections in the 1970s—when companies hire consultants, unions won only 23 percent of the time (Freeman and Medoff 1984:234). In addition, the number of decertification elections increased from 301 in 1970 to 856 in 1981 (Union busting today 1983:18). The AFL-CIO estimated that 95 percent of employers by the mid-1980s actively resist unions and 75 percent of companies now hire union-busting consultants because of their effectiveness (AFL-CIO Committee 1985:10).

The NLRB, which is supposed to protect workers in their right to organize without illegal pressures from companies, historically had been fairly even-handed. In the 1980s, however, three of its five members are antiunion, appointed by an antiunion administration (Compa 1984:24, 26; Union work 1984:12; Kisler 1984:104). One recent NLRB chairman publicly declared that "collective bargaining frequently means . . . the destruction of individual freedom and the destruction of the marketplace," and that "the price we have paid is the loss of entire industries and the crippling of others" (AFL-CIO Committee 1985:11).

An estimated 50,000 union activists a year bring suit for illegal discharge, but the NLRB finds only 30 to 40 percent of these unfair labor practice suits to have some merit. Kisler (1984:102) reasons that this lack of successful employee cases is due to the difference in legal firepower between workers and corporations. Even if the employee wins the case, the union's organizing drive has been damaged. Further, the financial penalties for illegally discharging an employee for union organizing are slight—back pay, minus whatever the employee earned at other jobs—and the posting of a little notice that the company will not engage in this illegal activity again. These notices are humorously known as "hunting licenses"; they let employees know how far the company is willing to go to defeat unions (Freeman and Medoff 1984:232–233). The chances of an employee's being fired are high. One out of every 20 workers who voted for a union was discharged for union activity in 1980 (Freeman and Medoff 194:232).

Not only can a worker still be fired for trying to organize, but, because of the *Helton v. Bill Johnson's Restaurants, Inc.,* Supreme Court ruling in 1983, an employer also can bring a libel suit against an employee for bringing the case to the NLRB (Libel and Labor 1983:25–27).

In addition, management can now rent a strikebreaker or scab during union organization periods or strikes from such suppliers as Payne and Keller in Houston or United Technical Services in California (Chernow 1981:24). Strikebreakers arrive in buses with barred windows to insure their safe delivery. Under Taft-Hartley, srikebreakers and other people hired for the occasion can vote in union certification or decertification elections one year after employment (Balanoff 1985:8).

Oddly enough, Quality of Worklife Programs (QWLs) and quality circles (QCs), which should empower the working person, are sometimes used against worker autonomy (Parker and Boal 1984; Parker 1985; Kochan, Katz, and Mower 1984; Watts 1982). The basic idea of these plans should be to allow the worker input into decision making (see Chapter 11). Under the NLRA Section 8(a)(2) it is unfair for any employer "to dominate or interfere with the formation or administration of any labor organization or contribute financial or other support to it. . . ." This statement has been interpreted to mean that QWLs must not be used to counter unions. However, as has happened, QWLs have been used to try to bust unions.

One example involves a union in a chemical company. The chemical company union had been trying for some years to convince management that the men and women employees needed separate shower facilities, because after each shift one group would have to wait for the other for their mandatory shower. A quality circle plan was put into effect, and one of the first efficiency suggestions from the circles was another shower room. Management quickly accepted the idea, and one was immediately provided. The message was clear: Now that you have quality circles, why do you need a union?

Even though the impact of these activities, subtle and not so subtle, legal and illegal, cannot be gauged specifically, Freedman and Medoff

(1984:238) estimate that about 25 to 50 percent of union decline can be traced to managerial opposition.

Technology and Unions

A final factor, which is proving to be very powerful, affects all workers—union and nonunion, blue collar and white collar. This factor is the increasing use of robotics and other computer-based technologies (Miller 1983; Zimbalist 1979). By 1990 robotics and other computer-based systems are expected to completely change the organization of production in the automobile industry (Dassbach 1986:57). Proponents of this transformation point out that new, more highly skilled jobs will be created in the production, programming, and maintenance of these robots. The monotonous and hazardous jobs created by earlier automation will be eliminated. Quality of life will be improved (Dassbach 1986:57).

In opposition, Harley Shaiken (1986), professor of information technology at the University of California at San Diego and a former machinist, questions the number of jobs this will create and wonders what will happen to the displaced high-skilled as well as low-skilled workers. Other studies support these doubts. In a study for the U.S. National Technical Information Service, William Tanner and William Adolfson (1982) estimate the impact on the automobile industry. In this industry the ratio of jobs eliminated to jobs created by robots stands at 20:1, and they expect the ratio to be about 30:1 by 1990 (quoted in Dassbach 1986:58).

A study of the Volkswagen Wolfburg plant found that the job elimination to creation ratio was only 5:1—Volkswagen made its own robots, however. The effect on the remaining work force was also interesting. Only one displaced worker was retrained; the others were reassigned to jobs at their current skill level or to lower level jobs. In addition, workers experienced increased stress, workload, machine pacing, and social isolation (Dassbach 1986:58). In this particular case, the quality of work-life did not improve. Similar findings have been reported for Japan and the United States, including the deskilling of jobs for many displaced skilled workers, such as welders and painters (Argote, Goodman, and Schkade 1983; Dassbach 1986:59).

Shaiken pointed out a serious long-term problem related to these concerns. Small aspects of technology may be neutral and value free, but the larger systems into which they are organized are not. In reviewing his own case studies and those of other researchers, he finds that systems are designed for social purposes and, currently, the purposes are those of management, reflecting the power arrangement in society. In other words, using the automobile industry examples, if the companies were interested in the workers' quality of life, they would have paid more attention to the design of the overall system and to worker retraining with that in mind.

In a history of the evolution of the design and use of automatically controlled machine tools, David Noble (1984) makes us aware that *technological determinism*—the seeming necessity of a particular design and use of technology—is a cultural myth. This myth blinds us to the options available in the technology's use and eliminates what should be publicly debated and decided. It also both conceals and legitimates the agenda of the people who make those decisions—the socially powerful (Noble 1984:xiv—xv). On a brighter note Noble points out that technology sometimes has consequences unanticipated by its designers; machines, like people, are often imperfect. However, he warns, we should not anticipate "the imminent collapse of the edifice of domination" (Noble 1984:325).

Technology can be used to free the creativity of workers or to remove the human element from the production process. Computers and microelectronics have enabled companies to centralize such activities as (1) planning from the home office, (2) executing at the machine station on the shop floor, (3) controlling inventory and getting it to the work station, (4) controlling robots on the assembly line operations, and (5) keeping detailed records of the entire process. Computer-aided design and computer-aided manufacturing (CAD/CAM) and numerically controlled machines (NC) have taken away the need for many skills from the blue-collar worker, who in most cases has no say about what technology will be used or about programming the new equipment. Electronic monitoring in communications and word processing have paced and stressed the office worker. This is all done in the name of efficiency and the alleged lack of a skilled work force (Noble 1984:335).

New technology appears in most U.S. firms in a plan already designed by management, in a climate of antagonistic union/management relations. In this situation, workers are trying to keep both their jobs and some minor measure of control over their work situation while management seems to be trying to deskill and control the workers. The introduction of new technology has resulted in petty grievances and tactics by unions and high-handedness by management. Unions have frequently resisted automation, but not in all industries. For example, the steel industry has long been urged to retool and modernize by its union. The United Mineworkers were in the forefront of urging automation on reluctant mine owners.

The problem, according to Shaiken, is that the introduction of new technology has not included the workers in planning, as is mandated by law in a number of European countries such as Norway, Sweden, and West Germany (Shaiken 1986:276; *Computerized Manufacturing Auto-*

mation 1984:10). Hence, automation has usually worked to the disadvantage of workers, and their organizations have resisted. The 1981 convention of the International Association of Machinists and Aerospace Workers (IAM) codified a Technology Bill of Rights for workers calling for such inclusion in planning (see Shaiken 1986:271–274 for text). Its basic point is the inclusion of the workers in planning for technological change and its attendant social costs.

The new technology has other problems as well as frequently routinizing and deskilling the blue-collar and office workers' jobs. The lack of input from the shop floor divorces the machinist, or other worker, from the designer in the planning department and thus may short circuit the creative process. Even the designer can be throttled by his or her limited choices. On complex work this can be a serious creative problem. One observer, formerly a senior design engineer at Lucas Aerospace in England, has referred to the computer as "the Trojan Horse with which Taylorism is going to be introduced into intellectual work" (Shaiken 1986:222; See also Noble 1984:329–330).

Computerization can alter existing power relationships within an organization. First, it can change access to information. For example, a middle-level manager who once kept relevant data in his head for some area of decision making, now finds he must share the data and lose some of his power in the computerized operation. Second, computerization modifies behavior as people change to fit the machine pace or some new task the program calls for. Third, Shaiken (1986:232–233) points out that information systems have their own symbolic aspects, such as some managers' refusal to use computers because keyboard work looks like something a secretary should be doing.

Computerization has also contributed significantly to off-shore sourcing, with companies buying components from their subsidiaries abroad or from other foreign companies. In 1981 5 percent of automobile parts on vehicles manufactured in the United States came from plants abroad. By 1986 this figure had become 15 percent of parts (Shaiken 1986:242; Rudolph 1986:59). With the capabilities of central planning in Detroit (or elsewhere) MNCs can easily off-source their parts and play off dual plants and the governments of their countries against each other (Shaiken 1986:240–241). This situation leaves the workers in higher wage countries extremely vulnerable and fearing a loss of any control they might have had over the production process through skill or union work rules. There is also the justifiable fear of their becoming structurally unemployed by robots.

If large computer manufacturers enter the market as expected, the number of robots introduced yearly in U.S. industry will reach approximately 200,000 by 1990. Some industry analysts estimate that 65 to 75 percent

of today's [1980] factory jobs could be done by robots in 1990. In addition
to the robotics revolution, other new technologies are restructuring
nearly every workplace. Researchers estimate that new technology will affect as many as 45 million jobs—about half of which are currently held
by union workers. Of this number, approximately 25 million workers will
be affected in the most drastic way—their jobs will be eliminated. (Kennedy, Craypo, and Lehman 1982:1)

Not all unemployment estimates are quite this drastic. The General
Accounting Office reported in 1982 that "whether automation will increase unemployment in the long run is not known" (quoted in Noble
1984:348). The Congressional Budget Office, however, estimated a loss
of three million manufacturing jobs by 1990 (Noble 1984:348). This figure does not include expected declines in middle- and lower-level management and clerical workers forecast by the Office of Technology Assessment report in 1984 (Computerized manufacturing automation
1984:7). Carnegie-Mellon estimates the loss of one million jobs by 1990
and three million by 2000 (Marshall 1984:10).

The estimate of 200,000 industrial robots by 1990 seems wide of the
mark. There were approximately 25,000 industrial robots in the United
States in mid-1987 (Japan had half of the 110,000 world total) (Moberg
1987a:7). Nevertheless, most observers seem to agree that there will be
a negative impact on individual workers, their communities, and on
income distribution in the United States if public-private planning for
re-education and income redistribution is not in place soon (Computerized manufacturing automation 1984; Marshall 1984; Noble 1984;
Shaiken 1986).

UNIONS REACT

In 1985 the AFL-CIO published the results of a two-year study on the
declining situation of unions (AFL-CIO Committee 1985). Some of their
suggestions for reversing this trend, along with ideas from other writers,
are presented here. The Committee emphasized better training for organizers, union officials, and members, more active participation of members, more information-sharing with the media and other unions, help
with union mergers, and the inclusion of more issues of concern to
workers in bargaining. Other writers have stressed early warning laws,
worker buyouts of firms being shut down, tripartite national planning,
participation in planning technology, and job creation through the use of
pension funds.

Clerical and Service Workers, Unite!

Some unions are beginning to awaken from the lull between the 1930s and 1970s, when they assumed that a liberal government would always protect their rights and that militant and charismatic organizing was an unnecessary thing of the past. With the shift in new jobs from the unionized sector to white-collar and service sectors, unions are beginning to attempt organizing in new areas. Women and other minority workers, long thought to be difficult to organize to any extent, have been the most receptive (Roberts 1984:30). Much is still to be done in this area, however, as only 14 percent of women workers are currently organized (Hewlett 1986:344).

The clerical union 9 to 5, which grew out of the women's rights movement, has been one of the most successful. Under Karen Nussbaum, a former clerk-typist at the Harvard Graduate School of Education, the organization has grown from 10 women in 1975 to some 12,000 members in 18 chapters affiliated with Service Employees International Union (SEIU) and has won 12 straight certification elections—5,000 members in one and a half years. Unions are discovering that the issue of women's right to equal pay for jobs of comparable worth has organizing appeal (Anderson et al. 1983). This dynamic union may have demonstrated to older unions what they have been missing for some time—charismatic leadership and an ideology, or at least a nobler sounding issue—equal rights and equal pay for jobs of comparable worth (Askin 1983:3, 11).

The American Federation of State, County, and Municipal Employees (AFSCME) has been successfully organizing university personnel and has won an important comparable-worth decision in the lower courts against the State of Washington for the 15,000 women and some men in traditionally low-paying women's jobs (Anderson et al. 1983:54). The case was settled out of court before the Supreme Court was asked to give a ruling. Ultimately, the Supreme Court will probably be called on to decide whether comparable worth will stand. Comparable worth as an issue makes good sense for a union with more than 600,000 women members out of its 1.1 million membership. Yale University workers successfully ended their strike for equal pay for comparable worth in January 1985. AFSCME's New York district has also pursued parental leave and flextime in its contracts (Hewlett 1986:346).

The United Autoworkers (UAW) has been organizing bank employees, even in the hometown of the famous Willmar Eight, who struck their bank employer for equal opportunity. Hospital employees and other service personnel are also being organized in increasing numbers.

As discussed in Chapter 3, comparable worth is an important organizing point for women who earn less than 65 percent of men's pay, because they are in traditional women's jobs that are underpaid for their skill requirements, responsibility, and working conditions. Arguments that comparable worth would ruin the economy are not convincing to these women. They point to other countries that have these laws, such as Sweden and Australia, and to the fact that women in the United States are the lowest paid compared to men of any industrial country in the world, except Japan (see Chapter 3, Table 3.6).

Other civil rights issues, such as sexual harassment and affirmative action in hiring, on-the-job training, and promotion, are useful in gaining union support from women and other minorities. In fact under the principle of "duty of fair representation" a female union member may sue a union when it does not respond to her sexual harassment grievance. This suit may be taken to the NLRB. Unions could use these civil rights issues to their advantage in recruiting, if they pursued these grievances with vigor.

In addition to women and other minorities organizing, another group long thought to be difficult to unionize is becoming active. Professional and technical workers, particularly in the public sector, where management is now less likely to be able to oppose organization than in the private sector, are turning to unionization. Teachers, performing artists, journalists, airline pilots, professional athletes, nurses, engineers, school administrators, and other government workers are growth areas in organization (Kisler 1984:98).

Buyouts and Early Warning Laws

Unions have taken two interesting approaches to plant shutdowns and capital flight. In more than 70 instances since 1971 workers have been hurriedly able to piece together a worker buyout to save their jobs (Rosen, Klein, and Young 1986:51). In union plants these efforts were spearheaded by the union. Employee ownership has been furthered by the Employee Retirement and Income Retirement Security Act of 1974 and subsequent acts, saving thousands of jobs. Four or five of these companies have since gone under, but the rest have continued to function, providing salaries and some dividends to worker/owners. (Chapter 11 discusses Employee Stock Ownership Plans [ESOPs] and other types of worker ownership.)

Another union approach has been to push for early warning laws. Currently the European Economic Community (EEC) is considering the Vredling proposal for member nations. This proposal would require that multinational firms inform and consult their employees before making major decisions about plant shutdowns or the introduction of new technology. Many European nations already have such a law. A similar bill was introduced in the United States by Representative Bill Ford (D-Michigan) as H.R. 2847. If passed, such a law would require firms with more than 50 employees to give one-year's advance notice before displacing more than 100 workers and six months notice before displacing from 20 to 100 workers. The law also provides for health and

welfare benefits to be continued and for the government to be responsi-·
ble for some assistance to affected communities and workers (Kilmnik
1983:8–9).

Naturally, U.S. multinationals are fighting this type of legislation
both at home and abroad. U.S. corporations had $77 billion invested
directly in EEC countries in 1980, plus the investment in the United
States that might be affected by forced disclosures. The multinationals
argue that such advance information would endanger their competitive
edge and give away confidential business information to competitors.
Early warning laws in Sweden, the United Kingdom, France, Greece, and
the Netherlands indicate that companies can learn to live with them. In
West Germany no plant may close without government permission and
an investigation of the impact of employment (Institute for Labor Education and Research 1982:365).

Tripartite Planning

The AFL-CIO is currently supporting the idea that tripartite national
committees should do more overall economic planning in the areas of
technology, job displacement, and community impact, as the Scandinavian countries have been able to do for the benefit of their entire societies. National economic planning by a board made up of management,
government, and labor representatives has its supporters and detractors.
In Sweden, for example, a tripartite planning commission has apparently
worked. There is disagreement on whether it would work as well in the
United States. The AFL-CIO apparently thinks it would be successful,
but other people feel that this could place unions in a "junior partnership" with management and their confederates in government (Moody
1984:32–33).

The AFL-CIO and the management of ten multinational firms have
already formed a labor/manangement committee that has deliberated
over such problems as illegal immigration, unemployment benefits, and
U.S. infrastructure (Big labor's comeback campaign 1983:41). The committee has had some success in agreeing on these issues. For unions and
the workers they represent, such a board for more overall industrial
planning could be either self-defeating or a means of gaining new leverage (Chernow 1981). Supporters of the idea argue that union involvement in planning will at least provide a foot in the door, where now the
workers can only react to decisions made in private, when it is usually
too late to do much about them.

Political and Public Relations Actions

Unions are particularly concerned about the negative public image they
continue to carry—from being un-American, to accusations of commu-

nist or gangster domination, to being blamed for U.S. corporations' failure to compete abroad. In 1983 unions spent $2 million on a media campaign through the new Labor Institute of Public Affairs (Big labor's comeback campaign 1983:41).

Unions also are paying more attention to politics. In 1984 the AFL-CIO unsuccessfully endorsed the Democratic candidate for president and contributed Political Action Committee (PAC) monies to the election of both Democrat and Republican Congressional candidates (Big labor's comeback campaign 1983:40–41). In 1982, 350 union PACs contributed $21 million to political campaigns; the 2,100 corporate and industrial PACs, however, spent $87 million (Rehmus 1984:43). In 1984 the 394 union PACs faced off against 2,510 corporate and trade PACs and another 1,100 unidentifiable PACs in the presidential race; this meant the unions' $26.3 million versus industries' $67.1 million, plus the contributions of unidentified PACs (Adamany 1986:21).

In an effort to get closer to the concerns of their membership, the AFL-CIO retained pollster Peter Hart to find out what the rank and file really think on various economic, political, and social issues (Anderson et al. 1983:53). In 1980, 44 percent of union families supported Reagan on public issues; thus, even though the unions have usually supported the Democrats at the national level, obviously not all rank and file are in agreement. To be politically powerful, unions not only have to counter corporate PAC money, but they also have to be able to deliver the vote of more of their members. Thus, more union activity is needed to get the issues before their membership and get them politically involved.

The most unusual suggestion for union political activism is that labor back its own Third Party as the unions in Europe do. In 1984, 76 million eligible voters stayed away from the polls. Was it apathy because these nonvoters are so well off, or was it the perception that both Democrats and Republicans seem to protect corporate interests to the detriment of workers? The argument is that a new labor party would assure that the issues workers are interested in came before the public. Either their own candidates would be elected or the Democrat Party would be forced to pick up some of the workers' issues to gain back their votes. The national labor organizations cannot be counted on to back a new party because of their long-standing ties to the Democrats. The efforts and funds must come from the grassroots—the local unions and their community-group allies (Mazzocchi and Leopold 1987).

Health and Safety Concerns

In addition to suggesting that unions should focus on obtaining civil rights for their workers and on saving jobs and communities when shutdowns occur, some writers suggest that unions should see that health and safety, including environmental protection, become public issues—both in union contracts and in public media (Deutsch 1982). Sweden and Saskatchewan have used labor teams in the workplace to check hazards. This requires protection for the reporting workers, an independent health agency to do research on possibly dangerous situations, and central agencies, such as OSHA and EPA, with mandates and resources to fulfill their functions. It also requires that workers receive training from the central agency and from their unions and that films, reports, and pamphlets and other materials be available for educating employees. We return to these issues in Chapter 9.

Participation in Technology Decisions

Some labor unions have been including clauses in negotiated contracts that attempt to deal with the human costs involved in introducing new technology. The American Federation of State, County and Municipal Workers (AFSCME), the Service Employees International Union (SEIU), the Communications Workers of America (CWA), and other unions are including items such as the following in their contracts (McLaughlin 1983:159; Weekley 1983:148–149):

- A requirement that the union receive advance notice when the employer intends to introduce new technology;
- Rate-retention obligations, should the newly structured job require less skill than it formerly did;
- Early retirement provisions;
- Employer-financed training and retraining rights;
- Interplant and intraplant transfer rights;
- The establishment of a joint labor-management committee, to deal with, among other things, health and safety problems;
- A severance pay provision;
- A restriction on time-motion monitoring or production quota setting;
- Spread-the-work provisions, such as longer vacations, more paid personal leave, shorter hours; and
- A provision that reduction in force due to the introduction of new technology will be by attrition or reassignment only, for those in place when the new technology is introduced.

Union Mergers and Information Sharing

What can be inferred from these ideas is that unions need to revitalize their thinking and old tactics; some have been doing that. Such revitalization takes conviction and organization for political power. To gain this power, unions have taken the following two steps: many unions have been merging into larger units, and many are participating in information sharing and the publication of that information to members and the general public. Mergers have occurred in the face of declining union membership and the increasing size and power of corporations. In recent times we have seen such mergers as (Early 1986);

- Food and Commerical Workers and the Insurance union
- United Steelworkers of America and the Upholsters
- Boilermakers and the Cement Workers
- Communication Workers of America pursuing deals with United Telegraph Workers and with the International Typographical Union (ITU)
- Service Employees International Union and National Association of Government Employees and California State Employees and some locals of 9 to 5.

Size does not guarantee strength, as the 1.5-million-member independent (not affiliated with the AFL-CIO) Teamsters union discovered in recent setbacks. Also, mergers have sometimes appeared as unfriendly takeovers. This means that time and resources sometimes seem to have been wasted in court battles between unions, in public relations campaigns against each other, and in political infighting—similar to mergers among businesses. Sometimes the situation has been quite brutal (Early 1986). The expensive suits of the Teamsters, the Newspaper Guild, and the Graphic Communications Union for mergers with popular ITU are cases in point.

The problem is twofold. First, this lost energy and money take away from the organization activities of the unorganized places in the union's traditional jurisdiction—as in the Teamsters' organizing outside their field when so many trucking establishments are unorganized. Second, the small unions that are taken over by the large unions may gain strike funds, and research, legal, and public relations departments available in the big unions; but because they are so small a part of the overall bureaucratic setup, their needs may not be met. In other words, they may suffer the same benign, or not so benign, neglect that subsidiaries in diversified corporate structures often suffer. They may be used and then ignored in favor of the larger entities. This is what the democratic and independent ITU is fighting.

In addition, unions must work together through their networking and public information activities to change the political/legal climate. This means they must work toward the situation present in other countries that allows for a more equal opportunity for organizing—shorter time periods between pledge-card signings and NLRB certifications, the outlawing of questionable consulting service practices, and stiffer enforcement of illegal antiunion practices, which the NLRB is now ignoring.

The publications of the AFL-CIO Committee on the Evolution of Work is one such information effort. Independent research and publication projects have also increased. The Labor Education and Research Project in Detroit is a nonprofit organization that does research, publishes useful monographs and a monthly newsletter, *Labor Notes* (1979–date), sponsors conferences, and acts as a clearinghouse for information on labor issues and organizations (see Slaughter 1983 for a list of resources).

Job Creation through Investment of Union Pension Funds and Public Ownership of Corporations that Default on Pensions

In 1980 the estimated assets of pension funds held privately in the United States was $240 billion; at least half this total were union pension funds (Freeman and Medoff 1984:75). In 1984 the privately held pension funds had grown to $948.2 billion (U.S. Bureau of Census 1985:369). Even though there are state and federal laws limiting the use of such funds, federal regulatory agencies have, since the late 1970s, been allowing some union funds to be invested in union projects. Job creation in socially useful areas on projects employing union labor is in its infancy but seems to be growing.

In California a consortium of twenty construction unions has invested pension funds in union construction projects. In other states similar investments are underway. Freeman and Medoff refer to this new use of tremendous union capital as "one of the few major innovations in industrial relations in the late-1970s–early 1980s with potential for strengthening the labor movement" (Freeman and Medoff 1984:77). Worker- and community-owned buyouts or new corporations could be funded by pension capital. In this way the community would also be serving its own priorities on what would be socially useful (Institute for Labor Education and Research 1982:364–365). The prospects are encouraging that with this source of capital workers and their communities could have more control of their own destinies.

Another radical idea has been suggested for corporations that default on their pension plans and turn them over to the federal Pension Benefit Guaranty Corporation (PBGC). If the government must pick up the tab for corporations such as LTV, which threatened to default on three of its pension plans in the mid-1980s, some politicians and workers suggest that the government take over these corporations' assets and turn the management over to the worker/community boards (Moberg 1987b). This action would further the worker/community control of basic industry.

THE OVERALL EFFECTS OF UNIONS

Have the unions done the working person any good? On balance, are unions good for society as a whole? Without a straight yes or no answer, we have to ask for whom, in what areas, and what might have been the consequences without them?

To try to answer these questions Freeman and Medoff (1984) have analyzed quantitative, and some qualitative, data from all the major data sources available on industries and firms, union and nonunion, and have collected their own survey data on points not well-covered elsewhere. They have also reviewed earlier studies. They examined wages, fringe benefits, profits, investment and capitalization, productivity, management practices, union structure, and political activities, such as backing various types of legislation. Even though it is sometimes difficult to generalize across industries and time, their findings indicate the following (Freeman and Medoff 1984:19–25, 246–251):

- Efficiency: In concentrated industries unions tend to encourage reduced employment, capital substitution (new technology and equipment), increased worker efficiency (better training, less turnover than nonunion firms even when wages are held constant), and often increased productivity (not true in all settings, but valid overall). Part of the increased efficiency is from the improved quality of management unionism seems to elicit. Apparently the effects of union featherbedding and work rules are greatly exaggerated in terms of their being widespread or having a great effect on efficiency.
- Distribution of income: Within companies unions tend to reduce inequality of wages among the various categories of workers (young/old, skilled/less skilled); they tend to lower profits in oligopolies (but not seriously since these are usually profitable industries; the higher productivity is not enough to counter the higher labor costs, hence, capital substitution); they tend to raise wages for other blue-collar workers in the region and in similar industries (which must compete for labor and also want to keep unions out of their companies); they tend to raise blue-collar earnings relative to the higher white-collar earnings (reducing inequality between those groups); they tend to increase fringe benefit packages, especially for deferred benefits of pensions and life, accident, and health insurance (a social plus); however, unions have historically tended to discriminate against minorities.
- Social organization: Unions appear to contribute to democracy in the workplace by allowing some worker representation. Freeman

and Medoff point out that most unions are democratic and that the corruption in a few unions has given the public an erroneous stereotype. In legislation unions have done fairly well recently in backing social legislation in the areas of civil rights, health and safety, and the environment but have faired less well on labor legislation, except in the 1930s.

All this leaves Freeman and Medoff with frustration as to the decline in union membership in the United States, which is counter to the increase in unionization in all other industrial nations. It also leaves us to ponder what happened to the neoclassical idea of paying a worker according to his or her marginal productivity/human capital value. As British industrial sociologist Michael Poole puts it, we are talking about power here and the resources on which it is based (Poole 1984:188). Marginal productivity turns out to be relative with regard to worker pay. The only means by which the individually economically powerless worker can gain any measure of power is through organization—to push for some measure of sharing industry profits.

On the negative side, workers who were there first with the skills have not helped to unite workers but to divide them. First, the skilled omitted the unskilled of their own ethnicity and gender from their organizations and from dealing with employers. Then, they excluded minorities and women from joining. Even though minorities and women sometimes formed their own unions, they did not deliver the impact of united working class organizations and in fact served to divide the workers into segments that the companies could then deal with one by one, sometimes playing one group against another, as when using minorities as strikebreakers.

From what we have seen in the historical approach in this chapter, power has not been on the side of workers—with the exception of a slight gain at the turn of the century, when socialist parties and the reform-mindedness of some of the middle classes called for both big business and the government to make a few changes. Every little gain through the years has been at high individual and social cost. The 1930s was the political peak of the organized labor movement, again during a period of threats of even more serious sytem change. Since World War II, however, the situation for organized labor has deteriorated in the private sector in the United States, and most organizing has been in the public sector, where extremes of managerial opposition have been curbed.

If we believe that competition is healthy and look at the data rather than accepting the questionable stereotypes in society, we might share two thoughts with James Madison. In the Federalist No. 10 in 1787 Madison wrote, "Division of society into different interests and parties" was inherent in human beings and "liberty is to faction what air is to fire" (quoted in Gersuny 1981:106). Without freedom and the power for factions to counter each other's interests and domination, we may risk seeing the fire go out in the United States.

The overall consequences of not having unions, considering their contributions, might have been somewhat less overt ethnic discrimination, but possibly a lower standard of living for the general public and no labor law protections—weakly enforced as they are. This scenario is hypothetical, of course, but seems to be possible when considering what it likely to happen if all the power is on one side, given the historical activities of the powerful. Freeman and Medoff contend that society as a whole would be worse off without unions. They are not optimistic about the future as it appears, unless the public reassesses the actual contribution of unions to our quality of life and our social system.

SUMMARY

This chapter has covered the following areas about unions:

1. Unions in the United States have historically found it difficult to organize to better the conditions of workers. The only exceptions have been during wartime and in the 1930s, when the public and the government looked on unions more favorably.

2. Tactics used against unions have included private and public armed forces, strikebreakers, blacklisting, yellow-dog contracts, lockouts, court injunctions, trials, and more recently threats of shutdowns, professional union-busting consultants, right-to-work laws, quality circles, Chapter 11 bankruptcy filings, suits against workers who take cases to the NLRB, and stacking the NLRB with antiunion members.

3. Unions have reacted to their recent declines in membership as a percentage of the work force by attempting to organize clerical and service workers; pushing in the courts for equal pay for work of comparable worth and an end to sexual harassment in the workplace; buying out shutdowns; pushing for early warning laws; supporting tripartite planning; increasing PAC contributions to politicians or initiating a Third Party for labor; urging health and safety and participation in technology decisions in contracts; union mergers and information sharing; and, more recently, and using some union pension funds to create jobs in socially useful projects employing union labor.

BIBLIOGRAPHY

Adamany, David. 1986. The new faces of American politics. *Annals of the American Academy of Political and Social Science* 486:12–33 (July).

AFL-CIO Committee on the Evolution of Work. 1985. *The changing situation of workers and their unions.* Washington, D.C.: AFL-CIO (February).

Anderson, Harry, Richard Manning, James C. Jones, Howard Fineman, Rich Thomas, Diane Weathers, David I. Gonzalez, and Peter McAlevey. 1983. The rise and fall of big labor. *Newsweek* 102, 10:50−54 (September 5).

Argote, Linda, Paul S. Goodman, and David Schkade. 1983. The human side of robotics: How workers react to robots. *Sloan Management Review* 24, 3:31−41 (Spring).

Aronowitz, Stanley. 1973. *False promises: The shaping of American working class consciousness.* New York: McGraw-Hill.

Askin, Steve. 1983. Female rights spell trouble for bosses. *In These Times* 7:3, 11 (July 27−August 9).

Auerbach, Jerold S., ed. 1969. *American labor: The twentieth century.* Indianapolis: Bobbs-Merrill.

Balanoff, Tom. 1985. The cement workers' experience. *Labor Research Review* 7:5−33.

Bankrupt but not broke: Chapter 11 lets management off the hook. 1983. *Dollars and Sense* 92:3−5 (December).

Berman, Daniel. 1978. *Death on the job: Occupational health and safety struggles in the United States.* New York: Monthly Review Press.

Big labor's comeback campaign. 1983. *Business Week* 2812:40−41 (October 17).

Boyer, Richard O., and Herbert M. Morais. 1971. *Labor's untold story,* 3rd ed. New York: United Electrical, Radio and Machine Workers of America.

Chernow, Ron. 1981. Grey flannel goons: The latest in union busting. *Working Papers for a New Society* 8:19−25 (January/February).

Commons, John R. 1918−1935. *History of labor in the United States,* Vols. 1-4. New York: Macmillan.

Compa, Lance. 1984. Stacked deck: The rules of the game won't let the unions win. *The Progressive* 48:12 (April).

Computerized manufacturing automation: Employment, education, and the workplace. 1984. Washington, D.C.: U.S. Congress, Office of Technology Assessment (April).

Dassbach, Carl H. A. 1986. Industrial robots in the American automobile industry. *Insurgent Sociologist* 13, 4:53−61 (Summer).

Deutsch, Steven. 1982. "Unions and technological change: International perspectives." In *Labor and technology: Union response to changing environments,* edited by Donald Kennedy et al., 191−202. University Park, Penn.: Department of Labor Studies, Pennsylvania State University.

Dubofsky, Melvyn. 1975. *Industrialism and the American worker, 1865−1920.* Arlington Heights, Ill.: Harlan Davidson.

Early, Steve. 1986. Mergers: Bigger isn't always better. *Labor Notes* 91:13 (September).

Edwards, Richard. 1979. *Contested terrain: The transformation of the workplace in the twentieth century.* New York: Basic Books.

Foner, Philip S. 1947. *History of the labor movement in the United States: From colonial times to the founding of the American Federation of Labor.* New York: International Publishers.

Freeman, Richard B., and James L. Medoff. 1984. *What do unions do?* New York: Basic Books.

Garson, Barbara. 1975. All the livelong day: The meaning and demeaning of routine work. New York: Penguin Books.

Georgine, Robert. 1980. "From brass knuckles to briefcases: The modern art of union busting." In *The big business reader: Essays on corporate America*, edited by Mark Green and Robert Massie, Jr., 89–104. New York: Pilgrim Press.

Gersuny, Carl. 1981. *Work hazards and industrial conflict*. Hanover, N.H.: University Press of New England for University of Rhode Island.

Gitlow, Abraham L. 1963. *Labor and industrial society*, rev. ed. Homewood, Ill.: Richard D. Irwin.

Gutman, Herbert G. 1976. *Work, culture, and society in industrializing America: Essays in American working-class and social history*. New York: Random (Vintage).

Hauser, Dedra. 1979. The union-busting hustle. *The New Republic* 181:16–18 (August 25).

Hewlett, Sylvia Ann. 1986. *A lesser life: The myth of women's liberation in America*. New York: William Morrow.

Hill, Stephen. 1981. *Competition and control at work: The new industrial sociology*. Cambridge: MIT Press.

Howard, Robert. 1982. Union or bust: The 11-month-old strike at Sterling Radiator is "a textbook case of union busting." *In These Times* 6:8–9 (February 3-9).

Institute for Labor Education and Research. 1982. *What's wrong with U.S. economy? A popular guide for the rest of us*. Boston: South End Press.

Kennedy, Donald, Charles Craypo, and Mary Lehman, eds. 1982. *Labor and technology: Union response to changing environments*. University Park, Penn.: Department of Labor Studies, Pennsylvania State University.

Kilmnik, Ken. 1983. Landmark European labor law nears passage. *Multinational Monitor* 4:8–9 (May).

Kisler, Alan. 1984. Union organizing: New challenges and propsects. *Annals of the American Academy of Political and Social Sciences* 473:96–107 (May).

Kochan, Thomas A., Harry C. Katz, and Nancy R. Mower. 1984. *Worker participation and American unions: Threat or opportunity?* Kalamazoo Mich.: W. E. Upjohn Institute for Employment Research.

Labor Notes. 1979–date. Detroit: Labor Education and Research Project.

Lagerfeld, Steven. 1981. To break a union. *Harper's* 262, 1572:18–21 (May).

Levy, Sheldon G. 1969. "A 150-year study of political violence in the United States." In *Violence in America: History and comparative perspectives*, edited by Hugh Davis Graham and Ted Robert Gurr, 89–91. New York: New American Library.

Lewis, H. Gregg. 1962. *Unionism and relative wages in the United States*. Chicago: University of Chicago Press.

Libel and labor: Bill Johnson's restaurant serves up a chill. 1983. *The Progressive* 47:25–27 (November).

Marshall, Ray. 1984. High tech and the job crunch. *The Texas Observer* 76, 7:1, 7–11 (April 6).

Mazzocchi, Tony, and Les Leopold. 1987. The politics of labor: A third party in the making. *Multinational Monitor* 8, 2:15–17 (February).

McLaughlin, Doris B. 1983. Electronics and the future of work: The impact on pink and white collar workers. *Annals of The American Academy of Political and Social Science* 470:152–162 (November).

Miller, Robert J., ed. 1983. Robotics: Future factories, future workers. Special issue of *The Annals of The American Academy of Political and Social Science* 470:1–214 (November).

Moberg, David. 1987a. The robotics industry discovers it's missing some key components. *In These Times* 11, 24:7 (May 13–19).

————. 1987b. Termination of LTV pension plans has brcader implications for economy. *In These Times*, 11, 11:6 (February 4–10).

Moody, Kim. 1984. Labor's misplaced hopes: Industrial policy may come back to haunt the unions. *The Progressive* 48:32–33 (November).

Nelson, Daniel. 1975. *Managers and workers: Origins of the new factory system in the United States, 1880–1920.* Madison: University of Wisconsin Press.

Noble, David F. 1984. *Forces of production: A social history of industrial automation.* New York: Alfred A. Knopf.

Parker, Mike. 1985. *Inside the circle: A union guide to QWL.* Boston: South End Press (Labor Notes Book).

Parker, Mike, and Ellis Boal. 1984. Will labor laws be weakened to permit expansion of QWL programs? *Labor Notes* 68:7 (September 27).

Pelling, Henry. 1960. *American labor.* Chicago: University of Chicago Press.

Poole, Michael. 1984. *Theories of trade unionism: A sociology of industrial relations,* rev. ed. London: Routledge and Kegan Paul.

Rehmus, Charles M. 1984. Labor and politics in the 1980s. *Annals of The American Academy of Political and Social Sciencies* 473:40–51 (May).

Renshaw, Patrick. 1967. *The Wobblies: The story of syndicalism in the United States.* Garden City, N.Y.: Doubleday (Anchor).

Roberts, Markley. 1984. The future demographics of American unionism. *Annals of The American Academy of Political and Social Science* 473:23–32 (May).

Rosen, Corey, Katherine J. Klein, and Karen M. Young. 1986. *Employee ownership in America: The equity solution.* Lexington, Mass.: Lexington Books.

Rosenstiel, Thomas B., and Henry Weinstein. 1984. Labor leaders rap bankruptcy ruling as union-busting. *Austin (TX) American-Statesman* A7 (February 23).

Ross, Philip. 1963. The role of government in union growth. *Annals of the American Academy of Political and Social Science* 350:74–85 (November).

Rudolph, Barbara. 1986. Singing the shutdown blues. *Time* 127, 25:58–60 (June 23).

Schwartz, Arthur R., and Michele M. Hoyman. 1984. The changing of the guard: The new American labor leader. *Annals of the American Academy of Political and Social Science* 473:64–75 (May).

Serrin, William. 1984. Labor leaders voice concern. *New York Times* 133, 45963:D25 (February 23).

Shaiken, Harley. 1986. *Work transformed: Automation and labor in the computer age.* Lexington, Mass.: Lexington Books.

Slaughter, Jane, 1983. *Concessions and how to beat them.* Detroit: Labor Education and Research Project.

Taft, Philip, and Philip Ross. 1969. "American labor violence: Its causes, character, and outcome." In *Violence in America: History and comparative perspectives*, edited by Hugh Davis Graham and Ted Robert Gurr, 270–379. New York: New American Library.

Tanner, William, and William Adolfson. 1982. *Robotics in motor vehicle manufacture, final report.* Washington, D.C.: U.S. National Technical Information Service (June).

Tausky, Curt. 1984. *Work and society: An introduction to industrial sociology.* Itasca, Ill.: F. E. Peacock.

Terkel, Studs. 1974. *Working.* New York: Avon.

Thompson, E. P. 1963 *The making of the English working class.* New York: Random (Vintage).

Union busting today: Rats teach new dogs old tricks. 1983. *Dollars and Sense* 85:8–9, 18 (March).

Union Democracy Review. 1979–date. Brooklyn, NY: Association for Union Democracy.

Union work. 1984. *The Progressive.* 48:12 (April).

U.S. Bureau of the Census. 1960. *Historical statistics of the United States: Colonial times to 1957.* Washington, D.C.: GPO.

———. 1983. *Statistical abstract of the United States: 1984.* Washington, D.C.: GPO.

———. 1985. *Statistical abstract of the United States: 1986,* Washington, D.C.: GPO.

Watts, Glen. 1982. Management incentives: Trick or treat? *Workplace Democracy* 9:2–4.

Weekley, Thomas L. 1983. Workers, unions, and industrial robotics. *Annals of the American Academy of Political and Social Science* 470:146–151 (November).

Wilson, Kinsey, and Steve Askin. 1981. Secrets of a union buster: Inside Modern Management, Inc. *The Nation* pp. 725–728 (June 13).

Wolf, Jerome. 1968. *Ferment in labor.* Beverly Hills, Calif.: Glencoe Press.

Zimbalist, Andrew, ed. 1979. *Case studies on the labor process.* New York: Monthly Review Press.

8

Work and Life-Style in the United States

This chapter looks more specifically at how *socioeconomic status* (SES) or position in society and the occupations related to each class stratum help influence life-style and preferences in many areas of life. In general, this is where that "long shadow of work" (Bowles, Gintis, and Meyer 1975) to which we referred in Chapter 2 becomes more personal—where we begin to see ourselves, family, and friends fit into the overall picture.

Occupation and SES are not the sole determinants of life-style for some people. Alternative life-styles have been and are being experimented with by some people for whom

> occupational and economic role no longer provided a coherent set of values and for whom identity has come to be generated in the consumption rather than the production realm, and affluence has permitted a choice of goods from which to make up a life-style package. (Zablocki and Kanter 1976:280)

Alternative life-styles are not random, either. Most people, however, through various stages in the life cycle, fit some fairly general pattern, with a few little deviations. This general pattern of life-styles in the different strata of the social stratification system is the subject of this chapter.

Most people have some belief concerning who gets what and why in society. Before we approach the specifics of life-styles, we first look at the two major opposing views of why societies have socioeconomic class structures—social stratification—and look briefly at a third view, which attempts a synthesis. Second, we see what kinds of factors people use in figuring out socioeconomic class in industrial societies— economic class, status/prestige, and power—and look at some data on how wealth and income are distributed in the United States.

TWO OPPOSING VIEWS ON SOCIOECONOMIC CLASS/SOCIAL STRATIFICATION AND LENSKI'S SYNTHESIS

In general people in the United States do not seem to be very class conscious. When asked by opinion-poll takers to place themselves in the class structure, people tend to place themselves in the middle class or, sometimes, in the working class if that option is given. We like to think of ourselves as a middle-class society. We know there are great differences in occupations, income, and wealth, but we like to think that most of our friends are somewhere in the middle and that we achieve our positions in that middle range on merit. Note that we do recognize a ranking system, even if we think most of us are in layers in the middle. These unequal ranks are what we call *social stratification.* Social stratification is the hierarchical ranking of persons with regard to the things that are important in the society—material wealth, social esteem, and power.

Most societies have some form of stratification system, as opposed to differences in status that are not ranked such as might exist in some hunting and gathering or simple technology horticultural societies. As societies become more complex, from advanced horticulture on, a social stratification system of some nature exists. As one sociologist stated, "The fact of social inequality in human society is marked by its ubiquity and antiquity" (Tumin 1966:53; see also Eisenstadt 1971 or Hodges 1968 for discussions of social stratification in different types of societies such as Chapter 2 reviews). Some societies with similar technology and economic systems, however, seem to differ greatly in degrees of inequality. Such differences in stratification also are present among advanced industrial societies. But how does this inequality happen and why is social stratification almost universal? Two basic opposing views try to answer these questions.

STRUCTURAL-FUNCTIONAL VIEW OF SOCIAL STRATIFICATION

The structural-functionalist perception of social stratification is related to the order/consensus view of the world outlined in Chapter 1. As you might suspect from what you know of this position, it appears to justify the social system more or less as is. It emphasizes the necessity and functionality (usefulness) of degrees of inequality in society in the following manner (Davis and Moore 1966; Tumin 1966:53-54):

1. Some positions in any society are "functionally more important than others, and require special skills for their performance" (Tumin 1966:53).
2. Only a few persons will have the talents that can be trained into skills needed for the positions of extreme importance to society.
3. A training period is required to convert talent into skills, and individuals must make sacrifices during this period.
4. Positions must have rewards sufficient to induce talented persons to undergo this training period.
5. Rewards attached to these positions must be valued by society and can be classified into things that contribute to (a) sustenance and comfort, (b) humor and diversion, and (c) self-respect and ego expansion.
6. Thus, institutionalized social inequality is based on these differential rewards.
7. Therefore, social inequality is useful and inevitable in any society.

In sum, this list means that differential rewards—some people receiving more than others of the things prized in society— are said to be necessary to motivate individuals to train for and diligently perform more difficult and more valuable tasks for society's benefit. Notice the neoclassical economics assumption here that people are rewarded according to what they are producing in a relatively competitive environment. You may also conclude that this view seems to imply that social inequality is justifiable and fair, since it is necessary.

Power/Conflict View of Social Stratification

An opposing view of socially structured inequality is the conflict view (see Chapter 1 for a discussion of the power/conflict worldview related to this position). The conflict social scientists argue the dysfunctionality of and lack of necessity for large degrees of inequality in social stratification, criticizing the seven points just listed in the following manner (Tumin 1966):

1. Assuming that the highly rewarded positions in society are the most necessary for society's survival is questionable; it is a short-run, value-laden view. Indeed, the same position in different societies may be rewarded quite differently because of differing cultural values, which may be basically unrelated to functional importance or survival for society as a whole (Grandjean 1975:551). For example, paying movie stars

and well-known football players enormous salaries may be functional for their corporations but should not be confused with functional necessity at the macro level.

2. The more rigid a stratification system, the less likely it is that we will know where the talented individuals are, in that many of them will not be given the opportunity to develop native talents. The people who have wealth and power are in a position to limit access to training or to social position (Grandjean 1975:548). By assuming open competition and ignoring power and conflict, the structural-functionalists overlook important factors in the distribution of training, rewards, and social positions.

3. The argument that individuals forego short-run earnings and must be paid more to undergo training does not consider that parents frequently pay for this training (and can sometimes secure these positions for relatively untrained or untalented offspring), that individuals reap immediate rewards in status for being in this type of training, and that sacrifices in earnings are recouped within a decade or so and every dollar after that is surplus earnings.

4. Highly skilled occupations are often very interesting in their job content, thus intrinsic job satisfaction may itself be enough to call forth the efforts cited by structural functionalists; therefore, conflict theorists argue it is not necessary to give some people all the rewards while others are going hungry and without shelter or are doing less interesting work at low pay.

5. Critics agree that social rewards are classified in the three categories structural functionalists describe, that is, rewards that contribute to (a) sustenance and comfort, (b) humor and diversion, and (c) self-respect and ego expansion.

6. However, critics disagree with the idea that large differences in rewards are necessary to elicit effort. In fact, in some societies such displays of differences in status are negatively sanctioned, that is, disapproved of. Again, this points up that the acceptance of large differences in status and rewards is itself a cultural value.

7. Finally, from these criticisms the conflict view sees such extremes that do exist in socially structured inequality as both unnecessary and dysfunctional for society. It is dysfunctional in that it limits the development of the individual in talent and self-esteem, robbing society of these contributions, and limits cooperation and commitment to membership in society by people who are not allowed to participate to their fullest. We return to this important point many times, particularly in the last chapter in the discussion of possible future scenarios.

Structural functionalists reply that they are not trying to justify the unequal system, just to explain it; that criteria for judging the importance of positions is not value-laden, just practical from the point of view of what needs to be done at any one time; that they are talking about positions, rather than individuals; that social mobility is limited by family, not by the positions in society, but (somehow) on the other hand people do not inherit their class standing in society but achieve it; further, they say the conflict criticism is "unsophisticated" because of a "lack of any clear notion of a social system as an equilibrium of forces of which the stratified positional scale is only one" (Davis 1966:62).

These arguments can be stated in an exceedingly simple form. Some people see social stratification as based on functional necessity—so society can fill important positions. Other people see stratification as based on power—a grab for a bigger share of the rewards prized in the society, with the dominant groups able to retain their positions over time, which is dysfunctional for society (Heller 1969:2−3, 479−531).

Lenski's Synthesis

Sociologist Gerhard Lenski (1966) bases his two laws of distribution in society on the ideas that even though persons must cooperate in society to survive, they will struggle with other groups to try to obtain more for their own group when decisions must be made about the distribution of surplus valued goods. The first law then is that people will share the product of their labors to an extent when it is necessary to ensure the survival of other people on whom they are mutually interdependent. Reciprocity of this kind dominates in simple technology groups, such as hunting and gathering or simple horticulture societies. "If I share my food with you today, you will share yours with me tomorrow."

When technology provides a surplus, however, law number two takes effect: Power will determine the distribution of most of the surplus the society possesses. The greater the surplus, the greater the percentage distributed by power; but some charity giving by the powerful is often useful for appearances. Lenski goes on to note that power can mean force and coercion, and the threat of its use is always there; the way power frequently works in societies, however, is to foster legitimation for the unequal distribution system. Legitimating myths can take the form of divine right of kings and nobility, or the form of greater ability, skills, and knowledge of the dominant group. Even though this view may be a synthesis, law two, which is certainly applicable to industrial societies with their enormous surplus, appears to be an extension of conflict stratification theory, with an indirect criticism of structural functionalism for providing legitimating myths.

What do people in our society believe about our social stratification system? Sociologists James Kluegel and Eliot Smith (1981:34—35) reviewed the various studies of our beliefs and found that the four most frequently held are as follow:

1. In general, there is opportunity for all people in the United States, although some groups may have a little less of it.
2. Inequality is necessary—although people at the top may be getting too much and workers at the bottom should receive at least a minimum liveable wage.
3. With opportunity available, the position of an individual in the social stratification system is a function of personal efforts, traits, and abilities, not the result of economic and social structure factors.
4. Hence, the system of distribution of rewards is relatively fair and just.

Given these views, we can easily discern societal beliefs about people living in poverty:

All methods of measuring attitudes towards the poor find the population divided into three groups: The largest group (the majority) believe the poor are partially to blame, the next-largest group attach total personal blame to the poor, and the smallest group see poverty as due entirely to structural factors (i.e., to supra-individual factors such as the failure of society to provide good schools or the failure of private industry to provide jobs). These findings support the somewhat polemical claim by Ryan (1971) that 'blaming the victim' is a dominant element of American thinking about poverty. (Kluegel and Smith 1981:31)

The key words *partially to blame* in the majority view refer to the idea that even though there are recognized obstacles to self-betterment by the poor, "such obstacles would be surmountable if it were not for the debilitating personal characteristics of the poor" (Kluegel and Smith 1981:31).

What is the origin of these generally held views that legitimate the on-going stratification system and what are some consequences of holding such views? Kluegel and Smith (1981:41) point out:

1. These views are part of our "culturally available beliefs" disseminated through the media and educational system. We referred to these beliefs early in Chapter 4 (social Darwinism, rags-to-riches, and the Protestant ethic, where wealth indicated you were among the Chosen and poverty put you among the Damned).
2. Other people suggest that blaming the poor may go along with industrialization and the rising expectations for social mobility it

brings. One can find these ideas in other industrial countries that did not have a Protestant reformation, such as Italy.
3. Social psychologists suggest that this tendency results from psychological ego-defensive mechanisms. "Projecting personal responsibility for failure onto the poor allows one to feel better about one's own limited success" (Kluegel and Smith 1981:41).

From whatever sources these ideas arise, the consequences are that this belief system or ideology privatizes activity toward the pursuit of individual monetary and commodity rewards and does not encourage alternative views of a just society (since this one is already assumed to be just) and does not lend itself to analyzing power or developing in-group/out-group consciousness and collective action. Even reformist public policy, such as affirmative action, is likely to be viewed as reverse discrimination if one assumes there is already almost equal opportunity (Kluegel and Smith 1981:53).

FACTORS IN DETERMINING SOCIAL CLASS IN INDUSTRIAL SOCIETY: ECONOMIC CLASS, STATUS, AND POWER

How do industrial societies establish a social stratification ranking system? Karl Marx's theory of social classes in industrial societies has strongly influenced how western societies perceive social class (see Heller 1969:14−23; Lopreato and Lewis 1974:7−37; Bendix and Lipset 1966b:6−11; Anderson 1974:1−24 for readings from Marx and for more discussion of this contribution). Even though Marx's collaborator Engels denied, in his 1890 letter to his friend J. Bloch, that he and Marx meant that class was determined entirely by a group's relation to the means of production, this idea still remained the basis for much subsequent theorizing on stratification.

According to the materialist conception of history, the *ultimately* determining element in the history is the production and reproduction of real life. More than this neither Marx nor I have ever asserted. Hence if somebody twists this into saying that the economic element is the *only* determining one, he transforms that proposition into a meaningless, abstract, senseless phrase. The economic situation is the basis, but the various elements of the superstructure—political forms of the class struggle and its results, to wit . . . political, juristic, philosophical theories, religious views and their further development into systems of dogmas—also exercise their influence upon the course of the historical struggles and in many cases preponderate in determining their *form*. There is an interaction of all these elements in which, amid all the endless host of accidents . . . , the economic movement finally asserts itself as necessary.

Marx and I are ourselves partly to blame for the fact that the younger writers sometimes lay more stress on the economic side than is due it. We had to emphasize this main principle *vis-a-vis* our adversaries, who denied it, and we had not always the time, the place or the opportunity to give their due to the other elements involved in the interaction. (Marx and Engels 1968:692−693; emphasis in original)

Why does Marx say the economy is so important, even if it is not the only factor involved? Marx said that history was made through human labor, which was immediately necessary to provide for biological needs, and that a person's work was his or her basic form of self-realization (see Chapter 4 for Marx's ideas on developing potential and self-realization through work). As the basic needs are met, new needs are created. Human beings cooperate to produce more, and the division of labor and the organization of production occur, eventually generating a social class system. With the advance of industrialization, urbanization, and communication among workers in larger factory settings, Marx foresaw the rise of class consciousness, organization for action, and eventually a revolution in which the owners of the means of production (capitalists or bourgeoisie) would be expropriated by the workers (proletariat), who had only their labor to sell.

In the meantime the downturns of the business cycle would have squeezed many middle-class small property owners (petite bourgeoisie) down into the ranks of the proletariat, and the position of the workers would grow worse and worse. The peasants cannot form a class for themselves by becoming class conscious because of the isolation inherent in their mode of production and lack of political organization (a point Mao Tse-tung later decided to ignore when he organized the peasant revolution in China).

While recognizing the importance of the economic system as a base for social class, German sociologist Max Weber (1946:180−195) also noted that the factors of economic class, status or prestige, and power must be examined separately. Whereas Marx had assumed that the people who owned the wealth (productive property) also had the status and power (and thus were able to oppress and manipulate the powerless) Weber insisted that the correlation of the three areas was problematic, not automatic. He also admitted they usually did correlate, as we will see. In addition, Weber seems to imply that power may not be dichotomous, but distributed on a continuum.

Other writers, such as Toennies, Schumpeter, Veblen, and Pareto, have added to our thinking about the three factors involved in social stratification systems as well as about caste and estate systems in pre-industrial societies (see Bendix and Lipset 1966a and Heller 1969 for readings on social class from these writers' works). However, sociologists and other social scientists still operationalize the three factors mentioned by Marx and Weber—economic class, status, and power—in their work today. Some variables in each category appear below.

Sociologist Marie Haug (1977) has written an informative bibliographic essay on how socioeconomic status (SES) scales have been developed in the United States, Canada, and Great Britain. All SES scales and indexes for these industrial societies begin with the selection of occupation as the "most feasible single indicator of relative position in a multiple social stratification system" (Haug 1977:53). To occupational prestige rankings (which reflect the subjective evaluations of society) are added educational and earnings information for each occupational group.

For two groups, however, occupation is not quite as useful for placement in the social stratification system. One group is the upper-upper strata of inherited wealth, for whom occupation is obviously not the salient feature for class placement and life-style. The other group is the lower-lower strata, for whom occupation is an intermittent experience and poverty is the defining factor in class placement and life-style.

Variables in Class, Status, and Power

Income and wealth are included in the first variable, economic class. Income is what accrues to people annually as earnings from occupation, interest and dividends on investments, and rent on land. Wealth includes property, stocks and bonds, physical plants, and land and other real estate that produce income, interest, dividends, and rents.

Status or prestige is the second variable. Status groups have their own ranking on prestige and honor in society, according to Weber. Status groups sometimes cross-cut economic class. "Both propertied and propertyless people can belong to the same status group." However, "property as such is not always recognized as a status qualification, but in the long run it is, and with extraordinary regularity" (Weber 1946: 187). One must often maintain a specific life-style in order to retain status group membership.

— Status includes both achieved and ascribed status. Achieved status includes occupational status, status from educational attainment, status from associational membership (which for some people might include religious affiliation, such as joining a more socially acceptable church) as well as other voluntary associations. Ascribed status refers to those statuses one is born into, such as ethnicity, race, religion (e.g., Jews), and old family name (e.g., Vanderbilt, Rockefeller). Another aspect is gender status, particularly important today because of its implications for the social position of female-headed households.

Power is the third variable. Social power was the goal of party, (associations, special interest groups) which might be backed by either class or status groups, both, or neither, according to Weber. By organizing to gain social power, groups could put into operation their own programs for self-interest or idealism, as the case may be.

Power is evident at two levels—national and community. Chapter 5 discusses theories of the distribution of power at the national level and power sources and positions influencing major public policy. The importance of large corporations and, perhaps, old-line wealth is pointed out. One has to read into Weber a broad meaning for the term *party* to encompass the mechanisms used by the powerful. Weber says, "parties may exist in a social 'club' as well as in a 'state'" (Weber 1946:194), so perhaps he had such a broad meaning in mind.

There have been a wealth of interesting community power studies (see reviews in T. N. Clark 1975; Bell and Newby 1972). Some but not all studies have purported to find a local power elite. Remember here that the entire range of the national stratification system will probably not be found in each community.

In small communities the local power may be in the hands of people who would be lower middle-class in a larger setting. Individuals who have moved from an elite position in a small town to a larger community may suffer culture shock when they become small ducks in larger ponds.

The research on community power structures includes studies such as the work of social anthropologist W. Lloyd Warner in Newburyport, Massachusetts (Yankee City); sociologists Robert and Helen Lynd in Muncie, Indiana (Middletown); sociologist Floyd Hunter in Atlanta (Regional City); political scientist Robert Dahl in New Haven, Connecticut; and social psychologist John Dollard's *Caste and Class in a Southern Town*.

Unfortunately, as sociologists Arthur Vidich and Joseph Bensman (1968) point out, few major decisions can still be made at the local level today, except for local taxes and pot hole and sewer repair, because no community is isolated from the decisions being made higher in the political structure, on economic matters, educational content, political possibilities, and welfare.

WEALTH AND INCOME DISTRIBUTION IN THE UNITED STATES

Economic factors are particularly important in terms of the social stratification system and in the distribution of power that influences public policy in industrial society. It thus seems useful to look at some figures on the actual distribution of wealth, income in quintiles of the population, median family income for some categories in society, and poverty in the United States. By examining these distributions we may be able to get a picture of the disparities before we discuss both social mobility in society and life-styles by class.

Table 8.1 indicates the amount and types of wealth (property, which produces income) held by the top 2 percent of families in 1983. Wealth is especially interesting to note for two reasons. First, the inheritance of great wealth is the basic factor in stabilizing (or fossilizing, depending on your viewpoint) our social stratification system in the form it has been since the late nineteenth century. Second, from the discussion in Chapter 5, we know that many people in this top 2 percent, and certainly their interests, must be considered as particularly influential in shaping public policy. Hence, their economic wealth base becomes germane to the direction society takes.

The 2 percent who own more than half of income-producing wealth will be recognizable when we discuss life-style by class as the upper-upper old-line wealth and lower-upper newly rich strata of the top class in the United States (Rast 1986). The top one-half of 1 percent may own as much as 35.1 percent of the wealth, up from 25.4 percent in 1963, according to the report issued in July 1986 by the Joint Economic Committee of Congress (Cockburn 1987). From the upper-middle classes down to near the bottom, occupation and the income from there become very important. The Bureau of Census has provided data on income distribution by segments of the population for some time. Table 8.2 presents an historical view of income distribution from 1910 to 1984. Note the shifts and lack of shifts in income distribution in this century.

Most of us seem better off than our grandparents or great-grand-

Table 8.1 Wealth Held by Top 2 Percent of Families, 1983

Type of Wealth	Percentage Held
All liquid financial assets	30
Privately held stocks	50
Tax-free bonds	71
Real estate	20
Individual checking accounts	23
Taxable bonds	39
Savings accounts	8
Money market and certificates of deposit	15

Source: Avery, Elliehausen, Canner, and Gustafson, "Survey of consumer finances, 1983," 289.

Table 8.2 Income Distribution by Fifths of the Population, 1910–1984

U.S. Population in Quintiles	1910	1918	1934	1945	1955	1968	1978	1984
Top 20 percent	46.2%	47.4%	46.7%	45.0%	45.4%	43.0%	41.5%	42.9%
2nd 20 percent	19.0	18.3	20.4	24.0	23.5	24.7	24.1	24.4
3rd 20 percent	15.0	14.9	15.5	16.0	16.7	17.4	17.5	17.0
4th 20 percent	11.5	12.6	11.5	11.0	10.5	10.8	11.6	11.0
Bottom 20 percent	8.3	6.8	5.9	4.0	3.7	3.9	5.2	4.7

Sources: Compiled from Budd, "Postwar changes in the size distribution of income in the U.S.," 247–260; Kolko, *Wealth and power in America*, 14; U.S. Bureau of the Census, *Statistical abstract of the United States: 1986*, 452.

parents at the beginning of the century or our relatives after World War II. Most of us have cars, television sets, video equipment, even indoor plumbing and other luxuries that our predecessors could never have dreamed of. Our standard of living has increased remarkably, which might lead us to believe there has been a redistribution of income. The distribution of income as shown in Table 8.2, however, points up another aspect of wealth. The pie has become larger, due to technological advances, but the shares of the pie have not changed that much, except for people at the bottom of the class structure, who are relatively poorer than at the turn of the century. Who has gained? The winners are the second 20 percent, which includes the top and some middle managers and the highest paid professionals, and the third 20 percent, who may have made gains from unionization in the skilled blue-collar primary economic sector (Lewis 1963: Chapters 6, 7).

Who has lost? A little has come from the top 20 percent, but most of the loss has come from the bottom 20 percent, who could scarcely afford it. Their small share of income has been cut almost in half since 1910. The 20 percent above them is still maintaining its slender share, 11 percent of income.

There are other ways to look at income distribution. Table 8.3 shows median family income from 1960 to 1984 for whites, blacks, and Hispanics. Chapter 3 discusses occupational distribution, structural unemployment, and educational attainment of these groups of workers and two alternative views attempting to explain the wage gaps between minorities and white males. Keep these factors in mind when looking at the family income data in Table 8.3.

Family income includes not only earnings but also other sources of income—interest, rents, transfer payments (assistance programs of various kinds, such as Aid to Families with Dependent Children, AFDC).

Table 8.3 Median Family Income, White, Black, and Hispanic, 1960–1984

Year	All Families $	White $	Black $	Hispanic $	Black as Percentage of White	Hispanic as Percentage of White
1960	$19,711	$20,465	$11,329	na	55.4%	
1965	22,903	23,871	13,145	na	55.1	
1970	26,394	27,381	16,796	na	61.3	
1975	26,476	27,536	16,943	$18,432	61.5	66.9%
1980	26,500	27,611	15,976	18,550	57.9	67.2
1981	25,569	26,858	15,151	18,731	56.4	69.7
1982	25,216	26,475	14,633	17,462	55.3	66.0
1983	25,594	26,814	15,150	17,626	56.5	65.7
1984	26,433	27,686	15,432	18,833	55.7	68.0

Source: Compiled from U.S. Bureau of the Census, *Statistical Abstract of the United States: 1986*, 450.

Family income also includes earnings of all workers that, as seen in the participation rate tables in Chapter 3, includes wives. Remember that more than 50 percent of married women have worked outside the home since 1980. For all the groups cited above, including Hispanics, note that more and more frequently the earnings of both husband and wife are necessary to maintain the standard of living. This is true not only because our expectations are high but also because real earnings (what money will buy after taxes) has fallen 6.2 percent since 1975. Real annual median family income dropped $3,152 from 1973 through 1984 (Seaberry 1985:D9,11). The bottom 20 percent of families lost 34 percent of their buying power during this period (Kantor 1986:A3; Rich 1986: Al, 8-9). In fact, according to House Majority Leader Jim Wright (D–Fort Worth), "Today, the average thirty-year-old American man earns about 12 percent less in real buying power than his father did at his stage in life" (Kantor 1986:A3).

The stability and recent decline of black median family income compared to white may come as a surprise given the rapid increase of median years of education for blacks in the last twenty-five years. Under the human capital view, we would expect to see some closing of the median income gap. Some, but not all, of the discrepancy between black and white median family income is the number of families who are female-headed. If you remember the large earnings gap between men's and women's wages, you will be aware that groups with many female-headed families are going to be lower in median family income. More than 40 percent of black families are now female-headed, as compared to 14 percent of white families. Several possible reasons for this trend should come to mind. The high labor force participation rate for black males has declined steadily since the end of World War II with the restructuring of occupations—automation, plant shutdowns—and its companion, structural unemployment. The central city, in which many black families live, has been losing blue-collar jobs at a rapid rate.

Other factors may also have a bearing on this trend. Many black males are in prison; nearly 50 percent of the inmates in federal and state prisons are black, cutting down on the number of possible mates. There are only 44 eligible, employed single black males for every 100 single black females. In addition, the structure of AFDC as administered by many states requires there be no male head-of-house, which encourages unemployed males to vacate the premises so the family will have some income. This phenomenon should not be cited as the cause of the female-head of household increase, however. During the period of mid-1970s and early 1980s, when median real AFDC payments fell by one-third, the share of female-headed families rose sharply (Hard times for black America 1986:6).

Obviously, jobs that pay a living wage for both men and women are in urgent demand for there to be more male heads-of-household and more children above the poverty level and off welfare, as families are currently structured. One economist estimates that paying women's jobs what they are worth (comparable worth) would get more than half the people off the welfare roles. For an excellent sociological analysis of the ghetto from this structural/occupational viewpoint, see William Tabb's *The Political Economy of the Black Ghetto* (1970). For an anthropological study of the black family and ghetto life, which reads like a novel and makes you feel a part of the scene, see Elliot Liebow's *Tally's Corner* (1967).

You should recognize these arguments as structural or institutional arguments, which address the demand-side—pointing out that demand has decreased for people traditionally in certain places holding certain jobs, and jobs do not necessarily pay what their marginal productivity is worth. The opposing supply-side argument returns to the human capital view presented in Chapter 3. This argument includes the lack of investment in education and training. It also includes the culture of poverty arguments that female-headed households socialize their children into short-run, fatalistic attitudes that do not suit them for the work force. However, this argument does not explain why those females are without more permanent males or without good jobs in the first place. The problem, as seen in this view, is that the workers have not invested in themselves to increase their productivity, not that the structure of the economy or other structural barriers are causing a problem.

By now these arguments should be exceedingly familiar and their applicability to various types of social problems should be apparent. *Social problems* are defined as problems that a society recognizes as problems; they do not include latent problems yet unrecognized. The next section uses these micro-human capital and macro-structural arguments again when briefly examining a related aspect of social stratification— social mobility in industrial societies.

The subject of income and wealth distribution requires a comment on poverty in the United States. In 1960, before the start of the Great Society programs and a major restructuring of the U.S. economy, 22.2 percent of all persons in the United States lived in poverty (*World Almanac* 1986:227). Even in the depths of the recession of the early 1980s, the percent in poverty was not as low as the 1960 level. However, in 1984 33.7 million persons were considered living in poverty in the United States, and some economists predict a long-term upward trend in this number. Some writers fear the formation of a two-tier society—the rich and the poor (Moberg 1986; Rast 1986; Tilly 1986; Marshall 1984; Computerized manufacturing automation 1984:153–156). Table 8.4 indicates the poverty levels for blacks and whites and female-headed households in recent years.

The reasons for this pessimistic view are many. There is a decline in the creation of middle-income jobs and a loss of better paid blue-collar jobs, as noted in Chapters 3 and 7. The percentage of U.S. households in the middle-income bracket (defined as between 75 percent and 125 percent of median household income) has slipped from 28.7 percent in 1967 to 23.2 percent in 1983 (Tilly 1986:11). This decline in the middle-income bracket has been due to both downward social mobility and upward mobility. The decline in the middle bracket might have been greater if wives had not joined the work force in large numbers. The increase in female-headed households, likely to have lower than average incomes, has added to the problem of downward social mobility, as shown in Table 8.4.

In addition to the problems created by a changing economy and attendant changes in family structure, there is a failure of political will to

Table 8.4   Black and White Poverty and Female-Head-of-Household Poverty, 1978–1984, in Percentages

Group	1978	1979	1982	1983	1984
Total U.S.	11.4%	11.7%	15.0%	15.2%	14.4%
White total	8.7	8.0	12.0	12.1	11.5
Female head	23.5	22.3	27.9	28.3	27.1
Black total	30.6	31.0	35.6	35.7	33.8
Female head	50.6	49.4	56.2	53.8	51.7

Source: *World Almanac and Book of Facts: 1987*, 227.

deal with poverty, according to some observers. University of Massachusetts economist Ben Seligman analyzed the programs of the Great Society, planned as they were by professionals and politicians at both the national and local levels. The programs did not attack the causes of poverty and did not include the poor in the planning—offering bandages rather than major surgery and political expediency rather than careful diagnosis.

Since Professor Seligman wrote, there has been a further decline in interest in antipoverty policies (Moberg 1984). This failure of political will to rethink the problems of the present system and where the system is heading make his cheerless prediction even more striking.

> In this book I suggest that getting rid of poverty is dubious in our own time. Hence I refer to poverty as a social syndrome, a condition so hardened and so fixed by our economic, political, and social circumstances that it is likely to remain with us in the calculable future. For so long as we adhere to our present values, so long as we adopt sudden make-do methods of dealing with issues such as poverty, so long as we refuse to exercise foresight, so long will the poor be with us. (Seligman 1968:unpaged preface)

SOCIAL MOBILITY IN INDUSTRIAL SOCIETIES

Social mobility usually refers to intergenerational shifts in occupations between fathers and sons (not much on mothers and daughters yet). The study of status attainment, meaning occupational status, has gone in two major directions. After World War II there was a marked increase in the number of both national and crossnational social mobility studies (see Matras 1980 for a review of these studies). Sociologists Lipset and Bendix (1959) published an early influential study concerning the importance of the level of economic development/industrialization in a society for the degree of upward social mobility. From their study of intergenerational social mobility in several industrial countries at various stages of development, they found that no matter what the political rhetoric of a country regarding openness or elitness, the degree of social mobility from manual to nonmanual jobs, in particular, seemed dependent on economic growth. The openness or closedness of the higher education system did seem to make some difference in who got into the higher professions and higher bureaucracy posts.

> Instead of supporting the assumption that value differences cause variations in mobility rates, the data support the hypothesis that mobility patterns in Western industrialized societies are determined by the occupa-

tional structure. The findings are compatible with Veblen's analysis of the ways in which consumption patterns spread down the class structure. Our hypothesis is that the desire to rise in status is intrinsic in all persons of lower status, and that individuals and groups will attempt to improve their status (and self-evaluation) whenever they have any chance to do so. (Lipset and Bendix 1959:73)

What Lipset and Bendix make clear here is that without economic development to provide occupational growth in the middle sectors, upward social mobility appears limited. What they also should have pointed out is that the desire to rise in status (aspirations) is often limited by the expectations of what is possible and by the lack of knowledge of the means of rising due to one's background. For example, I can aspire to make a million dollars but I do not expect, nor have the knowledge of the means, to get it without getting arrested. Lipset and Bendix are correct, however, in pointing out that people do aspire, and when the opportunity is there and becomes apparent, they take it. With regard to the opportunity's being there, the drawings in Figure 8.1 outline increasing opportunity available with an increasing technological and economic base.

In Figure 8.1, the division of labor in the hunting and gathering society is fairly homogeneous, except for sex and age (see Chapter 2). The social stratification system appears rather flat except for leaders who might arise from time to time to lead the hunt or religious rituals. The feudal society has a landed aristocracy at the top, a small middle of clergy, traders, artisans, functionaries for the aristocracy, and the mass are peasants at the bottom. The developing society has increased the

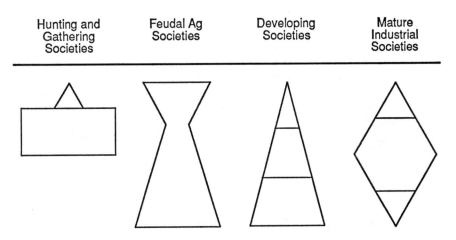

| Hunting and Gathering Societies | Feudal Ag Societies | Developing Societies | Mature Industrial Societies |

Figure 8.1 The Shape of Social Stratification in Various Economic Systems

middle jobs with more trade and more production of goods and services, although most people are still in agriculture; this breakdown resembles Kling's model of many Latin American states discussed in Chapter 6. The mature industrial society is diamond-shaped, with a fat middle. Note that industrial societies, such as Sweden, can eliminate the poverty group at the bottom of the diamond through social policy. During recessions some people in the middle will be pushed downward. During economic growth periods some people will be pulled up into the middle class.

What can we deduce from these sketches? Basically, we can surmise that the social stratification system is dependent on the number of middle-class jobs created by a society. Without job creation, there is nothing to pull people up into, no matter how much education they have. We can now appreciate Ivar Berg's commentary on the "great training robbery" and see why increased educational credentials do not mean better jobs for all people. In fact, we note in Chapter 3 that mature industrial societies seem to be producing more lower-paid, lower-skilled service or routine white-collar jobs than other kinds of jobs. Some middle-class young people with college educations may find it difficult to maintain their class position, or at least their standard of living, as they form their own families if the jobs with middle-class incomes do not exist. Even though educational advancement for the society does boost economic growth to some unknown degree, as the needs-achievement psychologically oriented theorists of development argue (McClelland 1961; Hagen 1962), the reverse really seems to be true. Economic growth puts to work people who have some education or who will obtain the necessary knowledge on-the-job.

In addition to the effects on social mobility of the amount of economic growth, crossnational and national studies focus on the importance of what we have called human capital and other life-history background characteristics of workers. These studies often couch their research question in a form such as: What are the returns for each year of education? Or, what are the effects of parents' education and occupation? Many of these studies replicate the early Blau-Duncan (1967) status attainment research. These Wisconsin school of social mobility studies have added a great deal to the understanding of these factors (Featherman and Hauser 1978, for example).

Not all studies on background effects are completely consistent, but they do seem to indicate (1) the very top and bottom strata in the United States seem more difficult to get into and out of, buffered by transition zones that are nearly impermeable; (2) the middle layers contain more flexibility for upward and downward mobility and more choices on occupation and life-style; and (3) some groups do not receive as much return on human capital investment as does the dominant group. These latter studies sometimes label their findings as "The cost of being black" (Siegal 1965) or "the cost of being Mexican American" (Poston, Alvirez, and Tienda 1976) or "the cost of being female" (Bibb and Form 1977; Blau and Jusenius 1977). Many of the studies also find that the effects of gender and ethnicity/race may be declining somewhat over time but not rapidly (Stolzenberg 1975; Featherman and Hauser 1976). Initial class placement is also cited as an ongoing problem (Wright 1978).

In case we are left with too optimistic a view on the social mobility available among the middle layers of the social stratification system in the United States, recognizing the added burden of being one of the minorities or in the lower-lower class, we have criticisms from researchers who study the education system itself and its effects on people in different strata of the social system. Their arguments on how the educational system reproduces the existing class structure should be taken seriously (Bowles and Gintis 1976; Jencks et al. 1972; Feagin and Feagin 1987). Table 8.5, based on Blau and Duncan's 1960s data but still relevant for today (Matras 1980), stresses the likelihood that blue-collar fathers are likely to produce blue-collar sons and white-collar fathers, white-collar sons. Note where farmers' sons were most likely to go occupationally. Social mobility in the past has been likely to be in small steps up or down, not in great leaps forward or backward.

This section illustrates how important the structure of the economy is to the shape of the social class structure and the ability of persons to shift up or down in it. Industrialization has enabled us to improve our standard of living and has enlarged the middle class, but it is not clear what the future of mature industrial nations will be. As Chapter 3 discusses, the majority of new jobs seem to be pulling away from manual labor, but they are not increasing earnings as expected from experience (McMahon and Tschetter 1986; Kutscher and Personick 1986). Increases in education raised expectations for better paid and more interesting

Table 8.5 Intergeneration Mobility in the United States

Father's Occupation When Son Was 16	Son's Occupation in March 1962			
	White Collar	*Blue Collar*	*Farm*	*Total*
White Collar	71.0%	27.6%	1.5%	100%
Blue Collar	36.9	61.5	1.6	100
Farm	23.2	55.2	21.6	100

Source: Parker, *The Myth of the Middle Class*, 215.

work. Instead, many people are finding themselves in fairly routine jobs at lower pay than anticipated. Entrance requirements in the form of credentials have increased, however.

Some of the new high tech and professional and managerial jobs are both stimulating and financially rewarding. Overall, however, there appear to be a small number of such jobs. Middle-income jobs have decreased slightly. Most of the people displaced from the middle seem to have ended up in the lower-income jobs; this is the job sector that has grown the most (McMahon and Tschetter 1986:25). The unanswered question is whether this is a short- or long-run trend. Is this trend an effect of the business cycle, due to the entrance of so many young workers and women into the labor force, or is it a more permanent result of more jobs in the less productive service sector? People who fear the latter talk about a slide into a bipolar class system—the high earners at the top, a few people in the middle, and the largest group at the bottom. This view raises questions about the shape of the stratification system and social mobility in such areas as the following: Are we deploying technology appropriately for the long-run good of society? Is the current system for distributing wealth and income functional for society as a whole?

We now turn to life-styles in the present and some general patterns we might expect to find today in the various strata of the class system. We observe expected patterns in the areas of types of occupation, income and wealth, education, housing, religion, family structure and roles and child-rearing practices, associations belonged to, and ideology. Keep in mind that these are only common patterns and that individuals in any stratum may vary greatly.

LIFE-STYLE AND SOCIAL CLASSES

The first thing people in an industrial society do when meeting a new person is to try to establish what that person, or her husband, or a young person's father, does for a living. Knowing the occupation establishes some idea of what that person's life chances are—the possible education, family structure, place and kind of residence, ideology and attitudes on social issues, clubs or groups belonged to, even, in a general way, the kind of religion (Kennedy 1986; Zablocki and Kanter 1978; Gans 1969). Sometimes we may be fooled on a few specifics, but the probabilities are that we will be fairly close in most guesses.

Table 8.6 is a brief summary of some kinds of life chances (what people in those social strata can expect). Some aspects associated with various strata—occupations, associations, ideology—are referred to, in part, in earlier chapters. See Zablocki and Kanter (1976) for a review of the literature on life-style up through the mid-1970s.

Occupation, Income and Wealth, and Education

Occupation, income and wealth, and education are listed first since we have seen what important roles these areas play. Indeed, some writers have referred rather scornfully to the SES ranking systems as "the money model" (Kluegel and Smith 1981:46). The upper class contains about 2 percent of the population and includes most of the people identified as the major wealth holders. The upper class is here divided into two strata to reflect the old-line wealth (acquired at least two, preferably more, generations back) and the newly rich (whose children may be partially acceptable to the old-rich, if their educational backgrounds in the right private schools and their clubs and associations and other life-style aspects are appropriate). Note the importance of the New England Episcopalian boarding schools (girls) and prep schools (boys) to the upper stratum. This is where children meet other youngsters of their station whose friendships will be important all their lives. Attending these schools also helps the elite young people firm up a similar value system, code of conduct, and class consciousness (Mills 1956:63–68).

The newly rich are frequently the top executive officers of the largest corporations and may include some of the top government and military elite, if they will go along with the appropriate life-style. Lower-uppers in the last categories quickly fall out of the blue book social registers when out of office, if they have not attended to their upper-class life-style.

The middle class is here divided into three strata that reflect certain differences. As discussed, the middle class has more upward and downward social mobility, so the transition zones between the strata are blurred. Upper-middle occupations and healthy incomes reflect the middle management positions of large corporations and the top management of smaller firms. Top professionals in their fields are here—people who are invited into policy-making associations and to sit on corporate boards of directors and whose life-styles allow them to fraternize with individuals in power positions (Dye 1983:191–217). Good educations and occupational achievement are prime necessities.

Middle-middle class persons are more numerous than those people in the strata above. They have achieved their white-collar business and professional positions through education or entrepreneurial activity. College is not likely to be Ivy League, however. Some middle-middles are upwardly mobile from blue-collar backgrounds. We meet these persons daily in their businesses around town, in the schoolroom, in the doctors' offices, and on the commuter train.

The lower-middle class contains both the better paid, skilled blue-collar and the not-so-well-paid, lower-skilled white-collar occupations. Retail sales and clerical work white-collar jobs and the unionized trades are included here. Education is less than the strata above for most members, but some college may be found. This strata together with the strata below, the upper-lower class semiskilled, blue-collar, are sometimes called the modern working class and make up approximately 46 percent of U.S. society. There may be some differences among these three occupational groups in life-style (see Table 8.6), but the higher income, suburbanization, and perhaps even the television viewing of the skilled blue-collar group members allow them to emulate the lower white-collar group, if they choose. This is not easy in the semiskilled blue-collars, but with a working wife, a lower-middle-class life-style may be available, if there is an inclination. Semiskilled blue-collar jobs include machinery operatives, including transportation, and a wide range of lower-skilled service jobs either blue- or white-collar in nature in hospitals, local government services, and restaurants.

On a technical note, we should mention that some social scientists do not place the lower white-collars in the working class; they divide the middle-class into only two sections (upper and lower) (Shepard 1984:283). The old working-class contained only manual workers and was divided from the white-collar middle class. This separation appears to overlook some distinctions and similarities between the lower-white collars and skilled blue-collars that are given in Table 8.6. Wilensky (1961) offers an alternative view of this blurring of distinctions between the lower-white-collar and upper-blue-collar groups. He feels this blurring is a result of the middle classes becoming more like the working class, "a theme echoed in analyses of the effects of bureaucratization on world view" (Zablocki and Kanter 1976:276). Occupation sets the limits on conditions of life but has "ceased to be a significant factor" in the integration of these "middle mass" strata (Zablocki and Kanter 1976:276).

The lower-lower stratum, which some social mobility researchers refer to as more difficult to get out of, is basically unskilled labor (Featherman and Hauser 1978:180). Lack of a high school diploma, lack of steady employment and employment in secondary labor market jobs, and poverty or near-poverty are apparent for many of these persons. This stratum may include 20 to 25 percent of the population, depending on the state of the economy (Shepard 1984:283).

Housing and Religion

Housing segregation is noticeable for the top three strata (upper-upper, lower-upper, upper-middle) and for the bottom lower-lower stratum. We have noted the economic effect of inner-city living. Working-class neighborhoods are an identifiable, popular subject for research. Working-class persons with more middle-class incomes can also be found in middle-class neighborhoods, when they choose that life-style.

Religion is interesting to look at by class. The English Church origins of the early East Coast settlers are predominant in the upper class and came to be the Episcopalian Church in the United States. This fact explains why the important private boarding schools have Episcopalian roots. Into the newly rich come some Catholics and Jews. The Catholic Church is exceptional for taking in the very rich and the very poor since feudal times. Protestant denominations that developed out of the Reformation period in Europe are more likely to be middle-class (see Weber 1958 for insight on this connection). People who emphasize religion in their lives in the lowest strata are more likely to belong to fundamentalist sects, which require more emotional commitment and adherence to church teachings than do the denominations. (See Demerath and Roof 1976 for a review of the research literature in religion and status attainment.)

Family Life and Health

Family life and health categories contain some interesting points. Extended-family relationships in an industrial society are found most in the top and the bottom strata, each for different money reasons (McKinley 1964:23–26; Zablocki and Kanter 1976:273). The top strata want to keep the family fortune intact, since it is more useful as a block. Here, the marriages of children are more likely to be alliances between families than in any other strata. Children are more likely to be raised somewhat isolated from immediate family members, through governesses and at boarding schools. Nonetheless, they are more likely to be subject to family control. They and other family members are presided over in a patriarchal manner by the senior male, who is still active in financial concerns. The male role is psychologically rewarding; he is a success and an authority figure in the eyes of society. Note under *Housing* in Table 8.6 that the family often is expected to gather at the summer compound. Emphases on the past and on family stories and lore are part of this life-style.

The middle strata are usually nuclear (mother, father, children) and geographically as well as socially mobile. Both of these aspects may contribute to less emphasis on kinship. Families are likely to be democratic-participatory, with all members participating in discussion and decision-making on family matters. Even though the father role is respected in varying degrees, the mother may be contributing to family income as well as decisions. In many cases of fathers who are busy in occupational pursuits, the family may be mother-centered; she keeps

Table 8.6 Life-Style by Social Classes in the United States

Class (and Percentage of Total Population)	Occupation and Income	Education (Reasons for Obtaining)	Housing and Location	Religion	Health and Family	Clubs and Assns.	Ideology and Reference Groups
UPPER-UPPER (UU + LU = 2%)	Old-line wealth; Top corp. execs.; Professionals in family investments (e.g., banking, law politics)	Private Epis. boarding prep schools in New England; Ivy League & other top universities	Clustered in own communities; family summer compounds; Park Ave. apts.	Episcopal; Unitarian; some Presbyterian	Some extended family–patriarchal	Private clubs (e.g. Links, Chicago, Bohemian Grove); policy-making assns. (e.g., CED, FPA, CFR, Brookings, American Assembly)	Liberal policy assns. & most foundations; also conservative Nat'l Assn. of Manufacturers & National Chamber of Commerce & new groups (e.g., Heritage Foundation)
LOWER-UPPER	New wealth; Top mgt., large corps, top govt, & military elite	Some private prep, some public; Ivy League, military & large univs. in home state;	L-U suburbs	Same as above, with some Catholic & some Jews	Nuclear, father controlled	Private clubs; Policy assns.	Small split as above
UPPER-MIDDLE (10%)	Middle mgt., big corps.; Top mgt, small corps.; Professions (e.g. corp. lawyers, some top college profs., scientists, physicians)	Good college (ed. prized); best suburban public or private schools	Suburbia or urban apts.	Protestant denominations; Jews; some Catholics	Nuclear, democratic-participatory	Professional assns.; Some private clubs & policy assns.	Liberal intellectual professional group; NAM conservatives in some smaller corps (depending on ref. group in upper-class & on occupation)

	Occupation	Education	Residence	Religion	Family	Associations	Values / Politics
MIDDLE-MIDDLE (22%)	Middle mgt.; Professionals & teachers; ministers; social workers	College or some college (ed. important for job & social mobility)	Suburbia & small town	Protestant denominations; Jews; some Catholics	Nuclear, mother-centered, dem.-participatory, egalitarian; geographic mobility; Health insurance	Chamber of Commerce; Voluntary assns, (e.g. Eagles, Rotary, Lions, Masons)	Conservative (U-C NAM & C of C as interpreted by local CofC); No real political orgs.; basically apolitical
LOWER-MIDDLE*	Lower white collar, sales; skilled blue-collar	High school; some college (vocational)	City fringe; small town	Protestant denominations, esp. Lutheran, Baptist, (church attendance high)	Nuclear, may be embedded in local family group Like M-M participatory, possibly more strict	Voluntary assns (e.g. Eagles, Moose, Odd Fellows, Masons, KofC); Some unions	Ref. group M-M (conservative to apolitical); some union influence
UPPER-LOWER*	Semiskilled blue collar mfg. & service	High school	Inner city; rural	Baptist, some Methodists; Catholics; Lutheran sects	Nuclear, may be embedded in kin group—authoritarian but not patriarchal, mother influential in socializing—youth peer group provides some role models; Medicaid in city; some union insurance	Few clubs or assns.; Some unions	May be liberal on some economic issues, conservative on social issues; some union influence; lower-middle-class reference group
LOWER-LOWER (20%)	Unskilled farm & nonfarm labor	Grade school	Inner city ghetto; Rural, esp. South & border states	Some Baptists; Fundamentalist sects	Nuclear authoritarian or female-head—may be in kinship network; Role compensation; Mental illness, esp. psychoses; higher in single men; Poor health care; Medicaid in city	Little interaction with voluntary assns. or politics; occasional urban org. run by M-C in name of poor	Liberal on economic & mixed on social issues depending on ethnic, regional subculture; Low expectations—may be fatalistic & defeatist in attitudes

• (LM + UL = 46%, often called the *modern working class*)

the social calendars and car pools running. With mothers now often pursuing careers, instead of just jobs, some shifts in family roles and responsibilities are often necessary.

White-collar middle-class child-rearing patterns are affected by occupation. In a ten-year study Melvin Kohn (1969; Bowles, Gintis, Meyer 1975) found that people tend to socialize their children into values and qualities they, as workers, have found useful. The most important variable is the amount of autonomy in their jobs (*autonomy* is an important word in Chapter 11). Middle-class parents emphasize curiosity, self-control, consideration, and happiness, and they foster communication and decision-making skills—all of which they will need in their middle-class work. Parents tend to punish children more for the intent of their transgressions than for the actual consequences of the acts. Obviously other useful pieces of knowledge regarding middle-class occupations and norms are also passed along.

Blue-collar working-class families tend to be more strict and may even be authoritarian, although they are not likely to be patriarchal at the same time, since the father may have less status as a role model than fathers in higher classes have. These blue-collar families have found, according to Kohn, that obedience, neatness, and honesty have been useful on the job. Hence, they emphasize these traits in socializing their children. Punishment is likely to be more harsh than in middle-class families and may be based more on the seriousness of the consequences of the acts than on the intent of the perpetrator. There is less discussion, give-and-take, and problem solving. Sociologist Mirra Komarovsky (1969:276–284) has written widely on the lack of communication in many blue-collar marriages. Kinship networks may be retained, because there is less mobility involved in many of these families. These relationships can help compensate for the failure to communicate within a marriage. A kinship network can also help as a reciprocity survival net in case of hard times. Upwardly mobile persons from this stratum may have to cut themselves off from this kinship network, both for status reasons as they try to become accepted in a higher stratum and for economic reasons as demands may be made on the successful cousin, for example. For many such people, being upwardly mobile may involve some psychological pain.

In the working class and in the lowest stratum, gender roles are more distinct than in middle class, and ethnicity may be emphasized by some members. These latter two ascribed categories (sex and ethnicity) lead to the subject of role-compensation.

In an achievement-oriented society those individuals who fail in the occupationally determined class system will turn to other roles for "achievement." This achievement will be sought not only in illegal achieved economic roles (e.g., crime, the syndicate), but also in the more ascribed roles regarding sex, the peer group, the "in-group," and the family. We will call this response "role compensation." (McKinley 1964:52–53).

Exaggerations of masculinity, patriotism, ethnicity, and other ascribed roles could be partly explained in this manner. Sociologist Robert Merton (1968:215–248) used a similar concept in his discussion of anomie and deviant behavior. Some persons who aspire to achieving but find their means blocked find substitute means and new definitions of achievement. For many examples of this description, think of the television character Archie Bunker, whose character fits the stereotype of the authoritarian personality, overcompensating with his ascribed roles for his marginal status position in society. This idea of marginality and role compensation should not be taken to mean that all working-class persons fit the Archie Bunker stereotype, nor do they mean that racists and bigots cannot be found in other classes (Sexton and Sexton 1971: 249–259). The struggle to maintain personal dignity in the face of such odds is, however, one of the hidden injuries of social class (Sennett and Cobb 1972).

Health care for the lowest stratum, in particular, becomes problematic. The mental strains and anxieties are particularly harsh, the compensations fewer. Medical care may be difficult to obtain. The prevalence of psychoses among lower-lower singles, particularly men but including bag ladies, has been dramatized in recent years in the homeless shelter movement.

Some writers indicate that they think family disorganization and pathology in the bottom stratum are overstated, with their emphasis on the number and pathology of female-headed households, for example. Sometimes stated bluntly (Billingsley 1973:431–439), these writers find this analysis more the product of middle-class white biases than of the reality of what they feel is more often a warm, supportive kinship network (Willie 1981). While the research and debate continues, according to the women themselves the situation is a difficult one that deserves immediate attention (Stallard, Ehrenreich, and Sklar 1983:27–36; Sheehan 1976).

One point to make before ending the discussion of family life and child socialization practices is that television seems to be working as a leveling device among middle- and working-class groups. Televised advice from the experts in intimate relationships fields and the life-styles portrayed in video fiction are undoubtedly affecting and, perhaps in some ways, homogenizing subcultures in society (Bronfenbrenner 1961; Erlanger 1974).

In sum, we see how really pervasive class and occupation are when the structures of our family relationships are so affected. Family roles and socialization practices are shaped by many factors, of which stratification seems to be one of the most powerful.

Associations and Ideology

Chapter 5 discusses some of these ideas with regard to the upper groups, in particular. We note a split in the ideology of the groups at the top of the stratification system and the entrance of new money to support the conservative views. Persons involved with small businesses, influenced in part by the Chamber of Commerce, also frequently tend to hold these more conservative views. Some of these views are carried over into other voluntary associations joined by people in the middle- and lower-middle strata. The intellectual part of the upper-middle class has traditionally identified more with the old-line liberal philanthropic view of social policy.

Notice that strata frequently look to the group just above them as a reference group on social policy, although occupation and organizational affiliations, such as clubs and unions, also have some impact. As we discuss in Chapter 7, however, unions often have trouble keeping their membership in line on policy.

The fatalism and low expectations, although not necessarily low aspirations, in the bottom stratum remind one of the culture of poverty view. This, however, should not blind one to the structural and institutional factors that have set the conditions and the barriers for the life-style of this segment of the population. We might remember with Merton that people who lack means are often rather creative in substituting (Merton 1968:230–235).

SUMMARY

Most societies, particularly from the advanced horticultural societies on, have some kind of social stratification—social ranking—system. In discussing social stratification, this chapter touches on these points:

1. Two opposing views on why social stratification exists and a synthesis:
   a. The structural-functional view sees a ranking system and unequal reward structure as necessary to encourage people to train for and perform important positions in society. This argument is related to the order/consensus view of the world.
   b. The conflict view argues that some people in society gain power and use it to garner more of the rewards society prizes and to keep other people from sharing and from developing

their talents; inequality thus is dysfunctional for society. This argument is based on the power/conflict view of society.

c. Lenski's synthesis points out that in societies when subsistence goods are scarce reciprocity occurs and people share for the good of the whole group, but when there is a surplus of goods these goods will be distributed by power.

2. In industrial societies the positions in the social stratification system are ranked according to evaluations on three broad categories:

   a. Economic class: income and wealth.

   b. Status or prestige: including occupational status, family heritage, religion (sometimes), and educational attainment.

   c. Power: from occupational position and interest group organizational affiliation.

3. Wealth and income distribution in the United States is quite unequal, and the relative shares of income to the various sectors (quintiles are used here) of the population have not changed much in this century, except that the poor are relatively poorer. The top 2 percent of the population controls much of the nation's productive wealth. Median family income for black families has not changed much as a percent of median white family income in the post–World War II period, declining from a high of 61.5 percent in 1975 to its previous 1960 level of 55 percent again in 1984. Hispanic median family is somewhat higher, varying from 65 to 69 percent of median white family income. Explanations for these income levels have been presented from both the human capital arguments (not enough education, incorrect attitudes, for example) and the institutional structure arguments (such as changes in occupational structure, technology). The number of female-headed households is increasing in the poverty-level stratum of the population.

4. Social mobility in society, studied both nationally and cross-culturally, seems to depend in large part on economic growth to generate middle-class jobs to pull people up into. The ideology of openness or elitness in a society does not seem to matter as much as the economy, although an open higher education system is useful in helping lower groups gain professional jobs. Studies also indicate that there are apparently barriers in getting into and out of the top and bottom strata of society. The middle strata are much more flexible. Still, there is some tendency for children to remain at the same socioeconomic status as their parents. Social mobility is usually incremental. There is some question about the future shape of mature industrial societies and the amount and direction of social mobility. In the short-run it appears that

these societies may be generating more new lower-paying jobs than middle- or higher-paying ones. Whether this trend is long-run and what can be done about it are the uncertainties.

5. Life-style by class has certain predictabilities, although some people do occasionally choose alternative life-styles. Except for the wealthy and the impoverished, most of us are placed in our stratum of the socioeconomic class structure by occupation, assisted by the educational level attained. Housing, religion, health, associations joined, ideology, and even family organization and child socialization are affected by class position, as summarized in Table 8.6. Role compensation in some of the lower groups that have not attained occupational and income levels seen as acceptable in society may account for certain traits found more frequently in those groups—including exaggerated gender role divisions, emphasis on ethnicity and subculture group norms, and deviance from dominant social norms in various ways.

BIBLIOGRAPHY

Anderson, Charles H. 1974. *The political economy of social class.* Englewood Cliffs, N.J.: Prentice-Hall.

Avery, Robert B., Gregory E. Elliehausen, Glenn B. Canner, and Thomas A. Gustafson. 1984. Survey of consumer finances, 1983. *Federal Reserve Bulletin* 70, 9:679–692 (September).

Bell, Colin, and Howard Newby. 1972. *Community studies: An introduction to the sociology of the local community.* New York: Praeger.

Bendix, Reinhard, and Seymour Martin Lipset, eds. 1966a. *Class, status, and power: Social stratification in comparative perspective,* 2nd ed. New York: Free Press.

Bendix, Reinhard, and Seymour Martin Lipset, eds. 1966a. Karl Marx's theory of social classes. In *Class, status, and power: Social stratification in comparative perspective,* 2nd ed., edited by Reinhard Bendix and Seymour Martin Lipset, 6–11. New York: Free Press.

Bibb, Robert, and William H. Form. 1977. The effects of industrial, occupational, and sex stratification on wages in blue-collar markets. *Social Forces* 55, 4:974–996 (June).

Billingsley, Andrew. 1973. "Black families and white social science." *The death of white sociology,* edited by Joyce A. Ladner, 431–450. New York: Random House (Vintage).

Blau, Francine D., and Carol L. Jusenius. 1977. "Sex segregation in the labor market." In *Woman in a man-made world: A socioeconomic handbook,* 2nd ed., edited by Nona Glazer and Helen Youngelson Waehrer, 194–207. Boston: Houghton Mifflin.

Blau, Peter M., and Otis D. Duncan. 1967. *The American occupational structure.* New York: Wiley.

Bowles, Samuel, and Herbert Gintis. 1976. *Schooling in capitalist America.* New York: Basic Books.

Bowles, Samuel, Herbert Gintis, and Peter Meyer. 1975. The long shadow of work: Education, the family, and the reproduction of the social division of labor. *Insurgent Sociologist* 5, 4:3–22 (Summer).

Bronfenbrenner, Urie. 1961. The changing American child—A speculative analysis. *Merrill-Palmer Quarterly* 7, 2:73–84 (April).

Budd, Edward C. 1970. Postwar changes in the size distribution of income in the U.S. *American Economic Review* 60, 2:247–260 (May).

Clark, T. N. 1975. Community power. *Annual Review of Sociology* 1:271–295.

Cockburn, Alexander. 1987. How rich are the rich? *In These Times* 11, 8:17 (January 14–20).

Computerized manufacturing automation: Employment, education, and the workplace. 1984. Washington, D.C.: U.S. Congress, Office of Technology Assessment. (April).

Davis, Kingsley. 1966. "Reply to Tumin." In *Class, status, and power: Social stratification in comparative perspective* 2nd ed., edited by Reinhard Bendix and Seymour Martin Lipset, 59–62. New York: Free Press.

Davis, Kingsley, and Wilbert E. Moore. 1966. "Some principles of stratification." In *Class, status, and power: Social stratification in comparative perspective,* 2nd ed., edited by Reinhard Bendix and Seymour Martin Lipset, 47–53. New York: Free Press.

Demerath, N. J. III, and W. C. Roof. 1976. Religion—recent strands in research. *Annual Review of Sociology* 2:19–33.

Dye, Thomas R. 1983. *Who's running America?: The Reagan years,* 3rd ed. Englewood Cliffs, N.J.: Prentice-Hall.

Eisenstadt, S. N. 1971. *Social differentiation and stratification.* Glenview, Ill.: Scott, Foresman.

Erlanger, Howard S. 1974. Social class and corporal punishment in childrearing: A reassessment. *American Sociological Review* 39, 1:68–85 (February).

Feagin, Joe R., and Clairece B. Feagin. 1986. *Discrimination American style: Institutional sexism and racism,* 2nd augmented edition. Englewood Cliffs, N.J.: Prentice-Hall.

Featherman, David L., and Robert M. Hauser. 1976. Changes in the socioeconomic stratification of the races, 1962–73. *American Journal of Sociology* 82, 3:621–651 (November).

Featherman, David L., and Robert M. Hauser. 1978. *Opportunity and change.* New York: Academic Press.

Gans, Herbert J. 1969. "Class subcultures in American society." In *Structured social inequality,* edited by Ceclia S. Heller, 270–276. New York: Macmillan.

Grandjean, Burke D. 1975. An economic analysis of the Davis-Moore theory of stratification. *Social Forces* 53, 4:543–552 (June).

Hagen, Everett E. 1962. *On the theory of social change: How economic growth begins.* Homewood, Ill.: Dorsey Press.

Hard times for black America. 1986. *Dollars and Sense.* 115:5–7 (April).

Haug, Marie R. 1977. Measurement in social stratification. *Annual Review of Sociology.* 3:51–77.

Hauser, Robert M., and David L. Featherman. 1977. *The process of stratification: Trends and analyses.* New York: Academic Press.

Heller, Ceclia S., ed. 1969. *Structured social inequality: A reader in comparative social stratification.* New York: Macmillan.

Hodges, Harold M., Jr. 1968. *Social stratification: Class in America.* Cambridge, Mass.: Schenkman.

Jencks, Christopher, M. Smith, H. Acland, M. J. Bane, D. Cohen, H. Gintis, B. Heyns, and S. Michelson. 1972. *Inequality: A reassessment of the effect of family and schooling in America.* New York: Basic Books.

Kantor, Seth. 1986. House leader cites drop in standard of living. *Austin (TX) American-Statesman* A3 (February 3).

Kennedy, Robert E., Jr. 1986. *Life choices: Applying sociology.* New York: Holt, Rinehart and Winston.

Kluegel, James R., and Eliot R. Smith. 1981. Beliefs about stratification. *Annual Review of Sociology.* 7:29–56.

Kohn, Melvin L. 1969. *Class and conformity: A study of values.* Homewood, Ill.: Dorsey Press.

———. 1971. "Social class and parent-child relationships." In *Sociology of the family,* edited by M. Anderson, 323–338. Baltimore: Penguin.

Kolko, Gabriel. 1962. *Wealth and power in America: An analysis of social class and income distribution.* New York: Praeger.

Komarovsky, Mirra. 1969. "Blue collar marriage." In *Structured social inequality: A reader in comparative social stratification,* edited by Celia S. Heller, 276–284. New York: Macmillan.

Kutscher, Ronald E., and Valerie A. Personick. 1986. Deindustrialization and the shift to services. *Monthly Labor Review* 109, 6:3–13 (June).

Lenski, Gerhard E. 1966. *Power and privilege.* New York: McGraw-Hill.

Lewis, H. Gregg. 1963. *Unionism and relative wages in the U.S.: An empirical study.* Chicago: University of Chicago Press.

Liebow, Elliot. 1967. *Tally's corner.* Boston: Little, Brown.

Lipset, Seymour Martin, and Reinhard Bendix. 1959. *Social mobility in industrial society.* Berkeley: University of California Press.

Lopreato, Joseph, and Lionel S. Lewis. 1974. *Social stratification: A reader.* New York: Harper & Row.

Marshall, Ray. 1984. High tech and the job crunch. *The Texas Observer* 76, 7:1, 7–11 (April 6).

Marx, Karl, and Frederick Engels. 1968. *Karl Marx and Frederick Engels: Selected works, in one volume.* New York: International Publishers.

Matras, Judah, 1980. Comparative social mobility. *Annual Review of Sociology* 6:401–431.

McClelland, David C. 1961. *The achieving society.* New York: Van Nostrand.

McKinley, Donald Gilbert. 1964. *Social class and family life.* New York: Free Press.

McMahon, Patrick J., and John H. Tschetter. 1986. The declining middle class: A further analysis. *Monthly Labor Review* 109, 9:22–27 (September).

Merton, Robert K. 1968. *Social theory and social structure.* 1968 enlarged ed. New York: Free Press.

Mills, C. Wright. 1956. *The power elite.* New York: Oxford.

Moberg, David. 1984. The poor still getting poorer. *In These Times* 8, 32:6–7 (August 22–September 4).

————. 1986. Middle class may be losing the economic war of attrition. *In These Times* 11, 2:9 (November 12–18).

Parker, Richard. 1972. *The myth of the middle class: Notes on affluence and equality.* New York: Harper & Row (Colophon).

Poston, Dudley L., Jr., David Alvirez, and Marya Tienda. 1976. Earnings differences between Anglo and Mexican American male workers in 1960 and 1970: Changes in the 'cost' of being Mexican American. *Social Science Quarterly* 57, 3:618–631 (December).

Rast, Bob. 1986. Middle class bind adds population to ranks of poor. *Dallas Times Herald* A4–5 (November 23).

Rich, Spencer. 1986. Average family's income up little over 11 years. *Washington Post*, 109th year, no. 263: A1, 8-9 (August 25).

Ryan, William. 1971. *Blaming the victim.* New York: Random House (Vintage).

Seaberry, Jane. 1985. Typical family's income has fallen. *Washington Post*, 108th year, no. 359: D 9,11.

Seligman, Ben B. 1968. *Permanent poverty: An American syndrome.* Chicago: Quadrangle Books.

Sennett, Richard, and Jonathan Cobb. 1972. *The hidden injuries of class.* New York: Random House (Vintage).

Sexton, Patricia Cayo, and Brendan Sexton. 1971. *Blue collars and hard-hats: The working class and the future of American politics.* New York: Random House (Vintage).

Sheehan, Susan. 1976. *A welfare mother.* New York: New American Library.

Shepard, Jon M. 1984. *Sociology,* 2nd ed. New York: West.

Siegal, Paul M. 1965. On the cost of being a Negro. *Sociological Inquiry* 35:41–57 (Winter).

Stallard, Karin, Barbara Ehrenreich, and Holly Sklar. 1983. *Poverty in the American dream: Women and children first.* New York and Boston: Institute for New Communications and South End Press.

Stolzenberg, Ross M. 1975. Education, occupation, and wage differences between white and black men. *American Journal of Sociology* 81, 2:299–323 (September).

Tabb, William K. 1970. *The political economy of the black ghetto.* New York: W. W. Norton.

Tilly, Chris. 1986. U-turn on equality: The puzzle of middle class decline. *Dollars and Sense* 116:11–13 (May).

Tumin, Melvin M. 1966. "Some principles of stratification: A critical analysis." In *Class, status, and power: Social stratification in comparative perspective,* 2nd ed., edited by Reinhard Bendix and Seymour Martin Lipset, 53–58, 62–63. New York: Free Press.

U.S. Bureau of the Census. 1985. *Statistical abstract of the United States: 1986.* Washington, D.C.: GPO.

Vidich, Arthur J., and Joseph Bensman. 1968. *Small town in mass society: Class, power and religion in a rural community,* rev. ed. Princeton, N.J.: Princeton University Press.

Weber, Max. 1946. "Class, status, and party." In *From Max Weber: Essays in sociology,* edited and translated by Hans H. Gerth and C. Wright Mills, 180–195. New York: Oxford (Galaxy).

———. 1958. *The Protestant ethic and the spirit of capitalism.* Translated by Talcott Parsons. New York: Charles Scribner's Sons.

Wilensky, Harold L. 1961. Orderly careers and social participation: The impact of work history on social integration in the middle mass. *American Sociological Review* 26, 4:521–539 (August).

Willie, Charles Vert. 1981. *A new look at black families,* 2nd ed. Bayside, N. Y.: General Hall.

The world almanac and book of facts: 1987. 1986. New York: World Almanac.

Wright, Erik Olin. 1978. Race, class, and income inequality. *American Journal of Sociology* 83, 6:1368–1397 (May).

Zablocki, Benjamin D., and Rosabeth Moss Kanter. 1976. The differentiation of life-styles. *Annual Review of Sociology* 2:269–298.

9

Work, Stress, and Health

We have seen that for most of us the work we do affects all aspects of our lives. The work our parents did and the work we do are the major determinants of our social class position and these, in turn, determine our life chances—including health. We have also seen that not all categories of people in U.S. society have the same types of jobs; we would thus expect health might differ in some respects among various groups—ethnic, gender, and class categories in particular. These differences are discussed briefly in this chapter.

Health includes both physical and mental health, and they are intimately connected. Work produces effects on both aspects of health. The most obvious physical health aspect of work is physical injury or death on the job. Less obvious is occupational disease. Even less apparent is the effect our work has on our mental health—and its impact, in turn, on our physical well-being.

This chapter examines these areas closely: (1) the relationship of longevity and work, (2) work-related stress, (3) what some companies or workers are doing to cope with stress, (4) physical injury and death on the job, and (5) occupational disease. After a brief report from Silicon Valley, the text discusses the Occupational Safety and Health Administration and its problems and then two successful examples of work environment programs from Sweden and Saskatchewan. Finally, a program for action in the United States to improve health in the workplace is suggested.

Before looking more closely at health and work in the United States, we ask if the United States is the healthiest, best cared for nation in the industrial world. A comparison on a few health indicators with other industrial countries is very interesting.

HEALTH INDICATORS IN SEVERAL COUNTRIES AND DISTRIBUTION OF DISEASE BY SOCIAL CATEGORIES IN THE UNITED STATES

International Comparisons

What is the state of our general health in the United States? As a nation we spend almost 10 percent of our gross national product on various forms of health care. That amounted to $425.0 billion in 1985 (*World Almanac* 1986:778). We should be well cared for.

The first thing we notice about two of the basic indicators of health—life expectancy and infant mortality—is that they differ by what category a citizen is born into. Life expectancy for people born in 1984 in the United States (*World Almanac* 1986:774):

Overall	74.7 years
White male	71.8
White female	78.8
Black male	67.3
Black female	75.2

Infant mortality per 1,000 live births in 1981 (*World Almanac* 1985: 782):

Overall	11.9 percent
White male	11.7
White female	9.2
Black male	21.7
Black female	18.3

How does the United States compare to other countries of the world on such health indicators as life expectancy, infant mortality, number of hospital beds, and suicide rate? Keeping in mind that we are the only industrial nation without a nationally funded health-care system, observe the statistics in Table 9.1. Note that the U.S. infant mortality rate has declined slightly from the 1981 figure of 11.9 cited above to 10.6 in 1984.

Obviously, the United States is not necessarily the healthiest industrial nation judging from the indicators in Table 9.1. A recent study comparing the United States with other nations on dozens of categories reveals the U.S. position in the following areas (Wallechinsky 1986:5):

- 13th in preventing infant deaths
- 15th in preventing maternal death during childbirth

Table 9.1   Life Expectancy, Infant Mortality, Hospital Beds per 100,000 People, and Suicide Rate in Several Countries, Latest Year Available

Country	Life expectancy M	Life expectancy F	Infant Mortality (per 1,000 Births)	Hospital Beds (per 100,000)	Suicide Rate (per 100,000)
United States	71.4	78.7	10.6 (1984)	550	11.8
Austrialia	70.0	76.0	9.9	1,244	10.9
Austria	69.3	76.4	16.0	1,106	27.3
Canada	69.0	76.0	15.0	875	14.8
Czech.	67.0	74.0	16.8	776	19.8
Denmark	71.3	77.4	7.9	853	30.0
France	70.2	78.5	8.9	814	19.6
German D.R.	68.8	74.7	13.1	1,029	na
Germany, F.R.	67.2	73.4	13.5	1,152	21.3
Italy	70.0	76.1	12.3	1,036	7.0
Japan	73.0	78.0	6.2	1,084	17.1
Netherlands	72.0	78.0	6.0	482	10.7
Norway	72.5	79.7	7.5	1,626	14.0
Poland	66.0	74.4	20.2	651	na
Sweden	73.4	79.4	6.8	1,496	17.5
Switzerland	73.4	79.4	9.0	1,141	23.5
USSR	64.0	74.0	27.9	1,248	na
United Kingdom	70.2	76.2	13.3	894	8.9
Yugoslavia	68.0	73.0	32.8	593	15.7

Sources: U.S. Bureau of the Census, *Statistical Abstract of the United States: 1986, 841; World Almanac and Books of Facts: 1986, 535–621; U.N. Demographic Yearbook: 1983, 450–468.*

- 25th in avoiding low birthweight in babies
- 9th in female life expectancy
- 19th in average male life expectancy
- 10th in health expenses per capita
- 21st in physicians per capita
- 31st in hospital beds per capita
- 1st in dentists per capita
  nutritionally, 4th in fat consumption per capita, 11th in protein consumption, 15th in calcium, 24th in vitamin A, 49th in iron, and 59th in vitamin C consumption.

The situation of people in less industrial societies is even more grim. Taking the world view of health, a past director general of the

World Health Organization (WHO) comments on health care in industrial and less industrial nations:

> The general picture in the world is of an incredibly expensive health industry catering not for the promotion of health, but for the unlimited application of disease technology to a certain ungenerous [small] proportion of potential beneficiaries, and perhaps, not doing that too well either. (quoted in Elling 1980:5)

People who work in *epidemiology* (the study of what groups in society get what diseases and why) have been uncovering interesting data and asking interesting questions. Some findings seem to support the previous quotation as accurate for the U.S. population; we are not paying enough attention to real causes of ill health. In their readable chapter on work and health, the HEW report (U.S. Department of Health, Education and Welfare 1973:76–92) made it clear that health and medical care are not synonymous.

Because much data seem to point to the importance of social variables, a new term is now being used. *Social epidemiology* focuses on the importance of social processes and the incidence of disease, which a medical model of illness ignored in the past as it concentrated on virology and biology (viruses and infections) alone. This broader social approach considers gender, social classes (both income and educational differences), and age, while also looking at possible genetic and personality differences for people in the various categories. Let us now discuss some findings on health among these segments of the population.

Gender Differences

Recent data indicate that some difference between the sexes is lessening in the United States as women increasingly practice habits once basically for men—smoking (heart disease, lung cancer and emphysema, probably accounting for about one-third of the difference between men and women in longevity), drinking (cirrhosis of the liver, traffic fatalities, other accidents, suicide), and working outside the home (arteriosclerotic heart disease and more exposure to accidents in the workplace or on the road) (Waldron 1986). The aggressive, competitive, and rebellious behavior long encouraged in males is now becoming more culturally acceptable for females, with some accompanying physical side effects for women (Waldron 1986:43).

A study of the incidence of coronary disease among working women and housewives found that working or having a family to care for in themselves were not related to higher incidence of coronary disease. What made the difference in the incidence of the disease were (1) the type of job held, and (2) the number of children (Haynes and Feinleib 1980). Researchers need to know more about women's lives (e.g., the effects of various domestic arrangements) in order to understand variations in health patterns.

Waldron (1986:44) ends on a positive note, however. In changing some aspects of their life-styles and reaping the negative effects on their health, women have underlined factors which have shortened men's lives. These factors include smoking, drinking, and work-related stress. Perhaps men, says Waldron, will seek to change behavior patterns and the social conditions that help to cause those behaviors. This hypothesis is based on the power/conflict perspective that when a social situation negatively affects people who have the power to influence social institutions, they will change those institutions. Critics from the power/conflict view of society have noted, for example, that as long as society held the idea that "drink is the curse of the working class" we had little concern. Now that alcoholism and other mind-altering drugs are seen as middle-class problems, we are quite concerned.

SES and Black/White Differentials

Health problems related to lower socioeconomic status (SES) and racial discrimination do not appear likely to be tackled with as much energy in the future as will the problems that gender comparisons bring to the fore, if power/conflict theorists are correct in their analysis of whose needs are met in society. Although lower SES people could conceivably be helped by attention to smoking, alcoholism and other drug abuse, and work stress, the underlying causes of poverty and racism are less likely to rank high on the agenda of the more powerful (if the power/conflict view is correct) because the powerful are less personally involved. Poverty leads to a number of factors involved in poor mental and physical health. Poorer and crowded housing, poorer nutrition, less adequate medical care, and psychological stress have all been cited as contributing to poor health (Syme and Berkman 1986; Reed 1986). Even though living in toxic and hazardous physical environments and not having adequate health care are obviously important health factors, people who study mortality (death) and morbidity (illness) in the social classes are beginning to emphasize the stress caused by the social and psychological environment as a major element in health problems (Syme and Berkman 1986).

A little stress is the spice of life, according to Hans Selye (1974), who is called the father of stress studies. Prolonged stress, however, can kill some people. We do not have a complete understanding of how undue stress translates into illness (see discussion below on biology and the immune system). We do know, however, that whites and blacks in lower SES groups have higher rates of hypertension (chronic high blood pressure) and diseases related to it than do people in the higher SES groups. We also know that even the normal blood pressures are higher for the lower SES groups (Syme and Berkman 1986:29). Hypertension is also inversely related to education. People who go to college, both blacks and whites, generally have lower instances of the disease than do people completing less than ten years of school (Schnall and Kern 1986:81).

Other points have been brought out about race and possible effects of the social and psychological environments on health. Blacks have more hypertension and higher rates of infant mortality than do whites in their same SES and educational categories; middle-class blacks also have higher infant mortality than do the lowest SES whites (Reed 1986:274). In addition, blacks with some college education have higher infant mortality rates than do whites with no more than an eighth-grade education—and this higher rate is definitely not all due to sickle cell anemia (which is more prevalent in blacks and other peoples with ancestry from malarial zones). The reasons for this higher rate are not yet clear. Education and higher income seem to help control hypertension to some degree for blacks, but they do not seem to affect infant mortality as much.

Cross-cultural data are particularly interesting for blacks in the United States. Their higher incidence of hypertension than whites, after age twenty-four for men and twenty-five for women, is apparently not genetic. Blacks living in tribal conditions in Africa do not display this tendency, although presumably the genetic background is the same (Schnall and Kern 1986:82). In his studies of blacks in Detroit, Harburg (1973) found internalized anger to be associated with increased incidence of hypertension. Schnall and Kern (1986:82–83) hypothesize that somewhere in their midtwenties blacks are "forced to recognize the reality of their social situation," leading to increasingly higher rates of hypertension.

Age Differences

Studies examining hypertension among different age groups have also found some interesting relationships. In the United States hypertension increases with age. However, cross-cultural comparisons indicate that this is not the case in other countries—particularly in nonindustrial groups (Schnall and Kern 1986:83–84). Researchers suggest that (1) stress is cumulative over one's lifetime and that industrial societies may present stresses not found in nonindustrial societies; and (2) that in our society aging itself is looked on negatively, and for many people this itself may be a stress factor (Schnall and Kern 1986:83–84). We noted the increase in hypertension rates for black men and women after the mid-twenties. This is true for all women. Their rate of hypertension begins to rise in the midtwenties, although men as a group have higher rates than women until age forty-five. Thereafter, women have more hypertension than do men (Schnall and Kern 1986:83). Again, this is likely to have social causes, such as role changes, which need further study to clarify. The association of coronary and other diseases with men's retirement is clearly sociopsychological and related to role change.

Researchers are beginning to find out that the immune system, which protects us from many kinds of ailments, is affected negatively by our mental condition—the kinds of depression and fatalism found so frequently in lower SES groups and sometimes in higher SES minorities. We discuss the immune system in more detail later in this chapter.

If we concede that mental state is important to physical health, then how is the mental state of the country? In the largest mental health survey conducted in the United States (20,000 persons in five communities around the country), the National Institute of Mental Health found some disturbing data (Seligmann and Hager 1984). Using the American Psychiatric Association's 1980 revision of its *Diagnostic and Statistical Manual of Mental Disorders* (DSM–III), the Institute found nearly 20 percent of American adults suffer some kind of psychiatric disorder, from disabling anxiety to schizophrenia. The rates were about the same for men and women, but the types of illness varied statistically and women were twice as likely to seek help. Depression and anxiety were more common in women; substance abuse and antisocial-personality disorders were more common in men (Seligmann and Hager 1984). The researchers are examining the data for clues on what contributes to these problems.

How does work fit into this health picture? For people who have jobs, the questions are related to hazardous physical conditions of work and to work-related stress. For people in the lower SES groups and for some retirees and the unemployed, health questions focus on stress from lack of work, or good work, or steady work.

LONGEVITY: JOB SATISFACTION, STRESS, DEPRESSION, AND THE IMMUNE SYSTEM

For some years we have known that one of the best predictors of longevity is "work satisfaction." Other good predictors are "perception of health"and "overall happiness" (U.S. Department of Health, Education and Welfare 1973:77–81; Palmore 1969, 1982). Heart disease, which kills nearly half of all people who die in the United States each year, is an interesting case in point. Proper diet, exercise, not smoking or drinking, and medical checkups if heart disease runs in the family: these factors account for only about 25 percent of the cause of heart problems. The other 75 percent, our ignorance coefficient, is attributable to "something else." If the fifteen-year study cited by the HEW report is correct, most of the "something else" is psychological and is strongly related to work (U.S. Department of Health, Education and Welfare 1973:79).

Why is stress so hard on the cardiovascular system? Stress causes the release of adrenaline (associated with uncertainty and depression of mood) and noradrenaline (associated with increased drive and elevation of mood, with premature aging of the cardiovascular system and released in greater amounts in Type A personalities) (Carruthers 1980). This is the body's way of getting ready for "fight or flight." If, however, the stress is prolonged (long-run combat fatigue conditions) the extra adrenaline and noradrenaline can work against the body. Beta blocking drugs stop the stress hormones adrenaline and noradrenaline from acting on their receivers in the nervous system.

In addition to heart disease, peptic ulcers, arthritis, gout, and other ailments to which stress was already linked, recent research on the effects of long-run stress and depression on the immune system links these factors with cancer and other diseases that may have a virus base (Foreman 1986; Squires 1981; Levy et al. 1985; Jaret 1986). Prolonged stress and depression can, in some people, affect the body's natural killer cells that fight disease. Studies on animals first indicated some kind of connection. Dogs and mice, put in positions in which they had no control over electrical shocks and thus learned to be helpless, had alterations in their immune systems.

More recently a study of cancer patients indicated that cancer was more likely to recur in people who were model patients—dependent, quiet, uncomplaining, depressed, and inert. Patients who fought the disease and tried to exert control were statistically less likely to develop cancer again. Biochemists are beginning to learn how this chemical process works. For example, stress causes an increased release of the steroid cortisol, which inhibits macrophage cells from alerting the natural killer cells that a virus has entered the body (Jaret 1986:733). A study by researchers from Harvard University Medical School, Boston University, and Northwestern University found this connection between stress and (1) lowered ability of natural killer cells to recognize and kill virus-infected cells and tumors and (2) lowered numbers of white blood cells important to the immune system (Squires 1981).

Researchers are also beginning to investigate the possible impact of the mind on the immune system with regard to the question of why some people who are exposed to AIDS contract the disease whereas others do not (Health Watch 1986).

WORK-RELATED STRESS

General Factors: Working Conditions and Personality

Occupational epidemiology can be approached in a number of ways, using a number of methods (see Kasl 1978 for a discussion of methods and some measurement problems that have made the study of the work environment, the stresses felt, and the mental and physical effects so difficult to discern). Some researchers describe the distribution of illness without attention to causes. Some researchers take a medical model and pursue toxic and other physical dangers in the workplace, such as the successful tracking of angiosarcoma of the liver in some workers to polyvinyl chloride as the probably cause (Creech and Johnson 1974). More difficult than this kind of detective work, however, is tracing illness to stressors in the workplace.

What factors (stressors) can cause stress? Taking a broad definition of stress, we can say *stress* is anything that leads to "inadequate person-environment fit, which includes" . . . also the relation of needs in the person to sources of satisfaction in the work environment to meet such needs" (Kasl 1978:13). The last part of the definition underlines the subjective aspect of stress—what is stressful to some people will not be to others.

In measuring the stressors in the workplace environment, Kasl (1978:14) suggests the following approach.

1. That stressors (the independent variables) be measured as objectively as possible (e.g., factual data from company records, fellow workers' reports, actual observation).

2. The workers' subjective perception of the stressors (the dependent variable) should be measured along with their current physical states.

3. Another category that must be measured is the personality of the workers, which might be a confounding factor (MMPI or other psychological tests are available). For example, certain personality types may be self-selecting (or the personnel office may be selecting certain types) into certain jobs. In this case, the jobs may not have any extraordinarily stressful tasks or roles, but the people who take the jobs may be anxiety-prone.

4. Another category to check includes outside influences of stress on the workers (family, finances, health, impending retirement, recent occupational mobility and support systems that might lessen work stress).

5. If one can do longitudinal prospective research (time and money), then the long-run health of these individuals can be monitored.

Intuition on stressors and subjective reports of workers are places to start. Ideally, however, the entire range of factors and possibilities should be examined. Examples of the circuitous route to finding causes are legion. One study, done to determine the causes of the higher incidence of coronary disease among London drivers of double-decker buses than among the conductors, began with the assumption that the cause was the amount of physical activity on the job. Then researchers noticed that the uniforms initially issued to drivers were much larger than the conductors', suggesting a self-selecting factor—more obese people became drivers. A follow-up reanalysis of the data finally pinpointed the stressor. The London drivers at risk were those who drove the central London buses. Those who drove in the suburbs, where there was less traffic, had lower coronary rates than did the London conductors (reported in Kasl 1978:8).

Figure 9.1 indicates a model of the factors that frequently appear to be related to stress on the job.

Related to the model in Figure 9.1, the following six objective working conditions have been identified thus far as being possible high risk factors associated with stress-related diseases (U.S. Department of Health, Education and Welfare 1973:79–81; Kahn et al. 1964; House 1986:64–72; Jenkins 1971; Margolis and Kroes 1974:136–138; Levi 1981):

1. Job dissatisfaction: Represented by tedious work, lack of recognition, poor relations with co-workers, and poor working conditions.

2. Low self-esteem: In both white-collar and blue-collar work, especially when plant shutdowns occur.

3. Occupational pressures: Work overloads, responsibility for people rather than things, conflict or ambiguity in occupational roles, shift work, time pressures regarding decisions or production, inadequate training for the job, inadequate resources to get the job done, a lengthy period of working long hours without a vacation, dealing with the external environment of one's organization that is changing and difficult to control.

4. Excessively rapid and continuous change in employment.

5. Incongruity between job status and other aspects of life: Status incongruity such as high education and low status employment, or vice versa.

Figure 9.1 Stress on the Job: A Model

Sources of Stress	Individual Reactions	Symptoms	Problems
Intrinsic to job	*The person*		
Working conditions			
Work overload			
Time pressures			
Physical danger	Level of	High blood pressure	
Lack of resources for job	anxiety	High cholestrol level	
Unfailing cheerfulness, calm, (internalizing emotions)			Coronary or other stress-related
Role in organization			physical illness
Role ambiguity		Fast heart rate	
Role conflict	Level of neuroticism	Smoking	
Responsibility for people			
Conflicts in organizational environment		Escapist drinking, drugs, extra-marital affairs	Mental ill health
Career development			
Overpromotion	Tolerance for		
Underpromotion	ambiguity		
Lack of job security			
Thwarted ambition			
Relationships at work			
Poor relations with boss, subordinates, colleagues	Personality type: Type A Workaholics	Reduced aspirations, burnout/lack of ability to function	
Difficulties in delegating responsibility			
Organizational structure and culture	*Extra-organizational sources of stress*		
Little or no participation in decision making	Family Life crises Financial		
Restrictions on behavior			
Office politics			
Lack of effective consultation			
Lack of recognition for work			

Source: Adapted from Cooper and Marshall, Sources of managerial and white-collar stress, 83.

6. Jobs that require the worker not to express personal feelings but to hold them within while maintaining a calm, cheerful, controlled exterior.

Even though these working conditions might put all workers under stress, studies indicate that some workers are under more stress by the same objective conditions than are others and therefore are at higher risk. Personality characteristics and the subjective experience of stressful conditions become important factors in mental and physical health. Some studies indicate that excessive drive, aggressiveness, ambitiousness, competitiveness, and urgency about time (Type A personalities and some workaholics might fit this category) are especially at risk (Chesney and Rosenman 1980).

Furthermore, House (1986:69) suggests that some people exhibiting these characteristics might be seeking social approval and the extrinsic motivations that show status, (higher pay, job status, and recognition) rather than the intrinsic motivations of interesting, self-satisfying work. Hence, some of these individuals might self-select themselves into high-pressure jobs. An earlier study by House (1972) indicates that this might be the case for white-collar jobs, but the opposite seemed true for blue-collar workers; that is, intrinsic motivation for this group was positively related to occupational stress and heart disease risk (perhaps because there seem to be fewer intrinsically rewarding jobs).

Another hypothesis suggests that people classed as Type A may also perceive stress more readily than others, and this subjective perception puts them at risk (Caplan 1971). These hypotheses need more empirical study to ascertain the interaction of personality and job seeking and stress perception.

One thing is clear from the studies yielding the previous list of objective working conditions and subjective perceptions of stress. A lack of stability, security, and support in the job environment is going to present problems for workers. Studies of NASA professionals, primary core sector workers, some Japanese workers, and others have shown that the presence of stability, security, and support is a positive influence on lack of stress. Perhaps these are areas for subsequent research and intervention at the organizational and political economy levels if we want to improve national physical and mental health in the United States.

Blue-Collar Stress: Objective Factors and Subjective Perceptions

Adam Smith and Karl Marx warned about the effects of routine jobs and lack of job control on factory workers. Most blue-collar jobs are in this category. They also often include additional aspects of modern industrialization—noise, dusts, mists, fumes, vapors, temperature variations, gases, and vibrations, plus low status in the general society and negative stereotypes of the blue-collar person. These factors are important in work stress, job satisfaction, and health for many blue-collar workers.

Arthur Kornhauser's (1965) early study indicating that 40 percent of autoworkers had symptoms of mental health problems has been supported by more recent work. His study indicated the importance of these factors:

1. Job satisfaction varied with the job's skill level, and higher level blue-collar workers had better mental health.
2. Job dissatisfaction related to the characteristics of jobs—dull, repetitive, unchallenging, low-paid jobs rated lowest in satisfaction and absenteeism correlated with dissatisfaction.
3. Work was the central focus of the lives of workers, but only 25 percent would choose the same work again.
4. Feelings of helplessness, withdrawal, alienation, and pessimism were predominant among half of the factory workers, compared with only 17 percent of the nonfactory workers.
5. Extrinisic factors such as wages, security, and physical conditions of work were not as important to mental health as was challenge of the job and other intrinsic factors.
6. Self-esteem correlated with job satisfaction and mental health.
7. The workers who scored lowest on mental health and job satisfaction were often escapist or passive in nonwork activities— they watched television, did not vote, and did not participate in community activities.

The boredom of machine-paced repetitive work (such as on assembly lines) is what most people relate to blue-collar stress. However, even in this type of work there are differences in people and in what they find dissatisfying. A few people say they do not find such work boring, although most do. It also is correlated with poorer mental health. However, Kornhauser thinks the dissatisfaction is more with the job's low status and the lack of being able to use one's abilities, then with fast pace and intensity of the work (Kasl 1978:28).

Some workers will deliberately allow work to stack up so they can rush to catch up, just for a change of pace (Garson 1975). Another common practice to relieve the monotony on the line is for one worker to cover two jobs while the other worker takes an unauthorized break. This doubling up practice is against the rules, which makes it part of the fun. Some workers feel they work better with short bursts of intensity than with the slower, tedious pace of brain and body (Loose bolts 1973).

The HEW report (1973:83–85), which cites studies of people adapting to their routine work, notes that the HEW Task Force members do not consider it mentally healthy for blue-collar and other workers to adapt themselves to their work and limit their aspirations for themselves. Blue-collar workers' aspirations tend to be more for their children, whom they hope will have a better, more rewarding life. This displacement of ambition to the children helps explain blue-collar and lower white-collar opposition to desegregating schools and integrating neighborhoods. These actions are interpreted as encroachments on their children's educational and inheritance (property value) chances. This same aspect of aspirations limited by jobs low in power and potential is further discussed in Chapter 10 in the arguments of sociologist Rosabeth Moss Kanter.

Society's negative image of blue-collar workers and working conditions, including their lack of control on the job, leads workers to role compensation factors, which are discussed in Chapter 8. The ascriptive ethnic group and religious group emphasis, along with excessive masculinity or femininity in social roles, compensate workers for esteem not found elsewhere. Shostak (1980:54–57) presents a lengthy list of traditional in-group/out-group ethnic and religious group conflicts that he says have traditionally Balkanized the U.S. working class and kept them fighting each other. A number of writers have emphasized the negative images the blue-collar worker receives in the popular culture and media—as a stupid lout who featherbeds, makes shoddy goods, is overpaid and causing inflation, gets in fights at the local bars when he is young, and thinks like Archie Bunker instead of his about-to-be-professional son-in-law (Sexton and Sexton 1971:255–259; Sennett and Cobb 1972; Terkel 1974:xxix; Shostak 1980). Manual labor is the out group and the professional is the in group (doctors, lawyers, business tycoons). Children get the message early.

This image, which the worker and the family can hardly ignore, is bolstered by the often degrading treatment on the job in many blue-collar situations. The blue-collar workers often have to punch time clocks (which they note the office workers do not do), work in surroundings made for machines rather than people, be paid an hourly wage instead of an annual salary, adhere to work rules that spell out virtually everything, put up with close supervision that says workers cannot be trusted, and receive no recognition for good work (Shostak 1980:43–69; Spencer 1977). In other words, it is difficult to maintain self-esteem under both societal and on-the-job put downs. Is it any wonder, these writers ask, that blue-collar workers, particularly the lower skilled, find life satisfactions off the job in family or other pursuits? (Kasl 1978).

To some extent the images and treatment on the job are self-fulfilling prophecies for many blue-collar workers. Many attempts to overcome job tedium and the only creativity sometimes available are in breaking the little rules and circumventing the supervisor when possible, or even an occasional bit of sabotage (although this should not be exaggerated as it is not very common). One thing on which the writers on the blue-collar strata seem to agree is that if this creativity could be allowed to focus on product and process and the overall "vision" (Garson 1975:211), then blue-collar workers would be more efficient and offer more ideas from below than Frederick Taylor could have imagined (Shostak 1980:61−65; Garson, 1975:210−221). In Chapter 11, we see that this idea receives support from some studies of alternatives in workplace organization that have tried to encourage more worker participation in decision making. Even the more limited programs, such as job rotation, cross-training, and more chances for education, for workers who want such things, can help. Two other points on which many studies agree are a need for a share in the gains made from the workers' increased efforts and also recognition of their contributions.

Alcohol and other drug abuse and extramarital affairs also are related to the dissatisfactions of work life, for both blue-and white-collar workers. Alcohol and drug abuse have an important link with physical health in addition to mental health. The extramarital affairs seem to occur more in the younger blue-collar set and then become less prevalent. The white-collar strata, however, tend to discover this escapist route in the middle years.

HEW lists several factors that studies indicate are linked to alcoholism and other escapist mechanisms: nonsupportive jobs with little feedback on performance, workaholism (in which workers are obsessed with work), occupational obsolescence (a particular problem for blue-collar workers), role stress on the job (role conflicts, role ambiguity), and unstructured environments for some personality types (U.S. Department of Health, Education and Welfare 1973:86). Suicide rates seem to be correlated with work and expectations, although we do not have national statistics by occupations for good comparisions. Workers with high expectations, for example, some professionals (discussed below), seem to have a high incidence of suicide and drug abuse. Earlier, it was noted that the HEW Task Force considers it mentally unhealthy for blue-collar and other workers to limit their aspirations. Apparently high aspirations and expectations also can be unhealthy.

The unemployed and retirees also seem to be at risk in these escapist areas. Certainly the blue-collar worker in many industries today is at risk in terms of unemployment, or the threat of it. As mentioned in Chapter 6, a number of sources are available on the effects of plant shutdowns and unemployment on blue-collar health and suicide rate (Shostak 1980:28−30; Briar 1978; Brenner 1973; Kasl and Cobb 1970). These factors lead one to conclude that "there is considerable evidence concerning the therapeutic value of meaningful work" that fulfills the workers' expectations (U.S. Department of Health, Education and Welfare 1973:87).

Meaningful work has often been successful in rehabilitating alcoholics, drug addicts, convicted criminals, juvenile delinquents, and others who have tried to escape from society. Meaningful work is something that the doer can be proud of and is important in its contribution to society. The examples of former alcoholics who have found a vocation in curing other alcoholics, of former juvenile delinquents who want to help other juvenile delinquents, and of retired business executives who are enthusiastic about helping other people get started in business are legion. All are coming back to do a meaningful job after being temporarily put on the shelf by society.

Three other factors particularly affect the blue-collar worker/work stress/job satisfaction/health connection. First, smoking is linked with work stress. It has been historically more prevalent in blue-collar strata and is correlated with ill health. We also now know that snuff, traditionally a working man's habit, is also a health hazard. Second, people with lower educations and/or lower SES backgrounds in higher status positions are at risk due to such things as fear of inability to perform work or an uncomfortable feeling of not fitting in socially with one's peers. Third, workers with long hours performed on the job (rather than being able to carry work home to do) and multiple job-holding workers are at risk. Both situations are more common in blue- than white-collar work (Kasl 1978:16–18).

One particularly stressful job is that of the supervisor or foreman/woman. This person is responsible for people, is caught in role conflict between doing management's bidding and representing the people on the front line under him/her, and sometimes also faces role ambiguity. For people who are sensitive to both management and labor roles and who are in the usual authoritarian structure, this is the most stressful position possible. We all know about the executive ulcer, but the foreman/woman is the person most likely to have the ulcer (Cobb study cited in Kahn et al. 1964).

White-Collar Stress: Objective Factors and Subjective Perceptions

Included in this white-collar category are white-collar professional, technical, and managerial workers, as well as the lower ranks of clerical, sales, and other support. Another group sometimes categorized as blue- and sometimes as white-collar workers are nonprofessional service jobs, such as hospital workers and restaurant workers that are low- and semi-skilled service workers. We are including them here because they usually work in the white-collar environment. The data on this latter group is a little skimpy, however.

The stress factors listed in Figure 9.1 are the same for white-collar workers, as discussed for blue-collar workers. However, the stressors manifest themselves in somewhat different ways in the white-collar environment, and some stresses are more influential than others.

In general, white-collar professionals are more satisfied with their jobs than are blue-collar workers. However, coronary and other stress-related diseases seem to be increasing in some white-collar groups. In her representative sample of 1,415 workers from different occupations Cherry (1978) indicates that the reports of nervous debility and strain at work were professional, 53.8 percent; intermediate nonmanual, 56.9 percent; skilled nonmanual, 44.3 percent; semiskilled nonmanual, 15.3 percent; and unskilled manual, 10.3 percent.

A 1979 study by the American Academy of Family Physicians, surveying 4,473 workers in six occupations, indicated that 81 percent of the business executives, 62 percent of the teachers and secretaries, 44 percent of the garment workers, and 38 percent of the farmers experienced significant work stress. This job overload stemmed particularly from pressures from superiors, deadlines, and low salaries. If these figures are representative, there is much basis for discussion on white-collar workers as well as blue (reported in Kasl 1978).

First, let us review some broad assumptions and findings regarding white collar versus blue collar.

1. Anywhere from slightly to a great deal more status is accorded white-collar jobs in western industrial societies. Self-esteem is higher for the high-status occupations.
2. The physical conditions are usually somewhat more pleasant and less overtly physically dangerous for white-collar than for blue-collar work.
3. Some of the higher-status white-collar work is less routinized and more autonomous (for professionals, in particular).
4. Education levels for the higher white-collar strata are higher, which correlates with better health.
5. Income and fringe benefits, including medical care, are often better for white-collar occupations.

Considering that stress is partially self-generated, depending on expectations, a number of factors could be causing stress. One writer refers to the white-collar illnesses as the "achievers' diseases" (Forbes 1979:149). Consider the following factors from our original discussion at the beginning of the chapter: (1) worker expectations and aspirations are higher than some in blue-collar positions, due to white-collar status, higher education, and probable white-collar SES backgrounds; (2) responsibility for people, which is a known stressor, is inherent in the middle and top management positions (as for the blue-collar supervisor);

(3) the middle and lower white-collar ranks, in particular, are still circumscribed in autonomy by bureaucracy, office politics, and the same problems with co-workers that blue-collar workers have; (4) some white-collar work is intrinsically interesting, but some is as routine and boring as an assembly line; (5) some jobs demand overextension, calling for more resources than the person or the position can muster in talent, time, resources, or underutilization, which does not allow people to use their personal resources; time pressures seem to be important here; (6) long hours in the office and excessive travel are part of some white-collar positions; (7) another part of the job is decision making, which may be expensive for one's career and the company, especially if the worker's resources are limited and many decisions must be made quickly (quantitative and qualitative overload) (Cooper and Marshall 1978). In addition, the white-collar workers are facing a loss of job due to mergers and new technology in the same way that blue-collar workers fear shutdowns, although the loss of white-collar jobs has been at a much lower rate.

Hazardous Duty

What does this mean in terms of specific jobs? Are some jobs more stressful than others? Why do general practitioners have more coronary heart disease than surgeons? Why do dentists have a higher suicide rate than other professionals? Why do secretaries and caseworkers suffer from *burnout* (mental, spiritual, and physical exhaustion that leaves one temporarily unfit to function and may lead to long-term debilitation)? Can we explain why telephone operators at AT&T are so susceptable to psychiatric disorders? Why do policeman (information is sparse on policewomen) have twice the divorce rate of white urban males and high rates of heart trouble, diabetes, ulcers, and other stress-related diseases (Kasl 1978; Forbes 1979; 173–189; Rice 1981; Howard 1981)? The one thing these occupations seem to share is a form of combat fatigue. Causes of combat fatigue are a constant, prolonged bombardment with stimuli while feeling unable to control the situation. The bombs come in various forms, but the employee must never change expression or yell back, internalizing the felt response.

Telephone operators are electronically monitored, incessantly oversupervised, and faced with elaborate productivity indexes and petty management rules at the twenty-three operating companies of the Bell System. As they work, however, they must be courteous and cheerful to the customers, whom they must often put on hold because they must answer another incoming call within twenty seconds of the first ring, and the supervisor may be listening on the line (Howard 1981:41–42).

Secretaries are commonly innundated by requests for work that must be done "now"—frequently by several people at the same time—while the phone is ringing and other people are queueing at the desk for assistance. At the same time secretaries are expected to be unfailingly polite, if not charming (Turi 1985; Stifled secretaries 1985). In the last decade or so clerical work has also been faced with encroaching technology in the form of the computer. The office worker who uses a computer for hours faces tedium, possible stress, eye strain, and in some instances radiation (Pechter 1983; Nussbaum 1983; Schiro 1983). *Ergonomics* (the study of how people and machines/technology/environment interact) has indicated physical and mental stressors in this area. The union 9 to 5 (the National Association of Working Women) suggests frequent rotation to other jobs and transfer of pregnant women to other tasks (Pechter 1983). Karen Nussbaum, the president of 9 to 5 (SEIU affiliated) also discusses the dilemma of clerical workers who do piecework at home at the terminal (without fringe benefits, in most cases) being displaced by overseas keypunch operators in Barbados and automated out (25 to 30 percent reduction in jobs by 1990 projected by European studies) (Nussbaum 1983). Boredom, stress, and fear of job loss are key factors in addition to other overload factors.

Social workers suffer from case overload. Handling more than 400 cases at a time is not uncommon. In addition, they must often try to help solve problems without adequate resources. Inadequate funds, time, and support staff are ordinary facts of life. Also, many clients' problems are with the larger political economic system, which the caseworker is, of course, unable to change (Eaton 1980). Both secretaries and social workers are notoriously underpaid.

Police officers must be constantly alert. Their duty shifts and work roles often conflict with family roles. They suffer from negative images from society and from the people with whom they deal in the line of duty. Also, they usually must cope with a military-type of administration in their own department, plus the bureaucracy of a court system with which they must interact. At the same time, they must be calm, stable, and unemotional while separating battling spouses, pulling people from wrecks, informing parents their child has been killed in a traffic accident, and answering lawyers' questions under cross-examination (Forbes 1979:174–177; Davidson and Veno 1980). They also are underpaid.

General practitioners must often make instant decisions, sometimes without adequate resources at hand, in order to keep up with closely spaced appointments. Meanwhile, a doctor's manner must inspire confidence in the patient. Dentists face hostility and fear of pain in their patients and must work quickly in small, isolated quarters—not for two hours in an operating room, but for eight or more a day to cover escalating overhead costs (Forbes 1979:187–188; Cooper 1980). Other researchers are studying the possible effect of exposure to X-rays, anesthetics, and mercury (Ashford 1976:11). In addition to having the highest rate of suicide for any professional group, dentists have excessively high rates of leukemia, diseases of the nervous system, and lymphatic malignancies.

By now you should recognize many of the stressors in various jobs—dangerous working conditions, time deadlines, responsibility for people, uncertainty in the societal environment, overload without adequate resources, and lack of self-esteem.

More Hazardous Duty: The Minority Worker in a Nontraditional Job

The hazards of specific jobs also apply to minority workers—black, women, Hispanics—in any job that is not traditional for their social category. Even though there may be some psychological pluses for being given a chance at a higher status, better paid job in which minority people can use their abilities, there are costs for being among the first. Most of these costs center around the fish bowl effect. Everyone is watching to see what the newcomers will do, often without the usual mentoring and help other newcomers would get. Furthermore, the newcomers may have to, or think they have to, work twice as hard to overcome stereotypes and to prove their worth.

The organizational culture is likely to be new for the minority persons who will feel uneasy in it—as will its traditional members who do not know how to treat the newcomers who look different from the rest of us. Not only are there stresses on the job, but life-style changes that go with upward mobility are also stressful, as we saw with upwardly mobiles from lower SES backgrounds. These factors put the new minority higher level white-collar workers at risk for the stress-related diseases (Kanter 1977:206–244; Forbes 1979:149–172).

Stressors from Outside

White-collar families are frequently under stress, as are blue-collar families. Changing and frequently conflicting social roles emerge as more women are in the workplace by choice or economic necessity in both types of families. The businesswoman (and sometimes the businessman, if his work is closer to home than that of his working wife) who must leave a meeting to retrieve an ailing child from school is under stress as much as the secretary or the factory operative who must explain to the boss why she has to leave suddenly. Long hours and out-of-town business trips affect white-collar families, just as long hours and shift work affect blue-collar ones. Even though the financial and unemployment crises may not occur as often for white-collar couples, they can happen.

Geographic mobility and being up-rooted are presenting problems for many white-collar workers. The cutting of ties with support groups, when one spouse is transferred by the company or takes advantage of a new job in another area, may contribute to the rising divorce rates among white-collar couples and appears to be a significant factor in the increase in teenage suicide in upper-middle-class suburbs (Donahue 1986).

The next section looks at how some organizations and individuals are trying to deal with such stresses.

COPING WITH STRESS: ORGANIZATIONAL AND INDIVIDUAL RESPONSES

Because dealing with people is more frequent in white-collar positions, relationships of trust and mutual support in such jobs are especially important (Cooper and Marshall 1978:88–94; Kahn et al. 1964; Margolis, Kroes, and Quinn 1974; Reich 1987). Some organizational cultures are more supportive than others, and thus, one might conclude, better for health of their workers. Organizational cultures and structures that foster group participation in decision making, for example, may be able to relieve subordinates' feelings of lack of autonomy, to take some pressure off people who have heretofore been making too many decisions with too few resources, and to reduce role ambiguity through communications. A participatory environment also offers people opportunities to learn and develop toward career goals, or to catch up if they have been overpromoted. Most organizations, however, apparently have not achieved this kind of supportive culture and remain closer to the traditional pressure cooker. Chapter 10 talks about organizational cultures that have a climate of distrust, and Chapter 11 discusses alternative workplace structures that are more conducive to open, participatory climates.

In addition to setting up an environment and structures for group decision-making participation, some organizations are also tackling both the on-the-job and off-the-job stresses in other ways. The issue of company liability for work-related stress has encouraged some firms to give attention to the employees' mental states (Ivancevich, Matteson, and Richards 1985). Flextime scheduling, assistance with child care, wellness programs, substance abuse programs, preretirement courses, and in-house counselors are now being offered by some large organizations and a few smaller ones. Some 5,000 companies, including about 60 percent of the top 500 corporations, now have some form of Employee Assistance Program (EAP). Most workers, however, are not yet fortunate enough to have such a menu of programs at their disposal.

Popular writers are now offering practical advice to individual workers on how to combat stress if the organizational climate is not being altered to help or if counseling and other programs are not available. Such advice includes (1) clarifying your values so you do not get bogged down in doing what you do not want to do; (2) talking to yourself regarding why you are so upset (cool yourself out on whether the issue is really important); (3) learning how to relax through meditation and regularized breathing; (4) exercising regularly, after a medical checkup. to let off steam and keep the body in tone; (5) getting leisure time doing something quite different from the work routine; (6) adopting dietary goals for weight stabilization where you want it; and (7) avoiding chemical haze of smoking, drinking, excess coffee, or drugs (Eliot and Breo 1984; Veninga and Spradley 1981).

PHYSICAL HAZARDS IN THE WORKPLACE AND THE ENVIRONMENT

Becoming Aware of the Problems

The two broad subdivisions of physical hazards are (1) immediate effects, such as death, injury, acute illness, and (2) chronic illness, which may have up to a thirty-year lag after exposure to the damaging substance before serious illness shows up in the victim. As a society, the United States has been slow in developing public policy in either area.

In the discussion of the effects of working conditions on mental health, we saw that noise, vibration, excessive heat or cold, unsafe equipment, toxic fumes, and exposure to chemicals, radiation, dust, and other hazardous physical conditions have negative psychological effects on workers. Of course, they also have more direct physical effects. In the late 1960s the public became more aware of some dangers of the workplace, and social consciousness and activism were high. Four factors came to the public attention and helped unions lobby successfully for occupational safety and health legislation. They were:

1. Industry's reported injury rate (including all reported injuries, not just the disabling injuries shown in Table 9.2) increased nearly 29 percent from 1961 to 1970. Several well-publicized mining disasters underscored the problem (Ashford 1976:3). The public was becoming aware of the inaccuracy of the reported disabling injuries as companies attempted to hide the number of actual cases (Stellman and Daum 1973:3–4).

Cases of injury may be underestimated by a factor of five (Ashford 1976:3).

2. In addition, the Department of Health, Education and Welfare (now divided into the Department of Health and Human Services and the Department of Education) was indicating the *occupational disease* rate (the long-term effects of exposure to chemicals, radiation, etc.) was much higher than previously thought—because accurate records are not kept in this area. The estimate was 390,000 new cases and 100,000 deaths due to occupational disease each year (that estimate has been increased to around a half million new cases annually).

3. The rapid rate of technological change and its effects on health were becoming apparent. There was an increasing rate in new chemicals used (more than 3,000 new ones a year) and new production processes in use. Also, new information was appearing on stress related to noise, heat, and vibrations. Some of the older occupational diseases, such as black lung (pneumoconiosis) of miners, brown lung (byssinosis) of textile workers, and cancers of uranium workers, were finally being recognized as occupationally related after years of being regarded as normal by company doctors and the general medical community (Stellman and Daum 1973; Smith 1986). People were becoming aware of the effects of the environment both in the workplace and in the wider community, but good information was not available on what long-run health effects these new hazards would have.

4. Further, the loss of production days due to injury and death and the high cost of medical coverage and workman's compensation were costs to companies at a time when foreign competition was making them conscious of needing to cut costs. For example:

> The total cost of occupational hazards—in terms of lost wages, medical expenses, insurance claims, production delays, lost time of coworkers, and equipment damage—was estimated by the National Safety Council at $9.3 billion during 1971—nearly 1 percent of the GNP. This figure, moreover, is likely to be a gross understatement of even the direct costs to the GNP of both occupational injuries and illness. An estimated 25 million workdays were lost through absenteeism during 1972. This reported figure is equivalent to a loss of 100,000 man-years of work. It has been estimated that reduction of one day per year in the annual rate of absenteeism among the U.S. labor force would add $10 billion to the GNP. Much disease resulting in absenteeism is probably occupationally related, although it is not reported or recognized as such .... Many of the other costs of chronic occupational illness—early retirement, reduced efficiency, family and community problems—are also not reflected in the Council's estimates. (Ashford 1976:17–18)

Even though most businesses were not lobbying for federal legislation in health and safety, the cost-cutting argument other companies used are cited as the rationale for the subsequent legislation. With these factors in mind, grassroots environmental groups and unions began to push for more government standards and inspection in these areas.

In 1970 the first comprehensive law was passed to improve workplace health and safety. The Occupational Safety and Health Act set up the Occupational Safety and Health Administration (OSHA) to determine standards and inspect workplaces. A similar comprehensive bill introduced in 1968 had been defeated by the business lobby, led by the U.S. Chamber of Commerce (Stellman and Daum 1973:7). Previous legislation had been aimed at specific industries—construction, mining, maritime, and businesses with federal contracts. Any other regulation was carried out at the state level, which was proving ineffective, according to the recorded statistics. (See Chapter 7 for a short history of how state workman's safety-compensation programs developed from 1910 to 1948, basically putting compensation funds in private hands, ignoring occupational disease, and lacking enforcement.) Under its power to regulate interstate commerce, Congress found "that personal injuries and illnesses arising out of work situations impose a substantial burden upon, and are a hindrance to, interstate commerce in terms of lost production, wage loss, medical expenses, and disability compensation payments" (Section 2 [a] of OSHA act quoted in *Guide to Occupational Safety and Health* 1977:8).

In terms of general public safety other legislative actions were also taken in the early 1970s. By 1974 Congress had enacted into law the Environmental Protection Agency (1970), the Consumer Product Safety Commission (1972), the National Traffic Safety Commission (1970), and the Mine Safety and Health Administration (1973) (Edsall 1984:113). The backlash from business and the economic recession and the rise of conservative social policy soon followed, as discussed in Chapter 5.

Death and Disabling Injury in the Workplace

The current situation of *disabling injuries* (*disabling* means the worker was unable to perform regular activities for a full day beyond the day of the injury) and deaths on the job shows some improvement since World War II, according to reported figures. Table 9.2 indicates death and disabling injuries in manufacturing and nonmanufacturing industries between 1945 and 1984 in the United States. Table 9.3 indicates the situation in specific industries. These tables show accident and injury statistics collected by the Bureau of Labor Statistics.

From a glance at Tables 9.2 and 9.3 for these more obvious kinds of workplace dangers, it appears that the period of the most rapid improve-

Table 9.2 Workers Killed or Disabled on the Job, 1945 to 1984

Year	Total Number (1,000)	Total Rate per 100,000	Manufacturing Number (1,000)	Manufacturing Rate per 100,000	Nonmanufacturing Number (1,000)	Nonmanufacturing Rate per 100,000	Disabling Injuries (1,000)
1945	16.5	33	2.7	18	13.8	39	2,000
1950	15.5	27	2.6	17	12.9	31	1,950
1955	14.2	24	2.0	12	12.2	29	1,950
1960	13.8	21	1.8	10	12.1	25	1,950
1965	14.1	20	1.8	10	12.3	24	2,100
1970	13.8	18	1.7	9	12.1	21	2,200
1975	13.0	15	1.6	9	11.4	17	2,200
1980	13.2	13	1.7	8	11.3	15	2,300
1981	12.5	13	1.5	7	11.0	14	2,100
1982	11.5	12	1.1	6	10.4	13	1,900
1983	11.3	11	1.2	6	10.1	12	1,900
1984	11.3	11	1.2	6	10.1	12	1,900

Sources: U.S. Bureau of the Census, *Statistical Abstract of the United States: 1984*, 422; U.S. Bureau of the Census, *Statistical Abstract of the United States: 1986*, 425.

Table 9.3 Workers Killed or Disabled, by Industry Group, 1984

Industry Group	Deaths Number (1,000)	Deaths Rate (per 100,000 workers)	Disabling Injuries (1,000)
Total	11.3	11	1,900
Agriculture, forestry, fishing	1.7	49	180
Mining and quarrying	.6	60	50
Construction	2.1	37	190
Manufacturing	1.2	6	320
Transportation and utilities	1.3	24	150
Trade, wholesale and retail	1.2	5	350
Service	1.8	6	400
Government	1.4	9	260

Source: U.S. Bureau of the Census, *Statistical Abstract of the United States: 1986*, 425.

ment was from 1945 to 1950, presumably when production on a crash basis for war was less urgent. Improvement slowed during the 1960s, picked up slightly in the early 1970s, and has slowed a little since then. The overall trend is for improvement in these obvious categories, assuming that the reporting habits remained the same throughout the time period.

Mining (which includes the high-risk oil-extracting industry) is clearly still the most dangerous industry in terms of work-related death, followed by farming, construction, and transportation. In manufacturing, which has a low death rate compared to some other industries, one of the highest subcategories is food and kindred products, especially meatpacking (see Johnson 1984 for an upsetting account of the operations in a large plant in the industry today). In terms of work-related injuries, OSHA figures for 1981 indicate the following percentages of injuries in these high-risk industries per year: meatpacking, 33 percent, different kinds of sawmilling, 27 to 33 percent; heavy construction, 20 percent; and anthracite coal mining, 13 percent (Johnson 1984:17). A 1985 EPA report found chemical plants averaged five accidents a day from 1980 to 1984. This includes 139 deaths and 1,500 injuries (Irwin 1986:11).

Why have not industries had lower death and injury rates in the 1970s and 1980s, after OSHA? OSHA's problems are discussed below after considering a few points on chronic occupational and environmental disease.

Chronic Occupational and Environmental Disease

In their clearly written introduction to health hazards in the workplace, Stellman and Daum (1973) discuss the physiology of occupational disease and some problems in dealing with it. We now examine these physiological factors and the problems involved in tracing the sources of occupational disease.

First, there is the difference between *acute reactions* to toxic substances (reactions that are immediate or occur within a few hours of exposure) and *chronic reactions* (reactions that may take several years to surface, during which time the victim and physician may not recognize the symptoms of on-coming illness). *Fulminant reactions* are acute reactions occurring so quickly and so severely that even immediate medical attention may be too late to prevent death or permanent disability.

Chronic diseases are diseases that arise from repeated exposure to small doses of irritating substances. Common chronic diseases seem to attack particularly the respiratory and circulatory systems or to cause cancer in the body.

Lung ailments, for example, such as chronic bronchitis and emphysema, can be caused by long-term exposure to small doses of chlorine, nitrogen dioxide, ammonia, hydrogen sulfide, cigarette smoke, cotton dust, or urban and industrial air pollution. Over the years, often accompanied by bronchial infections and further lung scarring, the air sacs can neither take in oxygen nor give off waste carbon dioxide from the body. Many of the inhaled insoluable substances stay in the lungs. Asbestos dust is now well-known to cause one form of the scarring occurring in this manner. Inhaling asbestos dust leads to pulmonary fibrosis, a chronic lung disease, and in some people, to cancer.

The fact that so many irritants can cause similar symptoms is itself a problem. Even after a person is diagnosed many years later as having a chronic disease, the symptoms in the lungs could be from any one of a number of things, including a cumulative effect of exposure to several substances. This multiple *etiology* (causation) has enabled industry and workmen's compensation to avoid its responsibility for occupational disease over the years; it also hampers epidemiological research (Ashford 1976:15–19; Hattis and Kennedy 1986).

Even though diagnosis is improving, finding the exact cause(s) for the condition calls for better and more frequent testing for diseases among occupational and geographic subgroups of the population and more thorough record keeping (including international information). Also, independent (not done by the industry) research is required. (See Hattis and Kennedy 1986 for an account of the problems of doing risk-assessment research on environmental factors.)

Other chronic diseases can be caused by inhaling soluable substances, which pass from the lungs into the blood stream and damage other organs. Other toxic substances, such as lead or arsenic, can enter the blood system through the mouth and digestive tract. This happens when contaminated hands, food, and/or cigarettes are put in the mouth. Toxins in the blood often settle in the liver, which acts to neutralize them and make them harmless. In the process, an overworked liver may be damaged. Many industrial chemicals also settle in the pancreas, kidneys, or the bladder (Ozonoff 1982:14; Stellman and Daum 1973:36–47).

In addition to breathing toxins into the lungs or ingestion through the mouth and digestive system, poisons can be absorbed through the skin. Phenol and carbolic acid can be absorbed through the skin without being felt; other substances may burn their way through with allergy-like reactions. Others, such as aniline, a common dye, are so insidious that they can be absorbed into the body through shoes and clothing (Stellman and Daum 1973:20).

Some chemicals and gases that in small doses produce chronic disease can produce acute reactions if exposure to larger quantities occurs. For example, chlorine, ammonia, and nitrogen oxides in large doses cause severe burns in the lungs, keeping the air sacs from transfering oxygen. This condition, pulmonary edema, causes the victim to drown on dry land.

Carcinogens (cancer-causing agents) in the environment are currently receiving some attention because of the seeming increase of cancer. At the present rate, one out of four persons can expect to have cancer sometime during his or her life. Researchers suspect that 70 to 90 percent of cancer is environmental in origin (Ozonoff 1982:13). How much of this cancer is due to exposure on the job in unknown. Current estimates range from 4 percent to 20 percent (Irwin 1986:12). A wide range of substances have been identified as carcinogens. They include such commonly found substances as asbestos in building insulation and durable goods, benzo(a)pyrines in cigarette smoke, and the effluents from power plants and diesel engines, ionizing radiation in nuclear power and medical X-rays, arsenic, cadmium, chromium, nickel, radium, and vinyl chloride (Irwin 1986:12−13).

No look at chronic occupational disease is complete without a few comments about the electronics industry. Once heralded as the clean industry of the future (no smokestacks), the 1,800 or so industries of Silicon Valley in California and those located elsewhere are more dangerous than originally thought. In an article in *Technology Review*, Dr. Joseph LaDou of the University of California-San Francisco School of Medicine noted "the semiconductor industry, which uses large quantities of toxic metals, chemicals, and gases, may be creating significantly greater health and safety problems for its workers than heretofore realized" (quoted in Nader 1984:6). Besides the more obvious dangers of burns and toxic fume inhaling, the article notes the probable reproductive problems such exposure causes—and 70 percent of the workers are young women of childbearing age. Further,

> the use of highly toxic and flammable materials also poses a serious threat to the safety of residents in surrounding communities . . . . For instance, the rupture of one cylinder containing a toxic gas such as arsine could cause widespread acute exposures among local residents. Recent findings also show that the industry is contaminating the groundwater of nearby communities and polluting the air with photochemical smog. (Nader 1984:6)

The California Department of Industrial Relations' surveys show high relative rates of semiconductor worker illnesses. The widespread use of arsine, phosphine, and diborane gases contributes to the problem. The workers, however, are not informed of exactly what they are working with in order to protect "trade secrets" (Nader 1984:6). Underground leaks of toxic materials from storage, waste and fuel tanks, and piping systems are contaminating underground drinking water supplies to which Nader refers. Reactive organic gases are the causes of the photo-chemical smog alluded to.

A Report from Silicon Valley

These general statements are given a little life by an eyewitness description of one plant. Investigative reporter Diana Hembree (1985; see also Martinez and Ramo 1980) described the small company, apparently typical, for which she worked in the Silicon Valley, California. She started at minimum wage with all the other printed circuit board assemblers; no medical insurance or other fringe benefits were provided. The local unemployment situation assured a steady supply of workers, and she felt lucky to get the job. As she clipped the tiny wires in place on the back of the boards, she began to yawn.

"It's the freon," the other workers explained. Six feet from the assembly line was the open vat of freon, dripping on the floor. The other workers told her of dizziness and stomach cramps when it was their turn to degrease the boards by dipping them barehanded into the tank. Examining the tank, she found a sign on the back toward the wall: DANGER! TOXIC CHEMICALS! DEATH MAY RESULT FROM CARELESSNESS! In small letters was the warning never to use the machine without proper ventilation. The other workers around her had never seen the sign and some admitted that they could not read English. Besides the local people, the employees were from Mexico, Iran, the Philippines, and Portugal. The plant's management was not unkind, but arbitrary in dispensing justice and ran the place like a "kindergarten," in the words of the other workers.

Noticing that some of the other assembly rooms were enveloped in an acrid smelling white fog, Hembree asked the workers if all these chemicals were dangerous. They did not know. The supervisor was miffed when asked. When hired, she had been told, "No, we don't really use any hazardous chemical in here. None that could really hurt you." So, Hembree closely observed her surroundings when she lunched with the other workers beside the drums thrown out back and found the following chemicals:

- Freon 113, which dissolves the skin's essential oils, causes rashes, and acts as a depressant on the central nervous system; symptoms of inhalation are drowsiness, nausea, giddiness, central nervous system depression, irregular heartbeat, and if inhaled in concentrated doses, death;
- Tin-lead solder, which when heated releases lead oxide fumes harmful if inhaled; when absorbed into the bloodstream it is stored in

tissues and can cause brain damage, paralysis, colic, miscarriages, and sterility. Symptoms of lead poisoning include fatigue, irritability, headaches, tremors, wrist drop, pain in joints, and blue line on gums;

- Acid flux, which is a corrosive liquid used to clean metal during soldering; when heated, may release fumes that can irritate the skin and respiratory tract;
- Isopropyl alcohol, which is highly flammable; exposure to fumes can irritate eyes, and inhalation of large quantities can cause vomiting, narcosis, and coma.

These chemicals can be used safely and are comparatively mild compared to chemicals used in semiconductor and electroplating plants. However, no one mentioned the proper use of these chemicals or provided training seminars on their dangers and proper uses; no protective clothing was handed out. Workers ran back and forth with coffee cans of freon to fill up the dipping tub. They smoked and ate near the empty drums out back marked "flammable" and "toxic." One can marked "To be disposed of carefully and used for no other purposes" was the paper towel receptacle in the bathroom. When one employee suggested they needed a union, another worker pantomimed operating a video camera while a third made police siren sounds. The message was clear: the power was on the side of the company, not the worker or any worker organization.

People just wanted to work; many were moonlighting at a nearby food-processing plant on a full eight- to ten-hour shift there, including Gloria, four months pregnant, who worked in the vapor-filled assembly room by day and on a brussels sprouts assembly line by night. She came to work in all kinds of garb—from her husband's work shirts to an evening dress one day because her clothes did not fit and she had nothing to wear. She was apologetic but too near exhaustion to care, although she did wonder what happened to the energy and the joy of life she had had as a child in Mexico.

Workers who got sick just lost their jobs and that was the end of it. After a bad week of particularly noxious fumes, when many employees vomited in the bathroom, several workers secretly called OSHA. No one showed up to investigate, at least no one whom any worker saw.

After leaving as an employee, Hembree returned as a reporter to interview the plant manager, Fred Freiberg. He was seldom on the plant site, usually leaving it in the hands of his assistant. In response to questions about lead fumes, he replied that they were not hazardous "because the body can't absorb lead." The plant had an excellent health record, he said; no accidents in twelve years. He did not add that sick workers were let go with no further company obligations and apparently no reports filed. If there were any problems with toxic fumes it was because:

> You know, we do hire a lot of 'low-end' people around here. People with bad attitudes. When employees won't follow the rules, then of course we have a problem." (Hembree 1985:24)

The basic problem, the reporter concluded, was that Freiberg did not understand the nature of the chemicals; he believed the salesmen and the company that as long as workers did not drink the chemicals or jump in them, they were safe. If the reporting was accurate, it raises many questions. What rules were the employees breaking when none were given? Why didn't the company offer training about dangers and supply the appropriate protective gear and ventilation? What evidence of bad attitudes were there on which Frieberg could blame the workers for any problems, except that they did not protest more? In addition, had he never read any material on the processes and materials in his industry?

A request made by a former worker to OSHA to see the report on the complaints filed by the workers produced a report copy marked "confidential." It claimed that a thorough inspection of the plant revealed no health or safety violations. The woman inspecting the plant had reportedly done so while Hembree was working there under the conditions described.

On this note, let us look at some problems OSHA faces in carrying out its mandate of protecting the worker at the worksite.

OSHA AND THE WORKPLACE ENVIRONMENT

OSHA: Mandate and Problems

The first part of the previous section on physical hazards outlines the factors that alarmed some groups and led to the passage of the first comprehensive safety and health law. When some hazards of the workplace were found to be spilling over into the environment, the Environmental Protection Act (1970) was passed in the same year. The Environmental Protection Agency and OSHA face similar problems in the areas of hazard research and risk assessment and in the same kinds of political barriers in enforcement.

In 1970 the Occupational Safety and Health Act provided for five agencies to be created to implement the act: (1) the Occupational Safety and Health Administration was established as the principal agency, to set standards for workplace health and safety, inspect worksites, and levy fines for noncompliance; (2) The National Institute for Occupational Safety and Health (NIOSH) was created to conduct research, prepare criteria documents, recommend standards, and assist companies in training and educating workers for health and safety or otherwise complying with standards; (3) the Review Commission (OSHRC) was set up to adjudicate disputes over fines; (4) a National Advisory Committee of Occupational Safety and Health (NACOSH) was appointed to advise the Department of Labor and HEW on matters relating to the administration of the act; and (5) the National Commission on State Workmen's Compensation Laws was temporarily created to carry out a study and evaluation of state workmen's compensation laws, to report in July 1972, after which it was dissolved.

What happened to this mandate to improve worker health and safety? Some of the following eight points will give us an idea:

1. Even initially there were too few inspectors to check more than a fraction (2 percent) of the 3 million or so worksites in the United States in a year. Furthermore, only 50 industrial hygienists were hired—they were the only people allowed to take air samples. Once in office in 1980, the Reagan administration immediately cut the inspection staff from 1,600 to 1,200 and replaced the head of the administration with pro-business leadership (OSHA's inspection force 1985). By 1985 the number of inspectors was down to 1,082 (Irwin 1986:3). The House Government Operations subcommittee found that recent OSHA policy seemed to be not to investigate a worker complaint unless there had been a death (Kantor 1985);

2. The American Conservative Union formed Stop-OSHA (which sometimes calls itself the Labor Task Force) to fight OSHA's penalties in the courts. Stop-OSHA helps companies pay court and litigation costs, which are tax deductible as business expenses;

3. These cases have innundated the 52 legal aides at OSHA, each of whom may be handling more than 100 cases at a time. Each case takes three to five years in court to settle; during that time the hazards charged by OSHA inspectors need not be abated. In 1979 companies took 47.8 percent of their serious health violation citations to court— 5,681 out of the 11,884 serious violations (O'Connor 1980);

4. In 1978, business, funded largely by Stop-OSHA, won the Barlow case in the Supreme Court, which now requires OSHA to have a court warrant to inspect. OSHA can no longer have surprise inspections (O'Connor 1980);

5. The fines levied were minimal in the 1970s and dropped 44 percent between 1980 and 1985. In a puzzling turnabout, in 1986 OSHA

levied a $1.4 million fine against Union Carbide for 221 alleged violations at its Institute, West Virginia, plant (Irwin 1986:3);

6. Many workers who cooperate with OSHA inspectors and point out problems are fired, despite the worker protection provided under the act (O'Connor 1980);

7. The hazards targeted by OSHA have frequently been trivial, and the more important dangers, such as factors involved in occupational disease, are usually ignored. One exception is the vinyl chloride industry, where OSHA has made some real improvements (Northrup, Rowan, and Perry 1978:181–418; Bollier and Claybrook 1986:53–54). "To date, OSHA has promulgated only 24 complete health standards plus some 500 'interim' standards for the estimated 45,000 potentially toxic substances in commercial use" (Irwin 1986:3). Standards appear to be more politically negotiated than the result of objective measures aimed at worker health and safety (Berman 1978; Ashford 1976; Bollier and Claybrook 1986). Most standards are derived from industry's research, not from independent investigation. Twenty-three states have passed tougher standards for the industries using chemicals and also have worker/community right-to-know laws, but court cases are invalidating the state laws and substituting the weaker OSHA standards (Right to know laws 1985);

8. Information films and materials meant to alert workers to workplace hazards and to train them on safety measures have been pulled from the shelves by the Reagan administration. The films were said to be antimanagement and would frighten the workers (Berkowitz 1982).

In essence, OSHA has not fulfilled its original mandate from Congress. Despite some enthusiasm in its administration in the early 1970s, OSHA has always been underfunded for research and inspection. Using the courts and the intimidation of workers, some people in the business community have made it more difficult for OSHA to operate. In the conservative political climate of the 1980s, the situation has worsened—with even less funding and with censorship of some of OSHA's educational materials (Noble 1986). (See Berman 1978; Elling 1986; Gersuny 1981; and McCaffrey 1982 for more on the politics of health and safety regulation.)

Safety Programs: Sweden and Saskatchewan

Faced with these limitations, many workers and their unions and environmental and health activist groups are calling for reform. In addition, many communities are forming their own Committees on Occupational

Safety and Health, or COSH. Frequently these groups point to the worker health and safety programs that are so successful in Sweden and in Saskatchewan, Canada. Since passage of the 1974 Work Environment Act by the Swedish parliament, accidental deaths on the job have been reduced by 50 percent and injuries by 17 percent (Engler 1986). These safety programs have a key ingredient that is missing in the United States—most of their workers are unionized, and unions have a great deal of power. Even though more than 84 percent of Swedish businesses are privately owned, the employers recognize the power of their workers' organizations and cooperate with them. In fact, they find that the workers make good suggestions and that the government intervenes less—only in cases in which the safety committee and employer cannot agree (Witt and Early 1980:27).

The safety committee and the safety steward are the bases of the Swedish system. National laws require that every workplace with fifty or more employees have a labor-management safety committee, with a majority of the committee elected from the union. Smaller workplaces that voluntarily form safety committees have a regional union representative to help them. Blueprints and plans for new construction, new machines and technology, and new production processes must have approval of the union representatives, in addition to the approval of the national Swedish equivalent of OSHA. Company doctors, nurses, industrial hygienists, and safety engineers must also work closely with the safety committee, on whose approval they were hired. Local occupational health clinics that service smaller businesses in the area must be union controlled before they can receive public funds. Companies must share all the information they have about workplace hazards with the safety committee, and chemical labeling is required by law.

> To monitor conditions union safety stewards must be elected to cover each work area on each shift in all Swedish workplaces with five or more employees. These stewards have the right to shut down dangerous operations until they can be corrected—without fear of punishment. All workers have the right to refuse unsafe work. (Engler 1986:16)

Another area covered by law and national contracts is work environment training for workers and safety stewards. The safety committee is responsible for scheduling and topics to be covered in training sessions. The Swedish Work Environment Fund helps defray the costs. The fund, created by law in 1972, also supports research on occupational safety and health and workplace democracy. It publishes a magazine for workers on the latest information in these areas. The magazine is sent to all safety committee members and safety stewards. Manuals on specific hazards are also published and can be found at the worksites likely to have a problem in that area.

In Saskatchewan, Canada, the system operates similarly. Each workplace with ten or more workers must have a safety committee trained by the government of the province to do its own monitoring of conditions. All company health records and records required by the government are open to the committee. The province also establishes standards, makes inspections when invited by the safety committee, provides technical advice and monitoring equipment, and oversees committee operations (Witt and Early 1980:22).

The safety program in each of these two places works because workers themselves do the inspecting, have the training and knowledge of environmental hazards, and have the power to make changes (Witt and Early 1980:22). Rather than relying on government regulation and inspection, the action starts from the bottom up with the local labor-management safety committees—going over plans together, getting and sharing information, and cooperating most of the time. The government supplies research, technical advice, and training assistance; helps set overall standards; and supplies investigators when called in to settle a dispute over conditions (Kelman 1984).

Suggestions for Workplace Environment Programs

As we have discussed, the people interested in a healthier workplace environment include workers and their unions, and also a range of health and environmental activists. Many of the substances that make workplaces unsafe when not properly used are spilling over into the neighborhood, seeping into the groundwater that provides our drinking water, and polluting our air. Canada is angry about the acid rain (airborne sulphuric acid) from the United States that is damaging that country's forests and lakes (Gunter 1984:20). The U.S. reaction to Canadian complaints about acid rain was the banning of a Canadian-produced film on acid rain and the suppressing of an Office of Science and Technology Policy (U.S.) report urging immediate action on air pollutant reduction (Gunter 1984). Given the lack of worker organization in the United States, is there any means by which workers can protect themselves at work and their families in the community?

The fact that a number of types of groups are beginning to be concerned about environmental hazards may allow some leverage for environmental/workplace protection. The following is a list of proven and suggested strategies for action (Berman 1978:189–196; Kelman 1984):

1. When Sweden began to decide about the same time the United States did that the workplace environment needed attention, the Swedes went about it differently. The safety steward is the center of the Swedish program. The Work Environment Fund was set up at the national level, funded by a surcharge on workmen's compensation premiums. The safety stewards were given extensive training by the fund, and their responsibilities back in the plant were extended to spread their new knowledge among other workers and the employers in study circles (not lectures). Study circle course materials were provided. Not only were safety stewards charged with making people aware of unsafe conditions. they were also to train other people on how to monitor those conditions. Workers also were urged to check their worksites for the hazards they were learning about in the study circles.

Further, the new safety stewards and safety committees were given the power to shut down the operations on the spot until an outside inspector arrived if the employer would not handle an unsafe condition found by an employee. This procedure has been used about 100 times a year since the plan went into effect in 1974 (Kelman 1984:362). This kind of worker-controlled committee program with its extensive training and power to back it up is indispensible. This type of plan would mean applying pressure on OSHA to pick up the training function at their regional centers and provide more training material, and an amendment to the law to put power in the safety committee's hands.

2. Union locals should coalesce with each other and with other environment/health groups to continue to form regional committees on safety and healthy (COSH groups, such as those in Chicago and Philadelphia) to collect their own data, share information, and lobby for local and national laws and enforcement.

3. Right-to-know laws, which guarantee workers and communities access to knowledge of the dangerous substances they face, such as twenty-three states now have, should be fought for in other states, and court cases to resist preemption of these by the (currently) weak OSHA standards should be undertaken. A national right-to-know law should also be sought.

4. The movement should expose the current ghettoization of occupational medicine, in which company medical records and corporate-sponsored research are disguising the real hazards faced by the workers and their communities. Medical schools need to emphasize occupational medicine. The new Health Maintenance Organizations (HMOs) to which companies and communities are entrusting health care should be worker- and community-controlled (following the Swedish community clinic example), if information on health and adequate health care are to be sought (Berman 1978:192).

5. If occupational (environmental) diseases are to be understood and preventative measures taken, then workers must demand national and international statistics and insist upon independent research. Networking with other U.S. groups and international groups is necessary to carry this out. Ultimately NIOSH is responsible for independent research and standard setting, and it must be pressured to perform these functions.

6. Other writers suggest that concerned citizens groups should demand a national workmen's (workperson's) compensation plan and national health care. Such plans would facilitate keeping statistics on occupational illness and keep the data from being buried in private insurance and company records. Another argument for public control of workpersons' compensation funds comes from the experience of the state-controlled programs. In Ohio, Washington, West Virginia, North Dakota, and Wyoming, the only states in which private insurance plans are not allowed to operate, 94 percent of the money taken in as premiums was paid out in workers' benefits. In other states private plans paid out only 53 percent of premium funds to workers (Berman 1978:64). The profits taken out could almost double workers' benefits without raising premiums to the employer.

Programs such as these, as outlined by critics of the current environmental system, need not be detrimental to the capitalist, private ownership system (with the exception of private insurance companies and some needed facilities). Cooperation in this area will, however, mean that employers will have to share both information and decision making. Sweden has been able to work this out to its satisfaction.

SUMMARY

This and subsequent chapters keep returning to the importance of worker participation, for various reasons. This chapter discusses the positive effects of participation from the bottom up as indicated by:

- Group decision-making in the workplace and an organizational structure and culture that foster real participation in an effort to find causes of and help relieve worker stress;
- Worker/union/community participation in planning and carrying out workplace health and safety programs, if they are to be effective. Ashford (1976:26–30) pointed out the current imbalance in resources (power) between employers and workers and their communities. We must work to change this situation if national health in the United States is to be a priority.

More specifically, the chapter has covered:

1. A few international health indicator comparisons among industrial countries; the United States could be doing better;

2. Health differences among various groups in the United States—gender, SES, black/white, and age; health varied among the categories, possibly from the effects of work as it interacts with other social factors;

3. An overview of contributors to longevity, including the importance of job satisfaction, and feelings of well-being and life satisfaction. Some new findings on the effects of state-of-mind on the immune system were introduced;

4. Factors in work-related stress, with specific stressors in blue-collar and white-collar occupations and stressors from outside the workplace;

5. How some organizations and individuals respond to the stress problem. Some companies are setting up EAPs, but most workers are left to deal with stress individually;

6. The physical hazards of the workplace and the environment, including both death/disability and occupational disease. Some workplace hazards and the lack of management and OSHA attention were highlighted in a vignette from Silicon Valley;

7. OSHA and its numerous problems—underfunding, understaffing, underenthusiasm in administration in the political climate of the late 1970s and the 1980s, court tie-ups, censoring, and intimidation of workers by companies. Examples of more successful work environment programs from Sweden and Saskatchewan and some suggestions were offered for improving health and safety in the workplace in the United States.

BIBLIOGRAPHY

Ashford, Nicholas Askounes. 1976. *Crisis in the workplace: Occupational disease and injury.* Cambridge, Mass: MIT Press.

Berkowitz, Mike. 1982. Talk of workers may be hazardous to your films. *In These Times* 6, 18:10 (March 31–April 6).

Berman, Daniel M. 1978. *Death on the job: Occupational health and safety struggles in the U.S.* New York: Monthly Review Press.

Bollier, David, and Joan Claybrook. 1986. Regulations that work. *Washington Monthly* 18, 3:47–54 (April).

Brenner, M. H. 1973. *Mental illness and the economy*. Cambridge, Mass.: Harvard University Press.

Briar, Katherine H. 1978. *The effect of long-term unemployment on workers and their families*. San Francisco: R&E Research Associates.

Caplan, Robert. 1971. Organizational stress and individual strain: A social-psychological study of risk factors in coronary heart disease among administrators, engineers, and scientists. Ph.D. diss., University of Michigan, Ann Arbor.

Carruthers, Malcolm. 1980. "Hazardous occupations and the heart." In, *Current concerns in occupational stress*, edited by Cary L. Cooper and Roy Payne, 3–22. New York: John Wiley.

Cherry, N. 1978. Stress, anxiety, and work. *Journal of Occupational Psychology* 51, 3:259–270.

Chesney, Margaret A., and Ray H. Rosenman. 1980. "Type A behaviour in the work setting." In *Current concerns in occupational stress*, edited by Cary L. Cooper and Roy Payne, 187–212. New York: John Wiley.

Cooper, Cary L. 1980. "Dentists under pressure: A social psychological study." In *White collar and professional stress*, edited by Cary L. Cooper and Judi Marshall, 3–18. New York: John Wiley.

Cooper, Cary L., and Judi Marshall. 1978. "Sources of managerial and white collar stress." In *Stress at work*, edited by Cary L. Cooper and Roy Payne, 81–105. New York: John Wiley.

Creech, J. L., and M. N. Johnson. 1974. Angiosarcoma of liver in the manufacture of polyvinyl chloride. *Journal of Occupational Medicine* 16:150–151.

Davidson, Marilyn J., and Arthur Veno. 1980. "Stress and the policeman." In *White collar and professional stress*, edited by Cary L. Cooper and Judi Marshall, 131–166. New York: John Wiley.

Donahue, Phil. 1986. "The Human Animal: Part 5, Family and Survival," ABC-TV Special (August 15).

Eaton, Joseph W. 1980. "Stress in social work practice." In *White collar and professional stress*, edited by Cary L. Cooper and Judi Marshall, 167–185. New York: John Wiley.

Edsall, Thomas Byrne. 1984. *The new politics of inequality*. New York: W. W. Norton.

Eliot, Robert S., and Dennis L. Breo. 1984. *Is it worth dying for?* New York: Bantam Books.

Elling, Ray H. 1980. *Cross-national study of health systems: Political economies and health care*. New Brunswick, N.J.: Transaction Books.

———. 1986. *The struggle for workers' health: A study of six industrialized countries*. Farmingdale, N.Y.: Baywood.

Engler, Rick. 1986. Political power aids health and safety. *In These Times* 10, 8:16–17 (January 15–21).

Forbes, Rosalind. 1979. *Corporate stress*. Garden City, N.Y.: Doubleday (Dolphin).

Foreman, Judy. 1986. Mental state called a link to immunity. *Austin (TX) American-Statesman* p. C1 (June 11).

Garson, Barbara. 1975. *All the livelong day: The meaning and demeaning of routine work*. New York: Penguin.

Gersuny, Carl. 1981. *Work hazards and industrial conflict.* Hanover, N.H.: University Press of New England for University of Rhode Island.

Guide to Occupational Safety and Health, 1977 ed. 1977. Chicago: Commerce Clearing, House.

Gunter, Pete. 1984. Damn the environment—Let's do business! *The Texas Observer* 76, 20:19–21 (October 12).

Harburg, E. W. 1973. Socio-ecological stress, suppressed hostility, skin color, and black-white male blood pressure. *Psychosomatic Medicine* 35:4.

Hattis, Dale, and David Kennedy. 1986. Assessing risks from health hazards: An imperfect science. *Technology Review* 89, 4:60–67, 71 (May/June).

Haynes, Suzanne, and Manning Feinleib. 1980. Women, work and coronary heart disease: Prospective findings from the Framingham heart study. *American Journal of Public Health* 70, 2:133–141 (February).

"Health watch." 1986. ABC-TV (October 3).

Hembree, Diana. 1985. Dead end in Silicon Valley: The high-tech future doesn't work. *The Progressive* 49, 10:18–24 (October).

House, James S. 1972. The relationship of intrinsic and extrinsic work motivations to occupational stress and coronary heart disease risk. Ph.D. diss., Department of Sociology, University of Michigan, Ann Arbor.

———. 1986. "Occupational stress and coronary heart disease: A review and theoretical integration." In *The Sociology of Health and Illness: Critical Perspectives,* 2nd ed., edited by Peter Conrad and Rochelle Kern, 64–72. New York: St. Martin's Press.

Howard, Robert. 1981. Strung out at the phone company: How AT&T's workers are drugged, bugged, and coming unplugged. *Mother Jones* 6, 7:39–45, 54–59 (August).

Irwin, Michael H. K. 1986. *Risks to health and safety on the job* (Public Affairs Pamphlet No. 644). New York: Public Affairs Committee.

Ivancevich, John M., Michael T. Matteson, and Edward P. Richards III. 1985. Who's liable for stress on the job? *Harvard Business Review* 63, 2:60–72 (March–April).

Jaret, Peter. 1986. Our immune system: The wars within. *National Geographic* 169, 6:702–735 (June).

Jenkins, C. D. 1971. Psychologic and social precursors of coronary disease. *New England Journal of Medicine* 284:244–255; 307–317 (February 4; February 11).

Johnson, Tom. 1984. Hog butcher's lament. *In These Times,* 8, 28:17, 23 (June 27–July 10).

Kahn, Robert L., D. M. Wolfe, R. P. Quinn, J. D. Snoek, and R. A. Rosenthal. 1964. *Organizational stress: Studies in role conflict and ambiguity.* New York: Wiley.

Kanter, Rosabeth Moss. 1977. *Men and women of the corporation.* New York: Basic Books.

Kantor, Seth. 1985. Safety official is accused of laxity on workplace hazards. *Austin (TX) American-Statesman* p. A5 (March 28).

Kasl, Stanislav V. 1978. "Epidemiological contributions to the study of work stress." In *Stress at work,* edited by in Cary L. Cooper and Roy Payne, 4–48. New York: John Wiley.

Kasl, Stanislav V., and S. Cobb. 1970. Blood pressure changes in men undergoing job loss: A preliminary report. *Psychosomatic Medicine* 32:19–38 (January–February).

Kelman, Steven. 1984. "Bureaucracy and the regulation of health and safety at work: A comparison of the U.S. and Sweden." In *Critical studies in organization and bureaucracy,* edited by Frank Fischer and Carmen Sirianni, 356–374. Philadelphia: Temple University Press.

Kornhauser, Arthur. 1965. *Mental health of the industrial worker.* New York: Wiley.

Levi, Lennart. 1981. *Preventing work stress.* Reading, Mass.: Addison-Wesley.

Levy, Sandra M., Ronald B. Herberman, Annette M. Maluish, Bernadene Schlien, and Marc Lippman. 1985. Prognostic risk assessment in primary breast cancer by behavioral and immunological parameters. *Health Psychology* 4, 2:99–113.

Loose Bolts. 1973. Peter Schlairfer. Film.

Margolis, Bruce L., and William H. Kroes. 1974. "Work and the health of man." In *Work and the quality of life: Resource papers for 'Work in America,'* edited by James O'Toole, 133–144. Cambridge, Mass. MIT Press.

Margolis, Bruce L., William H. Kroes, and R. P. Quinn. 1974. Job stress: An unlisted occupational hazard. *Journal of Occupational Medicine* 16, 10:654–661.

Martinez, Sue, and Alan Ramo. 1980. In the valley of the shadow of death. *In These Times* 4, 39:12–13 (October 8–14).

McCaffrey, David P. 1982. *OSHA and the politics of health regulation.* New York: Plenum.

Nader, Ralph. 1984. Update on Silicon Valley: Health threats. *Multinational Monitor* 5, 6:5–6 (June).

Noble, Charles. 1986. *Liberalism at work: The rise and fall of OSHA.* Philadelphia: Temple University Press.

Northrup, Herbert R., Richard L. Rowan, and Charles R. Perry. 1978. *The Impact of OSHA: A study of the effects of the Occupational Safety and Health Act on three key industries—aerospace, chemicals, and textiles.* Philadelphia: Industrial Research Unit, Wharton School, University of Pennsylvania.

Nussbaum, Karen. 1983. Office high tech is not here for good. *In These Times* 7, 25:12 (May 24–30).

O'Connor, John T. 1980. The '70 OSHA Act offers little safety. *In These Times* 4, 31:8 (July 30– August 12).

OSHA's inspector force needs a boost, not a cut. 1985. *Austin (TX) American-Statesman* p. A14 (November 16).

Ozonoff, David. 1982. Carcinogens at large: "A public health catastrophe." *Dollars and Sense* 80:13–14 (October).

Palmore, Erdman B. 1969. Physical, mental, and social factors in predicting longevity, Part I. *Gerontologist* 9, 2:103–108 (March).

———. 1982. Predictors of the longevity difference: A 25-year follow-up. *Gerontologist* 22, 6:513–518 (December).

Pechter, Kerry. 1983. VDT's and your health. *Spring* 2, 8:23–24 (October).

Reed, Wornie L. 1986. "Suffer the children: Some effects of racism on the health of black infants." In *The sociology of health and illness: Critical perspectives*, 2nd ed., edited by Peter Conrad and Rochelle Kern, 272–280. New York: St. Martin's Press.

Reich, Robert B. 1987. Enterprise and double cross. *Washington Monthly* 18, 12:13–19 (January).

Rice, Berkeley. 1981. Can companies kill? *Psychology Today* 15, 6:78–85 (June).

Right to know laws. 1985. *Dollars and Sense*. No. 109:17 (September).

Schiro, Anne-Marie. 1983. Secretaries' poll on computers, *New York Times* 132, 45617; B7 (March 14).

Schnall, Peter L., and Rochelle Kern. 1986. "Hypertension in American society: An introduction to historical materialist epidemiology." In *The sociology of health and illness: Critical perspectives*, 2nd ed., edited by Peter Conrad and Rochelle Kern, 73–89. New York, St. Martin's Press.

Seligmann, Jean, and Mary Hager. 1984. Mental state of the union. *Newsweek* 104, 16:113 (October 15).

Selye, Hans, 1974. *Stress without distress*. Philadelphia: Lippincott.

Sennett, Richard, and Jonathan Cobb. 1972. *The hidden injuries of class*. New York: Random (Vintage).

Sexton, Patricia Cayo, and Brendan Sexton. 1971. *Blue Collars and hard hats: The working class and the future of American politics*. New York: Random (Vintage).

Shostak, Arthur B. 1980. *Blue-collar stress*. Reading, Mass.: Addison-Wesley.

Smith, Barbara Ellen. 1986. "Black lung: The social production of disease." In *The sociology of health and illness: Critical perspectives*, 2nd ed., edited by Peter Conrad and Rochelle Kern, 50–63. New York: St. Martin's Press.

Spencer, Charles. 1977. *Blue collar: An internal examination of the workplace*. Chicago: Lakeside Charter Books.

Squires, Sally. 1981. Studies look at ways stress contributes to various diseases. *Austin (TX) American-Statesman*, p. C1 (August 29).

Stellman, Jeanne M., and Susan M. Daum. 1973. *Work is dangerous to your health: A handbook of health hazards in the workplace and what you can do about them*. New York: Random (Vintage).

Stifled secretaries. 1985. *Wall Street Journal* 205, 91:31 (May 9).

Syme, S. Leonard, and Berkman, Lisa F. 1986. "Social class, susceptibility, and sickness." In *The sociology of health and illness: Critical perspectives*, 2nd ed., edited by Peter Conrad and Rochelle Kern, 28–33. New York: St. Martin's Press.

Terkel, Studs, 1974. *Working*. New York: Avon.

Turi, Gemma. 1985. Job stress affects millions. *Austin (TX) American-Statesman* p. E7 (March 31).

United Nations. 1983. *U.N. demographic yearbook: 1983*. New York: United Nations.

U.S. Department of Health, Education and Welfare. 1973. *Work in America*. Cambridge, Mass: MIT Press.

Veninga, Robert L., and James P. Spradley. 1981. *The work stress connection: How to cope with job burnout*. Boston: Little, Brown.

Waldron, Ingrid. 1986. "Why do women live longer than men?. In *The sociology of health and illness: Critical perspectives*, 2nd ed., edited by Peter Conrad and Rochelle Kern, 33–44. New York: St. Martin's Press.

Wallechinsky, David. 1986. We're number one: Or so we think. *Parade Magazine* pp. 4–6 (September 21).

Witt, Matt, and Steve Early. 1980. The worker as safety inspector. *Working Papers for a New Society* 7, 5:21–29 (September/October).

World Almanac. 1985. *World almanac and book of facts: 1986*. New York: Newspaper Enterprise Association.

———. 1986. *World almanac and book of facts: 1987*. New York: World Almanac.

10

Organizational Structure and Culture and Their Effects on Economic Growth and Productivity

WHAT IS AN ORGANIZATION?

Without even knowing the word *Gesellschaft*, we know we are living in an organizational society. Practically everything we do—school, religious affiliation, work, clubs, health care, police, fire, taxes, and even leisure activities—is in some kind of organization. Organizations (and associations) are social entities formed for particular purposes. This chapter examines organizations and associations more closely for a better understanding of them.

What else is an *organization*? First, we said it was formed for a purpose—the production of some kind of good or service. Actually, an organization usually has several goals, some of which may conflict. (See Kanter and Brinkerhoff 1982 for a discussion of the multiplicity of goals of the modern organization and the difficulties of measuring effectiveness given the political context of varying organizational constituencies with their own objectives.) Second, it is a social entity—it is composed of people working together in some relatively patterned way to further the organization's goals. Third, it has an organizational structure carrying out its activities. This means that the *technology* (knowledge, skills, and equipment used to produce the goods or services) has been subdivided into separate tasks that have been coordinated. Fourth, an organization is a distinct entity with an identifiable membership—even if it is a corporation with branches in 120 countries or an association with affiliate chapters in thousands of towns across the country.

Now that we have the idea of an organization or association as having goals, some form of structural pattern dividing tasks to perform its functions, and an identifiable boundary (this is a structural functionalist definition), here is another view. By itself Herbert Simon's communications (symbolic interaction) definition seems a little vague, but it is a valuable way to put people back into the structure. In Simon's view:

The term *organization* refers to the complex pattern of communications and other relations in a group of human beings. This pattern provides to each member of the group much of the information, assumptions, goals, and attitudes that enter into his decisions, and provides him also with a set of stable and comprehensible expectations as to what the other members of the group are doing and how they will react to what he says and does. The sociologist calls this pattern a "role system"; to most of us it is more familarly know as an "organization." (Simon 1947:xvi)

In relation to levels of analysis, Chapter 1 indicates that organizations are in the middle or mezzo level of analysis. Organizations are in the middle—affecting both their external environments and the micro level groups of workers within the organization. The external environment includes macro institutional structures (economic and political, for example) and other mezzo level organizations and micro groups, and these, in turn, affect the organization. That is what writers mean when they refer to organizations as *open systems*. Within the organization, micro level groups and the individuals can also effect the nature of their organization.

This chapter comments on the following six aspects of organizations:

1. A brief history of organizational theory's recent development
2. The characteristics of formal organization or bureaucracy, which Max Weber described early in this century and which still provide a starting point for thinking about large organizations and some advantages and disadvantages of bureaucracy, including some effects of organizational size, bureaucratic routine, and internal labor markets on worker attitudes and behaviors
3. Some dimensions of organizations that researchers and theorists have used to analyze organizational structure and behavior: size, technology and work process, division of labor (task specialization), location of decision making, interdependence among departments, and communications
4. Management styles and organizational culture and their effects on workers
5. Productivity, economic growth, and organizational and social (political economy) structures
6. A short case history on an industry and its major company and how they were shaped by and also shaped their environment from the late nineteenth century to the present: U.S. Steel—the industry and the corporation.

SOME HISTORY OF ORGANIZATIONAL THEORY

Like industrial sociology, the field of organizational theory did not emerge until the post–World War II period. In 1946 and 1947 two works of Max Weber were published in English. Michels's (1949) work on bureaucracy and the reader edited by Merton et al. (1952) soon followed. Case studies of specific organizations began appearing more frequently. Scott (1975) lists these early works and goes on to describe the subsequent changes in the field. Initially many researchers took the individual organization's structure as given and examined how that structure or the informal groups within it affected the behavior of its members; this is a *closed system* approach, with structure as the independent variable and employee behavior as the dependent variable.

Several influences helped change the closed system approach. One influence was Udy's (1959) studies of production organizations in preindustrial societies and his challenging of the accepted Weberian model of western bureaucracies. Another influence was the input from business schools that organizations are decision-making mechanisms (Barnard 1938; Simon 1947; March and Simon 1958). Structural arrangements and the part they play in aiding or limiting decision making become part of what is to be examined. In England two research teams, the Woodward and Aston groups, began studying the effects on structure of different types of technologies used in production. A major influence came from the general systems theorists. They stressed the dependence of organizations on outside resources—raw materials (including clients and customers), personnel, state of technology available, markets, legitimacy with the public and with government, and legal system (Scott 1975:3). Researchers began to study organizations as open systems, which are confronted with uncertainty in the environment with which they must contend (see Galaskiewicz 1985 for a review of this literature).

Rather than the static structures of a closed system, open systems research emphasizes the aspects of the organizational structure that allow feedback information to inform decision making and even to produce adaptive changes in the structure. The explanation of dependent variables shifted from the behavior of individuals as they were shaped by their organizations to variation in the structural characteristics of organizations from its interaction with both internal and external factors.

At the same time that this shift was taking place in the kinds of organizational variables that could be studied, a shift in methodology was found to be necessary. Previous research had concentrated on the single case study, whereas now many researchers began testing their propositions by using social surveys on a number of organizations. This required much effort in the development of measurement techniques, sample design, and analysis procedures (see Scott 1975:3–4 and Lammers 1978). Fortunately, formal organizations also are record keepers and often must report to government agencies, stockholders, and others. Researchers thus will sometimes have available historical information for longitudinal studies on some kinds of variables. Unfortunately, however, some of the most relevant variables are not recorded and require some detective work by the researcher. For example, an organization's informal procedures and communications, both internal and external, are frequently much more important in terms of what gets done and how it is accomplished than is the information that shows up on written records.

In sum, the field of organizational theory has expanded tremendously in scope since its post–World War II days. Its expansion has, in some respects, paralleled the changes in management theory reviewed in Chapter 4—although not at exactly the same time. From a Tayloristic, rationalistic, bureaucratic, and human relations concentration on the organization as the unit of analysis—isolated, autonomous, and concerned only with internal operations and worker attitudes shaped by work conditions—the field has enlarged to include reciprocal effects with the external environment (structural contingency management ideas) and alternative possibilities for workplace organization (human resources management) (see Chapter 11 for a discussion of these alternatives).

WEBER'S CHARACTERISTICS OF MODERN BUREAUCRACY

Formal organizations and bureaucracies had existed before the industrial revolution. Examples include the settled agricultural or nomad-sedentary states of Egypt, the Byzantine empire, China (Han to Ching periods, 200 B.C. to 1912 A.D.), Mohenjo Daro, Rome, the Incas of Peru and the Aztecs of Mexico, the various African empires, Arab Caliphate and Arab Moslem states in the Mediterranean and Iran, the Ottoman Empire, the Spanish-American empire, and other European colonial empires, and, of course, the Roman Catholic Church. All of these large organizations had bureaucracies—scribes, managers, tax collectors, a military, and other functionaries (see Eisenstadt 1971:250–313 for discussion of some of these early bureaucracies).

Even though these organizations may have shared some structural features similar to modern industrial society bureaucracies, sometimes they also presented some interesting differences—such as the number of examinations on classical literature one passed as determining one's position in the Chinese bureaucracy. The literature had nothing to do with the job; it assured that the candidate was of high moral calibre from learning so much Confucian writing (Weber 1946a).

Weber's *Wirtschaft und Gesellschaft (Economy and Society)*, written primarily in the second decade of this century, did not reach English readers until after World War II. By this time people in the United States were aware of government bureaucracies as well as of those of big business, and even of education and religion. Weber had noted a tendency for an increased *instrumental* or *technical rationalization* (division of labor, hierarchy of authority, routines, and rules) in organizations in modern industrial societies. Even though in general he thought this rationalization was useful because it was efficient for large-scale tasks, as a liberal republican he was concerned with its possibilities for limiting individual independence and freedom and also for limiting creativity and flexibility in society. Technical rationality can be used, of course, for totally irrational ends. For example, a great deal of technical rationality can go into building a bomb that can decimate a large part of the world (Weber 1968:85–86).

Another kind of rationality—*substantive rationality*—refers to the ends or goals of organizations or individuals. Weber called these two types of rationality *Zweckrational* (instrumental technical) and *Wertrational* (values, ultimate ends) (Weber 1968:24–26).

In his general view of social change, Weber offers the only way he can see how the "iron cage" of bureaucracy can be periodically changed and made temporarily more flexible. He pointed out that historically charismatic leaders (indicating that not everyone is totally shaped by their institutional environment) arise to break with custom because something about them inspires people to believe in their ability and follow them. These charismatic leaders can alter traditional structures and beliefs, but over time their beliefs and the organization established by their followers set up another institutionalized system—either traditional or modern bureaucratic, depending on the economic and political structures existing in the society. Hence, structures again become fossilized, awaiting another charismatic alteration (Weber 1968:246–254). This tendency to go from flexible to more rigid organizational structure over time could be viewed as the life cycle of organizations.

In addition to the tendencies of industrial societies for increased division of labor and rationalization, Weber noted that these modern bureaucracies were based on a different type of *authority* (power recognized as legitimate) than were older bureaucracies or other forms of governance. Weber outlined three "ideal types" of authority. First, *traditional authority*, found frequently in the past, is based on the sanctity of age-old rules and powers, the encumbent receiving loyalty to his or her person, rather than to the office (Weber 1968:226–241). Second, the *charismatic* type of authority is based on the personality of the leader—on his or her extraordinary powers or qualities that make the leader's word law and cause people to follow that leader (Weber 1968:241–245; 1946c). This phenomenon is referred to in the previous paragraph regarding Weber's only hope for revitalizing fossilized bureaucratic structures.

The third type of authority, found in modern bureaucracies, is a *legal/rational* type of authority—a legitimacy based on "legality of enacted rules and the right of those elevated to authority under such rules to issue commands" within the scope of the office (Weber 1968:215). In the real world, these three ideal types of authority will sometimes overlap, as in the cases of a charismatic elected official or of a constitutional monarchy that reigns rather than rules. In both the examples, however, the system is still based on legal/rational authority if the legal system still continues to operate and its rules are followed.

Weber discussed several characteristics he felt these modern bureaucracies had in common. His arguments can be summarized briefly as follows (Weber 1946a; 1968:956–1005):

1. Division of labor (specialization of tasks) among offices with prescribed duties and functions
2. Hierarchy of authority (with centralized decision-making, channels of communication, powers of office holders delineated)
3. Written rules and procedures
4. Files kept for continuity as new office holders enter the organization
5. Impersonality—office holders achieve their positions by fulfilling certification requirements and taking exams—all relationships within and between offices are according to the prescribed rules
6. Separation of home and office—separation of worker from ownership of his or her tools
7. Positions are *careers* with promotion procedures established and salaries on a set scale
8. Secrecy between offices, except for communications between them to carry out functions.

THE ADVANTAGES AND DISADVANTAGES OF BUREAUCRACY

Advantages of Modern Bureaucracy

When thinking about bureaucracy, many, if not most people, will groan and think of red tape, royal run-arounds, interminable forms, long waits

in reception rooms, impersonal or even brusk treatment by minor officials, and other negative stereotypes. However, they will usually agree
with Weber that bureaucracies do large tasks that could not be done
otherwise—with varying degrees of efficiency. Modern bureaucracies are
certainly more efficient and impersonal or "universalistic" in that they
require certification for the office, except for the heads of the public
bureaucracies that are often political appointments. This universalism
has many advantages over patrimonial and other traditional types of bureaucracies of the past, discussed at length by Weber with regard to fa-
voritism and "particularistic" (nepotism, old boy network) practices
(1968:1020–1110). Weber's description, of course, is an ideal type, and
we all recognize that positions are sometimes filled and promotions
granted on bases other than merit in the real world, as noted in earlier
chapters with regard to the difficulties of minorities in the occupational
structure. On the whole, however, modern bureaucracy vastly increases
the opportunity for hiring, promotions, and pay on merit and more or
less efficiently handles the large-scale tasks of industrial societies (see
Perrow 1986:6–10).

Disadvantages of Modern Bureaucracy

The disadvantages bureaucracies may develop can be surmised from a
thoughtful look at Weber's list of characteristics. We comment on the
following problems: the centralization of decision making, the rigidity
bureaucratic structures form in the face of changing conditions or specific cases, goal displacement—both accidental and deliberate, effects on
personality characteristics of the worker, and secrecy.

The Centralization of Decision Making

First, the hierarchy of authority centralizes decision making in fewer
hands, as Weber noted. As bureaucracies have grown larger since his
time and become more widespread in almost all areas of life, fewer and
fewer persons are involved in the decision-making process. Organizational Sociologist Charles Perrow comments on the concentration of
power in a few hands and bureaucracy as a means of social control.

> Bureaucracy is a tool, a social tool that legitimizes control of the many by
> the few, despite the formal apparatus of democracy, and this control has
> generated unregulated and unperceived social power. This power includes
> much more than just control of employees. As bureaucracies satisfy,
> delight, pollute, and satiate us with their output of goods and services,
> they also shape our ideas, our very way of conceiving of ourselves, control
> our life chances, and even define our humanity. As employees, whether we

see ourselves as exploited or as pursuing "careers," we dimly perceive this fact; as citizens in a society of organizations, where large organizations have absorbed all that used to be small, independent, personal, communitarian, religious, or ethnic, it is rarely perceived. We grow up in organizations; to stand outside them is to see their effect on what we believe, what we value, and, more important, how we think and reason. (Perrow 1986:5)

The Rigidity of Bureaucratic Structures

The second major criticism is that bureaucracies tend to fossilize. Rules and procedures are set up for one set of conditions, but conditions have a way of continuously changing. Also, such rule systems do not handle special cases well. Innovation and creativity that could encourage adaptation are frequently discouraged in many bureaucratic organizations, as we see in the story of U.S. Steel at the end of this chapter.

Goal Displacement: Accidental and Intentional

A third criticism is of goal displacement. *Goal displacement* refers to the organization's losing sight of its original goals for some reason. An early view of the phenomenon of bureaucracies that did not fulfill their original goals well was that inefficiency developed in the system because functionaries became caught up in filling out forms and following the letter rather than the spirit of the rules in serving clients or producing products. A later interpretation of some goal displacement from the power/conflict perspective calls attention to the point that powerful groups in society may not want the bureaucracy to fulfill its stated goals and, therefore, leaders are appointed to ensure that goal displacement occurs (Perrow 1986:263–265). Examples of this phenomenon from previous chapters include EPA, OSHA, the NLRB, the World Bank, the IMF, and recent appointments to the U.S. Commission on Civil Rights.

Effects on Workers' Personalities

Another problem with bureaucracies involves the possible effects on some workers, as well as on the clients they serve. We have commented on the irritation some clients feel about the red tape and impersonal treatment. For some time researchers from several disciplines have studied the effects on the workers themselves. Some of these effects include a lack of commitment that large organizations seem to foster, a related tendency to steal from the organization, a bureaucratic or organization personality that limits individual development, and an alternative reaction to sabotage the goals of the organization. Some of these effects need a little explanation.

Organizational Size and Lack of Worker Commitment: One dominant feature of bureaucratic organizations is large size. The effects of organizational and even task group size on many human beings is well documented. Economist Mancur Olson (1965) was an early writer on the fact that large organizations and groups encouraged lack of commitment and a feeling of lack of individual responsibility among their members. The essence of the argument is captured in these frequently heard statements: "Why should I put out effort someone else will get credit for? Someone else will do it, therefore, I need not bother." Olson cites empirical and historical evidence of this phenomenon from labor unions, pressure groups, and corporations. His insight on why so many potentially powerful collectivities with common interests, such as consumers, the middle and lower social classes, and taxpayers, go unrepresented and unorganized in our mass society is as fresh and fascinating today as it was when it appeared more than twenty years ago.

News stories, such as the Kitty Genovese case in the borough of Queens, New York, in March 1964 give anecdotal support. Thirty-nine people looked out their middle-class apartment windows, saw her attacked, heard her cries for help. During the thirty minutes it took for her assailant to repeatedly stab and finally kill her (he left once, then returned to finish the job), no one called the police. The question of how people could allow this to happen stimulated study. Social psychologists Latane and Darley, in their "Lady in Distress" experiments, found that the larger the size of the group, the less likely the individual was to take responsibility and action to help other people (Latane and Darley 1970; Latane and Nida 1981). In other words, large organizations and groups encourage most of us to let the other person act. Being a small cog in a large operation, rather than producing in a more independent craftspersonlike manner, similarly lends itself to lack of commitment and sometimes to poor quality work.

Organizational Size and the Exploitative Orientation: Related to this lack of commitment and individual responsibility is what Gracey (1967: 607–610) called the "exploitative orientation" and Perrow (1986:14–20) referred to as "feathering the nest." Large organizations seem to invite stealing of various kinds—from paper and pencils, to expensive equipment, to the appropriation of products produced or sold, to stealing company time for personal projects. This ethical problem is not limited to only the middle-ranking or lower workers. Boardroom crimes—from price-fixing, juggling the books, stealing ideas from competitors or deliberately putting them out of business through underhanded tactics, selling products known to be unsafe, and bribery—are also included in the exploitative orientation (Gracey 1967:607–608).

Lest we think that this happens only in capitalist organizations, a sociologist from an Eastern European country stated several years ago that in his country the state expected one car in five to disappear from the assembly line in small parts; the workers felt it was their due and the government-owned company would never miss it. Similarly, why did respectable middle-class housewives steal shirts from Gimbel's Department Store when they could have afforded to buy them? This group had the highest theft rate (next to the employees) in a study done in New York in the late 1960s. The guilty parties made such statements as: "They are a big company. They'll never miss a few shirts. That's what they carry insurance for. If I don't take the goods, someone else will. They probably overcharge on what I do pay for, so we are coming out even."

The anonymity of being in a large group encourages many people to do things they would never dream of doing if they thought they would be held individually accountable. Adults are usually less inclined to steal from the small mom-and-pop store on the corner, where they know the owners and other customers. In a round-about way we are back to Olson's point that in small groups we can see the effect of our actions and our benefits from doing something "constructive," while in large groups we do not.

Effects on Workers of the Internal Labor Market and Ritualism in Bureaucratic Structures on Workers: Kanter (1977:245–253; see also Edwards 1975 and Piore 1975 and Baron 1984) has described the internal job market in large organizations—its rewards and upward mobility attributes—in terms of how the people in these jobs are affected by (1) opportunity for advancement and growth, (2) power—the ability to mobilize resources, and (3) proportions of a group filling that level position (that is, whether one is a token).

How do people feel when they perceive that their job is low in opportunities for mobility and growth? They tend to limit their aspirations by not valuing more responsibility and participation, have lower self-esteem, seek satisfaction outside of work, have a horizontal orientation to peers rather than to superiors, be critical of or fail to identify with higher-ups, not be active in seeking change in the structure (through collective action, for example), discourage peers from upward mobility, define success in ascriptive rather than task terms (role compensation), be more attached to a local unit than to the overall organization, not expect to do any better (fatalism akin to the culture of poverty) and value only extrinsic rewards (social or economic). Presthus (1962:218–221) has also noted this lowering of aspirations. According to Kanter, people low in power tend to foster lower group morale; be more authoritarian; restrict opportunities for the growth of other workers, especially subordinates who might rival them; judge themselves by their subordinates to gain a superior feeling; and hang on to their own turf.

On the other hand, people whose jobs are on career ladders and who perceive opportunity for growth will have an opposite orientation: high aspirations, orientation to people above them and the larger organization, more orientation toward action groups when blocked, and more orientation to competitive and upward mobility with work as a central life interest. People who perceive themselves higher in power tend to encourage group morale, behave in less directive and authoritarian ways, provide opportunities for subordinates to move up with them and encourage their growth, and project a helpful and positive image.

Hence, we find that people in dead-end jobs, whether in the secondary labor market or at the bottom jobs in primary sector bureaucracies, begin to select themselves out as well as being selected out already by other people. The self-fulfilling prophecy affects both the workers and those who judge their worth. For example, women have been said not to be career oriented historically, which may have been true for many women. However, men in dead-end positions, which are similar to the majority of women's jobs in that respect, are also not career oriented. The jobs may be shaping aspirations and expectations more than the people being different initially in these respects. This seems like a strong possibility until proven otherwise. It also makes nonsense out of the functionalist/status attainment argument that only the superior and deserving reach the top. Kanter's position is that people are adaptive and make the best of the organizational positions in which they find themselves. They strive for some dignity—"reduction of dependency"—in that position, which takes what the upwardly mobiles would call "self-defeating" forms (Kanter 1977:251).

Kanter's third point refers to the effect on workers in an organization when they are visibly different from the others in the same position. Workers who are in a small proportion (minority in numbers) tend to be on display, feel pressure to conform and make fewer mistakes, try to disappear socially, find it difficult to be creditable to peers and superiors, feel isolated, be excluded from informal peer networks and the informal power structure, be sponsored less often by a mentor, find themselves stereotyped and withdraw, and face more personal stress—as noted in the last chapter on health.

For blacks, Hispanics, women, Native Americans, Asian Americans and other visible minorities this means that the tokenism in nontraditional jobs puts them in a stressful, nonsupported, display position for which they must be well prepared if they want to retain their mental health.

Bureaucracy also demands conformity and attention to rules and routines, which may foster ritualistic traits or behavior. This behavior, which may affect many workers at different levels, is particularly apparent among the lower levels of a bureaucracy, where power and autonomy are low. At the individual level such behavior becomes goal displacement—the routines (the means) have become the ends (Merton 1952:361–371; Presthus 1962:205–256). In this way the worker keeps himself or herself covered and cannot be criticized for not doing the job as described.

For the upwardly mobiles who have not given up on their careers, ritualism takes a somwhat different form. The emphasis is not just doing enough to cover oneself and get by, but on reading the organizational culture and one's superiors to see what will be needed to rise in the system. Alan Harrington's fascinating but disturbing account of *Life in the Crystal Palace* (1959) describes how to adapt to and rise in the pleasant, uneventful, non-boat-rocking atmosphere of one large company.

Riesman (1967:610–616) refers to this chameleonlike quality as the "other-directed man." Riesman is referring not just to people who successfully adapt themselves to whatever it takes to rise in the corporation, but also to the wider meaning that in an industrial society we play so many roles in so many places and organizations that we become adept at reading whatever script is handed to us in a new situation. Riesman's metaphor is not so often that of role playing but of using our radar—a technological metaphor for a technological society. By this self-preservation mechanism some people lose the inner-directedness of a basic set of ideas and values socialized into us at an early age, which would make us try to shape our roles to us, rather than vice versa. Inner-directedness is a relic of earlier, less interdependent times. Our values and behaviors become situational. This other-directedness is the organization man when placed in an organizational structure such as Harrington's Crystal Palace. William H. Whyte (1956) popularized the term *organization man* and his penchant for adapting to the social ethic. Whyte describes the process in this manner:

> By social ethic I mean that contemporary body of thought which makes morally legitimate the pressures of society against the individual. Its major propositions are three: a belief in the group as the source of creativity; a belief in 'belongingness' as the ultimate need of the individual; and a belief in the application of science to achieve the belongingness. (Whyte 1956:7)

Naturally, in order to do this we must convince ourselves that our individual needs and interests are the same as those of the corporation, the group with the most telling imprint on our lives. Whyte's book ends with a tongue-in-cheek chapter on how to take personality tests the corporate personnel department will administer so you will look fairly conformist and conservative and give back the corporate values without being inconsistent and caught lying (Whyte 1956:449–456).

The people fewer in number who choose to resist conformity (such as Studs Terkel's autoworker who puts a little dent in each product as his trademark) remind us that resistance for those who want to conform completely can take many shapes (Terkel 1974). The Hawthorne studies of workers trying to set their own work pace and the combative relations between labor and management outlined in Chapter 7 remind us that workers in small groups and larger associations have often seen their interests as different from those of the organization and attempt to resist by whatever means are at hand.

Secrecy

A final possible disadvantage of bureaucracy is secrecy. Despite bureaucracies' many written records regarding some things, much within a bureaucracy is hidden. Sometimes information does not work its way up the chain of command, as workers attempt to cover tracks, hide the bad news from superiors, and maintain a little control over their work. In such a case even top management may have incomplete information on which to make decisions. In other cases, as implied in the section on exploitative orientation and also in other chapters, corporate executives are eager to keep some corporate operations out of sight of competitors or the public. At other times the secrecy is not purposeful as much as it is a lack of communications or reason to document what is occurring. From these general ideas about bureaucratic organization and some of its successes and problems, we turn to studies and classification schemes developed in the last thirty years or so for the analysis of organizational structures and processes.

TYPES OF ORGANIZATIONS: VARIOUS DIMENSIONS

As noted earlier in this chapter, organizations and associations are established to further particular purposes. Organizational structure can be defined as "the division of labor and means of coordination (integration) used to link the technology, tasks, and people in an organization to achieve the desired goals" (Hellriegel, Slocum, and Woodman 1983:311). Organizational theorists have studied and sorted into types the nature of these purposes, the kinds of power they hold over their members and the reasons people become members of them, the size and age of organizations, the nature of technology and structure of production, the nature of the organization's environment, management styles, and organizational culture (climate).

Like other typologies or ideal types we have encountered—political and economic systems and types of authority—these are based on one or a few defining characteristics in order to make broad classification possible. They do not enable us to predict everything about organizations within the category because those organizations may vary in other important ways. In addition, studies designed to test relationships among the characteristics, such as size, differentiation of structure, and number of levels of management, do not always agree. Some typologies are useful because they sensitize us to the dimensions along which organizations are similar and different.

Two Very General Typologies

We begin with two typologies so broad that they have not been useful in generating research. Because they are so general, however, they provide a place to begin thinking about organizational structure and related attributes.

Peter Blau and Richard Scott (1963:46−67; Olsen 1978:64−65) classified associations/organizations into four categories on the basis of who benefits from the attainment of the organization's dominant goals and the kinds of problems they encounter:

1. Business associations: the main goal is to make money for the owners; the distinctive problem is operating efficiently in order to show a profit.

2. Mutual benefit associations: the dominant goal is to benefit their members in some way—occupational and professional associations, labor unions, political parties, literary and artistic societies, civil rights associations, social and recreational organizations, churches, and other special interest groups. The organizational problem is that the members must be able to retain internal control so that their association will really benefit them (remember Michels's "iron law of oligarchy" that even socialist parties and unions may end up in the control of the few).

3. Service associations: the dominant goal is to provide services of some variety to clients—schools, hospitals, social service agencies, real estate firms, law firms, police departments, and prisons, for example. The problems are maintaining the clients' best interests and not exploiting them since they are dependent.

4. Commonwealth association: the dominant goal is to serve the entire community, including government organizations and agencies, military, public health, libraries and museums, and scientific institutes. The prevailing problem is maintaining public control so that elite or inside interests do not turn the benefits away from the common welfare to their own ends (see Chapter 5 for examples).

Organizational sociologist Amitai Etzioni (1961:3–21) developed a "compliance" based typology, which is different from the technology/task approaches outlined below. His classification is according to the goals and rewards the organization offers to attract and keep workers and to legitimate their existence to the wider environment. First, he identifies three types of power an organization can have over its members:

1. Coercive: application or threat of *physical* sanctions—from forcibly withholding food, sex, or comfort to restriction of movement, to death
2. Remunerative power: control over *material* resources and rewards—salaries and wages, fringe benefits, services, commodities
3. Normative power: allocation and manipulation of *symbolic* rewards and deprivations—prestige symbols, ritual, acceptance.

Second, Etzioni classified the kind of involvement members themselves feel they have with the organization. These feelings are on a continuum listed here from the most negative to the most positive:

1. Alienative: intense negative orientation, such as slaves might frequently have to masters, inmates in prisons and concentration camps, and some enlisted personnel in basic training
2. Calculative involvement: a more neutral orientation of relatively low intensity, such as in regular business relationships and prison inmates who have established themselves with the authorities as informants
3. Moral involvement: a positive orientation of high intensity, such as the faithful member of a church and a devoted member in the party. Moral commitments are of two types: pure, based on internalization of norms and identification with authority; and social commitment, which rests on sensitivity to pressures of other people—such as Riesman's "other-directed" man.

Some combinations of these six categories are highly unlikely; others are more congruent. The congruent types are:

1. Coercive-alienative
2. Remunerative-calculative
3. Normative-moral.

What does this mean to organizations? According to Etzioni:

Congruent types are more effective than incongruent types. Organizations are under pressure to be effective. Hence, to the degree that the environment of the organization allows, organizations tend to shift their compliance structure from incongruent to congruent types and organizations which have congruent compliance structures tend to resist factors pushing them toward incongruent compliance structures. (Etzioni 1961:14)

However, people belong to organizations for different reasons, and the types of involvement and its intensity must be an empirical question in any study. Also, organizations and even units in the same organization may emphasize compliance structures of different kinds, or combinations of compliance rewards (coercive, material, symbolic). These structures must be carefully studied, as well. Shifting, seasonal, and intermittent structures are also interesting to observe as organizations are forced to change compliance and reward systems to fit changing social conditions. Also, because types are frequently found together in the real world and thus seem congruent, this should not blind the student of organizational structure and behavior to alternative possibilities and the successful cases that do not follow the implied pattern.

This typology does not seem overly helpful in differentiating what goes on within the organization. Even if we label all prisons and reformatories as coercive organizations, we find they do not all operate the same. Some are strictly punitive, custodial warehouses. Others make a strong attempt at rehabilitation and are nearer the goals and structure of what we expect from schools, especially prisons in Sweden. Also, some schools look more like coercive prisons and reformatories than we would have expected.

Technology, Tasks, Department Functions, and Interdependence

In Weber's bureaucratic model of the organization, we focused on internal aspects—hierarchy of authority (which also designates channels of communication)—division of labor into offices and departments, rules and regulations, record keeping, and impersonal (universalistic) personnel procedures. Added to this bureaucratic model is the scientific management idea of applied research to find the most efficient means of breaking down jobs into specific tasks and performing them in the most efficient manner. So far, we are talking about structure and not much about people and their various motivations. Of course the technology of how production is organized is implicit within the organization.

Woodward and Aston Group Studies

In Chapter 4 we learned we owed a debt of gratitude to British industrial sociologist Joan Woodward (1958, 1965), whose studies of 100 industries in South Essex revealed that structure and successful management practices differed according to the technology of the industry. We reviewed her classification of industries by the technical complexity of the manufacturing process: large batch or mass production, small batch or custom production, and continuous process (such as liquids and gases). When the 100 industries in her study were organized into these categories, some regularities began to appear. With increasing complexity of the process (from low complexity in large batch to high complexity in continuous process), the levels of management, the ratio of management and support staff to labor, the skill of the labor force, the amount of verbal communication, the decentralization of decision making and informal procedures all increased. Woodward noted that the successful firms most nearly adapted their structures to the nature of their technology (Daft 1983:162–165). The less successful firms all deviated significantly from the median of their industrial category.

Also studying technology was the research team from the University of Aston in Birmingham, England (Hickson, Pugh, and Pheysey 1969). In their research on fifty-two manufacturing and nonmanufacturing firms they identified three areas that seemed to affect the structure of the workflow within organizations:

1. Automation of equipment: This includes the number of tasks performed by machines rather than by people.
2. Workflow rigidity: This includes the amount of skill of workers and the number of purposes to which machines could be adapted, as well as the degree of standardization of the sequence of operations.
3. Specificity of evaluation: This ranges from exact, quantitative measurement to more subjective, qualitative evaluation by managers.

James Thompson

We were also introduced to the work of theorist James Thompson (1967) in Chapter 4. He considered the amount of interdependence among units or departments in the technological process in the following typology:

1. Pooled interdependence: Each unit or department makes a discrete contribution to the entire process. The interdependence among the units in the organization is not great so the demands on management for communications and decision making are low and the service can be fairly standardized. Sales departments and real estate offices are examples of pooled interdependence.

2. Sequential interdependence: Interdependence among units or departments is sequential so there must be some planning and coordination on the part of management. Assembly line operations are good examples of sequential interdependence.

3. Reciprocal interdependence: The departments in the organization pass the product back and forth among them several times and are reciprocally interdependent, which makes high demands on management to allow for frequent communications, coordination, and decision making in this complex interaction. Surgical units and psychiatric hospitals are examples of reciprocal interdependence.

Charles Perrow

Chapter 4 also contains typologies from the work of structural contingency theorist Charles Perrow (1970). Perrow's work is particularly useful in understanding departmental structures and their technologies, since departments within organizations differ along the dimensions he observed. We combine his ideas with those of other theorists who take into account the differing effects of environment on departments shown in Figure 10.1.

Perrow first analyzed the tasks according to variety—a continuum on whether the tasks were routine and predictable, to the extreme of unexpected situations with frequent problems. The second dimension of technology dealt with the analyzability of work performed. If work procedures and cause-effect relationships in technological process were clear, a manual of procedures could be written. If work procedures were not straightforward and relied on experience, intuition, and judgment,

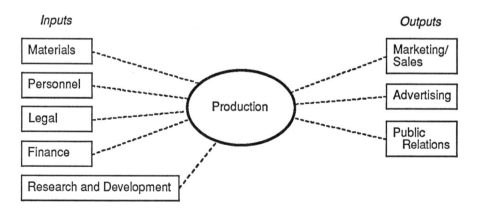

Figure 10.1 Departments within Organizations, Including Buffers that Deal with the Environment

then it was not an analyzable technology. Combining these two dimensions, Perrow arrived at four types:

1. Routine: Little task variety and easily standardized procedures, such as assembly lines and bank tellers routines
2. Craft: Fairly predictable tasks but not very analyzable, resting on much training and experience, such as glass blowers and performing artists
3. Engineering: Variety of tasks overall, but relying on set knowledge, formulas, and techniques; exemplified by engineering and accounting
4. Nonroutine: Tasks with much variety and a conversion technology that is not well understood; for example, sciences that are on the frontier or are in the frontier stage (require much knowledge and a certain amount of intuitive know-how from experience); exemplified by social sciences, strategic planning, and applied research.

Before looking at influences from outside the organization, we comment on the amount of technological determinism involved in an organization. We have seen some convincing statements that successful organizations adapt themselves to their technology. Apparently, more is involved. Subsequent studies have not always been so positive about the strength of technological determinism. Size of organization and the nature of their environment are also powerful determinants (Daft 1983:180). In addition, there may be a choice of alternative technologies and the manner in which they are used. For example, Volvo deliberately chose not to employ large-batch assembly line technology in the production of autos; instead, the company successfully employed a work-team approach usually associated with small-batch production. Such examples appear in Chapter 11.

Influences from the Environment

The resource dependence model of organizations (variously called a political economy model, dependence exchange approach, or structural contingency approach) recognizes that organizations depend on their environments for raw materials and other inputs, personnel, markets, political and legal influences (see Pfeffer and Salancik 1978). Chapters 5 through 7 show organizational decisions made regarding many types of environmental conditions—vertical integration to assure supply or distribution, horizontal integration to limit competition, political lobbying and related activities to gain favorable legislation, interlocking directorates for various reasons, public relations to gain legitimacy, and a whole range of activities to establish or maintain a favorable climate in which to operate at home and abroad. Various departments in the organization have responsibility for coping with different aspects of the environment and stabilizing conditions for production.

In their review of the literature on organizations and their environments, organizational sociologists Aldrich and Pfeffer (1976:84) note a range of choices or strategies is available to organizations. The influence of internal subunits and sometimes the demands of external groups affect the outcome of organizational decisions on how to deal with its environment. In other words, an organization can act in a number of ways and still survive. This is not a model of complete determinism. Some theorists take a natural selection approach to the shaping of organizations over time by their environment that is more deterministic and carries the assumption that the organizations that survive are more fit. We do not discuss that model here (see discussion in Aldrich and Pfeffer 1976; Carroll 1984).

Buffer Departments and the Production Core

Environmental uncertainty has an interesting effect on the internal structure of organizations. Note the buffer departments dealing with various parts of the environment in Figure 10.1. When an external uncertainty is perceived as particularly important to an organization's survival, then the internal unit that deals with it becomes more important. This reaction might account for the tendency in Japan for chief executive officers (CEOs) to have science and engineering backgrounds and the increasing tendency in the United States for CEOs to come from finance or legal backgrounds. The part of the environment that large corporations perceive as most important to be dealt with in each country seems apparent. One is looking at product quality, the consumers, and foreign competition because of a small home market; the other is more concerned with cost efficiency and how the juggling of assets can contribute to the quarterly earnings statement (Rosen 1981; Peters and Waterman 1982:36–39; Reich 1987).

Figure 10.1 sketches the functions of various departments commonly found in corporations. The buffers must deal with varying degrees of uncertainty in their parts of the environment. From the previous discussion, we recognize that this means these departments must be more flexible, informal, and collegial in nature. Business students will see in Figure 10.1 the line-staff conflict inherent in some organizations due to differences in department organization, differences in age and training (staff in the buffer departments often tend to be younger and professionally trained as opposed to production/line workers, who may have been working for many years and may be less credentialed). Large service organizations also develop buffer staff departments. For example, university professors (line workers) and department chairs (foremen/women) have been heard to grumble about the necessity of all the staffers, all their directives, and the paperwork and reports they can demand.

Thompson's and Mintzberg's Attempts at Inclusive Typologies

Thompson's typology concerns the interdependence of units in the organization. In his second typology of organizations he considered the clients as types of inputs in the technological process. This process included service organizations as well as goods production and extended our thinking from internal structure to inputs from outside the organization. He uses the term *technology* here in its broad meaning, to refer not only to machines, but also to the entire work process in the following types of technology:

1. Mediating technology: These organizations link clients from the outside with each other, providing a service, such as banks, real estate firms, stockbrokers, employment agencies, and retail stores.
2. Long-linked technology: Operations from one stage become inputs for the next, and so on until the product is ready for the consumer—assembly-line production, for example.
3. Intensive technology: Organizations provide a collection of specialized services for clients and may bring about some kind of change in the client or other inputs—hospitals, schools, airlines, and their respective maintenance departments, for example.

Henry Mintzberg (1979) developed five classifications of organizations that seem to tap more aspects of organizations than do some of the earlier studies. His classifications are:

1. Simple structure: These organizations are usually new and quite small. Work procedures are informal and directed by the entrepreneur. If they are adaptable (not to mention lucky in finding venture capital and not being clobbered by the larger organizations in the field), they can react quickly in a changing environment and succeed.

2. Machine bureaucracy: These organizations are typically large, with routine large-batch production. Large technical staff in buffer departments deal with the outside environment and try to keep production stable, as in Figure 10.1. Since these bureaucracies do not usually adapt well in a changing environment, they are often found in the sunset industries.

3. Professional bureaucracy: These organizations are bureaucracies, even though they are composed of professionals who have a lot of autonomy and need little of the more rigid control mechanisms usually found in bureaucracy. Technical support groups are minimal. These organizations often provide services in a complex environment. Examples are hospitals, large law firms, and consulting, investment, and engineering firms.

4. Divisionalized form: These are large firms divided into product or market groups. Direction from the home office may be minimal, perhaps including some planning and research, and the work falls on the divisional manager. Internal structure of the division depends on nature of the product or service—large batch, small batch, or custom. Some of the sunset industry companies mentioned have adopted the divisional idea (General Motors, for example) to try to gain flexibility.

5. Adhocracy: This flexible form has developed in high technology industries, such as electronics and aerospace, to deal with complex and rapidly changing environments. A matrix form of structure often develops, with the professional workers sharing information across departments and making many decisions in small temporary task teams (reminiscent of Likert's linking-pin committees) in a decentralized manner. IBM was a pioneer of this form.

These classifications touch on but do not emphasize two possible dimensions of organizations. The excluded dimensions relate to each other in that they all deal in some way with worker personality, motivation, and behavior. One dimension is how the internal structure of organizations affects worker attitudes and behaviors, both on and off the job. Another dimension related to worker attitudes and behaviors includes management styles and the overall corporate culture possible in organizations, although Mintzberg deals briefly with corporate culture as a "missionary configuration" or ideology.

Earlier we discussed the first dimension in Kanter's discussion of the effects of specific positions within the organization's internal labor market on worker personality and behaviors, aspirations and expectations. The next section turns to Likert's four management styles and organizational culture/climate as it affects workers' attitudes and behaviors in more general ways.

MANAGEMENT STYLES AND
ORGANIZATIONAL CULTURE: TWO VIEWS

The Connection between Management Styles and
Organizational Culture

Chapter 4 traces management styles over time in the United States revealing that the thinking on the best ways to manage changed somewhat with experiences and changing social environments. Still, we recognized that many current U.S. management practices are firmly rooted in a bureaucratic, rationalistic model and in Taylorism, often with a dash of human relations management (Likert's first three styles, McGregor's Theory X). We cling to this early management style despite the presence of other styles in the business literature. These prevalent management practices have assumptions of economic rationality and technical answers to our problems, whether the emphasis is on efficiency in production of goods and services, researching the market, or communicating with employees for purposes of increasing profit. Recall Likert's (1961) general typology of management styles:

1. Authoritative: coercive, money only reward for workers
2. Paternalistic: velvet glove on the iron fist
3. Human relations: consultative, groups address problems but pseudoparticipation in that decision making is still centralized
4. Participative: encourages decision making in groups, cooperative organizational culture fostered, flexible structure.

The first three types are authoritarian in lessening degrees as we approach the fourth system, which is quite different. These four types are often used in survey research questionnaires to ask workers and managers (1) which style their supervisor (or they themselves, if they are managers) have, and (2) what style they would like to see used. Implicit in each type is the general nature of the organizational culture or climate one might expect to find. *Organizational culture*, in broad terms, is the organization personality and way of life.

To elaborate on his four management types, Likert (1967) listed fifty-one aspects of organizations, divided into eight broad clusters or categories, and described how each of the four management styles would handle each aspect. The eight groups into which these aspects fell are (1) leadership processes, (2) character of motivational forces, (3) communications, (4) interaction-influence processes, (5) decision-making processes, (6) the setting and prioritizing of goals, (7) control processes, and (8) performance goals and training. As Perrow (1986:101) noted, this list goes a little further than just leadership.

When one reads down the list of how a particular management style would handle the various areas, one begins to get a sense of at least a stereotype of its organizational culture and how it might feel to work there. Also, Perrow states, no manager reading the list would want to admit openly that he or she was not a System 4 (participative) manager because System 4 is so consistent with our democratic ideals. However, in social surveys using these management styles, managers usually choose System 4 less frequently than their subordinates as an appropriate style for their organization.

Where does an organization's culture come from? We already know that the external social environment exerts an influence. The wider social environment (both structural and cultural) and the environment of subsets, such as the specific industry of which the organization is a part (social work, steel, or publishing, for example), set some conditions and pass along perceptions of the world. Organizational sociologists Aldrich and Pfeffer (1976; Pfeffer and Salancik 1978) present an interesting account of how environments can influence organizational cultures. For example, the ideas of business schools or other training and educational establishments, our professional associations, our voluntary associations (including groups such as the Chamber of Commerce) and the media all socialize us into our perceptions of the environment and our cultural beliefs. Even though there is a certain homogenizing effect across many organizations from some of these socializing agencies within any particular society, sometimes specific folk wisdom and industry rules of thumb emerge as being taken for granted within a particular industry.

The effect of national culture on organizational cultures deserves special mention. Social psychologist Geert Hofstede (1984) of the Netherlands has made an impressive attempt to compare the impact of the national cultures of forty nations on four clusters of variables important to organizational culture and management styles.

The first cluster he calls "Power Distance"—the degree of inequality and type of decision making the culture encourages, including the degree of fear of workers to disagree with superiors (Hofstede 1984:65–109). The second factor is "Uncertainty Avoidance"—the amount of ritual and rule orientation, employment stability, and stress (some cultures are very anxious indeed—they even drive faster) (Hofstede 1984:110–147). The third cluster he calls "Individualism"—communal orientation or individual orientation *(Gemeinschaft* to *Gesellschaft)* (Hofstede 1984:148–175). The fourth factor he calls "Masculinity"—the stereotype of the male role of aggressiveness, achievement orientation, being unemotional, competitive versus cultures emphasizing feminine qualities of interpersonal relations, cooperation, and intuition (Hofstede 1984:176–210).

From thinking internationally we again think of particular organizations in the United States. When an organization is small or in the hands of a dominant entrepreneur, the organizational culture may strongly reflect the personality of the founder, even sometimes resisting influence from the outside world. The Ford Motor Company apparently had a culture for many years that was very much the personality of its founder, Henry Ford. Its culture was said to have changed significantly under the leadership of Henry Ford II, which must have been a great relief for workers who had been there for some time and had their social lives closely scrutinized by the puritanical founder. The consumers also probably appreciated having their preferences taken into account.

Management style helps set the tone for an organization's culture over time. If a new manager comes in with a new style, he or she may meet some resistance from employees who are used to doing things the old way—as Alvin Gouldner (1954) reported so graphically in his description of a gypsum company and its surrounding community near one of the Great Lakes. The new manager eventually changed the structure and corporate culture of the above-ground plant, but he was never able to change the organizational culture of the mine, where the new bureaucratic style was inappropriate for the operation and the miners were also adamant in resisting change. Organizational sociologists Kanter and Stein (1979:16) point out the necessity for leaders' coming in from outside the organization paying homage to some of the organization's rituals before going on to induce change by chipping away at the old system of rewards and by replacing key personnel.

Two Different Ways to Study Organizational Culture: Bureaucratic Technological Rationality and Humanistic Participatory Models

Now that we have noted how closely interlocked management styles are with the overall organizational culture, we can consider more specifically what aspects are included in the term *organizational culture* and how organizational culture has been and can be studied. At the outset, note that it can be studied with different research techniques, at varying levels, and with emphasis on different variables by researchers with different agenda in mind. (See Ouchi and Wilkins 1985; Putnam and Pacanowsky 1983; Uttal 1983; Webber 1969; Harrison 1972; Organizational Culture 1983).

The study of organizational culture owes much to concepts from anthropology, which has been documenting and analyzing cultures in societies and subcultures in groups for decades, although applied anthropologists have not yet entered the field of organizational culture in large numbers (Nelson 1983; Reynolds 1987). We gave a definition of *culture* in Chapter 1 as "all the material and nonmaterial aspects of a society passed on to succeeding generations by means of symbols." Researchers in organizational culture have looked at organizational stories, language (including slang and jargon), jokes, rituals and ceremonies, myths and heroes, values, stated organizational objectives, structural arrangements (including network of social roles and role sets), standard ways of doing things (including informal procedures), intentions of members, and what members think they must know to get by in the organization (see Fine 1984: 243–244; Deetz and Kersten 1983:157; Neff 1985:131–136).

Getting right to the point of what they are looking for, one text puts it into more operationally specific terms. Organizational culture or climate is "the degree of trust, communications, and supportiveness that exists in the organization" (Hellriegel, Slocum, and Woodman 1983:590). Similarly, other writers say it is "the stimuli, constraints on freedom, and rewards and punishments that affect worker attitudes and performance" or "anything in the working environment that affects worker satisfaction and/or productivity" (Bass and Barrett 1981:175). One study of "excellent companies" puts it this way: "their value set *integrates* the notions of economic health, serving customers, and making meanings down the line" (Peters and Waterman 1982:103).

These last definitions begin to lean in the direction of expected outcomes or at least of criteria by which to judge the effects of organizational culture. When criteria are being specified, the careful reader will begin to guess about the agendum(a) of the researcher(s). For example, researchers who want to include the human resources approach to management (in varying degrees) have attempted to list characteristics of the cultures of the so-called best companies to work for (Peters and Waterman 1982; Deal and Kennedy 1982; Levering, Moskowitz, and Katz 1984; Dowie and Brown 1985; Leff 1986; Rosen, Klein, and Young 1986).

Why are they best? First, of course, they are successful in surviving and being profitable. However, these are not the basic criteria—other companies can survive and make money and yet not make the "best" lists. These companies are on the lists because they offer, more than other companies, greater organizational flexibility, informal communications, and creativity. These factors lead to an increased degree of individual freedom, to participation in decision making, and to development (Likert's System 4 again). In other words, these companies seem to try to fulfill the multiplicity of goals from varying constituencies Kanter and Brinkerhoff (1982) referred to at the beginning of this chapter. The seeming paradox of firm corporate cultural values and a loose structure can be explained this way:

Perhaps culture was taboo as a topic following William H. Whyte, Jr.'s *The Organization Man* and the conformist, gray flannel suit image that he put forward. But what seems to have been overlooked by Whyte, and management theorists until recently, is what . . . we call the 'loose-tight' properties of the excellent companies. In the very same institutions in which culture is so dominant, the highest levels of true autonomy occur. The culture regulates rigorously the few variables that do count, and it provides meaning. But within those qualitative values (and in almost *all* other dimensions), people are encouraged to stick out, to innovate. (Peters and Waterman 1982:105)

Before continuing, let us consider the kinds of organizational structure this culture fosters. This loose-tight environment would encourage Likert's linking-pin committees, which form task forces across departmental lines to handle temporary problems and projects; Pinchot's (1985) "intrapreneurship," in which groups within the organization are encouraged to act in entrepreneurial ways to compete with other internal or external groups; Peters and Waterman's (1982) "skunkworks" researchers, who are given minimal funds, staff, and a time limit in which to produce an innovation; and Kanter's (1983) "change master" management. In other words, the goals are set in meaningful terms to the workers, and they are given positive reinforcement to pursue them in their own ways. Workers are turned loose, but loose to be creative toward agreed on goal(s).

To return to the "best" list criteria, sometimes the writer also includes as part of the criteria that the company must be notable for socially useful projects; this is a plus for both society and for the satisfaction and commitment of employees. These factors are all high on the humanist agenda. The importance of the humanist agenda to researchers varies widely, from those who emphasize it as a way to increase worker productivity and profits, to those who see it as a way for individuals to take back some control over their lives. The former are nearing the camp of the other view—the researchers from the bureaucratic/technological answers to any problem perspective who discount humanist goals as unscientific or less rational than the pursuit of profits alone.

Researchers studying organizational culture from the bureaucratic/technological perspective will not be very interested in examining power arrangements within organizations or in the external environment; they will be more concerned with how consensus is developed by negotiating parties. Statements of goals, operating procedures, and worker satisfaction will more likely be taken at face value without looking for anything below the surface (basically, power arrangements). Organizational sociologists and psychologists and other researchers fall into both camps.

Social scientists who study organizational culture from the inside are usually applying some form of interpretive or symbolic interaction perspective that emphasizes how the social actors involved develop meanings, that is, the social construction of reality (see Berger and Luckman 1967 for a more complete account). Initially this view was usually micro-oriented, focusing on the social actors and their interaction to develop meanings; it also was often accused of ignoring power differences in the formation of meaning.

In recent years, however, the resource dependency (or political economy) approach, which looks at how organizations attempt to generate and use power to stabilize their environments, has been joined by a new critical interpretive approach for analyzing organizational cultures. This perspective developed out of the writings of the Frankfurt Critical School in Germany (Habermas 1971, 1973, 1975, 1979). The approach combines (1) the Marxian tradition of looking for domination in structures and traditional ideologies, both of which are barriers to the fulfillment of humanist ideals; (2) the hermeneutic tradition of understanding of linguistic texts; and (3) the Freudian tradition of looking for distorted communication. The focus in critical research is on the historical conditions of domination that cause distortion in communications (Deetz and Kersten 1983:147–171). This might be called the humanistic participatory model for examining organizational cultures.

Proponents of this view argue the importance of making a critical analysis of society and organizational cultures for the following reasons. They observe that technical rationality and instrumental reason (*Zweckrational*, which leads to domination of nature and people) have become ends in themselves and that our society has lost sight of the real end (*Wertrational*)—a liberating humanism. From this point of view, this behavior could be called a case of goal displacement by society; that is, a concentration on technical means has replaced the desired goals or values. Remember that one of the earliest criticisms of bureaucracy is a loss of freedom for the individual. Adorno and Horkheimer (1972) describe this undivided attention to economic goals as the "eclipse of reason." In terms of organizations:

> This eclipse of reason is evident in a number of aspects of organizational life. First, organizational goals are commonly viewed in terms of economic growth, profit, or continued organizational survival. Other goals, such as the welfare of organizational participants, are subordinate to this goal and have only instrumental importance. Humanistic and participatory programs, for example, are valued only for their ability to increase productivity. . . . Job redesign and job enrichment are usually introduced to increase productivity rather than to accomplish employee development. (Deetz and Kersten 1983:153)

The humanistic values that are presumably widely held in society, such as democracy, freedom of speech, and individual development, must be left outside the door of many organizations. We excuse this on the grounds of technical rationality; human rights get in the way of, or are irrelevant to, organizational goals. In other words, critical research on organizational culture and communications has an emancipatory interest in promoting conditions (Habermas's "ideal speech situations") in which meanings are shaped and individual development takes place without domination (Ford 1978: Part IV on similarities between Mills and Habermas). Organizations, so much a part of our lives, shape our social development, even in the nonorganizational aspects, as discussed in Chapter 8. Critical research theorists hold that if we are to maintain the values of freedom, democracy, human dignity, and development that we proclaim, then we cannot allow our organizations to ignore and deny them. At the same time, organizations do not operate in a vacuum; researchers must thus also understand how the organization has been influenced by the economic, political, and ideological environment in which it is historically situated.

In reviewing all of those items listed as possible variables in the study of organizational culture earlier in this section, critical researchers must do more than researchers from other perspectives. Structural functionalists/technical rationality researchers have developed concepts with which they will make a "literal description of recurring features of organizational behavior and members' psychological states" (Deetz and Kersten 1983:159). Naturalistic researchers from the interpretive/symbolic interaction approach, like good ethnographers, will endeavor to describe what the actors themselves understand their meanings to be (Weber's *Verstehen*). Critical researchers, however, think of this as the surface level. The real meanings and questions ultimately lie in the deep structure of power and domination—which may not be apparent to some or all of the actors.

Freud probed the individual's unconscious for the causes of his or her meanings and actions; the critical approach attempts to probe the deep structures of domination in organizations and the social environment that cause our surface meanings and actions. If organizations are "socially constructed realities," the critical researchers want to know not only how this happens (through organizational processes, worker rewards, rituals, and/or stories) but also why this particular meaning system happened. They assume it was not entirely by chance and not by free and friendly negotiations among equals on neutral territory, at least until critical examination proves otherwise (Edwards 1979). Examining surface structures may offer choices *within* contexts; examining deep structures may offer a choice *of* contexts.

Fortunately, not all organizations are equally dominating, so researchers can find a range of types to study. Some organizations operate to promote varying degrees of humanistic values—freedom, human dignity, and development, for example. Chapter 11 looks at alternative workplace organization (alternatives to Taylorism with a veneer of human relations) that offer varying degrees of domination-free communication—depending on how the alternative is implemented. The degree of domination is thus an empirical question for critical approach researchers and is top priority on their agenda. Lest we take this agenda to mean antimanagement or anticapitalism (even though it may be for some individuals, this need not be the case in the critical approach itself), speech communications/organizational analysts Deetz and Kersten (1983:166) note:

> The thrust of critical research, in terms of organizational development, is proliberation and anticlosure rather than proworker and antimanagement. There is no inherent contradiction between emancipation and economic development of organizations. Many organizations fail because domination-based closure prohibits adaptation to current social conditions. The critical interest opens systems of domination to rational assessment, not necessarily to a different organizational structure. To change structures merely constitutes a shift in the origin of closure (domination) from one source to another. The critical interest rests in *how* the structuration process proceeds rather than the content of its outcome.

This is why the implementation of alternatives to technical, rationalistic bureaucracies is so important. It is not enough just to introduce an alternative that looks good on paper. Note once more that the purpose behind this approach is not only to make the worker more productive, but also to promote the humanist ideals of Likert's System 4.

Postscript

Organizational sociologist Charles Perrow (1986) divides the same structures of domination into bureaucratic and nonbureaucratic models; presumably the first three of Likert's management styles are bureaucratic and the fourth is nonbureaucratic. An organization is

> a tool that masters use to generate valued outputs that they can then appropriate. . . . This theory emphasizes hierarchy, specialization, formalization, and standardization. . . . The formal structure of the organization is the single most important key to its functioning. (Perrow 1986:260)

But the complete control of the masters, he says, is limited by *bounded rationality* (incomplete knowledge or anything else that limits understanding; Simon's idea, which we discussed earlier); therefore, informal and formal groups both inside and outside the organization occasionally have some leverage. There are unintended consequences of purposeful actions, which we often try to justify after the fact by rethinking what our original plans and purposes must have been. Also, workers, and presumably consumers, are not completely passive and occasionally throw a monkey wrench into deliberate manipulation. A nonbureaucratic model would have included these groups into the planning of organizational action in the first place.

Ultimately Perrow (1986:272–278) returns to an amusing account of what history might have been like if the early industrialists had not been able to get the state to intervene on their behalf. The message of his little tale is this: If you are inclined to believe that particular bureaucracies evolved because they were somehow fittest to survive, you need to examine power relationships in society and the externalities (costs to people who are not direct beneficiaries) that these organizations produce.

POLITICAL ECONOMY STRUCTURES, ORGANIZATIONAL STRUCTURES, AND THEIR CULTURES: WHAT THEY MEAN FOR REAL ECONOMIC GROWTH

What has caused the slowness in economic growth and the economic problems of recent years in the United States? Many reasons are given: inflation, unemployment, inadequate resources (worldwide decline), decline in capital expenditures, overregulation, excessive government spending and economic policy or lack of it, the overpriced dollar, the decline of the Protestant work ethic, and unions.

Other people say the problems are of a structural and cultural nature. Structures in the overall political economy and within large organizations inhibit innovation and entrepreneurship: overconcentration of power, lack of access to credit and equity for potential entrepreneurs, government policy that focuses almost exclusively on needs of big business (e.g., tax breaks and other subsidies that increase corporate profits but do not lead to increased production) (Rosen 1981). Our overall culture and corporate cultures overemphasize individualism to the point of creating a climate of distrust that discourages cooperation for the good of the whole (Reich 1987). We return to the factors on these lists after looking at what seems to have been involved in past economic growth and productivity.

This section looks at what creates economic productivity and growth and what part organizational and social structure and culture might play in this economic growth. The following chapter returns to more on the contributions to productivity and real economic growth of worker attitudes and worker satisfaction under alternative workplace organization.

Innovations

Most real *economic productivity* (the amount of goods and services produced per worker hour) and growth seem to come from innovations in three areas: new processes, new products, and new markets (Rosen 1981). Why is innovation so important? Innovation provides more of an economic good at a lower price or a new process or product that did not exist before—increasing demand and providing jobs. Capturing the market, either new or increased, is then the key. If the innovation does not find a market and get used, ultimately there is no economic growth (Rosen 1981).

Innovation of any kind requires research and development (R&D) by someone and then diffusion into the market. Innovation becomes particularly important when one considers that it is more controllable than, and can make up for a lack of, other factors that can aid growth—supply of resources, and such demographics as population growth, age structure, rural to urban movement, and educational attainment. That is, innovation is more controllable when we understand from where it is likely to come and what aids or impedes it.

Where has innovation come from historically? Jewkes and his associates (Jewkes, Sawers, and Stillerman 1969) found 61 important innovations between 1900 and 1958. More than half had been developed by small firms and independent inventors. Only 20 to 25 percent of the inventions could be attributed to organized research by large corporations. Even in steel and autos the smaller companies, not the industry leaders, developed the major innovations. The remainder came from the research of middle-sized firms. Similar findings from other studies have been cited by the U.S. Department of Commerce (U.S. Dept. of Commerce 1967): For example, Hamberg found two-thirds of inventions between 1946 and 1965 came from small firms and independent inventors. Peck's study of the aluminum industry found big producers had only one in seven major inventions. Enos reports the seven major inventions in petroleum were all made by independent inventors. Apparently, size of organization has been an important variable in innovation, at least in the past.

Von Hippel of MIT (1978) has given us a little insight as to why people outside the big laboratories come up with so many good ideas. In his study of innovation in the scientific instruments business (such as the gas chromatograph, the nuclear resonance spectrometer, and the transmission electron microscope) he found that the major breakthroughs, and the major and minor improvements came almost entirely from users. All of the eleven first-of-type major inventions were from users outside the companies. Eighty-five percent of the sixty-six major improvements were from users, as were 67 percent of the eighty-three minor improvements. The inventor would usually build a prototype and try it out. The invention would diffuse to other users, and then the companies would become interested. Once a major new product is adopted the large companies turn to incremental innovations in the production process (Abernathy and Utterback 1978).

This process has also been true in the computer field. IBM reports that its early innovations, including the company's first computer, were made in conjunction with its biggest customer, the U.S. Census Bureau. Digital, Wang, and Allen-Bradley report the same. Their customers start building prototypes or at least tell the companies what to build (Peters and Waterman 1982:194–199). Hewlett-Packard puts engineers onto user premises to work with customers on applications and design.

Proctor and Gamble have had an 800 telephone number on their products for some years to encourage customers to phone in with their ideas, suggestions, and complaints. The company says this is its major source for product ideas (Peters and Waterman 1982:193–194).

In an extensive study of innovation, the SAPPHO (Scientific Activity Predictor from Patterns with Heuristic Origin) team led by economist Christopher Freeman (SAPPHO 1972; Peters and Waterman 1982:196–197) analyzed 39 innovations in the chemical industry and 33 in scientific instruments. Fifteen of the 200 measures of aspects of innovation used proved to be statistically significant. The top factor in successful innovations in both industries turned out to be that successful firms understand user needs better. The second factor for both was that successful innovations have fewer problems (because the industries had worked out the bugs with their leading customers before the innovations went on the market). Their analysis of why innovations sometimes did, not succeed was, in essence, that companies failed to listen to customers comments or were too committed to a preconceived design to change.

In another report Freeman and colleagues (Freeman, Clark, and Soete 1982) noted that when observed over time (they used the Jewkes data from 1920 to 1970), innovations tend to cluster. One innovation will lead to others in another field or in a related field. This process, in turn, initially enhances employment in those fields, followed by a period of tightening up and trying to increase productivity per employee (Rostow 1983:10–11). Rostow reports that attempts to tie these innovative clusters to Kondratieff-type business cycles has thus far not been convincing. The hypothesis behind this attempt was that innovative clusters might lead to periods of economic expansion, an upswing in the business cycle.

Other researchers (Hayes and Abernathy 1980; Hayes and Garvin 1982) argue that innovations must now come from technology-oriented rather than from market-oriented sources; that is, basic research in the lab needs to be emphasized. Apparently, both approaches are necessary. Companies must continue and even increase their R&D expenditures at the same time they are working closely with their creative customers, who may be more at the cutting edge of innovation than some engineers and researchers in the labs.

To underline the point of size, the National Science Foundation found that firms with fewer than 100 employees were twenty-four times more innovative per R&D dollar than were firms with more than 1,000 employees. Firms in the middle range of 101 to 999 employees were four times as innovative per dollar as the larger firms. A staff study done by the Congressional Joint Economic Committee came up with similar findings. Small businesses created 66 percent of all new jobs and generated twenty-four times as many innovations per research dollar as did the largest companies (Joint Economic Committee Rx 1981:85).

Several questions now come to mind: What is the innovation/new job creation connection that keeps appearing in statements in these studies? What is it about size or structure that makes small companies and individuals creative and large corporations less so? What sectors are currently doing R&D, how much is being spent and by whom, and what is happening in other advanced industrial nations in R&D and the mix of sectors doing research?

Job Creation

Dun and Bradstreet, in their annual employment forecast survey, indicated that U.S. businesses planned to create nearly 3 million new jobs in 1986—quite an improvement over the 2 million jobs added the previous year (Galante 1986). The article added that small business would "once again" do most of the hiring, with companies that employ fewer than 100 workers providing nearly two-thirds of the expected new jobs. Companies employing 25,000 or more workers planned to increase employment .6 percent, or only about 3 percent of the new jobs. Firms with 500 or more workers would provide 24.6 percent. The "so-what-else-is-new" tone of the report reflects the idea that job creation by the smallest firms is now common knowledge.

MIT's David Birch (1979) found that firms with fewer than 20 employees created 66 percent of all net new jobs between 1969 and 1976. The Fortune 500 industrials created less than 1 percent, even though they have 80 percent of all industrial workers; they are not planning to add many. Most new jobs, as we know, are outside the manufacturing sector in services. Job-creating firms are often young, most of them four years old or less. Many will go out of business within the first year, to be replaced by new entrepreneurial starts.

Structural Features: In Organizations and in the Political Economy

Competition and flexibility appear to be the important factors for innovation. Industries are innovative during their competitive periods—when industries are new or when they are deregulated and new firms can enter. The uncertainty in a competitive environment seems to encourage a risk-taking attitude in order to corner a share of the market. Organizational structure must be open to change, have fewer levels of hierarchy, and experiment more. Small firms, for example, are likely to have very flat organizational structures, be managed by their owners (Mintzbert's first category) who take a long-term view of success, and be concentrating on one or a few new products for which they are aggressively trying to carve a niche. Workers in small firms are likely to be generalists rather than specialists. Richard Caves (1967) notes that between 1897 and 1955 innovations were in industries in which there was a lack of economic concentration, or at least in which entry barriers for new firms were low and experimentation could flourish.

On the other hand large organizations tend to be bureaucratic and oligopolistic, have a tall organizational structure with layers of management and highly specialized jobs, reward conformity rather than individuality, not likely to compete but to service existing markets, and have capital invested in current technology. In addition management in large firms has a short-run view of profit making, which does not encourage long-run investments in R&D (these managers will probably stay on that job for about three to five years, the stockholders want a good P/E ratio and dividends now, and managers' bonuses are tied to quarterly profits). Management backgrounds are likely to be finance and law rather than technical and oriented to paper entrepreneurship rather than to product development and marketing. They thus will be prone to cost analyses and number crunching, which favor retaining current technology and what has worked in the past (Rosen 1981:23–24). Rationally, large organizations can take a "strong second" approach; they can wait for smaller firms to innovate and then buy them out. However, this technique does not work well if the entire industry is made up of large firms that have agreed not to compete with each other (Rosen 1981:25). Under these conditions, innovation languishes.

Two points stand out in what has been said. First, organizations that are large and have bureaucratic structures, particularly those in industrial sectors that are oligopolistic and do not have easy entry to the field by small firms, must rethink their management styles and organizational structures, including the reward systems, to gain more flexibility, internal competition (intrapreneurship), and innovation. The adhocracy of which Mintzberg spoke, the "bias for action" and "skunkworks" of Peters and Waterman, Kanter's "change masters" (1983), the "corporate cannibals" of Foster (1986), and Pinchot's (1985) "intrapreneurs" are examples of what organizations caught in this position can consider.

Second, jumping to the macro level, the political economy as a whole must be considered as to whether it can provide a more favorable climate for the emergence of small firms that innovate. Consider the following five points.

First, in Chapter 5 we noted the tendency for both economic concentration in specific sectors and the centralization of economic power across sectors.

Second, we also noted that government tax policies have been beneficial to the large corporations and encouraged the tendency for merger and paper entrepreneurship, but not for promoting R&D and industry reinvestment. The smaller firms may not yet have the profits against which those tax breaks would be beneficial. In fact the medium-sized and smaller companies both paid taxes and reinvested at higher rates than the large corporations; the big companies found other noninnovative uses for their tax credits. The small companies are innovating and creating jobs.

Third, what these small firms need are not tax breaks but places that will lend them seed money and venture capital at reasonable rates. Because most investment, as discussed, is now in the hands of a small and declining number of large institutional investors, who tend to invest in Fortune 500 stocks and bonds and real estate tax shelters, small firms are not likely to get funds from this sector. (Note: Federal and state pension laws have encouraged this concentration of financial markets by requiring that pension funds be in nonrisk investments.) Clearly what is needed is a mechanism, such as an expanded cooperative bank, that lends to small firms with new ideas. This mechanism, however, needs to be adequately funded so it will reach enough firms to have an impact on the economy. This does not mean spending enormous amounts of money. "A doubling of the total annual amount of venture capital in the United States would still provide less capital than was spent on mergers and acquisitions in one typical week in 1981" (Rosen 1981:62). During that same year $1 billion was spent on venture capital and $50 billion was spent on advertising. Some states, including California, Alaska, New York, Georgia, and Indiana, currently provide equity capital to small ventures. Alternatively, lower capital gains taxes on investments in small firms that invest in a certain minimum R&D might be given. Other financial mechanisms that could be used are Small Business Participating Debenture and royalty financing (see Rosen 1981:63).

Fourth, the government could set aside more of its R&D funds for contracts with small firms, where it will get more for its money, as we discuss in the next section. The National Science Foundation already has a successful small business set-aside grant program, and the Department of Defense has a similar program (Rosen 1981:49—50).

Fifth, Rosen (1981:52—54) also sugggests that the government could set up a technology exchange in which technologies developed as spin-offs by the private sector and government R&D could be bought and sold. Of the 8,000 inventions funded by government R&D every year only 3 percent are used. Smaller companies might be willing and able to carry some of these forward.

The R&D Mix

As implied in the previous section, investment is not necessarily the same as innovation. Individuals and firms can invest in any number of ways that do not lead to innovation, including real estate tax write-offs, certificates of deposit, mergers and acquisitions, and old technology instead of new. Presumably, investments in R&D will produce innovations and contribute to long-run economic growth and productivity. With this in mind, it would be interesting to see where official R&D money is spent and by whom. By *official*, we refer to the money labeled *R&D* in the national accounts. This does not include the unofficial money spent by many individuals and small groups funding their own experiments.

First, we note that almost half of the official R&D funds come from the federal government. In 1985 the federal government spent an estimated $50.5 billion on R&D. Of these government R&D funds, 76 percent were for defense—space-related research—$38.4 billion (U.S. Bureau of the Census 1985:577, 579). In earlier years approximately half of all government R&D was used in-house by government agencies; the other half went to private firms and individuals. In the private sector, 80 percent of these funds have gone to fewer than 200 large companies. This leaves about 4 percent (perhaps $2 billion in 1985) of federal R&D for small firms, in which the returns are likely to be much higher, as we have mentioned. The small-business share has been the same since the mid-1960s (Rosen 1981:48).

Who is spending for R&D in the private sector? The large corporations receive the lion's share. In fact, although there were somewhere between 10,000 to 15,000 firms doing some kind of research, 20 firms spent 50 percent of funds, and 4 of those firms spent 20 percent of all R&D effort, according to a Congressional study of where funds went in 1978 (Joint Economic Committee Rx 1981:85). There is no reason to believe that this distribution of R&D funds has changed significantly.

In what kinds of research are the government and private sector engaging? Two broad areas receive 43 percent of the funds: aircraft/ missiles and electrical equipment/communications (Joint Economic Committee Rx 1981:85). This means that defense R&D rather than consumer-oriented research is being emphasized. This allotment does not give the United States a leading edge for competition in the market, particularly since Japan and West Germany are putting their research in the civilian industrial area.

How does the United States compare in R&D expenditures with Japan and West Germany? As a percent of GNP, civilian R&D in the United States was 1.3 percent in 1963, 1.5 percent in 1970, 1.59 percent in 1979, 1.69 in 1981, 1.75 percent in 1983, and 1.73 percent in 1985 (Bentsen 1985:4A; U.S. Bureau of the Census 1985:577). West Germany, which had been outspending the United States since World War II, invested 2.53 percent of its GNP in 1981, and Japan spent 2.3 percent in the same year. France also spends a higher percentage than the United States on civilian R&D (Thurow 1983:80).

A number of economists have been calling for private industry to form consortia and pool their research efforts in the manner of Japan. A pool of this nature recently formed in the U.S. electronics industry— Microelectronics and Computer Technology Corp. (MCC) in Austin, Texas, organized by Control Data and headed initially by Bobby Ray Inman. Economist Lester Thurow (1978:71, 1983:80) suggests the formation of a "Ministry of Technology" to channel funds to such consortia for industrial research and development. This would allow industries to take longer and relieve the government from being accused of supporting individual company's operations when they allocate research grants. He and other economists hope it would help the United States regain the lead against foreign competition. This might, however, include basically the large firms.

While not denigrating the importance of the consortia approach, other writers remind us that this may not be enough to regain a lead in technology. With many examples, Peters (1985:D4) illustrates that large research labs that receive a lot of money usually produce dismal results. Innovations still seem to come from small, agressive, underfunded, "skunkworks" labs under time pressures to produce quickly.

Culture and Economic Impasse

Economist Robert Reich (1987:18–19) would have us look a step beyond these structural problems to see what might lie in U.S. culture that inhibits innovation. He describes a culture of "opportunistic individualism." This is a climate of distrust in which management distrusts workers, who gain too much knowledge and leave the company to sell its new ideas to competitors; workers and communities distrust management, who ask for wage concessions and subsidies so the company can invest in new plant and equipment and the company spends it on a merger instead. Or, the company innovates and is bought up by another company, which forgets about the concessions and subsidies. Or, the company innovates, fires the now surplus workers, and threatens to move the plant unless additional concessions are made. The stockholders do not trust management on long-run investments or even in mergers in which management bails out in a golden parachute after the deal is completed. Golden parachutes, so popular in the mergers of the 1980s, give severance pay and bonuses to the departing executives—at the investors' expense.

Reich is saying that innovation requires "collective entrepreneurialism" in the sense that investors, workers, community, and management are willing to share ideas and work toward the same ends in a climate of trust (Reich 1987:18–19). What does Reich offer as a way out of this impasse?

> To the extent our place in the world economy is determined by our success at collective endeavors, the central problem of economic policy is how to create the kinds of organizations in which people can pool their efforts, insights, and enthusiasm without fear of exploitation.
>
> One possible approach to this problem is to encourage versions of worker ownership. . . . The point is that some form of employee ownership and control could provide a superior context for forging joint commitment and fostering trust. Reciprocal dependencies would be clearer. Relationships would be longer-term, and reputations correspondingly more important; the slacker and exploiter would bear the burden of their actions. Such arrangements could go far to reduce the appeal of opportunism and increase the perceived advantages of collaboration, and thus lessen the dilemmas that give rise to economic gridlock. (Reich 1987:19)

In essence, Reich is saying that if our current structures and culture do not suit what we need in order to progress, then we must try structures that foster a climate of cooperation. This conclusion leads to the next chapter on alternative workplace organization, which includes employee and community ownership.

First, however, let us examine a concrete case of an industry and its major company that represent some problems of blockage and lack of innovation discussed in this chapter.

THE RISE AND FALL OF AN INDUSTRY: U.S. STEEL

The story of the steel industry in the United States and particularly of the principal character in the plot, U.S. Steel (renamed USX in July

1986), brings together a number of points made in this and other chapters about lack of innovation, past and present. Early in its history, steel was a competitive, fairly innovative industry. Then, as an oligopoly, it failed to innovate. Today, as a conglomerate, it rearranges its assets on paper to show a profit. This is an interesting story in and of itself, however, and worth telling.

The steel industry grew in the nineteenth century partly as a result of the railroad industry's demand for steel. The entire output of the early Bessemer plants went into rails. The railroads were interlocked, through ownership and shared board members, to steel companies to insure a steady supply. Andrew Carnegie, for example, had been an executive with the Pennsylvania Railroad before founding his steel corporation (Chandler 1977:267).

By the early 1890s the steel industry in the United States was intensely competitive. Companies had been forced to cut costs in order to compete, which meant constant efforts to cut wages and ignore poor working conditions. One of Carnegie's favorite sayings was "Watch the costs and the profits will take care of themselves," and he was good at both (Chandler 1977:267). The bloody Homestead Strike in 1892 was an all-out war between the Pinkertons and the unions. It ended with the breaking of the unions, but this did not solve the owners' problems. It was necessary for companies to innovate continuously in order to cut costs and compete for short-run advantages. Between 1890 and 1898 prices of steel rails, one of their most important products, dropped 45 percent (Steel 1982:8).

Andrew Carnegie seemed to be coming out on top as the best at keeping wages and other costs low and was about to put his rivals out of business. Financier J. P. Morgan and other bankers who had invested large sums in the rival companies were not happy at the thought of possible bankruptcy. At the turn of the century they were able to buy out the Carnegie holdings, and in 1901 they combined their major steel companies into one large corporation—U.S. Steel. This move placed at least 65 percent of the nation's steel capacity into one company and completely changed the nature of the industry. Stone (1981:352), however, reports that U.S. Steel controlled 80 percent of the U.S. output of steel in 1901. It was a virtual monopoly. Prices were set by U.S. Steel's "price leadership" ("Pittsburgh-plus-freight"), and markets were divided up in a gentlemanly manner over lavish dinners. The dinners gradually ended over the years, but the oligopolistic nature of the industry and lack of competition remained. Profits came, not from innovating or cutting costs, but from setting prices in unison, giving the customers no choice.

As expected in oligopolistic situations, the laws of supply and demand were repealed. When demand went up, so did prices, as they would in a competitive situation. However, when demand slumped, prices still went up. Even wages seemed to have no effect; prices increased whether or not wages went up. The company's power was still strong in the 1950s, when steel prices rose 90 percent, almost three times the rate of other industries (Steel 1982:8).

The situation was rapidly changing, even as the oligopolies enjoyed their 1950s profits. In 1950 steel companies in the United States produced 47 percent of the world's steel production. By 1960 that share had fallen to 26 percent, and by 1980 it was 14 percent (Steel 1982:8). The competition came from Japan, West Germany, South Africa, South Korea, and Brazil, who all began exporting aggressively. By 1959 the United States was no longer a net exporter of steel. By the mid-1980s, the United States imported about 22 percent of its steel, and the situation would be more extreme if the government had not imposed voluntary import quotas on European and Japanese steel companies and heavily taxed imports thought to be dumped (offered for sale at prices lower than what the U.S. government figures it cost to produce).

How did this happen? The industry tends to blame the workers, foreign government subsidies to their steel industries, and environmentalists. Japanese steel workers were once paid much less than U.S. workers. Between 1960 and 1984, however, the Japanese steel workers' wages increased tenfold to about half that of the U.S. workers, although their other benefits bring the costs closer together than the direct wage figure implies (Anderson 1984:D.C.11). Since then the devaluation of the U.S. dollar and the give backs negotiated in union contracts have made steelworkers' wages in the two countries even closer.

In terms of the costs of pollution control, the "Japanese steel companies have outspent their American counterparts both in terms of absolute dollars and as a portion of their total investment" (Steel 1982:9; Von Hoffman 1983).

How much do state subsidies affect steel prices? The Office of Technology Assessment, attached to Congress, reported in 1984 that some 45 percent of world steel production is state-owned both in Europe and in the Third World, but it is not necessarily subsidized (Collier 1984:13). The report went on to state that this was not the cause of the industry's decline, since the domestic industry has had some import protection since the 1960s. In addition U.S. companies have received generous tax breaks to modernize during the last twenty years (Anderson 1984:D.C.11; Von Hoffman 1983). The argument that they are in a free trade situation seems to be an illusion of the U.S. steel industry, according to the report. The industry "has neither preserved jobs among workers, nor has it modernized facilities among the integrated [from ore to finished product] producers," according to the Congressional Budget Office (Collier 1984:13). As one economist stated, "The steel industry's abrupt collapse springs not so much from imports as its obsession with imports" (Samuelson 1984:78). Instead of trying to compete, the industry relied on continued demand (which was grossly overestimated, as it turned out) and on government quotas and tax breaks.

One of the two most important points seems to be the industry's failure to modernize and use new technology. When the basic oxygen furnace (BOF) and continuous casting were introduced in the postwar period, the steel industry in the United States continued to expand its capacity with the latest edition of their old open-hearth furnaces—the state-of-the-art since World War I. BOF was an innovation in the 1950s from a small nationally owned Austrian company. The BOF's ability to make a load of steel in forty-five minutes with fewer raw materials was quickly recognized in Europe and Japan. That same load takes nine to ten hours in an open-hearth furnace.

The continuous casting process, introduced in Europe in the early 1960s, uses about half of the steps in heating and cooling raw steel that the older processes use. This saves labor time and energy use and also wastes less raw steel. Again, Europe and Japan saw its advantages. In 1957 the U.S. Congress urged the steel industry to adopt BOFs; the Steelworkers Union urged its adoption, too. U.S. companies had always used open hearth and had never had foreign competition; they stood firm against any risky new technology and against cutting current profits for long-run growth for some time. In the 1960s they did begin to replace the worn out prewar furnaces with BOFs, but it was too late with too little. The second major problem, the drop in demand for steel products, was at hand.

The second problem appears to be the ultimate difficulty—lower demand. The recession of the 1970s, the lighter weight autos demanded by the newly gas-conscious public, the loss of much of the tin-can market to aluminum, and the lower amounts of steel needed in construction with reinforced concrete did not promote expansion or investment of profits back into the steel industry. Capacity had outrun demand worldwide since the mid-1970s. The industry could have chosen to be in the forefront in developing the new lightweight construction materials, but it did not innovate in new products just as it had not done in new processes.

Since the 1960s the medium-sized companies, such as Inland, Republic, and McLouth, have modernized and have developed exceedingly modern, small, and efficient plants. However, the lack of demand and foreign competition have made it difficult for these producers. The minimills, such as Nucor Corp., Raritan River, and Korf Industries, have succeeded temporarily in producing specialized, high priced, and quick supply small steel products from recycled scrap. Currently these minimills are big competitors and have 20 to 25 percent of the U.S. steel market. If scrap becomes scarce, however, they will have to decide in which direction to go. The larger companies, U.S. Steel (USX) being the prime example, took their profits and diversified, shut down most of their old outdated plants, and almost got out of the steel business. Only 25 percent of USX's assets are now in steel, hence, the company's name change from U.S. Steel.

A summary of a few events in the industry in 1985 and 1986 indicates the various directions the different steel manufacturing companies are currently taking (Greenhouse 1985:D2; Flint 1986; Bensman 1986, Moberg 1986). USX announced a joint venture with Pohang Iron and Steel (POSCO) of South Korea to import POSCO's semifinished steel to finish in a plant in Pittsburg, California. A Japanese company owns the continuous caster in USX's Gary Works, which it leases to its U.S. partner. Nippon Kokan (NKK) now owns half of the National Steel Corporation, and Nisshin Steel has bought into Wheeling-Pittsburgh, which had gone through the Chapter 11 route. New joint ventures with foreign companies are expected to continue in the industry.

Other companies in the steel industry are updating their plants and equipment or trying to cut costs in various ways. Inland Steel introduced a $200-million continuous caster that will save $40 million a year in energy and labor costs. Bethlehem Steel (the third largest steel producer) cut back its pension plan for the white-collar workers to save $30 million a year and planned to install a continuous caster in 1986.

United Steelworkers of America issued a report asking banks and management to join labor in making sacrifices and new contracts in 1986. These contracts were negotiated on a plant-by-plant basis rather than industrywide and produced lower wages and fewer work rules in return for job security, company stock, or participation in management. One round of contracts produced $1.4 billion in wage concessions; the one before that lost the workers $3 billion in concessions (Moberg 1984:11).

Weirton Steel was bought out by its employees and, together with McLouth and California Steel (formerly Kaiser Steel), have reduced their costs more than 15 percent. LTV, the nation's second largest steelmaker in addition to its energy and aerospace holdings, has filed for reorganization under a Chapter 11. This reorganization is expected to put pension plans for 15,000 employees and retirees in jeopardy and cut off medical and life insurance payments for all 78,000 retirees (Hayes 1986:F12). Currently LTV owns Jones-Laughlin Steel, Lykes (which is the parent of Youngstown Sheet and Tube), and Republic Steel.

USX has changed its strategy. In its remaining plants, which leaves it still the largest single producer of steel, USX has up-dated a little. It has defied its union contracts to subcontract to nonunion workers and has ignored work rules to combine jobs and streamline production.

These methods increased steel production per worker by 49 percent between 1983 and 1985 (Bensman 1986). With this new efficiency and cost cutting, USX then began a round of price cutting to try to drive its competitors out of the market. This is a stark contrast to the price fixing of the oligopolistic period in the industry. The new methods have been accompanied by increased rates of accidents, deaths, and stress among workers (Moberg 1986). USX is sending mixed signals. The company is still taking more in depreciation than it is putting back into new plants and equipment. It has cut its own investments in steel while trying to drive other companies out. The current plan is for USX to be the last big integrated steel company when good times return.

Overall in the last decade or so, the steel industry shut down almost 700 steel-manufacturing and related facilities between 1974 and mid-1986 (Brown 1986:K3). The United States is now the only advanced industrial nation incapable of supplying its own domestic steel needs, if it should have to (Morse 1986:8). Seven years ago the United States had 200 blast furnaces still operating; now only 46 are left to supply raw steel.

The number of workers in the industry fell from 453,000 in 1979 to 200,000 in 1985, with another 30,000 drop expected by 1990. A 10 percent reduction per year in steel-making capacity is projected, placing capacity in 1990 at 120 million tons. Another estimate, from an economist at the Iron and Steel Institute, envisions production at 91 million tons by 1990 and perhaps bottoming out at 75 million tons by the year 2000 (Salpukas 1984:D1, 6). Given the way the U.S. steel industry has been reacting to the crunch, this latter estimate does not seem unrealistic. The United Steelworkers of America lost nearly half of its 1.4 million members in the last ten years, and most of the remaining members are not making steel, as the union has been taking a tip from the industry and diversifying into office workers and chemical workers in the last few years. The steel mills were operating at 70 percent of capacity in 1985, an improvement over the 55 percent of capacity in 1982. Production costs were down at the integrated mills from $611 per net ton in 1982 to $473 per net ton in 1985. Still, the industry is losing money because low demand is keeping prices down.

Other problems for the U.S. economy and society should also be noted. First, USX has been sabotaging worker/community buyouts of its shutdowns. The company is doing this because of the opportunities to go into joint ventures with foreign multinationals and its desire to be the surviving producer. The joint venture with POSCO will allow USX to shut down its slabmaking facility at Geneva, Utah. This is a similar arrangement as the 1984 attempt to set up imports of slabs to the East Coast from Scotland and shut down the slabmaking facilities at its Fairless (Pennsylvania) Works rather than update those facilities (Morse

1986:9). Worker/community-owned plants would be in competition with the foreign partner.

A second problem for the overall economy that should not be overlooked is that while the steel industry was receiving tax breaks and import controls, the price of steel remained higher in the United States than elsewhere. This means that other U.S. producers, such as automobiles and appliances, paid more than their foreign competitors for the steel in their products. Automobiles, for example, paid 30 percent more for steel than did their Japanese competitors (Von Hoffman 1983). This raised costs for these U.S. producers, limited their sales at home and abroad, and lost jobs for workers in those industries.

What is the future of the steel industry and USX? Until the recession of the early 1980s the steel industry as a whole had been operating at about a 7 percent profit rate, which is not high enough for the large corporations. The minimills are as efficient as any in the world, but they do not produce raw steel; they rely on recycled steel and small specialty products. Some of these minimills will remain, as will some of the medium-sized efficient producers. The large integrated producers may continue to shrink to the year 2000, although USX currently expects to remain in the steel industry. An upward shift in demand might encourage some mills to maintain capacity, but steel has been replaced by other materials (aluminum, reinforced concrete, and even plastic in automobiles) in many of its big markets. There is little reason to expect that substitution will not continue in the future.

The United States could increase demand if the nation decided to rebuild some of its crumbling infrastructure or to introduce mass transit. A 1982 estimate for the cost of infrastructure repair was $3 trillion—and bridges still use steel. Two other factors may help increase demand. Quality is up from a 5 to 10 percent rejection rate a few years ago to only 2 percent rejection, rivaling Japan. Also, the devalued U.S. dollar is making the U.S. product more competitive with those of other developed nations, but not yet with the Third World exporters.

Some economists applaud the restructuring of the steel industry, which they have seen as a dinosaur in its clinging to large open-hearth works, bureaucratic structure, and management by hubris (pride). The survivors currently are medium-sized BOFs and electric furnace minimills, mostly nonunion and close to their markets. The days of shipping from Pittsburgh and Chicago appear to be over. If communities want to keep their steel mills open and if United Steelworkers want to have members who are steelworkers, they will have to buy them out as Weirton has done, but they will have to fight the steel companies who have more loyalties to foreign companies and to their other investments outside the steel industry. They can expect no help from U.S. banks or the government (Steel: The new global order 1983). As of 1982, with the purchase of Marathon Oil and Texas Oil and Gas, U.S. Steel (USX) is now more in the oil business than in steel. The same thing is happening with West German and other EEC steel giants, except that the state is assisting in retraining displaced workers. Worldwide the steel industry is declining.

SUMMARY

This chapter has examined aspects of organizations, both internally and externally. We have observed the following important points:

1. The field of organizational theory has expanded to include not only organizational structure and the behaviors of the individuals within the organization, but also the environment of the organization and the reciprocal effects as they interact.

2. The formal characteristics of large organizations/bureaucracies were listed. Bureaucracies have advantages (more efficient for large tasks and more universalistic in hiring, promotion, and pay) as well as problems for their functioning and for society as a whole (centralization of decision making, rigid structures in the face of changing conditions, goal displacement, sometimes negative effects on personality characteristics of workers, and secrecy).

3. Various dimensions of organizations have been studied: size of organization (which may include the stage of the lifecycle of the organization), type of technology, the division of labor and location of decision making among departments—especially with respect to their relationship to the outside environment and to their internal interdependence within the organization.

4. The chapter discussed four basic management styles and their connection to organizational cultures and what this means for flexibility and innovation within the organization—including two different views on how to look at what is happening, with bureaucratic technological rationality or with a humanistic participatory approach.

5. Structures of both the political economy and the large organization and their cultures affect real economic growth and productivity. Real economic growth demands innovations in new products, processes, and markets, and structures and culture may not be providing the setting for cooperative creativity and innovation.

6. Finally, we saw an example of an industry and its leading firm that incapsulates the structural and cultural features of an old oligopo-

listic industry faced with a changing world and the directions in which various parts of the industry have gone in reaction to the changes. The major producer and the other large firms in the industry have not innovated but have diversified and have settled, largely, for rearranging paper assets.

In sum, organizational structures and management styles/ organizational cultures that lend themselves to flexibility, communications, and agreement on goals and that encourage innovation and creativity can be both efficient producers and more satisfying places in which to work. The next chapter continues to explore some of these alternative modes of organization.

BIBLIOGRAPHY

Abernathy, William, and James Utterback. 1978. Patterns of industrial innovation. *Technology Review* 80, 7:41–47 (June/July).

Adorno, Theodore W., and M. Horkheimer. 1972. *Dialectic of enlightenment.* New York: Herder and Herder.

Aldrich, H. E., and Jeffrey Pfeffer. 1976. Environments of organizations. *Annual Review of Sociology* 2:79–105.

Anderson, Jack. 1984. Steel industry may never recover. *Washington Post*, 107th year, no. 360:D.C.11 (November 29).

Barnard, Chester I. 1938. *The functions of the executive.* Cambridge, Mass.: Harvard University Press.

Baron, James N. 1984. Organizational perspectives on stratification. *Annual Review of Sociology* 10:37–69.

Bass, Bernard M., and Gerald V. Barrett. 1981. *People, work, and organizations: An introduction to industrial and organizational psychology*, 2nd ed. Boston: Allyn and Bacon.

Bensman, David. 1986. Steel standoff. *The Nation* 243, 5:132–133 (August 30).

Bentsen, Lloyd. 1985. Industry: U.S. staying ahead of the competition. *San Marcos (TX) Daily Record*, 4A (February 20).

Berger, Peter L., and Thomas Luckmann. 1967. *The social construction of reality.* Garden City, N.Y.: Doubleday (Anchor).

Birch, David. 1979. *The job generation process.* Boston: MIT Program on Neighborhood and Regional Change.

Blau, Peter, and Richard C. Scott. 1963. *Formal organizations.* San Francisco: Chandler.

Brown, Warren. 1986. A sign of the times: LTV's troubles were no surprise to analysts of an ailing industry. *Austin (TX) American-Statesman* K3 (July 20).

Carroll, G. R. 1984. Organizational ecology. *Annual Review of Sociology* 10:71–93.

Caves, Richard. 1967. *American industry: Structure, conduct, performance.* Englewood Cliffs, N.J.: Prentice-Hall.

Collier, Andrew. 1984. Steel industry's cries of "foul play" ignore basic realities. *In These Times* 9, 1:13 (November 7–13).

Daft, Richard L. 1983. *Organization theory and design*. St. Paul: West.

Deal, Terrence E., and Allan A. Kennedy. 1982. *Corporate cultures: The rites and rituals of corporate life*. Reading, Mass.: Addison-Wesley.

Deetz, Stanley A., and Astrid Kersten. 1983. "Critical models of interpretive research." In *Communication and organizations: An interpretive approach*, edited by Linda L. Putnam and Michael E. Pacanowsky, 147–171. Beverly Hills, Calif.: Sage.

Dowie, Mark, and Theodore A. Brown. 1985. Taking stock: The best and worst of American business. *Mother Jones* 10, 5:20–25, 37–39 (June).

Edwards, Richard C. 1975. "The social relations of production in the firm and labor market structure." In *Labor market segmentation*, edited by Richard C. Edwards, Michael Reich, and David M. Gordon, 3–26. Lexington, Mass.: D.C. Heath.

———. 1979. *Contested terrain: The transformation of the workplace in the twentieth century*. New York: Harper & Row (Torchbooks).

Eisenstadt, Samuel N., ed. 1971. *Political sociology: A reader*. New York: Basic Books.

Etzioni, Amitai. 1961. *A comparative analysis of complex organizations: On power, involvement, and their correlates*. New York: Free Press.

Fine, Gary Alan. 1984. Negotiated orders and organizational cultures. *Annual Review of Sociology* 10:239–262.

Flint, Jerry. 1986. Hold the obits. *Forbes* 137, 5:80–86 (March 10).

Ford, Ramona L. 1978. C. Wright Mills: A plain Marxist. Ph.D. diss., Department of Sociology, Southern Illinois University, Carbondale.

Foster, Richard. 1986. *Innovation: The attacker's advantage*. New York: Summit Books (Simon and Schuster).

Freeman, Christopher, John Clark, and Luc Soete. 1982. *Unemployment and technical innovation, a study of long waves and economic development*. Westport, Conn.: Greenwood.

Galante, Steven P. 1986. Small business: White House choice at SBA may rouse backers. *Wall Street Journal* 207,62: 21 (March 31).

Galaskiewicz, Joseph. 1985. Interorganizational relations. *Annual Review of Sociology* 11:281–304.

Gouldner, Alvin. 1954. *Patterns of industrial bureaucracy*. Glencoe, Ill.: Free Press.

Gracey, Harry L. 1967. "Morality in the organized society." In *Readings in introductory sociology*, edited by Dennis H. Wrong and Harry L. Gracey, 607–610. New York: Macmillan.

Greenhouse, Steven. 1985. Painful moves in steel go on. *New York Times* 135, 46629:D2 (December 20).

Habermas, Jurgen. 1971. *Knowledge and human interests*. Boston: Beacon.

———. 1973. *Theory and practice*. Boston: Beacon.

———. 1975. *Legitimation crisis*. Boston: Beacon.

———. 1979. *Communication and the evolution of society*. Boston: Beacon.

Harrington, Alan. 1959. *Life in the Crystal Palace*. New York: Alfred A. Knopf.

Harrison, Roger. 1972. Understanding your organization's character. *Harvard Business Review* 50, 3:119–128 (May–June).

Hayes, Robert H., and William Abernathy. 1980. Managing our way to economic decline. *Harvard Business Review* 58, 4:67–77 (July–August).

Hayes, Robert H., and David A. Garvin. 1982. Managing as if tomorrow mattered. *Harvard Business Review* 60, 3:70–79 (May–June).

Hayes, Thomas C. 1986. LTV seeks protection in Chapter 11. *Austin (TX) American-Statesman* Fl, 12 (July 18).

Hellriegel, Don, John W. Slocum, Jr., and Richard W. Woodman. 1983. *Organizational behavior*, 3rd ed. St. Paul: West.

Hickson, David, Derek Pugh, and Diana Pheysey. 1969. Operations technology and organization structure: An empirical reappraisal. *Administrative Science Quarterly* 14, 3:378–397 (September).

Hofstede, Geert H. 1984. *Culture's consequences: International differences in work-related values*, abridged ed. Beverly Hills, Calif.: Sage.

Jewkes, John, David Sawers, and Richard Stillerman. 1969. *The sources of innovation*. New York: Macmillan.

Joint Economic Committee Rx: Modification of U.S. policies needed to encourage R&D. 1981. *World of Work Review* 6, 11:84–85 (November).

Kanter, Rosabeth Moss. 1977. *Men and women of the corporation*. New York: Basic Books.

———. 1983. *The change masters: Innovation for productivity in the American corporation*. New York: Simon and Schuster.

Kanter, Rosabeth Moss, and D. Brinkerhoff. 1982. Organizational performance: Recent developments in measurement. *Annual Review of Sociology* 7:321–349.

Kanter, Rosabeth Moss, and Barry Stein, eds. 1979. *Life in organizations: Workplaces as people experience them*. New York: Basic Books.

Lammers, C. J. 1978. The comparative sociology of organizations. *Annual Review of Sociology* 4:485–510.

Latane, Bibb, and J. M. Darley. 1970. *The unresponsive bystander: Why doesn't he help?* New York: Appleton-Century-Crofts.

Latane, Bibb, and Steve Nida. 1981. Ten years of research on group size and helping. *Psychological Bulletin* 89, 2:308–324 (March).

Leff, Laurel. 1986. Firms of endearment. *Savvy* 7, 5:47–52, 81–84 (May).

Levering, Robert, Milton Moskowitz, and Michael Katz. 1984. *The 100 best companies to work for in America*. Reading, Mass.: Addison-Wesley.

Likert, Rensis. 1961. *New patterns of management*. New York: McGraw-Hill.

———. 1967. *The human organization*. New York: McGraw-Hill.

March, J. G., and Herbert A. Simon. 1958. *Organizations*. New York: John Wiley.

Merton, Robert K. 1952. "Bureaucratic structure and personality." In *Reader in bureaucracy*, edited by Robert K. Merton, Ailsa P. Gray, Barbara Hockey, and Hanan C. Selvin, 361–371. New York: Free Press.

Merton, Robert K., Ailsa P. Gray, Barbara Hockey, and Hanan C. Selvin, eds. 1952. *Reader in bureaucracy*. New York: Free Press.

Michels, Robert. 1949. *Political parties: A sociological study of the oligarchical tendencies of modern democracy*. New York: Free Press.

Mintzberg, Henry. 1979. *The structuring of organizations.* Englewood Cliffs, N.J.: Prentice-Hall.

Moberg, David. 1984. Monopoly's inevitable legacy: Steel closings. *In These Times* 8, 7:9, 11 (January 11–17).

———. 1986. Steelworkers brace for USX's next move. *In These Times* 10, 35:f5, 22 (September 17–23).

Morse, David. 1986. Surrender Dorothy. *In These Times* 10, 13:8–9 (February 19–25).

Neff, Walter S. 1985. *Work and human behavior,* 3rd ed. New York: Aldine.

Nelson, Hal. 1983. Review of *Corporate cultures: The rites and rituals of corporate life. Human Organization* 42, 4:368–370 (Winter).

Olsen, Marvin. 1978. *The process of social organization: Power in social systems,* 2nd ed. New York: Holt, Rinehart and Winston.

Olson, Mancur, Jr. 1965. *The Logic of collective action: Public goods and the theory of groups.* Cambridge, Mass.: Harvard University Press.

Organizational Culture. 1983. Special issue, *Administrative Science Quarterly,* 28, 3:331–501.

Ouchi, William G., and Alan L. Wilkins. 1985. Organizational culture. *Annual Review of Sociology* 11:457–483.

Perrow, Charles. 1970. *Organizational analysis: A sociological view.* Monterey, Calif., and London: Brooks/Cole and Tavistock.

———. 1986. *Complex organizations: A critical essay,* 3rd ed. Glenview, Ill.: Scott, Foresman.

Peters, Thomas J. 1985. The curse of cash stifles innovation. *Austin (TX) American-Statesman* D4 (December 9).

Peters, Thomas J., and Robert H. Waterman, Jr. 1982. *In search of excellence: Lessons from America's best-run companies.* New York: Harper & Row.

Pfeffer, Jeffrey, and Gerald R. Salancik. 1978. *The external control of organizations: A resource dependence perspective.* New York: Harper & Row.

Pinchot, Gifford III. 1985. *Intrapreneuring: Why you don't have to leave the corporation to become an entrepreneur.* New York: Harper & Row.

Piore, Michael J. 1975. "Notes for a theory of labor market stratification." In *Labor market segmentation.,* edited by Richard C. Edwards, Michael Reich, and David M. Gordon, 125–150. Lexington, Mass.: D.C. Heath.

Presthus, Robert. 1962. *The organizational society: An analysis and a theory.* New York: Random (Vintage).

Putnam, Linda L., and Michael E. Pacanowsky. 1983. *Communication and organizations: An interpretive approach.* Beverly Hills, Calif.: Sage.

Reich, Robert B. 1987. Enterprise and double cross. *Washington Monthly* 18, 12:13–19 (January).

Reynolds, Peter C. 1987. Imposing a corporate culture: An anthropologist examines a failed attempt to create an open culture behind closed doors. *Psychology Today* 21, 3:33–38 (March).

Riesman, David. 1967. "The other-directed man." In *Readings in introductory sociology,* edited by Dennis H. Wrong and Harry L. Gracey, 610–616. New York: Macmillan.

Rosen, Corey. 1981. Entrepreneurship, innovation and economic growth. Unpublished ms. for Control Data, Arlington, Va.

————, Katherine J. Klein, and Karen M. Young. 1986. *Employee ownership in America: The equity solution*. Lexington, Mass.: Lexington Books.

Rostow, W. W. 1983. Technology and unemployment in the Western world. *Challenge* 26, 1:6–17 (March–April).

Salpukas, Agis. 1984. A restructured steel industry: Plants will be smaller, more cost effective. *New York Times* 13:D1, 6 (February 2).

Samuelson, Robert J. 1984. The economics of self-pity. *Newsweek* 103, 10:78 (March 5).

SAPPHO. 1972. *Success and failure in industrial innovation: Report on Project SAPPHO*, by the Science Policy Research Unit, University of Sussex. London: Centre for the Study of Industrial Innovation (February).

Scott, W. Richard. 1975. Organizational structure. *Annual Review of Sociology* 1:1–20.

Simon, Herbert A. 1947. *Administrative behavior*. New York: Macmillan. (2nd ed., 1957)

Steel: The new global order. 1983. Special issue, *Multinational Monitor* 4, 6:1–23 (June).

Steel: Too little, too late: An industry trapped by its past. 1982. *Dollars and Sense* 80:8–9, 12 (October).

Stone, Katerine. 1981. "The origins of job structures in the steel industry." In *Complex organizations: Critical perspectives.*, edited by Mary Zey-Ferrell and Michael Aiken, 349–381. Glenview, Ill.: Scott, Foresman.

Terkel, Studs. 1974. *Working*. New York: Avon.

Thompson, James D. 1967. *Organizations in action*. New York: McGraw-Hill.

Thurow, Lester C. 1978. Eight imperatives for R & D. *Technology Review* 80, 3:64–71 (January).

————. 1983. The need to work smarter. *Newsweek* 102, 14:80 (October 3).

Udy, Stanley H., Jr. 1959. "Bureaucracy" and "rationality" in Weber's organization theory. *American Sociological Review* 24, 6:791–795 (December).

U.S. Bureau of the Census. 1985. *Statistical abstract of the United States: 1986*. Washington, D.C.: GPO.

U.S. Department of Commerce. 1967. *Technological innovation: Its environment and management*. Washington, D.C.: U.S. Department of Commerce.

Uttal, Bro. 1983. The corporate culture vultures. *Fortune* 108, 8:66–72 (October 17).

Von Hippel, Eric A. 1978. Users as innovators. *Technology Review* 80, 3:31–39 (January).

Von Hoffman, Nicholas. 1983. Traitors: Cut off tax breaks for America's dirty steel industry. *San Marcos (TX) Daily Record* p. 4 (April 21).

Webber, Ross A. 1969. *Culture and management: Text and readings in comparative management*. Homewood, Ill.: Richard D. Irwin.

Weber, Max. 1946a. "Bureaucracy." In *From Max Weber: Essays in sociology*, edited by Hans H. Gerth and C. Wright Mills, 194–244. New York: Oxford.

————. 1946b. "The Chinese literati." In *From Max Weber: Essays in sociology*, edited by Hans H. Gerth and C. Wright Mills, 416–444. New York: Oxford.

————. 1946c. "The sociology of charismatic authority." In *From Max Weber: Essays in sociology*, edited by Hans H. Gerth and C. Wright Mills, 245–252. New York: Oxford.

Thinking Ahead

11

Alternative Workplace Organization

The 1970s and 1980s have seen corporations in the United States thinking they are playing a game of catch-up. The social conditions had changed, and management practices developed during earlier times had to be re-examined. The need to develop new strategies and tactics was evident. In order to maintain profits and compete (and even survive) companies could (1) turn to the government for various favors, (2) diversify through mergers and acquisitions, (3) begin to develop new products or adopt new processes, and/or (4) implement cost-cutting and more efficient operations. The latter two tactics took the shape of establishing plants abroad, and automating and other new technologies. They also included a growing interest in worker participation for an expected increase in ideas for improving the work process, in worker commitment, in quality of product, and in worker productivity. This chapter discusses this area of alternative workplace organization for increased employee participation.

Many U.S. managers were already aware of the studies regarding the success of human resources management and the example of Japan's use of it.

Best seller book lists included Ouchi's *Theory Z* (1981), Naisbitt's *Megatrends* (1984), Peters and Waterman's *In Search of the Excellence* (1982) and Halberstan's *The Reckoning* (1986). These books stress human resources and worker participation in an overall participative corporate culture. Following the civil rights movement and its emphasis on self-actualizing, human resources research, and such international phenomenon as the 1968 general strike of white-collar workers and students in France (the "events of May"), U.S. management could not avoid being affected in some way. The message projected from these sources was that workers could work more efficiently and could offer important ideas to improve product and work process, if given the opportunity.

Attention began to focus on experiments that reorganized work in some way to elicit this input. Unions, as discussed in Chapter 7, were usually suspicious of management intentions, although in a few instances they helped initiate the planned changes.

The following section reviews some kinds of worker participation programs and alternative workplace organization that have been attempted in the United States and elsewhere. We look more closely at the political economy and management practices of Japan and review the organization of the successful Mondragon cooperative system in Spain. In addition, we summarize some studies on the effects of worker participation in decision making on job satisfaction and productivity. Finally, we offer a few comments on social scientists and their connection to implementing worker participation programs.

WORKER PARTICIPATION PLANS IN THE UNITED STATES AND ELSEWHERE

Companies in the United States have used several types of worker participation plans. The best known producer co-ops are the Northwest plywood cooperatives, 16 of which still exist (Zwerdling 1980:95; Berman 1967; Bernstein 1974). Scanlon plans have been in existence since the 1930s, and a 1967 estimate placed the number at 500 (Frieden 1980:27; Jenkins 1974:222). A New York Stock Exchange (1982:35) study indicated that 15 percent of U.S. companies with more than 500 employees had Scanlon or some other form of gain-sharing plan. Other companies have been using profit-sharing plans, job enrichment, workteams, quality circles, and Employee Stock Ownership Plans (ESOPS). Some companies have adopted more than one plan. For example, the shopfloor can be reorganized into workteams at the same time that a profit-sharing plan or an ESOP is introduced. Some companies that already had a profit-sharing plan kept it when they adopted an ESOP.

In examining these forms of alternative workplace organization, one might want to ask the following questions: (1) Does the plan offer shopfloor decision making, middle-level decision making at the departmental level, or top management decision making at the company level, with representation on the board of directors? (2) Does the plan return a share of profits from sales or increased production value to the workers for their increased efforts? (3) Does the plan offer stock ownership to the workers, how much of the stock is in the hands of nonmanagerial workers, and can they vote their stock on important company issues? (4) Is there potential for workers to increase ability for leadership and decision

making by training in problem solving and by gaining experience in decision making in a favorable organizational culture fostering mutual
trust and information sharing by the company?

In addition, Michael Maccoby of the Harvard Project on Technology,
Work and Character, and Neal Herrick, formerly with the Department
of Labor, cited four general criteria that successful workplace plans
must consider when analyzing alternative workplace programs:

1. Security—both job and income security;
2. Equity—fairness in hiring, promotions, and pay; no discrimination against women and other minorities; a share in the profits if
   productivity is increased;
3. Individuation—restructuring should take into account the individual worker's needs and desires for development, rather than a
   consultant or management deciding this for the worker (participation in the planning of restructuring);
4. Democracy—workers should be guaranteed free speech, due process, and participation in decisions which affect them (quoted in
   Zwerdling 1980:44).

Job Enlargement, Job Rotation, Flextime, Job Enrichment

Job enlargement refers to assigning more tasks to the worker—the opposite of the Tayloristic notion of breaking down tasks to their smallest
parts. *Job rotation* refers to shifting workers from one task to another to
alleviate the boredom of routine tasks. Job rotation may require bargaining with the union regarding work rules. *Flextime* or flexible work
schedules consider the worker's outside obligations, such as child care.
Flextime has had some beneficial results for parents and is reported to
cut down on absenteeism and job turnover. All of these approaches,
however, do not deal with the overall content of the job in terms of
responsibility or intrinsic interest, although they can be helpful in the
shortrun.

By *job enrichment*, Herzberg meant that the content of the job
should be expanded to allow the worker more autonomy and responsibility. Many companies that have attempted to restructure jobs, however,
have not had encouraging results because of how it was implemented.
Often, management or social scientist consultants have simply rewrit-
ten job descriptions and enlarged the job with more repetitive tasks,
rather than enriched jobs with more responsibility or opportunities for
worker decision making or growth (Jenkins 1974:168). If the worker is
not consulted in the job change and if no structures for group decision

making are included, then a chief mechanism for democratic discussion, leadership training, and decision making is lost. If workers are included in the restructuring of their jobs and if the jobs are enriched with responsibility and opportunities for decision making, however, this can be a useful means of increasing intrinsically rewarding work and job satisfaction.

Profit-Sharing and Gain-Sharing Plans

Profit-sharing plans have been in the United States since 1887, when Proctor and Gamble initiated one. The impetus for such plans is the idea that employees will work harder and produce more if they know they will receive some of the benefits. A 1973 estimate places the number of firms with deferred and combination plans at 150,000 and with cash plans at 100,000. These profit-sharing plans covered 10 million employees and held between $25 and $30 billion in trust assets (Metzger 1974:40−41). A more recent estimate placed the figure of gain-sharing plans (some are based on increased productivity, rather than on profit) at 15 percent of all companies with 500 or more employees (New York Stock Exchange 1982:35).

Under a *profit-sharing plan* the company pays a percentage of profits on sales to all employees, either directly in cash or stock or indirectly to employee accounts held by a trust to be paid later at death, disability, severance, or retirement. Some companies use a combination of deferred and cash payments. The amount of stock distributed in this way is usually quite small and is not voted by the employees. Financial participation is hereby encouraged, but these firms generally ignore employee participation in shopfloor and managerial decision making—no employee committees formed (Frieden 1980:79). Productivity has been significantly increased in firms after the introduction of profit-sharing plans (Frieden 1980:79−81; New York Stock Exchange 1982:35; Metzger 1980). Comparisons of firms with both profit-sharing and employee participation in decision making are currently underway (Conte and Svejnar 1981).

Gain-sharing plans have also been devised to increase worker efforts. Improshare (improved productivity through sharing) was developed in the 1970s by industrial engineer Mitchell Fein. Under this plan, workers receive periodic bonuses that are linked to increases in their output, rather than profits as in the profit-sharing plan. More than 100 companies have adopted this idea, including General Electric, Firestone, Phillips Petroleum, Weyerhaeuser, and Bell and Howell. The Rucker Plan is a similar suggestion system. Recognition is given for suggestions, and cash bonuses are given when labor costs as a percent of production value drop below a predetermined standard (Productivity sharing plans 1981:77–78). Scanlon Plans are another form of gain-sharing that share the increased profits made through implementing new ideas suggested by employees. These plans are discussed later in this chapter.

Labor-Management Committees

Labor-management committees, which vary in joint decision-making levels from plantwide production to minor social functions, began in the United States during World War II under the aegis of the War Production Board, with the blessing of the AFL-CIO. Only the conservative National Association of Manufacturers was reluctant to support such committees, seeing them as an attempt to dilute management's prerogatives (DeVos 1981:87). By 1944 there were some 5,000 plant committees, which represented more than 7 million workers. Many committees limited themselves to blood banks, car pools, and the war bond drives, but the memory lingered, and in some areas, such as the steel industry, the committees continued to function. The 1970s and 1980s saw a resurgence of these committees in various forms. Some included only labor and management, some included the community in a tripartite form.

Quality Circles

At the shopfloor level two major modes of employee participation in decision making are being tried in the United States: quality circles and workteams. They are often part of a broader Quality of Work Life (QWL) program or Participative Management Program (PMP). *Quality circles* involve usually eight to twenty workers who work together in an area of production. They meet every week or so to discuss possible production problems and improvements that might be made in the work process or in product quality. The workers then present these ideas to management for approval.

The idea for quality circles was introduced into Japan in the 1950s by William Edward Deming from the United States. The idea had been rejected by U.S. managers but appealed to the Japanese as a means of improving quality control. Today, quality circles are the most popular means of shopfloor participation in the United States. By February 1980 at least 65 large companies had active quality circles, and by 1983 the International Association of Quality Circles estimated there were more than 1,356,000 circles operating in 8,000 locations and including more than a million workers (DeVos 1981:95; Parker 1985:8). These companies include some giants, such as General Motors, J. C. Penney, Uniroyal, GE, Firestone, International Harvester, Northrup, Lockheed, Rockwell International, Phillips Petroleum, Ford, the U.S. Navy, and the Federal Aviation Administration, as well as many smaller organizations.

The reason quality circles have now spread to hundreds of companies in the industrial nations may be that they can be organized without having to restructure the shopfloor into teams, requiring employee stock ownership, or otherwise threatening the managerial hierarchy. In essence, management can attempt to make gains from employee input without having to give up any prerogatives.

Alan Watts, president of the Communication Workers of America, noted that an Oregon State University report found that 75 percent of the quality circle programs die within a few years because the manner in which they are implemented leaves the worker feeling manipulated (Watts 1982:3). Even though many of these quality circles have a certain amount of autonomy, are cost effective, average about 80 percent of their suggestions being accepted by management, tend to boost morale initially, promote some leadership and decision-making training, and may sometimes include bonuses or profit-sharing, they do not go far in dealing with company-level problems (DeWar 1979:15, 24, 26–27, 30).

Why do some quality circle programs succeed and others fail? In an issue of *Workplace Democracy*, union leaders and social scientists gave opinions based on their experiences with such programs (Watts 1982:4; Simmons and Bluestone 1982:20; Sachs 1982:9, 19). Their list of do's and don'ts for quality circles includes these seven points.

1. Quality circles must be structured from the beginning by both top management and by workers' representatives acting together on an equal footing, so that management goals of increased productivity and profits do not overshadow worker goals of participation in creating a satisfying workplace.
2. The initial contract between workers and management must contain a guarantee of worker rights—such as job security and voluntary participation.
3. Collective bargaining must be clearly separated from the Quality of Work Life program (QWL) if a union in involved, so that QCs will not be used as union-busting mechanisms.
4. Meetings must be regularly scheduled with time allowed for them.
5. Management must follow through on ideas.
6. There must be complete communications with and training for participation for all employees.
7. Management must share quality circle savings with employees.

Implicit in this list is the idea that mutual trust must engender complete autonomy and information sharing so that the circles can have the ability to consider and implement larger and larger issues. The entire body of literature points to the necessity of worker input into decision making growing over time, as workers become more knowledgeable about the company and more skilled in group decision making. Also, the haste with which some plans have been put into place has meant not enough preparation and education on how to operate the circle and what to expect. Participants become discouraged by early poor results.

A negative example of what can happen when these considerations are not made comes from Nissan (Datsun) in Japan. Here participation in quality circles for assembly workers is not voluntary, and the union, purportedly representing the workers, is a sweetheart union—following managements' goals and getting rid of dissident workers. How the quality circle plan was put into practice generated competition among quality circles and a speed up of the assembly line, which left the workers breathless trying to keep up with it. The implementation of the plan engendered anything but trust, sharing, and worker satisfaction. Workers who wanted to participate in a more democratic way have been forced out or made submissive by threats of ostracism and stymied pay and promotion (Junkerman 1982). Apparently Toyota operates similarly (Kamata 1982). We return to the organization of the political economy, some history and culture, and quality circles in Japan in a later section in this chapter.

Scanlon Plans

Another plan reminiscent of quality circles, but often aimed at the department level, is the Scanlon Plan pioneered by Joseph Scanlon in the 1930s to save a company during the depression. The plan's basic concern was to increase productivity. The wider company-level issues that can occasionally arise in quality circles are not treated. *Scanlon plans* send up production innovations from the shopfloor or departmental committee to management- or to plant-level worker-manager committees for consideration (Zwerdling 1980:179). A base line of worker productivity is decided at the start, and subsequent profits are based on the increased value of produced goods, rather than on profits from sales. Such profits are divided among employees (Frieden 1980:27). Usually, 75 percent of increased profits are reserved for the workers, and 25 percent for the company.

There appears to be less group interaction and training in problem solving under Scanlon plans than in quality circles. Eight studies of Scanlon Plan applications indicate production gains in most instances and tremendous gains in a few cases (Friedan 1980:27). In both the Scanlon Plan and most quality circles, however, the problems considered for solution are at the shopfloor or departmental level, rather than at the company level.

Workteams

Another form of shopfloor participation that calls for more restructuring of the workplace than does the quality circle is the shopfloor workteam. *Workteams* are formed in contiguous work areas and are allowed a great deal of freedom to plan their own production and scheduling, sometimes electing their own supervisor on a rotating basis from among their members. The best known example of the workteam in the United States was the General Foods Gravy Train plant in Topeka, Kansas. The eight-person processing team and sixteen-person packaging-warehousing team—one team each on three shifts—had a great deal of autonomy. The workteams decided who would do what job that day. There were no job categories, and each worker was paid according to the number of jobs learned. The teams also did their own hiring and firing, maintenance and cleanup work, and quality control (Jenkins 1974:225–231; Zwerdling 1980:19–29). Productivity and profits and quality were higher than at similar conventional plants. The project was eventually scuttled, however, because it worked too well and management and home office staff became nervous about workers' being obviously able to manage themselves (Frieden 1980:43).

The Rushton Mining experiment with workteams of miners was also successful in terms of extra training, morale building, productivity, and safety, but it was not introduced companywide. Jealousies from miners not in the experiment and from supervisors who did not have special training and feared their loss of power ended the experiment by a companywide vote (Zwerdling 1980).

Harman International Industries in Bolivar, Tennessee, adopted a Harman-United Auto Workers work improvement program that included virtually every worker in the factory. Shopfloor committees were developed to make their own workplace decisions. All committees contained union, management, and worker representatives. The new employee-run newspaper presents real debates and issues on company and community topics. The enthusiasm generated by the program at Harman has spilled over into the community in other ways, such as in joint courses on a wide range of subjects offered to the community using plant facilities. Although it has taken several years and many heated arguments to develop this system, the workers have continued to develop problem-solving skills and have maintained their workplace participation even after the company was sold and new management assumed control (Zwerdling 1980:31).

An example of workteams from abroad is the Volvo auto company in Kalmar, Sweden. Positive effects attributed to the introduction of workteams have been lower absenteeism and turnover as well as reduction in the white-collar job sector. The workers have a major role in deciding who will do what job, in training new employees, in ordering materials, and in quality checks. The automated trollies move the car bodies from one area to another, with buffer zones in between to allow each team to work at its own pace, and each team of from fifteen to twenty workers completes a significant part of the assembly (Volvo's Kalmar plant 1977). Elected team leaders are contact persons with other teams and management to coordinate operations.

A similar example, but more limited in scale, is the workteam organization at Saab-Scania, the third largest automotive producer in Sweden. Worker representatives also sit on the plantwide Works Council. At its Scania operation in Soedertaelje, workteams of three or four assemble an engine in thirty minutes. Making the parts for assembly, however, is done on a traditional assembly line. This was the case in 1974, when a group of auto workers from the UAW in the United States reviewed the operation. The U.S. workers liked the cleaner, quieter, smaller plant, its safety record, the plant's recreational facilities and better bathrooms, and less close supervision, they also thought the product might be higher quality than what they built in Detroit.

However, at the end of their four-week stay, the six U.S. workers concluded that Saab-Scania's workteam approach was probably too much work and too fast paced to appeal to U.S. workers, although three of the six thought they would like it themselves (Goldmann 1979:15–55). The U.S. workers thought the hard-working Finnish guest workers liked the team concept better than the Swedes; however, 90 percent of the Swedish workers at Volvo indicated a preference for the team concept when it was put to the vote. Job control seems to have been the key factor in this approval. The team concept plants cost more to build than does the conventional assembly line plant, but savings in other areas, the apparent worker satisfaction, and high product quality seem to make it a qualified success. Despite the fact that Sweden now has one of the highest labor costs in the world, Volvo and Saab-Scania are competitive and remain among the top companies in profitability in Sweden.

Like Japan, Sweden is a small country (about the size of California) with limited natural resources, except for water power. Unlike Japan, however, it is not heavily populated, with a population of 8.3 million in 1985, about the size of the Chicago Standard Metropolitan Statistical Area. When Swedish national planners contemplated the future (see later section on national tripartite planning), it appeared that they would have to sell to foreign markets and that the tight labor market, the high rate of absenteeism in the labor force, and the unrest exhibited in the late 1960s were problems to be dealt with. Both foreign competition and job satisfaction thus became high priorities when considering workplace reorganization (Gyllenhammar 1977).

A few guest workers from other countries have been allowed into Sweden, primarily to fill the less desireable positions, as in the case of the Finnish workers at Saab-Scania. In addition the planners decided to encourage the entry of women into the workforce, rather than to try to attract too many foreign workers. Therefore, support systems (day care, parental leave, income tax breaks for dual career families, for example) and more equitable wages for work performed were offered to women workers (O'Kelly and Carney 1986:182–199).

Employee Stock Ownership Plans (ESOPs)

The Employee Stock Ownership Plan (ESOP) offers individual profit-sharing through stock ownership and may also offer a great deal of worker participation, depending on how it is set up. This idea was originally suggested by investment banker Louis Kelso in the 1950s. In 1973 he enlisted the aid of the powerful Senator Russell Long, whose father, Huey Long, was well remembered for his populist sentiments. Senator Long was chiefly responsible for the legislation that allowed ESOPs to qualify for tax breaks—the Employee Retirement Income Security Act (ERISA) of 1974, as amended (Rosen, Klein, and Young 1986:14–16). ESOPs increased rapidly in the 1970s and 1980s, and an estimated 7,000 companies had such plans in 1986 (U.S. General Accounting Office 1986:7).

The growing popularity of the ESOP is due to several factors: (1) to receive the tax advantage to the corporation setting up an ESOP trust (ESOT) (this is the primary impetus); (2) management's desire to increase productivity and profitability through a more committed workforce during tough economic times; (3) to enable workers to buy out the company when faced with plant shutdowns; (4) to enable companies to borrow capital more cheaply; (5) to avoid a hostile takeover by placing stock in the accounts of employees; (6) to provide owners of closely held firms (companies whose stock is not traded publicly on an exchange or over the counter) with a built-in market for their stock when the owner wants to divest without selling out to a conglomerate or a competitor; (7) to discourage unions—a point management does not like to discuss; (8) in return for concessions on wages and workrules—a recent phenomenon; and (9) occasionally for the owner's ideological reasons—a conviction that employees should be participating owners. Such owners obviously want to develop the appropriate organizational culture and mutual trust that seem to be important characteristics of successful ESOPs (Rosen, Klein, and Young 1986:18–32).

An ESOP works as shown in Figure 11.1.

1. The corporation (partnerships and proprietorships are not eligible) sets up an ESOP plan, hopefully with the assistance of worker representatives to aid participation from the start and legal advice because tax laws are complex.

2. The plan must then be approved by the Internal Revenue Service.

3. If the company is publicly traded, the value of the stock is what it sells for on the market. If the company is closely held, an independent evaluator must be hired to figure the value of the shares about to be issued. This is an added expense to the company but required by law to keep a company from overstating value to the IRS and to the employees.

4. A trustee, usually a local bank, must be assigned to handle employees' accounts and stock purchases. If the company wants extra capital, a leveraged trust is set up to borrow money and to allocate stock to the employees' accounts. The trust gives the borrowed money to the company in exchange for company stock. The company pays the trust back out of its profits each year. The trust then pays back the lender and distributes the paid-for shares of stock into employee accounts.

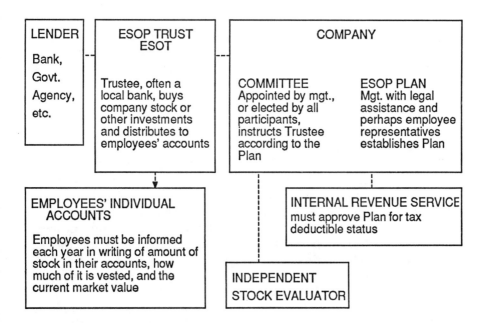

Figure 11.1 How an ESOP Is Organized

The employees are vested with ownership of the stock at some percentage per year—usually 10 percent, meaning that after eleven years in the plan the employee will be vested with the entire amount in the account. (*Vested* means that if the employee leaves the company, that amount of stock, or the value of it, is given to him or her by the company. The unvested shares in the employee's account are then divided among the other employees' accounts.) All contributions to the trust are tax deductible from the company's income before taxes. In a leveraged trust, the principal and interest are both deductible.

If the company does not want to borrow money (leverage), the trust accepts contributions of unpurchased or newly issued stock and/or cash profits from the company with which it can buy outstanding shares of stock or other investments and distributes them among the employees' accounts according to the formulae agreed on in the plan. The distribution to employees can be either as a percentage of the employee's earnings or, less frequently, equally among employees. Sometimes seniority is added to the equation on how to distribute. Again, these contributions from the company to the trust are in pretax dollars. The loan has been acquired cheaply, and the employees are the recipients of stock in the company in a sweat equity manner. Employees have not had to purchase stock; it has been earned through working for the company.

In more than half of such ESOP plans today the employees are not allowed to vote their stock, although voting privileges are now required by law in companies with publicly traded stock. In the seventy or so cases of employee buyouts to avoid shutdown, all of the company stock is usually owned by employees or employee/community members. Ownership does not automatically translate into control, however, unless control mechanisms are specifically built into the original plans. Even though most ESOP plans have increased worker morale, productivity, and profits in the short run, if employees' expectations regarding increased participation in decision making are unfulfilled a period of strong dissatisfaction usually follows. The well-known case of South Bend Lathe demonstrated this in 1979 when the worker-owners struck their own company to gain more control (Zwerdling 1980:65–79). The potential for meaningful worker participation exists but will remain dormant until structural changes are made in the organization through committees at the shopfloor level, up through representation on the board, and through the right of employees to vote their stock.

A number of companies have done exceedingly well by introducing the ESOP plan and offering a real worker participation corporate culture (see Rosen, Klein, and Young 1986). A company that has had widespread media coverage is Weirton Steel in Weirton, West Virginia. This is the largest employee buyout to date, and it was accomplished through the use of an ESOP. As well as immediately saving 7,000 jobs, in the first year of the plan the company got out of the red and into the black, hired 1,000 laid-off workers, and had the highest profits of any integrated steel mill in the country (Rosen, Klein, and Young 1986:27−28).

Another example of successful implementation is W. L. Gore Associates. A number of features about this company make its story worth commenting on.

> Gore is a 3,000-employee high-tech manufacturer known for its "Gore-Tex" fabric coating. It has been growing at almost 40 percent per year in recent years. All of its 'associates,' as employees are called, are considered 'non-managers.' According to the Gore credo, no one is a manager at Gore. There are no formal job titles or defined hierarchies, but rather a 'lattice' structure in which any employee or group of employees can communicate with any other. This approach might be considered anarchy by some, but it is a very profitable anarchy. Gore limits plant size to 200−400, although the manufacturing economies of scale would be larger, because the company believes larger plants lose human economies of scale.
>
> Gore employees, including the Gore family, own 95 percent of the company. It has an ESOP which owns a substantial (they will not say how much) and increasing share of the stock. Gore is regularly cited as one of the best places in the country to work. Although it is best to take the company's description of itself with some caution, by all accounts it is a most unusual and successful example of employee ownership and involvement. (Rosen, Klein, and Young 1986:26)

Quite recently ESOPs have been used to give employees some kind of equity in exchange for wage concessions. The transportation industry, which has had some hard times, offers a number of cases. In a number of trucking firms employees have gained more than 40 percent of the stock. In airlines employees have received 9 percent of Continental, 13 percent of Pan Am, 15 percent of Republic, 15 percent of PSA, and 33 percent of Western (Rosen, Klein, and Young 1986:31).

Anecdotal stories are interesting and informative, but aggregate data is sometimes more helpful in seeing what contributions an ESOP can make. Studies on employee productivity and job satisfaction discussed later in this chapter use aggregate data to compare factors in companies with various types of alternative workplace organization.

Cooperatives

Hypothetically, the most democratic form of employee participation is the cooperative, because it is both 100 percent employee owned and also equitable in voting rights. The cooperative allows one vote per owner-employee, no matter how many shares each voter owns. Theoretically, then, each worker-owner is equal. There may be about 800 cooperatives in the United States at the present time (Rosen, Klein, and Young 1986:17). The plywood cooperatives of the Pacific Northwest, which have been outproducing their conventionally owned and operated competitors since the 1920s, present an interesting case. Some of these coops have retained complete worker control over decision making; some have abdicated in favor of allowing management to make all decisions (Berman 1967; Zwerdling 1980). Some have not provided a means of transference of stock from outgoing to incoming members, creating outside ownership and workers who are not owners.

The three basic problems co-ops face are in (1) assuring mechanisms for continued employee involvement in decisions, (2) providing a means by which all employees are owners, and (3) assuring that ownership does not go outside the company through employee turnover or retirement. This latter situation can happen if departing employees can sell their stock outside the company. To assure that ownership does not pass outside the firm and that new employees can become stockholders (shares in some plywood companies have appreciated to more than $20,000 each), a trust can be set up to purchase the stock of departing employees on a right of first refusal basis. (Right of first refusal means that the departing employee must offer his or stock to the company for purchase before going on the market with it or willing it to another person.) New employees can be allowed to purchase this stock through sweat equity over a period of time, as in an ESOP.

To keep worker-owners actively involved in the decisions, in addition to the annual vote for the board of directors, owner-employees could participate in overlapping committees from shopfloor to plant level. Later in this chapter we discuss the highly successful Mondragon cooperative system in the Basque area of Spain; it is unique in its growth, its capital intensity, and its potential for ethnic communities in the United States.

BOARDROOM DEMOCRACY AND TRIPARTITE
NATIONAL PLANNING

When the Chrysler Corporation asked the U.S. government for a bailout of its financial difficulties, Doug Fraser (then UAW president) was appointed to the board of directors by Congress. Lee Iacocca, the president of Chrysler, claims the appointment was his idea, but other people in both union and management could not envision a union man on a corporation board (Iacocca 1984). The relationship between the union and management was supposed to be adversarial. How could having their representative on the board of directors help the workers? Would he not be co-opted? How could managers let the opposition know what was going on?

In Europe such labor-management cooperation is not new, even though Europe does have a long history of labor-management disagreement. After World War II the Allies required the coal and steel industries of West Germany to have one-third of their boards be worker representatives. In Germany such representation is called *codetermination* (*Mitbestimuung*). The Allies were trying to dilute the old power blocks. What subsequently happened was that the West German industries found this arrangement to be a great aid in their planning, and so laws were passed to require it of all large companies.

Not only are labor representatives on the company boards, but a labor director is also in the management structure. Worker councils oversee hiring, job evaluation, and training. Because the labor representatives must be separate from unions in West Germany, this situation seems to have led to some division in the labor movement, caused by dual representation (Jankowski 1986).

Other European countries saw the advantages of worker representation on boards of directors. By 1981, at least six EEC countries had mandated by law that the boards of directors of companies of a certain size or nationally owned must have worker representation, usually one-third of the board (Schwartz 1981:5). Three other countries with nationally owned companies also have workers as board members in those companies, without force of law. Other private companies in Europe have followed, without being required by law.

Since 1972 Sweden has had a law mandating worker representation on the boards of joint stock companies with more than 100 employees. Swedish law allows codetermination to operate through the unions. Even strikes are allowed in pursuit of codetermination issues. Hence, Sweden has not suffered factionalizing in the ranks of labor, as has West Germany (Jankowski 1986). This is something to consider when implementing worker representation at boardroom or national planning levels.

Worker representation at the company level was so impressive that a number of EEC countries have initiated a tripartite system in national economic indicative planning. Probably the best known indicative planning system in Western Europe is in Sweden, which has had some form of economic planning since 1932. The Governing Body of the Labor Market Board that sets national guidelines is composed of two planners from the government, three representatives of the Confederation of Employers (SAF), three representatives of the Confederation of Trade Unions (LO), two directors from the salaried employees association (TCO), and one director from the professional staff association (SACO). In addition, a board member is appointed to represent the interests of women workers and another member represents agriculture (Jones 1976:14–33). Through its tax-incentive policies, its influence over investment funds, and its personnel training programs, the Labor Market Board encourages business and labor to cooperate for the benefit of the entire society.

This chapter begins by commenting on another economically successful society—Japan. Many observers are crediting that success to Japanese human resources management methods. Other writers mention the Japanese educational system, the part played by the government economic ministry, and Japanese culture itself, which is said to foster group cooperation and effort. The next section briefly describes Japanese culture, structure, and management to serve as a background for the ongoing discussion of the factors involved in that country's economic success.

JAPAN: SOME HISTORY, CULTURE, POLITICAL ECONOMY, AND MANAGEMENT PRACTICES

On your first day on the job in a company in Japan, you might be asked to rise from your desk, sing the national anthem, do a few calesthenics with the rest of the workers, and hear announcements of when the various quality circles would meet, when the gym was open for recreational use, and when other programs—from technical courses to flower-arrangement—were available. You would expect a great deal of decorum in your dealings with colleagues and supervisors, but also a certain amount of informality and a playing down of status differences that seem quite different from most U.S. companies. (See Alston, 1985, for a primer on doing business in Japan.)

From the manager down, all plant workers wear uniforms, with first names above the pocket. As he greets you in one of his walks among the workers, the manager asks about your various family members since he knows about each one of your relatives, if the company division is not too large. In fact, the quality of relationships with subordinates is an important point on which the manager will be evaluated, usually about three times a year. The offices, you notice, do not seem to reflect the status level of the office-holder. The company parking lot is first come, first served, with no slots saved for the bosses by name. Everyone eats in the same cafeteria, and the management mingles with the nonmanagement employees. There are status differences, but they seem to be much less than in the United States. In fact you notice a certain homogeneity in ethnicity, gender, and status.

How has this general pattern come about? How does Japan differ from the United States both structurally and culturally? Such things would be useful to know before adapting any Japanese management practices to U.S. companies.

The Country

Japan is made up of a string (an archipelago) of 3,500 islands. Most of the population are on the four main islands; Japan has a total of 142,726 square miles of land—about the size of North and South Dakota together. Eighty percent of the area is mountainous, 190 volcanoes are still active, 70 percent of the land is forested, and about 15 to 16 percent is cultivatable. The population stood at 120.7 million in 1985, half that of the United States. Japan has little in the way of minerals or other resources, except timber, which is often difficult to get to because of he terrain.

Some History

Artifacts have been found dating from 4000 B.C. The *shoguns* (military dictators) ruled from 1192 – 1867 A.D., when the Meiji Reformation began. Emperor Meiji (ruled from 1867–1912) began modernization by sending students abroad to study Western technology, education, and business. By learning the secrets of the industrial revolution, Japan hoped to raise its standard of living for its large population in a land with so few natural resources and so maintain its independence from the West, which then seemed intent on dominance in Asia. Finance, industry, and trade were developed by the *zaibatsu* (powerful family corporations). Japan not only borrowed and adapted from the more developed countries, but also did some innovating. Japan developed central banking before the United States did. The country also developed a mass transit system.

By the time of the Russo-Japanese War in 1905, the West had to recognize that Japan had become an industrial power—certainly Russia had to recognize it after its embarrassing defeat by a country a fraction of its size. In the 1930s recession the government was taken over by a military regime and sided with Nazi Germany, signing an Anti-Comintern Pact in 1936 (relations with the USSR have been strained for many years). In 1941 Japan attacked Pearl Harbor, initiating the U.S. war against the Japanese. After Japan's defeat in 1945 Japan and the United States developed a new constitution for Japan and in 1951 the San Francisco Treaty was signed, granting Japan's independence again. The constitution forbidding military build-up and containing the educational system the United States helped establish are still in effect. There seems to be growing dissatisfaction in Japan with both of these areas as they exist today.

The Modern Political Economy

After World War II, U.S. economists predicted that Japan would be dependent on outside help for the rest of the century. Currently Japan has the third largest economy in the world. Initially the U.S. occupation forces required the dismantling of the *zaibatsu*, but this was changed in 1948 and they were allowed to reform, not around family-controlled holding companies but around banks. Japanese corporations fund 70 to 80 percent of their operations on loans (as compared to usually less than 30 percent for U.S. corporations). The banks thus have a great deal of control because they control most of the money. The old ruling families and management of the large companies during the war were not allowed to return to management after the war. Today the *zaibatsu* are the center of the Japanese economy and the most powerful force in the political economy. The Japanese Diet (parliament) seems relatively weak (Vogel 1979; Roberts 1983b). A brief sketch of the actors in the economy follows (Japan 1983:12–14).

Zaibatsu

Each of Japan's six *zaibatsu* groups is organized around its own bank and has a trading company (*soga shosha*) that operates for the whole group. The CEOs of the companies in a *zaibatsu* meet monthly to coordinate planning; for all practical purposes the *zaibatsu* acts as one company. Our interlocking networks of companies discussed in Chapter 5 seem very loose in coordination by comparison. These corporations are also tied to large companies in the United States through stock ownership, licensing agreements, or joint ventures. The six *zaibatsu* and a few of their U.S. connections are:

1. Mitsubishi: The largest and most powerful of the groups; company products range from beer, through defense contracts, transportation (Honda), petroleum, and trust banking, with U.S. connections including Westinghouse, Monsanto, Getty Oil, Caterpillar Tractor, Reynolds, Kentucky Fried Chicken (operates about 30 percent of its overseas shops), and Chrysler.
2. DKB (Dai-ichi Kangyo Bank Group): Second largest group; emphasizes manufacturing (Kawasaki Heavy Industries, Kawasaki Steel), defense contracts, and food production, with ties to Siemenn, Alcoa, Alcan Aluminum, B.F. Goodrich, Oscar Meyer, and Borden.
3. Sumitomo: Big in mining, manufacturing, chemicals, and telecommunications, with connections to ITT, AT&T, Upjohn, 3M, GTE, and Ford.

4. Mitsui: Fourth largest group leads in textiles, sugar, coal, and photographic supplies, with foreign friends in DuPont, Kimberly-Clark, Continental Carbon, Dow Corning, Mobil, Exxon, and Sperry Rand.
5. Fuyo: Strong in steel, electronics (Hitachi, Canon, Sharp), and transportation (joint venture with Nissan), with ties to Scott Paper, Union Carbide, Mobil, and Raytheon.
6. Sanwa: Smallest group, emphasizes banking, insurance, textiles, and construction, with friends at Borg Warner and Firestone.

Konzerns

In addition to the six *zaibatsu* are seven *konzerns* (German word), which are independent of banks (although some have loose ties to a *zaibatsu*) and are integrated vertically in an industry or in related industries. These Japanese *konzerns* are Nippon Steel (world's largest steel company), the Hitachi Group, Nissan, Toyota, Matsushita Group (National and Panasonic brand names), Tokyu Corporation, and Toshiba-IHI group, whose largest shareholder is GE. The *zaibatsu* and the *konzerns* often compete fiercely with each other; they also have joint ventures.

Soga shosha

Each *zaibatsu* has a trading company (*soga sosha*) that markets at home and abroad for the entire group. In addition there are three independent trading companies large enough to qualify as *soga shosha* and thousands of small trading companies. The nine large trading companies maintain more than 1,000 offices overseas and have a staff of 75,000 employees around the world (Roberts 1983a:15–16). The large traders, with their ties to *zaibatsu* banks, have virtually limitless credit lines. Other countries are beginning to attempt to emulate the success of this approach with trading companies of their own. In 1982 the United States passed the Export Trading Company Act to encourage banks to invest in export trading companies through their holding companies.

Zaikai

Behind the scenes operate five business councils (*zaikai* means financial circles), composed of the most powerful businessmen (no women) in Japan and some foreign multinationals (including Coca-Cola, Pepsico, IBM, Borg-Warner, Philips, and Olivetti) (Roberts 1983b:16–18). They head the major businesses; their power also extends to shaping government economic and other policy. The political officeholders do not seem to have the independence one might expect to find, even in the

United States, and the policies seem to have been agreed on before they reach the floor of the Japanese Diet. The *zaikai* lobbies have already done much of the deciding. They are also reported to have ties to the underworld. Their policies include opposing consumer protection and early-warning laws (such as the Vredling proposal) and also promoting anti-unionism and monopoly mergers and militarism. The five *zaikai* are:

1. *Keidanren*: The most powerful, dominated by heavy industry and electronics.
2. Japan Council on Economic Development (CED): Slightly more liberal, at least initially, doing research on various business issues—funded in the beginning by Ford Foundation and assisted by the U.S. CED.
3. *Nikkeiren*: The Japan Federation of Employers Organizations handles the antilabor propaganda in the mass media and tries to see that labor does not organize industrywide but remains company unions.
4. Japan Chamber of Commerce and Industry (JCCI): Ideology similar to *zaikai*'s (conservative, anti-union, private enterprise), acts as an indoctrination agency to convince the smaller businessmen of their solidarity with big business.
5. *Sanken*: Formed recently (mid-1960s), small, and containing members outside the *zaibatsu* as well as within it; its function is not well known. Because it is select and contains members from across the spectrum of groups, it is often called the Headquarters.

Ministry of International Trade and Industry (MITI)

MITI assists industries, particularly growth industries, with research and development funds; it does not appear to chose the industries itself but usually relies on advice from the *zaikai* (Roberts 1983b:16−18). It also smooths the way for joint ventures and assists in getting funding and insurance for these large ventures when necessary. MITI also offers high quality information and analysis, so that when a venture has its blessing, it usually can obtain private credit (Bluestone and Harrison 1982:214−220). For industries and ventures it wants to promote over the long run, MITI can provide patient money at low interest or even no interest rates from the Development Bank of Japan or from one of the other eleven government lending agencies. In 1986 MITI was in the middle of sponsoring a ten-year program to develop fifth generation computers that think like human beings and that can be applied to "medical diagnosis, fully automated factories, more advanced office automation, computerized corporate decision making, language translation, voice-operated typewriters, and more powerful personal computers" (Crane 1986:39). (See Johnson, 1985, for historical details.)

Standard of Living

According to Japanese government publications, the Japanese had a per-capita GNP of U.S. $9,022 in 1982 (compared to $11,107 in the United States that year) with a 20 percent savings rate. Another source gives the 1983 GNP per person at $10,100 (with a savings rate at 18 percent) in Japan and $14,090 (and 6 percent saved) in the United States. The Japanese are somewhat less consumer-oriented than people in the United States, as the savings rate implies.

In terms of durable goods Japanese families owned the following: color television, 98.8 percent; refrigerators, 99 percent; automobiles 62.9 percent (despite the rapid transit alternative). Housing is expensive and crowded by U.S. standards. Also, homes are less likely to have central heating, and one-third of Japanese houses lack complete plumbing, compared to 2.4 percent in in the United States. One author reported the life-style in Japan as similar to that of a U.S. family in the 1950s (Christopher 1983). Japanese clothing is less varied but of better quality. The people's diet is leaner—2,740 calories per person compared to 3,647 in the United States (more vegetables, less meat).

A person's standard of living is likely to decline significantly after retiring at age fifty-five. Social security is minimal, and private pensions are relatively limited except for employees at the top of the pay scale. Many retirees work at low wages in the smaller firms to supplement their incomes. The situation is particularly acute for elderly women, nearly half of whom have no income and who have the highest suicide rate in the world for this category (Higuchi 1984:387).

Education

Educational enrollment in Japan is high: primary, 100 percent; intermediate, 95 percent; and higher education, 37 percent of the respective age groups. Ninty-five percent graduate from high school. Students are under tremendous pressure to work at the top of their ability—most children learn to read in preschool before they start the primary grades. The school year in Japan consists of 240 days, compared to 180 days in the United States. The school day in Japan also is longer—7 hours instead of 5.5 to 6 in the United States (Bell 1985). Altogether a Japanese student has four more years of school than a U.S. student has at high school graduation. In Japan college is said to be almost a vacation after the difficult public school years (Reischauer 1977).

The school curriculum differs somewhat in Japan. Students begin to study a second language early, and the first foreign language learned is English. Math and science are stressed. Student scores on standardized tests are higher in Japan than in any other industrial country, and the variability around the mean is low—meaning a high widespread average. One report indicated that one out of 25 Japanese citizens is trained in engineering or science; as mentioned in the previous chapter, 65 percent of the board members of large Japanese corporations are engineers by training. In the United States about the same percentage on corporate boards are trained in law, finance, or accounting (Reich 1983:159–160). In the United States there is one lawyer for every 400 citizens; in Japan, there is a lawyer for every 10,000 (Reich 1983:159).

Some parents and other Japanese are complaining that the centrally standardized curriculum, the rote learning required, the uniformity of the products, the pressure-filled atmosphere of the public school program are beginning to become a detriment. Critics argue that creativity and innovativeness are discouraged and that this lack is beginning to be evident in the high tech fields, which require these traits (Duncan 1986:35–36). Parents complain about the pathological side of the system, which they say has led to increasing uniformity, suicide, and anguish (Duncan 1986:36).

Many older Japanese women are looking back with regret on the years they spent cajoling and pushing their children to excel in school—instead of enjoying a more companionable relationship. They claim their attitude has put a wall between themselves and their grown children, who sometimes harbor deep resentment about their unhappy childhood (Higuchi 1984:386). In addition, the education system is seen as a legacy of the U.S. occupation, and nationalism is reported to be increasing in Japan (Halberstam 1983:7).

The Workplace and Employment

Unions

More than 20 percent of the Japanese workforce is unionized. Most unions, however, are company unions with strong ties to management, rather than industrywide independent unions. Company officers have often spent some years as union officials, and personnel is interchangeable (Shorrock 1983a:6). The militant unions were crushed, mostly in the 1950s, by unified business and government policies. Grievances against the company cannot usually be taken to the union for redress, and the union will assist the company in firing disgruntled employees in the same industries, notably autos and steel (Junkerman 1982, 1983; Shorrock 1983a, b; Kamata 1982).

Public sector unions seem to be more independent. There appears to be little worker solidarity between unionized workers in the primary/core economic sector and the nonunionized workers in the secondary/periphery sector (Taira 1986:36).

Despite this predominance of company unions in the private sector, there were still 893 strikes and lockouts in Japan in 1983. However, the strikes are very brief—2.3 days on the average, compared to 22.6 days for the average U.S. strike (Alm and Walsh 1985:43). Between 1976 and 1981, Japan lost 5 days per 100 workers, whereas the United States lost 50 days per 100 workers (Evans 1985:37). Labor economist Robert Evans, Jr. (1985:37), explains part of this phenomenon (62 percent of days lost due to strikes in 1981) as the annual hour-long strikes at collective bargaining time in the spring. This seems to be a preprogrammed ritual allowed by government and industry as part of the formal *Shunto* bargaining process. The *Shunto* system includes the collection of national economy, industry, and specific company figures by the government. These figures provide bases for negotiating at the individual firm and union level, with a cap set by the government limiting wage increases to increases in productivity.

Lifetime Employment

"A man is known by the company that keeps him." The practice of lifetime employment was introduced in the large Japanese companies in the post-World War II period, according to most observers, although there were some attempts at it before World War I (Cole 1979; Koshiro 1984). Permanent employment includes about one-third of the workforce, and almost all "permanent workers" are male, although one observer places the figure at only 16 percent of the total workforce (Taira 1986:36). This lifetime employment practice in the internal labor market in the primary/core sector firms allows for extensive company training and retraining of employees since they will be remaining with the company. This promotes much cross-training and lateral promotion before vertical promotion so that employees know all the jobs under them. Permanent employment enables companies to introduce new technology since workers have less fear of being replaced by machines, and it promotes commitment and common purpose since the fate of an employee hangs on the fate of the company. For example, job turnover and absenteeism are lower in Japan than in the United States, and part of these low rates can be attributed to lifetime employment.

Lifelong employment does not always mean automatic promotion or even permanency. The company often expects individuals to resign if they do not keep up with their fellows in the merit reviews for pay and promotion—usually three times a year (Koshiro 1984). Thus there is a great deal of competition to out perform one's peers. In addition, during recession a worker may be demoted or transferred to a small affiliate that does not have a permanent employment policy. Before a company resorts to this measure, shareholder dividends are cut (Evans 1985:39). This is an internal labor market within the primary sector of the dual labor market, par excellence.

In the current worldwide recession, as Japan's growth slows with maturity, as the United States enacts more import quotas, and as the yen rises in value in relation to the U.S. dollar, large companies are not expanding fast enough to offer movement upward. The early retirement age of about fifty-five in most large Japanese companies means a worker must keep moving up steadily if he is ambitious or wants to retire with a respectable pension. Some junior members of management are reported to be restless; others have lowered their expectations and grown apathetic under the lack of opportunities for promotion (Kotkin and Kishimoto 1986). Yet the opportunities to work elsewhere are limited. If a worker leaves one large company, the others will not take him. When Lee Iacocca was fired from Ford, he became president of Chrysler; that would probably not happen in Japan. Some workers have dared to try working for one of the smaller, risky firms. A few have found places in foreign companies.

Educated young women are especially eager to work in foreign companies, where male chauvinism is less blatant. Many young women are reported to be having eye operations to try to look more European, in hopes of increasing chances of employment in foreign firms. This occurence seems to be commenting on racism as well as sexism. Many young people who expected lifetime employment in a large company are finding themselves in small companies at jobs with low pay because the big corporations are hiring fewer workers.

The Other Two-thirds of the Workforce

Most of the workforce is not in the privileged position of the workers who have lifetime employment. Small- and medium-sized firms, together with large corporations who hire temporary workers, employ the other two-thirds. The shift of the workforce out of agriculture in the last twenty years or so has put an additional burden on the smaller firms to create jobs. These smaller companies are often subcontractors and suppliers for the large corporations. Their ability to supply high quality goods on time is legend. Since the parts can be counted on to arrive on time and be perfect, the big company does not have to keep a large inventory of those items on hand, which is a major aid in keeping down operating costs. This is the *Kanban* or just-in-time system.

As in the secondary labor market in the United States, these smaller companies lack an internal labor market. The jobs in these companies are likely to be lower paid, have few fringe benefits, and be temporary and dead-end. Here are employees who were not the top students in their class, did not attend prestigious universities, most women workers, the retired who are supplementing their incomes, and workers who have washed out of or do not care to work for large corporations. The recession has hit this group particularly hard, and many women have given up and dropped out of the labor force, as their declining participation rate indicates.

Culture, Japanese Management, and Quality Circles

How can management practices from the Japanese culture be used in the United States, where rugged individualism, competition, and adversarial relations between management and labor are said to be the norm? Japan is said always to have been a cooperative culture, perhaps shaped by the necessity of cooperating to survive in such a densely populated area (for opposing views on Japanese culture, past, present, and future, see Vogel 1979 and Cumings 1983).

Under the concept of *ringi*, consensus on decisions is frequently sought before decisions are made, although the ultimate decisions are still with top management. This process takes a little longer but more input may go into decisions. Since the managers have worked their way up through the internal career ladders within the corporation, they know all the jobs and maintain their networks of relationships with other employees. This network is useful in facilitating the information upward and downward in the organization. Once the decision has been agreed on, however, it can be implemented more quickly, since it is understood and accepted by the lower ranks, who will do the implementing. Japanese organizations also have less hierarchy, fewer layers of bureaucracy between the top and the bottom. Foremen at Toyota report directly to the vice-president for operations (Reich 1983).

Another aspect of Japanese management is the amount of training the young managers receive. They are frequently sent to training schools for lessons in religion and humility. In addition, they may spend some time working in the hands-on part of production, learning the processes, the product, and their fellow workers. The many lateral transfers in various departments, before they are promoted up, give young managers a wide knowledge of the operations. This knowledge appears to be invaluable in terms of knowing what is going on in production, knowing the product, and knowing other workers. *Ringi* works because these networks are in place. Managers are role models. They are supposed to be out among the workers, seeing and being seen, and they are to work longer hours and harder than their subordinates. Men in management will not expect to see much of their families.

Even though democracy is not part of the traditional culture, listening to subordinates, politeness, and paternalism do seem to be. In addition, management practices downplay status differences (including differences in pay) and promote informality, unlike U.S. managerialism. Japanese companies operating in the United States with some modified form of their practices seem to charm many of their U.S. employees by what appears to be a true concern and attention. They cooperate and have high productivity on cue ("People and Productivity" 1982; Schrage 1985).

Quality circles, as mentioned earlier this chapter, have received favorable press in the United States. When they operate as they are supposed to—as places to generate and polish new ideas with autonomy—they are good for product quality, productivity, and morale.

Some observers, however, are revealing that in many industries in Japanese quality circles are not voluntary. Raises and promotions are sometimes tied to participation. Quality circles, sometimes urged by their supervisors, find themselves requesting work speed-ups and other ideas unlikely to have come freely from the workforce. They can be used as a means of worker control, even oppression, rather than as a means of democratic participation in decision making (Junkerman 1982; Kamata 1982; Shorrock 1983a, b). Obviously not all quality circles work in this oppressive manner, even on the shopfloor. U.S. workers and their unions will have to keep these possibilities in mind, however, in companies using QCs in the United States and will have to watch implementation closely to keep such programs truly democratic.

Attitudes toward Work

Japanese workers in Japan and Japanese-American workers in Japanese companies in the United States seem less satisfied, in general, with their jobs than are U.S. (non-Japanese) workers in United States-run or Japanese-run firms. That is, Anglo Americans seem more satisfied with their work than Japanese workers are with theirs. This conclusion has shown up in a number of studies (Lincoln, Hanada, and Olson 1981). Why should this be the case when presumably Japanese management is supposed to bring the worker into sharing in decision-making opportunities and engender commitment and it seems to do that at some levels and in some companies? One study suggests that the Japanese worker may expect more from the company and job than does the U.S. worker (Lincoln, Hanada, and Olson 1981:112–113).

Many older Japanese are concerned that younger people have lost the work ethic and become Westernized (enjoying music, disco, jeans, and skiing weekends). While some Japanese bemoan the point that the Japanese educational system and Japanese culture do not promote the individualism needed for creative research and risk-taking, others note that too much individualism and privatization of goals are being imported. Because the value systems and the perceptions of observers are opposite, we can hope that the observers are unduly anxious about the situation and that the young people will survive whatever stage they are going through to combine in their own way their goals and motivation. Since the Japanese political economy does not seem to be very democratic, this may mean a certain amount of disruption in the short run, assuming that individualism is becoming an issue. With the concentration in political and economic power, the contest may not materialize overtly.

MONDRAGON COOPERATIVES IN SPAIN

After the Civil War in Spain, the Basque region, which speaks a different language and has a different culture, had been flattened by the conquering facist dictator Francisco Franco (1892–1975) (Thomas and Logan 1982; The Mondragon Cooperative System 1982). The Basques had resisted to the last and lost. The region, which consists of four provinces nestled in the Pyrenees Mountains on the border with France, was basically a sheepherding area with some privately owned iron mines. During the rebuilding period after the war a Catholic priest named Don José Maria Arizmendi-Arrieta (1915–1976) had been teaching a group of boys in a technological school he had established in the regional capital of the Basque area, Mondragon. Eventually, some young men had gone on for engineering degrees. Unhappy with the authoritarian conditions in the local foundry, the young men appealed to Don José for help.

Having read the social doctrines of Catholicism, Marx, and Gandhi, and the experiments of the cooperative movement in England, especially the Rochdale Pioneers, Don José suggested the young engineers establish their own company along cooperative lines. The initial company, ULGOR, was so successful with its paraffin cookers (oil stoves) and Aladdin space heaters that they wanted to expand. Don José developed a plan whereby a set of cooperative rules for an individual enterprise and a cooperative bank could be established. The bank could offer a slightly higher interest rate to depositors under Spanish law and could fund and act as advisor to new spin-off cooperatives, if and when that should be necessary.

The subsequent success of the venture is a marvel to the few people who know about it—and that is not many in the United States. Currently there are more than 173 cooperatives in the system.

- Ninty-three are capital intensive production industries, some with automation and high tech;
- Seven are agro-industries;
- Fourteen are building companies;
- Others are service oriented (second-order co-ops), such as the ele-

mentary schools and kindergartens (teaching the Basque language and customs), the food cooperatives, the housing projects
(where all strata of society live near one another), the university
(which includes women—Don José insisted women needed education and employment), the ultramodern research center
(doing research in robotics and electronics, among other things),
the hospital and clinics, and the social security system (under
Spanish law cooperative members are self-employed and cannot
participate in the Spanish social security system);

- The co-op bank—La Caja Laboral Popular (CLP)—is the heart of
the entire network. The CLP had 132 branches (including a new
one in Madrid, the first co-op to be established outside the
Basque region) and had about U.S. $1 billion in assets in 1984
(Gutierrez-Johnson 1984:36);

The entire co-op system had more than 18,000 worker-
owners in 1984, about 5 percent of all jobs in the four-province
Basque area and 15 percent of the jobs in the province of Gipuz-
koa, where the city of Mondragon is located (Guitierrez-Johnson
1984:36).

The answer to how this happened may be twofold: The ethnic solidarity of the Basques and the organization of the cooperatives as set forth by Don José around the funds and technical
advice of the CLP. In general, the system in each cooperative
operates as shown in Figure 11.2.

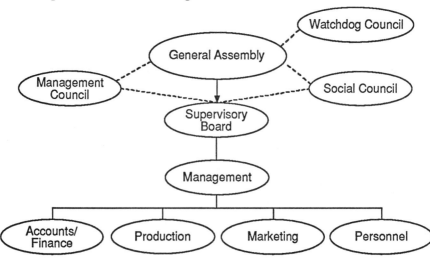

Figure 11.2 Organizational Structure of the Cooperatives in the Mondragon
System

Source: Thomas and Logan, *Mondragon: An economic analysis*, 27.

1. The General Assembly consists of all the workers who each own a share of voting stock. It elects the Supervisory Board, the Social Council, and the Watchdog Council.
2. The Supervisory Board, nine members who meet at least once a month, is the board of directors. It sets policies and appoints the manager for a minimum of four years.
3. The management (a group of managers, in some large co-ops, who manage as a collegial body) is responsible for day-to-day operations, often appoints department heads, serves on the Management Council, and can attend Supervisory Board meetings but has no vote.
4. The Management Council is an advisory committee only and consists of the manager, the department heads, and any outside consultants called in for their expertise. The Council meets at least once a month, reports to the manager and the Supervisory Board, and may attend board meetings but without a vote.
5. The Social Council, each member of which is elected by a section of the co-op, acts as a union and deals with personnel issues (such as wages, benefits, social security, safety, grievances) and manages the Social Fund for contributions to community projects. The Council's decision in these matters is binding. Each member must meet weekly with his or her section, and the full Council sits in plenary session quarterly.
6. The Watchdog Council consists of three persons elected by the General Assembly for four years. It oversees all operations and looks for any misdeeds or oversights of management and the Supervisory Board. It may call on assistance from the CLP when needed. It reports back to the General Assembly.

Overall, or behind this, stands the CLP, which is tied in by computer to all service and capital-intensive cooperatives. It does feasibility studies for spin-off cooperatives, monitors problems, and offers managerial or technical advice, and provides capital.

Over the years the co-op system has learned that if enterprises exceed 500 members the communications system breaks down. (This is a point the W. L. Gore Associates made in setting up their ESOP and is implied in the studies of social psychologists in Chapter 10.) The only strike the Mandragon co-op system has had was in a large co-op; three members had to be dismissed. Since then, when organizations become too large they are divided into two co-ops so this does not happen again.

Other features of the co-ops are wages and how income is distributed. The salary scale is 3:1; that is, the top management and professionals are limited to receiving only three times what the bottom worker receives. This scale has been a problem for medical doctors, some of whom have gone elsewhere to earn more money. Basque pride has been important in this arena, keeping most highly trained professionals and technicians from leaving the system. Management, scientists, and other professionals have tended to stay for less money than they could command elsewhere in Spain in order to further the goals of their group and remain in their culture.

Profit is distributed based on the following ratio:

- 10 percent is allocated to community improvement, such as schools and health care (this is the Social Fund administered by the Social Council of each co-op).
- 20 percent goes to the particular company for capital and other improvements.
- 70 percent goes into the workers' accounts to be collected on retirement or when they leave the cooperative system.

In other words, 90 percent stays with the co-op for a while for the members to reinvest and use. Interest is paid on the workers' accounts, building up for retirement.

How do the Mondragon co-ops compare in productivity and profitability to their private counterparts? British economists say they are more productive and profitable (Thomas and Logan 1982:109–113; The Mondragon Cooperative System 1982). There has been only one co-op failure so far—a fishing co-op that could not get permission to fish in territorial waters. In the recession period of 1973 to 1982, when private companies in the region were going out of business and the region's unemployment rate was about 18 percent, the co-op network not only protected its 11,000 existing jobs but also created 7,000 new ones. During these hard times the annual sales increased 25 percent, the industrial investment grew at an average annual rate of 15 percent, and 37 new co-ops were established (Gutierrez-Johnson 1984:36).

The bank—with its feasibility studies, capital lending, advice, and ability to tie together a powerful network—has been a key factor in the success of the system, along with Basque pride and diligence.

WORKER SATISFACTION AND PRODUCTIVITY STUDIES

Worker satisfaction on the job has been a topic of interest even before, and certainly since, the industrial revolution, when more rapid technological and organizational change seemed to indicate various forms of alienation. Marx wrote about it in the mid nineteenth century. In the late eighteenth century, Adam Smith, in *The Wealth of Nations*, noted:

(as mentioned before). "The man whose life is spent in performing a few simple operations . . . has no occasion to exert his understanding or to exercise his invention in finding out expedients for removing difficulties . . . and generally becomes as stupid and ignorant as it is possible to become" (Smith 1952:340 First ed. 1776).

Some Factors Involved in Worker Satisfaction

In the post-World War II period social scientists were concerned with trying to measure the effects on the worker of different technologies (both material and nonmaterial aspects), division of labor, and other job characteristics. Some looked at technologies applied in various industries. Others focused on characteristics of jobs across industries because these vary even within a single firm. Some attempted to look at the effects of the characteristics of the workers that they brought with them to the job—work ethic, age, education, rural-urban backgrounds, and SES origins, for example. Still others are interested in the effects of the job on the workers' behavior and attitudes off the job in the wider society. Sociologist Jon Shepard (1977) in his review of the literature on job satisfaction through 1977, provides a summary figure modified here to include other variables and relationships used in these studies (see Figure 11.3).

There are two basic reasons for our interest in job satisfaction. First, people are interested in the quality of life in society. Work is not the only factor involved in quality of life, but it certainly is one of the most important ones. Not only do most of us spend many hours of our adult lives working, but work also affects our nonwork lives in many ways. Hence, the quality of our work seems extremely influential on our overall quality of life. For this reason, phenomenologist Alfred Schutz called our world of work our "primary realm of reality" of which all other realms of reality may only be modifications (Schutz 1971:226–233).

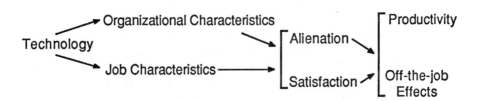

Figure 11.3   Schematic Summary of Variables and Their Relationship to Job Satisfaction

Source: Adapted from Shepard, "Technology, alienation, and job satisfaction," 2.

The second reason for an interest in job satisfaction is to try to increase productivity to ensure the health of the organization and the overall health of the economy. This assumes some connection between the job satisfaction, motivation, and productivity. The existence and nature of this connection interests managers and social scientists alike.

The human resource researchers, some of whose basic studies we reviewed in Chapter 4, have been saying for some time that workers want to self-actualize on the job—with more autonomy and control over their own work. These researchers emphasized that the content of the work increased motivation and creativity. Studies by psychologists of the conditions under which individuals are creative indicate that creativity occurs "when they feel motivated primarily by the interest, enjoyment, satisfaction, and challenge of the work itself—and not by external pressures" (Research notes 1985:7).

Professor of social work David Macarov (1982), in his review of the literature on job satisfaction, motivation, and productivity, states that the link between these concepts has not been proven. Do self-actualizing people work harder? (Proponents of human resources, of course, indicate they are not asking people to work harder but to work smarter.) Macarov does not think that it necessarily follows, except in one area. Evidence indicates that job satisfaction does improve the quality of service provided in the service professions—teaching, social work, and sales—where the quality of the relationship with the customer/client is of prime importance. He feels that the methodological problems of many studies that have been done have clouded their findings, and he calls for more rigorous methods.

Other studies have also found problems in the job satisfaction-productivity connection. Lawler and Porter (1971) found the causal relationship to be reversed in their study—people who performed well were more satisfied. Cummings and Molloy (1977) reviewed 78 studies of job redesign and found a mix-and-match on whether attitude and productivity changed. It seemed that no matter what kind of redesign was done, some kind of improvement occurred in either attitude or productivity, or in both. Macarov suggests this could be due either to a Hawthorne effect on the workers or to their improved communications and information. If some productivity increases we are seeing are due to the Hawthorne effect, then changes are bound to be short-run (Berg, Freedman, and Freeman 1978). However, studies continue to report some connection between job satisfaction (or at least job involvement) and productivity that is sometimes of long-standing, as we discuss.

What really seems to bother the critics of worker satisfaction studies is not so much that faulty studies produce fuzzy conclusions, but that the hype of the quick fix is being sold to management and unsuspecting workers and that these workers are not going to get participation in decision making in any really meaningful sense. We return to this problem in the last section of the chapter.

"I'm from Gallup Poll: How Satisfied Are You with Your Job?"

How satisfied are U.S. workers, in general, with their jobs? The answer depends on which opinion poll and social survey you believe. In the late 1960s and 1970s a number of articles and surveys (including the University of Michigan's third Quality of Employment Survey in 1977) appeared concerning the increasing dissatisfaction of the workforce. The phrases *blue-collar blues* and *white-collar woes* and *dehumanization of work* became well known in the mass media (U.S. Department of Health, Education and Welfare 1973; Sheppard 1971; Sheppard and Herrick 1972; Gooding 1970a, b, c; Staines and Quinn 1979; Zimbalist 1975; Braverman 1974). Anecdotal evidence, such as Studs Terkel's interviews with workers in *Working* (Terkel 1974), seemed to support these opinions. Reasons given for this malaise include the workforce changes in education, composition, and increased expectations. All these things were true, as we have noted, but did they create a deepseated or permanent change in worker expectations?

At the same time as some writers were finding major shifts in workers' thinking, however, national surveys conducted by the University of Michigan (the Survey of Working Conditions 1969–70, the Quality of Employment survey in 1969 and 1972–73, and the Quality of Life survey in 1971 and 1978) and the National Opinion Research Center (NORC) survey of 1973 and 1977 found no significant decline in workers' satisfaction with their jobs (Chelte, Wright, and Tausky 1982). According to these latter surveys more than 60 percent of workers could be relied on to say they were "largely satisfied" or "completely satisfied" with their present job. The same percent strongly agreed that their work was "interesting." More than two-thirds said they would continue to work if they became independently wealthy, although at what job is not always clear. Many workers criticized these aspects of their jobs: autonomy, good pay, job security, chances for promotion, physical surroundings, and time and resources to get things done (Chelte, Wright, and Tausky 1982).

What does the conflicting evidence mean? Perhaps it *might* mean that (1) at least two-thirds of U.S. workers see work as exceedingly important in their lives—apparently the work ethic is not dead; (2) people try to believe their work is interesting and meaningful and will only admit it is not when a skillful interviewer like Terkel or James Wright (O'Toole 1974:6–7) talks to them for some time; (3) there are some job characteristics that people would like to see improved. People interested in management, productivity, and quality of life focus on this third area. Two general findings may relate to this area.

Two apparently related findings have emerged from the general job satisfactions surveys. The first is that satisfaction relates to the hierarchy of job status. People with higher job status report being more satisfied—that is, doctors are more satisfied than nurses, and judges more satisfied than truck drivers. The independent professions seem particularly satisfied with their work.

Second, the type of technology is related to job satisfaction. Satisfaction follows the chronological introduction of types of technology in a U-shaped curve (Shepard 1977). Using Woodward's typology of technologies, we can trace this phenomenon. The crafts-type jobs prevalent before and in the early days of the industrial revolution are relatively high in worker satisfaction (mechanics and printers, for example). The mass production jobs introduced in the middle period (such as assembly-line work) are the least satisfying. Workers in the higher-tech jobs created more recently (the continuous process jobs in chemicals, for example) are as much, or more, satisfied than the craftspersons. Their satisfaction may be related to several factors: autonomy, status in the eyes of self and others, and pay.

A word of caution is in order here about job satisfaction survey questions. Even though research is more sophisticated than merely asking one global job satisfaction question ("How satisfied are you with your job?") and now asks many related questions (e.g., "Would you recommend this job to your son or daughter?"), it is still difficult to know exactly what is being measured. To some people in our work-oriented society, the question "Are you satisfied with your job?" gets a quick "Yes, very." This answer may really mean, "I'm very satisfied that I'm not unemployed." Macarov refers to this phenomenon as "fatalistic contentment" (1982:117). In other words, rather than being satisfied that two-thirds of the workforce is "very satisfied," it may be more important to find what could make this "very interesting" work even more interesting, meaningful, and productive.

Studies on Alternative Workplace Organization

Opinion polls and other surveys indicate the following responses:

- Workers' first concern for their jobs was that the work be interesting—good pay came in fifth (U.S. Department of Health, Education and Welfare 1974:13).
- Fifty-five percent of respondents to a Hart poll indicated that they would like to work in an employee-owned company.

A number of studies done in the last twenty years or so, including some individual case studies, examined the effects of introducing some form of worker participation/human resources to the workplace. More recently the data have been aggregated to compare companies' performance and the success of their programs on various measures, such as increased productivity, profits, job creation, company longevity, and cost reduction. Some studies have also used a matched control group of similar companies that have not made human resource changes. Some findings of those studies are summarized here:

- The HEW task force concluded its study of thirty-four cases in which worker participation was introduced with the following statement:

It is imperative, then, that employers be made aware of the fact that thorough efforts to redesign work—not simply "job enrichment" or "job rotation"—have resulted in increases in productivity from 5 to 40 percent. In no instance of which we have evidence has a major effort to increase employee participation resulted in long-term decline in productivity . . . it appears that the size of increase in productivity is, in general, a function of the thoroughness of the effort. (U.S. Department of Health, Education and Welfare 1974:112).

- A University of Michigan Survey Research Center study (Conte and Tannenbaum 1978, 1980) done for the Department of Commerce found that the 98 employee ownership companies in their sample were 1.5 times as profitable as comparable conventional firms. The amount of equity owned by the employees appeared to be the most significant variable.
- A study reported in the *Journal of Corporation Law* (Marsh and McAllister 1981) found that employee-owned companies with employee stock ownership plans had twice the average annual productivity growth rate of comparable conventional firms.
- A General Accounting Office study of thirty-six firms with productivity gain-sharing programs (Scanlon, Improshare, and Rucker Plans) found that these firms made a substantial savings in labor costs per unit of output. The longer the plan had been in effect, the greater the savings. Companies with plans in effect fewer than five years saved an average of 8.5 percent; companies with plans in place more than five years saved almost 29 percent (cited in New York Stock Exchange 1982:35; Productivity Sharing Plans 1981:77–78). Rewards—both monetary and psychological—were credited with causing the increased savings.

- In a dissenting study, fifty-one ESOPs which each had more than 1,000 employees in the plan were matched with fifty-one companies of the same size and industry that did not have a plan. The non-ESOPs were found to be more profitable overall than were the ESOP firms. The ESOP firms, however, had lower risk levels and thus might be more likely to survive (Brooks, Henry, and Livingston 1982).

- A New York Stock Exchange survey of firms (the sample was drawn from the 49,000 companies in the United States with 100 or more employees) with various types of participation and gain-sharing plans concluded that human resource programs had positive effects on increasing employee morale, increasing productivity, cutting costs, improving service, raising product quality, and reducing employee turnover, absenteeism, lateness, and grievances (New York Stock Exchange 1982). The study concluded that other corporations in the United States should follow suit and improve the quality of life in the workplace, which would boost productivity and generate a higher quality of life for society at large.

- A study done by the National Center for Employee Ownership (NCEO) found that companies in which a majority of the employees owned a majority of the stock (the importance of amount of equity again) created nearly three times more net new jobs per year than in comparable conventional firms (Rosen and Klein 1981). That figure adds up to 31 percent more jobs in ten years.

- A McKinsey and Company (1983) study found that a relatively broad distribution of ownership was one defining characteristic of the fastest growing mid-sized companies.

- An NCEO study done for the New York Stock Exchange found that publicly traded companies that were at least 10 percent owned by their employees outperformed 62 to 75 percent of their competitors on various measures of company performance (Wagner 1984).

- Some research offers case studies and anecdotal evidence of the best companies to work for—with employee ownership and participation in decision making as basic factors (Peters and Waterman 1982; Levering, Moskowitz, and Katz 1984).

- More recently the NCEO has conducted a study involving fifty-four companies with some variety of ESOP (Rosen, Klein, and Young 1986). The most important variables for increased performance appeared to be amount of stock owned by employees, participation in decision making (but not as important as equity in this sample), and corporate culture (a sincerely democratic atmosphere that constantly reinforces the ideas of participation and ownership).

- An ongoing U.S. General Accounting Office Study (1986) reported its initial findings on a matched sample of ESOP (before and after introduction of the plan) and non-ESOP firms. The report gives descriptive data (where, what kinds of ESOPS, and in what industries). The bottom line in this interim report is that between 1975 and 1982 corporate savings from the depreciation deduction against taxable income totaled about $515.6 billion, and most of this money went for capital expenditures (U.S. General Accounting Office 1986:44, 50). Various subsamples have produced the following results (1) 125 ESOPs had a higher productivity growth than their industry's average; (2) 10 matched firms did not show any advantage in the 1978–81 period; (3) a majority employee-owned firm sample showed greater employment growth; (4) another subsample showed a higher ratio of net sales to net worth; and (5) another subsample had a 50 percent higher profit than the average for their industry (U.S. General Accounting Office 1986:54–55). In the final report the GAO will summarize the productivity and profitability gains of all ESOPs in their total sample.

- An elaboration of one GAO subsample with a matched comparison of firms found no difference in the profitability of employee-owned and non-employee-owned firms (Tannenbaum, Cook, and Lohmann 1984).

- In a recent study data on forty-five ESOPs before and after the implementation of their plans were collected. In addition, each ESOP was matched with five or more non-ESOP firms in the same industry of about the same size, and, when possible, from the same geographic region. Information was obtained on sales growth, employment growth, and growth in the ratio of sales per employee as a rough productivity measure. The ESOPs outperformed their preplan records and those of the non-ESOPs. ESOPs grew 3.5 to 3.8 percentage points per year faster than before the plan or than their competitors—that is a 46 percent increase in jobs and a 40 percent increase in sales when projected over ten years. The most significant factor was participation in job-level decision making. Also highly correlated were management philosophy, voting rights, and employee board representation (Quarrey 1986:47). The primary factor behind all this appeared to be management's willingness to encourage employees to participate actively in decisions and act like owners (Quarrey 1986:48).

It is clear that quality circles, workteams, and employee ownership can make a difference, but only under certain conditions. James O'Toole said it very well more than a decade ago in his HEW report companion volume of commissioned papers:

> Responsible managers, union officials, and academic leaders acknowledge that while it is true that the redesign of jobs *can* have a positive impact on morale, productivity, social problems, and the quality of goods, it will *not* produce these marvels either automatically or invariably. To really improve the quality of working life requires hard work, careful planning and diagnosis, commitment, time, and a willingness to abandon old ideas and to accept some sound advice from those experienced in the field. If this effort leads to genuine participation by workers in decision making and profits, the desired outcomes will very likely follow. But in many cases the return on the investment will be only marginal, particularly if it is measured in traditional, narrow economic terms. (O'Toole 1974:15–16, emphasis in original)

C. WRIGHT MILLS AND THE ROLE OF SOCIAL SCIENTISTS IN WORKER PARTICIPATION

In 1948 sociologist C. Wright Mills castigated applied sociologists and other social scientists who accepted the human relations school of management (human resources had not made its appearance yet) for lending themselves to management as consultants (Ford 1984). In his critique, he charged that the human relations school was trying to create a psuedo-*gemeinschaft* atmosphere in an authoritarian industrial setting by manipulating workers and their informal groups to follow cheerfully the directives of management. Manipulation occurred through consulting with workers and listening sympathetically to their complaints in order to gain their cooperation and confidence. The human relations counselor might even be able to compete with the shop steward or co-opt the union into promoting collaboration in the pursuit of a collective goal. Intelligent human relations management should make workers happy and cooperative by changing the social nature of the workplace— that is, without making any real change in the power structure.

Why did Mills see this as a problem when it would appear that human relations/human resources management works and that management, share-holders, and workers are happier? Morale, productivity, and profit should rise. Alienation, absenteeism, turnover, strikes, and industrial conflict should decline. With a simple grid shown in Figure 11.4 Mills shows the subjective and objective possibilities of worker morale and explains why this school of management is a sophisticated conservative approach that does not liberate the worker.

Mills is saying that the pseudoparticipation of human relations

Individual's Subjective State	Objective Power Structure	
	Participates	Does Not
Cheerful, willing	1	2
Sullen, unwilling	3	4

Figure 11.4 Mills's Morale Analysis Model
Source: Mills, "Contribution of sociology to studies of industrial relations," 24.

management, if it is successful, places the cheerful robot in Cell 2 of the figure. It does not really allow the worker decision-making participation, as in Cell 1. Cell 1 participation implies that either the social structure available to the old-fashioned craftsperson who was self-managing or that workers' control under some new structure is in effect. Cell 3 contains workers who participate but do not like the work—hopeless malcontents who remain unadjusted to authoritarian control but who ritualistically perform their tasks. Cell 4 contains workers who are alienated, as in Cell 3, but who have not been manipulated into false consciousness like the cheerful robots of Cell 2. Cell 4 is what results if management misapplies or does not apply human relations methods. Cell 4 includes the active organizer or saboteur.

Mills holds that what social scientists should be seeking is not the management goal of Cell 2, but the humanist marxian goal of Cell 1. Mills considered himself a lower-case *m* nondogmatic marxist. Sociologists and other social scientists have been willing to allow the structure of the workplace to shift from the left side of worker participation in decision making to the right side of authoritarian power relations without any apparent moral qualms, he noted. In pursuing their own career development, social scientists have accepted management's definition of the problems of morale and productivity, allowing their political range of alternatives to narrow and atrophy. Mills castigates the social scientists of the 1940s for being so apolitical in their pursuit of the technician role that they cannot sell out something they do not have.

Mills's preferences for self-managing and workers' control can be distinguished (1962). He does not want either economic influence or political direction from a small financial capitalist class, or the authoritarian dictates of a bureaucratic state-controlled economy. He advocates a form of social democracy exemplified in the theories of Kautsky, Luxemburg, syndicalist G. D. H. Cole, and grassroots economic democracy incipient in the Yugoslavian workers' council and Mondragon experiences. The latter, of course, were yet to come when Mills was writing. Decentralized decision-making should be based on worker control/

industrial democracy in the economic sector. Is one pattern good for all the world? No. The "sociological imagination"—one of Mills's favorite terms—knows that in each culture and historical time, grassroots democracy might work itself out differently. The paths to that devolution of decision making for the average person will be different in different settings.

Social scientists should be on the forefront of exposing how people have been shaped by their social structures and cultural symbols and of learning how they can consciously reshape their future structures through public policy decisions.

We have seen more recent theorists express these sentiments. Berg, Macarov, Mike Parker, Jenkins, and many others have been wary of human resources programs that promise much participation and deliver so little. If social scientists are to be tied to both research/theory and applied experiments, they will have to avoid selling patent medicine and pay attention to how their findings are used. Are we to be limited to working only with democratic 100-percent employee-owned companies? Not necessarily.

Mills was always an active researcher and knowledge disseminator. At this time, he might advise us to take the jobs that can expand our knowledge and give us a chance to share findings with management, colleagues, and the workers. How can this be done when management defines the problems for the researcher of the consultant? What if the report is company property and strictly confidential? To answer the first question, which is an ethical dilemma social scientists have discussed for many years, the researcher might decide to enlarge the assigned task. Instead of taking a social engineering approach and dealing only with the problem as given, the social scientist might give clients more than they requested. Enlargement of the task means that the social scientist can bring a broader framework to the research project in theories, in a knowledge of other research, and in adding alternative hypotheses— sharing this information with management to expand their knowledge of and thinking on the situation.

The second question of confidentiality deals more with sharing knowledge in the other direction, with colleagues and workers. Before accepting an assignment, it is advisable for the social scientist to agree explicitly with the client on what findings can be shared, and in what form. (No firms I have approached in doing studies, for example, have balked at sharing all kinds of information with the research center with which I sometimes work, although they may request that their own company name not be included in reports to the public.) They seem eager to contribute to public knowledge and scientific research on organizational structure, management, worker morale, and productivity.

Today, C. Wright Mills might be an active member of the International Cooperative Association, the National Center for Employee Ownership, the Association for Workplace Democracy, or the Center for Economic Alternatives, or he might work at the Institute for Social Research at the University of Michigan on the effect of worker participation on productivity, or at the New York State School of Industrial and Labor Relations at Cornell University. He might even found his own applied industrial research institute. He would be irritated that things were not progressing faster toward industrial democracy but would probably throw his energies into finding out more to enable a foot-in-the-door approach to industrial democracy.

Of all sociologists, Mills best understood the value of organization and research and of getting the information to the public. He never lost sight of his original goals.

SUMMARY

This chapter briefly reviewed some experiments in workplace organization in the United States and elsewhere. It looked at some specifics of the political economy of Japan and its management and of the cooperative system of Mondragon in Spain. We surveyed worker job satisfaction/motivation/productivity studies regarding job satisfaction in general and in alternative workplace organization settings. Finally, we turned to C. Wright Mills's views on the place of the social scientist in applied industrial work. The discussion can be summarized as follows:

1. Human resources management and social science studies have promoted:
   a. Flextime, job enlargment, job rotation, job enrichment (only the latter involves real human resources thinking in that it expands responsibility and involvement in decision making)
   b. Labor/management committees
   c. Profit-sharing and gain-sharing plans (including Scanlon plans)
   d. Quality circles
   e. Workteams
   f. ESOPs
   g. Cooperatives
   h. Co-determination (boardroom representation of workers)
   i. National tripartite planning (management, government, and workers).
2. From Japan we have learned that the Japanese culture and political economy have promoted, or adapted from the West, a system of worker participation and management, parts of which can be effective in the United States, if adapted to the culture. The Japanese political economy is, however, highly concentrated and centralized in power.

3. Mondragon in Spain is a more democratic and open system of cooperative ownership and decision making. Although it too is centralized around the cooperative bank, it apparently remains democratic in its decision-making structure. Its model might conceivably be adaptable for ethnic communities in the United States, perhaps as an alternative to free enterprise zones in depressed areas.

4. The general job satisfaction studies in the United States are almost uniformly high but leave some question as to what this means. The various studies on alternative workplace organization tend to be very positive, although they are also criticized for their frequently vague methodology. Even so, there is an undeniable connection between job content and organizational culture, worker satisfaction or motivation to be involved in the job, and productivity, other things being equal. They do indicate that high status jobs and jobs that offer some autonomy (crafts and continuous process) are more satisfying intrinsically. Human resources programs of various types appear to work well, if implemented properly.

5. The role of the social scientist in helping implement human resources programs in the workplace is a sticky one—because what appeared to be a good idea on paper may turn out to be worker manipulation and pseudoparticipation in practice. This is a problem if one is concerned about industrial democracy. Management often wants the benefits but in many cases tends to resist real worker participation out of fear of loss of power. When the top management is fearful of loss of power, the problem may not be solvable unless the workers can eventually buy out the company. The social scientist is advised to keep his or her goals clear and wits in good tact.

BIBLIOGRAPHY

Alm, Richard, and Maureen Walsh. 1985. America vs. Japan: Can U.S. workers compete? *U.S. News & World Report* 99, 10:40–44 (September 2).

Alston, Jon P. 1985. *The American samurai: Blending American and Japanese business practices.* Berlin: Walter de Gruyter.

Bell, Terrel. 1985. Japanese Schools: "There is much we can learn." *U.S. News & World Report* 99, 10:43 (September 2).

Berg, Ivar, Marcia Freedman, and Michael Freeman. 1978. *Managers and work reform: A limited engagement.* New York: Free Press.

Berman, Katrina. 1967. *Worker-owned plywood companies: An economic analysis.* Pullman: Washington State University Press.

Bernstein, Paul. 1974. Worker-owned plywood companies. *Working Papers for a New Society* 2:24–34 (Summer).

Bluestone, Barry, and Benjamin Harrison. 1982. *The deindustrialization of America: Plant closings, community abandonment, and the dismantling of basic industry.* New York: Basic Books.

Braverman, Harry. 1974. *Labor and monopoly capital: The degradation of work in the twentieth century.* New York: Monthly Review Press.

Brooks, Leroy D., James B. Henry, and D. Tom Livingston. 1982. How profitable are employee stock ownership plans? *Financial Executive* 5, 5:32–40 (May).

Chelte, Anthony F., James Wright, and Curt Tausky. 1982. Did job satisfaction really drop during the 1970's? *Monthly Labor Review* 105, 11:33–36 (November).

Christopher, Robert. 1983. *The Japanese mind: The Goliath explained.* New York: Linden Press/Simon and Schuster.

Cole, Robert E. 1979. *Work, mobility, and participation.* Los Angeles: University of California Press.

Conte, Michael A., and Arnold S. Tannenbaum. 1978. Employee-owned companies: Is the difference measurable? *Monthly Labor Review* 101, 7:23–28 (July).

———. 1980. *Employee ownership.* Ann Arbor: University of Michigan Survey Research Center.

Conte, Michael A., and Jan Svejnar. 1981. Measuring the productivity effects of worker participation and ownership. Typescript. (December 28).

Crane, David. 1986. A new research drive: Competing in the world marketplace. *World Press Review* 33, 3:39 (March).

Cumings, Bruce. 1983. High technology and ideology: America's Japan mythology. *The Insurgent Sociologist* 11, 4:5–22 (Spring).

Cummings, T. G., and E. S. Molloy. 1977. *Improving productivity and the quality of work life.* New York: Praeger.

DeVos, Tom. 1981. *U.S. multinationals and worker participation in management: The American experience in the European community.* Westport, Conn.: Quorum Books.

Dewar, Donald L. 1979. *Quality Circles: Answers to 100 frequently asked questions.* Red Bluff, Calif.: Quality Circle Institute.

Duncan, Tim. 1986. Japan's identity crisis: Thorny nationalist questions. *World Press Review* 33, 3:35–36 (March).

Evans, Robert, Jr. 1985. Lessons from Japan's incomes policy. *Challenge* 27, 6:33–39 (January–February).

Ford, Ramona L. 1978. 1984. C. W. Mills, industrial sociology and worker participation programs. *Free Inquiry in Creative Sociology* 12, 1:13–19, 24 (May).

Frieden, Karl. 1980. *Workplace democracy and productivity.* Washington, D.C.: National Center for Economic Alternatives.

Goldmann, Robert. 1979. "Six automobile workers in Sweden." In *American workers abroad,* edited by Robert Schrank, 15–55. Cambridge, Mass.: MIT Press.

Gooding, Judson. 1970a. "Blue-collar blues on the assembly line," *Fortune* 82, 2:69–73, 112–117 (July).

———. 1970b. The fraying white collar. *Fortune* 82, 4:78–81, 108–110 (December).

———. 1970c. It pays to wake up the blue collar worker. *Fortune* 82, 3:133–135, 158, 162, 167–168 (September).

Gutierrez-Johnson, Ana. 1984. The Mondragon model of cooperative enterprise: Considerations concerning its success and transferability. *Changing Work* No. 1:35–41 (Fall).

Gyllenhammar, Pehr G. 1977. How Volvo adapts work to people. *Harvard Business Review* 55, 4:102–111 (July–August).

Halberstam, David. 1986. *The reckoning*. New York: William Morrow.

Higuchi, Keiko. 1984. "Japan: The sun and the shadow." In *Sisterhood is global: The international women's movement anthology*, edited by Robin Morgan, 382–388. Garden City, N.Y.: Anchor/Doubleday.

Iacocca, Lee. 1984. *Iacocca: An autobiography*. New York: Bantam.

Jankowski, Richard. 1986. Worker councils and unions: Competition or cooperation? *Workplace Democracy* 54:21–22 (Fall).

Japan: Industrial saint or trade demon. 1983. *Multinational Monitor* (special issue) 4, 10:1–23 (October).

Jenkins, David. 1974. *Job power: Blue and white collar democracy*. New York: Penguin Books.

Johnson, Chalmers. 1982. *MITI and the Japanese miracle: The growth of industrial policy*, 1925–1975. Stanford, Calif.: Stanford University Press.

Junkerman, John. 1982. We are driven: Life on the fast line at Datsun. *Mother Jones* 7:21–23, 38–40 (August).

———. 1983. Blue sky management: The Kawasaki story. *Working Papers for a New Society* 10, 3:28–36 (May/June).

Kamata, Satoshi. 1982. *Japan in the passing lane: An insider's account of life in a Japanese auto factory*. New York: Pantheon.

Koshiro, Kazutoshi. 1984. Lifetime employment in Japan: Three models of the concept. *Monthly Labor Review* 107, 8:34–35 (August).

Kotkin, Joel, and Yoriko Kishimoto. 1986. "Theory F": All those studies on Japanese management overlook the one ingredient that makes it all work: Fear. *INC* 8, 4:53–60 (April).

Lawler, Edward E. III, and L. W. Porter. 1971. *Pay and organizational effectiveness*. New York: McGraw-Hill.

Leff, Laurel. 1986. Firms of endearment. *Savvy* 7, 5:47–52, 81–84 (May).

Levering, Robert, Milton Moskowitz, and Michael Katz. 1984. *The 100 best companies to work for in America*. Reading, Mass.: Addison-Wesley.

Lincoln, James R., Mitsuyo Hanada, and Jon Olson. 1981. Cultural orientations and individual reactions to organizations: A study of employees of Japanese-owned firms. *Administrative Science Quarterly* 26, 1:93–114 (March).

Macarov, David. 1982. *Worker productivity: Myths and reality*. Beverly Hills, Calif.: Sage Publications.

Marsh, Thomas, and Dale McAllister. 1981. ESOPs tables. *Journal of Corporation Law* 6, 3:613–617 (Spring).

McConnell, Campbell R. 1979. Why is U.S. productivity slowing down? *Harvard Business Review* 57, 2:36–60 (March–April).

McKinsey and Company. 1983. *The winning performance of America's mid-sized companies*. Washington, D.C.: McKinsey and Company.

Metzger, Bert. 1974. Profit-sharing: Capital's reply to Marx. *Business and Society Review* 11:40–41 (Autumn).

———. 1980. *Increasing productivity through profit sharing*. Evanston, Ill.: Profit Sharing Research Foundation.

Mills, C. Wright. 1962. *The Marxists*. New York: Dell.

———. 1970. The contribution of sociology to studies of industrial relations. *Berkeley Journal of Sociology* 15:11–32. Originally published in *Proceedings of the First Annual Conference of the Industrial Relations Research Association*, edited by Milton Derber. Urbana, Ill.: The Association, 1:199–222, 1948.

Moberg, David. 1979. *Shutdown*. Chicago: In These Times.

"The Mondragon Cooperative System." 1982. London: British Broadcasting Corporation.

Naisbitt, John. 1984. *Megatrends: Ten new directions transforming our lives*. New York: Warner.

New York Stock Exchange, Office of Economic Research. 1982. *People and productivity: A Challenge to Corporate America*. New York: NYSE.

O'Kelly, Charlotte, G., and Larry S. Carney. 1986. *Women and men in society: Cross-cultural perspectives on gender stratification*, 2nd ed. Belmont, Calif.: Wadsworth.

O'Toole, James, ed. 1974. *Work and the quality of life: Resource papers for "Work in America."* Cambridge, Mass.: MIT Press.

Ouchi, William G. 1981. *Theory Z: How American business can meet the Japanese challenge*. Reading, Mass.: Addison-Wesley.

Parker, Mike. 1985. *Inside the circle: A union guide to QWL*. Boston: South End Press.

"People and Productivity: We learn from the Japanese" (film). 1982. Chicago: Encyclopaedia Britannica Education Corporation.

Peters, Thomas J., and Robert H. Waterman, Jr. 1982. *In search of excellence: Lessons from America's best-run companies*. New York: Harper & Row.

Productivity sharing plans can cut costs, boost productivity. 1981. *World of Work Review* 6, 10:77–78 (October).

Quarrey, Michael. 1986. *Employee ownership and corporate performance*. Arlington, V.: National Center for Employee Ownership (October).

Reich, Robert B. 1983. The next American frontier: A provocative program for economic renewal. New York: Penguin.

Reischauer, Edwin O. 1977. *The Japanese*. Cambridge: Harvard University Press.

Research notes: Interest in work. 1985. *The Chronicle of Higher Education* 31, 2:7–8 (September 11).

Roberts, John G. 1983a. Captains of global trade. *Multinational Monitor* 4, 10:15–16 (October).

———. 1983b. Councils of business elders: The powerful lobbies behind Japanese politics. *Multinational Monitor* 4, 10:16–18 (October).

Rosen, Corey, and Katherine J. Klein. 1981. Job-creating performance of employee-owned companies. *Monthly Labor Review* 106, 8:15–19 (August).

Rosen, Carey, Katherine J. Klein, and Karen M. Young. 1986. *Employee Ownership in America: The Equity Solution*. Lexington, Mass.: Lexington Books.

Sachs, Stephen. 1982. Union negotiates worker ownership and participation. *Workplace Democracy* 9:8 (Summer).

Schrage, Michael. 1985. Japanese companies in U.S. outperform local counterparts. *Austin (TX) American-Statesman* p. C14 (April 6).

Schutz, Alfred. 1971. *Collected Papers: Volume I: The Problem of Social Reality*, edited by Maurice Natanson. The Hague: Martinus Nijhoff.

Schwartz, William. 1981. The changing structure of labor-management relations. *The Social Report: Progress in Social Economy and Social Policy* (Boston College) 2:4–5 (May).

Shepard, Jon. 1977. Technology, alienation, and job satisfaction. *Annual Review of Sociology* 3:1–21.

Sheppard, Harold. 1971. Discontented blue collar workers—A case study. *Monthly Labor Review* (April).

Sheppard, Harold, and Neal J. Herrick. 1972. *Where have all the robots gone?* New York: Free Press.

Shorrock, Tim. 1983a. Nissan: Portrait of a global giant. *Multinational Monitor* 4, 10:4–7 (October).

———. 1983b. Toyota's factory of despair: An interview with journalist Kamata Satoshi. *Multinational Monitor* 4, 10:7–8 (October).

Simmons, John, and Barry Bluestone. 1982. Workers have brains, too. *Workplace Democracy* 9:5–7, 16–17, 20 (Summer).

Smith, Adam. 1952. *An inquiry into the nature and causes of the wealth of nations.* Chicago: Encyclopaedia Britannica. (Originally published in 1776).

Staines, Graham L., and Robert P. Quinn. 1979. American workers evaluate the quality of their jobs. *Monthly Labor Review* 10–2, 1:3–12 (January).

Taira, Joji. 1986. Labor market segmentation in Japan: How rigid it it? *Monthly Labor Review* 109, 6:35–37 (June).

Tannenbaum, Arnold, Harold Cook, and Jack Lohmann. 1984. *The relationship of employee ownership to the technological adaptiveness and performance of companies,* Report to the National Science Foundation. Ann Arbor: University of Michigan Institute for Social Research.

Terkel, Studs. 1974. *Working.* New York: Avon.

Thomas, Henk, and Christopher Logan. 1982. *Mondragon: An economic analysis.* London: George Allen & Unwin.

U.S. Department of Health, Education and Welfare. 1973. *Work in America.* Cambridge, Mass.: MIT Press.

U.S. General Accounting Office. 1986. "Employee stock ownership plans: Interim report on a survey and related economic trends," Washington, D.C.: GAO (February).

Vogel, Ezra. 1979. *Japan as number one: Lessons for America.* New York: Harper & Row.

Volvo's Kalmar plant: Bold experiment a qualified success. 1977. *World of Work Review* 2, 2:22–23 (February).

Wagner, Ira. 1984. Report to the New York Stock Exchange on the performance of publicly traded companies with employee ownership plans. Arlington, Va.: National Center for Employee Ownership (September). Typescript.

Watts, Glen. 1982. Management incentives: Trick or treat? *Workplace Democracy* 9:2–4 (Summer).

Zimbalist, Andrew. 1975. The limits of work humanization. *Review of Radical Political Economics* 7, 2:51–59 (Summer).

Zwerdling, Daniel. 1980. *Workplace democracy: A guide to workplace ownership, participation, and self-management experiments in the United States and Europe.* New York: Harper Colophon Books.

12

Future Scenarios for the U.S. Political Economy, Labor, and Organizational Structure

A BRIEF SUMMARY OF WHERE THE UNITED STATES STANDS

Before looking at where various thinkers would like to see the United States go and their programs for how to get there, let us see where the United States currently stands with regard to the restructuring of the political economy. The following seven points stand out from what we have discussed so far:

1. Economic power and decision making in the private sector have become more centralized since the late nineteenth century.

2. The U.S. government has become increasingly involved with the private sector, and the concentration of power in the political economy has strongly influenced the direction of national public policy.

3. With the advent of foreign competition noticeable since the late 1960s, multinational corporations have increased their capital investment movements between regions in the United States and to foreign countries, causing major trauma to many workers and their communities.

4. The job structure in the United States and other mature industrial countries has shifted from manufacturing in the old basic heavy industries to the service sector. The replacement jobs are of a different skill mix, are in different geographical areas, and are predominantly lower paid than were the lost heavy manufacturing jobs.

5. Competition has fostered an emphasis in companies to cut costs and to maintain short-run profits on which managements' reward systems are based—leading to paper entrepreneurship; increased mergers and acquisitions; demands for favorable legislation from the government regarding taxes, import quota agreements, and easing of regulations;

concessions bargaining with employees regarding wages, benefits, and work rules; demands for subsidies from communities; and implementation of programs to gain more productivity from employees in some corporations.

6. Changes in technology have occurred in many industries; in the old heavy industries this has been particularly true of the medium-sized and smaller companies and in the sunrise industries, in general. These changes have meant the loss of some jobs and the forecast of more losses to come and have also begun the restructuring of the nature of many jobs and workplaces.

7. These dramatic shifts have led some people to a rethinking of the quality of life in mature industrial societies and to alternative policy suggestions for the future, both in the United States and in mature European industrial nations.

TRYING TO PREDICT THE FUTURE: A RISKY BUSINESS

Looking back over the social changes in the history of the United States, we suspect it would have been difficult to have predicted the major changes ahead of time. It is not even easy to recognize major changes when they are taking place around us. For years social change theorists have been trying to find patterns—business cycles or other social change cycles—in U.S. history. U.S. policy swings seem to run in thirty-year cycles—the Progressive era around the turn of the century, the New Deal in the 1930s, the Civil Rights movement in the 1960s, and another predicted liberal policy period in the 1990s. Whether it is precisely predictable, the point is a truism that policy swings can be expected as social factors change and people react or overreact.

The business cycles noted through the nineteenth century and up to World War II, with a depression occurring about every twenty years or so, have subsided. However, monetary and fiscal policies have not been able to cope with periodic recessions, and the U.S. faces possible long-term structural unemployment problems. Not all economists are willing to agree, however, that structural unemployment will continue to increase. Lack of human social predictability is either aggravating or charming, depending on whether one likes the direction of the change. Keep in mind that after Weber wrote optimistically about charismatic leaders' breaking the "iron cage" of bureaucracy, the next charismatic leader in Germany was Hitler.

Even though we cannot be certain in prediction, it is worthwhile to consider what possible policy directions we might take. Even though power shifts among groups in society and unforeseen historical events will ultimately pull us in one direction or another, we want to consider in broad terms what some possible directions might be. We also realize that the events as they unfold might lead us down paths not yet thought of.

We have addressed some of the different possible views of society and some of the assumptions behind them—particularly in Chapters 1 and 5. We reviewed the major worldviews in U.S. society, the order/ consensus and the power/conflict views, which provide some of the general assumptions behind more specific theories. We saw opposing views spun off of these worldviews on the distribution of power, the stratification system and income inequality, theories of Third World development and the operations of multinationals, and even management theories and ideas on organizational structure—whether to judge by technical rationality or a substantive humanistic rationality.

This chapter considers four views of.what the future ought to be, according to their various proponents. Every ideology contains underlying assumptions about how the world operates (worldviews), some examples illustrating and reinforcing these beliefs, myths and rhetoric to attract and hold a following to their principles, a program for what ought to be, and some ideas on how to get from what they see as today's society to what they want tomorrow's society to be. Two programs for the future based on the order/consensus worldview are (1) the conservative neoclassical economic view and (2) the postindustrial society view of the old-line liberals. The other two views based on the power/conflict worldview are (3) the late-capitalism view of the democratic left and (4) the more orthodox Marxist left. This final chapter then considers specific programs currently being offered by economists and other social scientists coming from some of these views. Table 12.1 outlines some major points in the four approaches discussed.

FOUR IDEOLOGICAL APPROACHES

The Conservative Neoclassical Economic View

Both the economic and political aspects of this view assume a wide distribution of power among competing groups. The basic principles underlying this view are (1) the classical economics of Adam Smith's invisible hand, which assumes relatively pure competition among firms and the same among free-flowing factors of production and, (2) a wide distribution of political power based in Jeffersonian democracy. Not all theorists holding this worldview would assume that some degree of unequal power does not exist, but the policies put forth usually ignore power distribution as a problem.

Figure 12.1 An Outline of Four Ideological Views of the United States

	Order/Consensus Worldview	
	Conservative Neoclassical Economic View	*Postindustrial Old-line Liberal View*
Current economy seen as:	Smith's pure competition model, but with some barriers to free-flowing factors of production	Neoclassical economics and Keynesian theory; decentralization of power to knowledge workers
Current political system seen as:	Decentralized checks and balances of power pluralism	Checks and balances of power pluralism; professionals scientifically solve social problems
Basic problems seen as:	Impediments to market—government regulations, unions; lack of capital accumulation	Lack of national planning
Current social class system seen as:	Those on top produce more of what society needs; those at the bottom lack motivation and/or ability	Mostly fair, but some barriers for people at the bottom who need some extra assistance
Role of the state should be:	Small as possible; no regulation except to eliminate barriers to competition; small budget	Important role as great arbitrator to protect the public; monetary and fiscal policy, welfare. Social problems handled scientifically by professionals in government
What they want:	Laissez faire environment for business; free enterprise zones, lower taxes, few regulations	Tripartite national economic planning; federal bank to assist sunset industries; govt. R&D for sunrise industry consortia and venture capital for small businesses
Some theorists and groups who hold some form of the view:	Milton Friedman and the Univ. of Chicago School of Economics; NAM, C of C, Heritage Foundation, AEI, IMF	Rohatyn, Thurow, Bell; Business Roundtable, older liberal foundations and policy-making assns.

| | Order/Consensus Worldview | |
	Power/Conflict Worldview *Late-capitalism View* *Democratic Left*	*Neo-orthodox* *Marxist View*
	Power/Conflict Worldview *Late-capitalism View* *Democratic Left*	*Neo-orthodox Marxist View*
Current economy seen as:	Centralization of economic power—top corps., and banks	Same centralization of economic power
Current political system seen as:	Concentration of power in a power elite—when centralized economic power penetrated the political sphere	Same
Basic problems seen as:	Decision making and wealth in the hands of a few, which limits long-run prosperity and innovation	Private ownership and control; individual greed
Current social class system seen as:	Dominant groups exploting subordinate groups	Same
Role of the state should be:	Tripartite national planning for economic prosprosperity and social justice	Plan for social justice rather than acting on behalf of big business
What they want:	Tripartite national planning; worker and community ownership; full employment; more equal wages; more public information, debate, and participation in decision making; venture capital for small firms; economic conversion to socially useful production and infrastructure	State ownership control of means of production; politically conscious unions
Some theorists and groups who hold some form of the view:	Bluestone, Harrison, Reich, Kuttner, Gordon, Bowles, Weisskopf; Institute for Policy Studies	

The neoclassical economic program can be seen in the monetarist, cost-push, supply-side, and similar conservative policies both in the United States and abroad. According to the neoclassical view, a remedy is needed for defects in market mechanisms. The theorists see these defects as being caused by government and union interference. If the government would stop creating money by financing its deficits and stop trying to regulate, including such things as minimum wages and interference with private industry in the areas of environment and health and safety, and if unions were not pushing for higher wages and setting up work rules, then the market would regulate itself and supply and demand would set the price and allocate resources.

Neoclassical economic conservatives also see the current economic problems as being caused by a lack of capital formation, hence the call for cutting taxes for corporations and the wealthy so they can expand investment. On the other end of the stratification system, they feel that welfare programs not only boost government spending, but also discourage people from working. Without minimum wage, more jobs would be created. Without welfare, poor people would be forced to take these new below-minimum-wage jobs, which presumably would be good for their Protestant work ethic development.

Abroad these policies are imposed on the Third World through the International Monetary Fund. The IMF follows the policies of the Chicago School of Economics, which has long been under the influence of the teachings of Milton Friedman and other people at the University of Chicago. This program follows a line consistent with neoclassical economic thinking: cuts in domestic spending (except for the military budget), deregulation and curtailing of regulatory agencies, discouraging of unions, cuts in taxes for the wealthy, cuts in welfare programs, and similar policies (Solomon 1982; Baumol and Blinder 1985).

This view of a new competitive world with less government interference has been given a boost since the mid-1970s in influence on public policy and on public thinking. The National Association of Manufacturers and the U.S. Chamber of Commerce have been joined by new money supporting think tanks to produce policy papers and research from this point of view. The Heritage Foundation and various other Scaife family foundations have been particularly influential at the national level. The American Enterprise Institute has been influential through the dissemination of its materials on the free enterprise system into the U.S. public schools. Regulatory agencies have had their budgets cut and have been restaffed by conservatives in the important posts (the goal displacement noted by Perrow in Chapter 10). The 1981 tax reform lightened the burden for the wealthy. Social programs for the poor and regulatory agencies' budgets have been slashed.

In other words, people holding this view observed with horror the growth of government beginning in the 1930s. The long-run view toward which they are currently working is of complete independence for business, which will benefit society by working in its own self-interest (Smith's invisible hand). This view also entails independence within the firm to bargain individually with employees and structure the organization as the management sees best. State right-to-work laws, which make the union shop impossible and give a fairly free hand to union-busting, have been helpful on this latter point.

The Postindustrial Society: The Old-Line Liberal View

We have seen that in the 1930s many people found the intervention of the state useful in bolstering the capitalist system. In the 1940s and the 1950s, as the large corporations became tied more closely to big government, these old-line liberals developed what came to be called the postindustrial society concept.

Postindustrial refers to the point in mature industrial societies at which the new jobs are basically in the service and information sectors, rather than in the manufacturing of goods or in agricultural production. In these growth sectors as well as in manufacturing, knowledge becomes of utmost importance and joins the other three factors of production—land, labor, and capital. The new working class of technicians, engineers, programmers, educators, and other professionals with valuable information in our age of increasing high technology would demand and get more power. Decision making would become more decentralized, as these persons held the knowledge on which society operated.

Social issues and problems would now be decided by professionals operating in their various bureaucracies; thus, the need for political debate would be less. Technical rationality and science could solve any problems in the social system. Because other industrial nations would be facing the same technical problems and solving them scientifically, we would expect a convergence in how nations would progress in their beliefs, views, and activities. This use of technical rationality to solve problems common to industrial societies might lead to a convergence in thinking among mature postindustrial states and in the long run to an end of ideological differences.

Another aspect of the postindustrial society would be the high productivity from the new technology. This would mean that fewer workers would be necessary and shorter work weeks would be the rule—the four day work week has already arrived in many organizations. Some theorists predicted a ten-hour work week. Work would be a privilege eagerly sought after by the new working class of professionals and technicians.

Early postindustrial writers foresaw that the low skilled would become structurally unemployed. These people might be taken care of by a national guaranteed income or negative income tax, which would replace the demeaning welfare system, and perhaps by a national health care service, such as the other industrial nations have. For these more-or-less permanently unemployed persons, a leisure ethic would have to replace the work ethic. A privatization of goals must occur so these people would not be unhappy about being unemployed.

More recently, faced with international competition, a different program for the poor based on the free enterprise zone concept has been proposed to revitalize inner cities and employ the low-skilled worker there. This proposal is similar to the privileges offered corporations in such freeport zones in Third World countries. The guaranteed income for these people was put on the back burner by a stagnant economy. Sixteen of the twenty-three states passing free enterprise zone legislation since 1981 have set up such zones granting tax breaks to corporations locating there and allowing varying degrees of freedom from regulation (Lembcke and Hart-Landsberg 1985:18). Regional and local competition for corporate subsidiaries is seen as healthy for the economy (see Ford 1983 for a critique of free enterprise zones and an alternative proposal).

The postindustrial society view does not call for any shifts in the power system. Power is not considered as a factor, except as becoming more decentralized. Government interference is useful in terms of what it does for business, such as the relief from taxes and regulations called for in free enterprise zones. Initially, in better days, the plan was for the government to become even more useful in the social service reforms called for to support people who have been factored out of the labor market. The changing circumstances make that idea seem outmoded. Some regulatory agencies are acceptable, as long as they are staffed by suitable people. This view sees power pluralism as growing in an increasingly representative democracy, with the decentralization of decision making to professionals and technical personnel in political and economic bureaucracies.

Other areas of government involvement are also called for. Training must be readily available for people who want to change jobs or enter the workforce. The Job Training Partnership Act, subsidizing employers to hire low-skilled workers, has replaced the earlier job creation under the Comprehensive Education and Training Act (CETA). Portable pensions, suggested by writers in the earlier days of postindustrial society thinking, are seldom mentioned now. They would have replaced the current private pension system, which locks many people into the current job they do not care for and that many workers lose, in one way or another, and never get to collect on retirement. Since the mid-1970s such plans as portable pensions, guaranteed income, and national health care have dropped out of postindustrial society discussions. Still part of the program, however, is the idea that the government must take the lead in establishing more economic planning on tripartite boards and in channeling funds into sunrise industries' research to further the U.S. international competitive position.

Private international planning agencies, such as the Trilaterial Commission, should function to keep international competition stable and orderly. Joint ventures at the international level assist in this effort. Earlier postindustrial writers did not consider the international level; the United States still enjoyed hegemony at that time.

Late-Capitalism View of the Democratic Left

The late-capitalism view of the democratic left is in some respects across the great divide in intention from the order/consensus worldview programs. Parts of the programs, however, sound interestingly similar. Coming from the power/conflict worldview, this perspective emphasizes who gains and who loses from the existing policies and structures. Espousers of this view see concentration of power as a serious problem (power elite view), undermining democracy in the United States and abroad and halting Third World social reforms and development. Rather than leaving social issues, agenda, and problems in the hands of professionals in bureaucracies, they argue for more public information, debate, and input on these affairs. Economic revitalization must include more democracy at all levels.

Their want list includes more local community/employee ownership and control of business, more participation in decision making by employees and the average person both in the workplace and in the political sphere. Above all this view calls for more information to be widely disseminated to the public. Instead of tax incentives for the rich, they would prefer inheritance taxes, a clamp on corporate tax loopholes and subsidies, and a loosening of venture capital for smaller and medium-sized firms. In other words, they reject the supply-side argument that revitalization can occur only if the wealthy accumulate more money. More attention should be paid to infrastructure and the providing of public goods, such as mass transit and national health care. Economic conversion from some less socially useful goods to goods that provide social utility, as we saw Lucas Aerospace workers try to do in England, would save jobs and also stimulate job creation. Job creation, with pay scales set at a living wage and at what each job is worth, is a high priority. This view puts more emphasis on the Keynesian demand-side—decent wages, full employment, job creation—than on the conservative supply-side trickle down effect.

And yet, even though this late-capitalism view sounds different from the postindustrial package, it also encourages worker/management/government planning at the national level and worker/management and sometimes community participation on company boards, noted as flourishing in Europe. The reasoning is that given the current international division of labor, reindustrialization in the United States cannot occur without this kind of cooperation by all people concerned, if the United States is going to maintain a privately owned capitalist system. Reasonable concessions in wages, cost-of-living allowances, and work rules can be made with widespread worker participation in decision making, company ownership, and profit sharing. At face value this program is not very different from the postindustrial view. The difference seems to be that the democratic left wants real participation, not pseudoparticipation and cooptation. They are concerned that this will be tried on the workers by people with more power, but at least participation provides a beginning for gaining information and also provides learning opportunities for the currently disenfranchised.

The democratic left continually warns the worker to be wary of the possibilities of manipulation—a point not discussed by the postindustrial people, who rely on the disinterestedness of professionals with scientific answers. Also, this view places more emphasis on employee and employee/community buyouts of shutdowns and on government encouragement of this local ownership through provision for loan backing or actual lending and technical training and assistance. Community/employee ownership offers an opportunity for greater control over life conditions and participation in the profits.

Neo-Orthodox Marxist Left

Similarly, the more orthodox left is looking at who benefits, the concentration of power, and the damage they think this causes in the United States and abroad. However, this view still sees state ownership (nationalization of the major corporations) as the solution. They argue that this would put power in the hands of the people through their government. Rather than taking the USSR as their model, most of the neo-orthodox left refer to the successes of public ownership of some enterprises in Western Europe or Yugoslavia. Their analysis is based on the difference in power of the segments of the class structure, and their aim is to find tactics that will gradually shift power to the hands of the less powerful majority. The long-run strategy is to make the public sector self-sufficient.

Some writers in this group see the growth of more militant unions

in the public (governmental) sector as the key. In the current organization of the political economy the public sector must rely on the private
sector for both tax support and policy approval. They argue that the
public sector must push for public ownership of some of the basic industry that provides supplies to the public sector—for example, capital
goods for the rebuilding of infrastructure. Governments can use the
power of eminent domain to salvage facilities when community or national economic health is endangered. Public employees' pension funds,
which currently supply about 16 percent of capital equity in the United
States (Lembcke and Hart-Landsberg 1985:16) should be used to fund
publicly owned projects, instead of the funding of the private sector, as
is currently practiced. Publicly owned manufacturing can receive set-
asides for materials from publicly owned resource materials—that is
price breaks. Payment-in-kind to public employees in the areas of
health, housing, and transportation, for example can cut the wage bill
and help offset the loss in taxes from the private sector.

The neo-Orthodox view usually does not give much attention to a
job's intrinsic rewards. It apparently assumes that the opportunities for
increased participation in decision making at the company and higher
levels will handle the more micro level satisfactions, although this lack
of emphasis on the micro level does not preclude job enrichment and
other alternatives. Participation in democratic unions, particularly in
the public sector, are a necessity for the program to be successfully implemented. Third World nations must also press for control of their own
industry and must place limits on the power of corporations, nationaliz-
ing those seen as important to the country's independence and
autonomy.

EXAMPLES OF SPECIFIC PROGRAMS FOR
ECONOMIC GROWTH AND SOCIAL BETTERMENT

The four general perspectives just discussed give us some idea of the
ideological assumptions of specific writers when we read their proposals
for how the United States can improve its economic growth and provide
a better life for its citizens. This section examines eight such plans from
the four general categories of thinking.

Conservative Neoclassical Policy: Reaganomics

This model is fairly well observed in the government policies of the
1980s. Brookings economist Robert Lawrence (1983) and other Reaganomics enthusiasts—monetarists and cost-push inflationists, supply-
siders—see no problems that cannot be handled by neoclassical

economic policy. They find no deindustrialization in the economy. Lawrence, for example, claims that the jobs lost in heavy manufacturing for
about fifteen years are not deindustrialization, but a function of the
business cycle.

Supply-side economics tax cuts for corporations have been made to
try to stimulate investment. Federal spending in domestic programs related to welfare and regulation have been cut to try to lessen government influence on the market. Minimum wage has been allowed to decline in real terms and as a percentage of the average wage. Military
spending has been increased, this is the one area of federal spending
approved by conservative philosophy. These policies are in basic accord
with the neoclassical conservative program (Solomon 1982; Friedman
and Friedman 1979; Kemp 1979; Wanniski 1978; Baumol and Blinder
1985).

In terms of economic policy for depressed urban areas, the free enterprise zone idea, commented on in the previous section has been imported from England. The plan was to give tax breaks, freedom from
import and export duties, and relief from many regulations to companies to place plants in the ghettos and barrios to employ the poor in
much the same manner that Third World free trade zones operate. "Re-
creating Hong Kong" is a phrase used by advocates of the plan. The
nature of the jobs created, or moved from other sites in the United
States, was expected to be secondary labor market type—low-skilled
and low-paid. Tax breaks, as noted, are not what small business ventures need, since they usually do not have profits to tax; they need long-
term venture capital. The beneficiaries of the plan would be the large
corporations. Critics have suggested other means of revitalizing distressed areas that they feel might be more beneficial to the communities
and the workers themselves (Ford 1983).

Throughout the preceeding chapters, we have encountered the neoclassical and supply-side arguments on the various issues mentioned
and have seen critiques of these arguments, including in such areas as:

1. The assumption that the marketplace sets price (despite evidence
   of oligopoly and concentration of economic power)
2. A marginal productivity/human capital theory of wages (despite
   evidence of dual, split, and internal labor markets and various
   discriminatory barriers, including premarket barriers, such as in
   the education system)
3. Insistence on tax breaks to stimulate capital investment (despite
   data that there is an inverse relationship between corporate taxes
   and productive investment)
4. Free trade zones to lift the depressed urban areas (despite the evidence that they do not provide good jobs and that there are better
   ways of aiding ailing communities)

5. A call for relief from environmental and health and safety regulations in order to compete (despite the fact that the competitors abroad are doing more in this area)
6. A call for less unionization (despite the points that the United States is the least unionized of all mature industrial nations and that other countries have learned how to negotiate with their employees so they have both low inflation and more rapid economic growth).

For a more detailed middle-of-the-road account of the problems of the neoclassical approach, see Thurow (1982). For a short, but clear and devastating account, see former Secretary of Labor, economist Ray Marshall (1984). It is fairly easy to criticize the neoclassical school of policy making, especially if what is happening in other industrial nations is considered. What is not so easy is to decide which alternative program to use in place of this view of how the world operates. The programs differ widely; some of the most talked about are presented below.

Postindustrial Liberals: The Rohatyn Model

Investment banker Felix Rohatyn (1983) of the Wall Street investment firm of Lazard Freres is know by both friends and foes as Felix the Fixer. He was encouraged by the apparent success of his plan to bail out New York City from bankruptcy in the mid-1970s and by the equity he has gained for ailing giant corporations through the mergers he engineered. He has now suggested a national plan—a national development bank and a tripartite planning council, composed of labor, management, and government representatives, to assist national economic development.

In the 1970s President Carter set up a committee to examine what the economy needed. The committee was composed of Rohatyn, Lane Kirkland of the AFL-CIO, and Irving Shapiro, former chairman of the board of DuPont. In 1984 the committee produced a pamphlet calling for the formation of a tripartite planning council and a Reconstruction Finance Corporation (RFC). The latter would be a revival of the bank set up by Herbert Hoover in 1931 as the means of making order out of a chaotic political economy. The government would become the ultimate banker, the lender of last resort, for major U.S. corporations. Companies would never again have the embarrassment of going through Congress for money, as in the Chrysler and Lockheed cases.

The bank and planning council must require a performance bond from the large corporations before the government would assist them with capital, tax breaks, or quotas. This performance agreement would include at least two things. It would set out the concessions from workers, the major ingredient in the New York City bailout. It would stipulate how the companies would invest the money for capital improvements or other means of increasing production. The latter would prevent the loans from being used to buy up other companies or other such unproductive moves. These agreements should establish a political climate for labor and management to cooperate—each knows the other must work toward the goal of increased production.

Why would labor agree to sitting down to make concessions? In today's international free-floating capital situation, labor is already forced to make concessions without a chance to help plan. The AFL-CIO sees this as an opportunity to expand its level of decision making from more than just wages, hours, work rules, and working conditions—and from a weak position. This kind of overall investment planning might also keep more sunset industry jobs in the United States, as well as give legitimacy to unions again (Watkins 1984:16).

What do corporations have to gain? Probably nothing from the bank, unless the corporation was in the situation of Chrysler and Lockheed and had to be bailed out of financial ruin by the government—and with very few strings attached by Congress. The 1980s tax breaks and quotas from the government also have no strings attached concerning how the money saved is to be spent. It is difficult to imagine why large companies who can fund themselves on the private market would voluntarily opt for restrictions on their planning by borrowing from the RFC.

The RFC in the 1930s ended up bailing out some of the nation's largest banks and railroads. The first loan went to Bank of America, the second to the largest rail network of the time. The corporations used this money to prop up their credit ratings, rather than to create jobs. This effect prompted humorist Will Rogers to quip that the RFC confused money with water. Instead of trickling down to the workers whom it was intended to help, as water would have, gold (money) seems to run uphill. "You can drop a bag of gold in Death Valley, which is below sea level, and before Saturday it will be home to papa J. P. [Morgan]" (quoted in Bluestone and Harrison 1982:213).

There is something corporations can gain, however, from participating in the planning council, according to historian James Livingston (1981). This is an opportunity to legitimate executive planning and isolate it from Congress and local and state governments that occasionally speak for other constituents. Livingston quotes Rohatyn's complaint that

> a government of checks and balances has become all checks and no balances. . . . Today, we could not build our road system, the TVA, or the Manhattan Project. Between the Congress, the courts, and numerous interest groups, these projects would all die on the vine. (Livingston 1981:11)

Does this mean that the centralization of planning under such a board would ensure that big business was the first among equals and would steer the planning away from social programs, pump-priming for demand-side consumption, or job creation? Are the numerous interest groups too many? Or are there too many interest groups in the areas of social concerns—the poor, the structurally unemployed, the minorities, the environment, and consumers? Livingston (1981), Watkins (1981, 1984), Bluestone and Harrison (1982:210–214), and Reich (Rothenberg 1983) are among those suspicious of the intent behind the backing of this corporatist idea of planning by the business leaders. Corporatism "looks to active government intervention to serve traditional capitalist ends" (Watkins 1981:46).

The Rohatyn proposal has been very appealing to some members of the Democratic Party, as well as to the unions and big business. The idea of cooperation among the groups involved is attractive, as is the idea that the nature of restructuring could in this way be shaped to deal with unemployment and regional problems, if all partners were equal in the planning. The plan also has the appeal that the policy decisions would be handled by the professional economists and technical experts, presumably in the rational scientific manner admired by postindustrial thinkers. These questions remain, however: Why would companies participate in the bank, and who would do most of the planning?

From observing Rohatyn's handling of the New York City case and from listening to his comments on politicians, University of Texas government professor Al Watkins makes the following observation about the effect of Rohatyn's plan:

> Since Rohatyn believes democratic institutions will resist massive budget cuts, he now wants to give an RFC many of the same powers as New York's EFCB [Emergency Financial Control Board]. This way, an RFC could not only help meet corporate financing needs, but also extract concessions from political and labor leaders and institutionalize substantially greater corporate power over national policy.
>
> Ironically, Rohatyn proposes to use a New Deal-style strategy to roll back many New Deal and Great Society social programs. Perhaps that helps explain why Rohatyn is so nicely camouflaged. (Watkins 1981:49)

More Postindustrial Liberals: Thurow Model

Economist Lester Thurow also urges more national planning in the sense of directing investment to growth, or sunrise, industries. He would not like to prop up dying industries, as might be the case in the Rohatyn model of bailing out corporate giants. Rather, Thurow (1983) would like to see a government cabinet position or tripartite corporate finance committee channel grant monies for R&D to consortia of industries on the frontiers of technology and long-term venture capital to smaller firms with potential. The aim of this committee is to make the U.S. companies competitive with foreign firms. An obvious cue for this investment in growth industries comes from the example of the Japanese Ministry of International Trade and Industry, which we noted in the previous chapter assists new industries to grow and old declining industries to merge or go out of business gracefully with new ones coming in to absorb their workforce.

So far, the old unionists of the AFL-CIO have not responded positively to the high tech idea. New jobs do not seem to be forthcoming fast enough from this area, and the AFL-CIO base is in the older industrial areas, which are supported more in Rohatyn's plan than in a sunrise industry plan (Lekachman 1984:41).

A Democratic Left Model: Bluestone and Harrison

One of the first critiques of the political economy under Reaganomics and corporate boardroom practices of the 1980s came from economists Bluestone and Harrison (1982). One of their major contributions to the thinking about the economic malaise is their analysis of capital flight and the subsequent deindustrialization of the United States—denied by some of the far right (some of their data and arguments appear in Chapter 7 in the discussion of shutdowns).

As with other programs of the democratic left, Bluestone and Harrison emphasize that the United States needs to rethink the validity of taking for granted how the U.S. political economy works. The current assumption that the United States must allow business to do anything it wants to relieve the country of its problems overlooks the point that the narrow conceptions business holds of what is good for society helped create the problem. The democratic left asks people to rethink what the agenda should be and how to get there.

Priorities need to be realigned with the firm knowledge that there is no incompatibility between economic efficiency and social justice, unlike such previous assumptions of incompatibility. For example, the authors ask people to rethink these current situations: Why should human development and preventative health care take a back seat to military R&D, when military overkill is already so enormous? Why is infrastructure allowed to crumble when luxury items are a glut on the market? Why should a fifty-year-old bricklayer pay more taxes than one of the nation's largest banks? Why should a profitable plant be shut down and leave workers and the community to wither and die? Why should we kid ourselves with the fiction that General Dynamics, Lockheed, IBM, and General Electric are private corporations when they are highly subsidized by the government, "either through cost-plus procurement contracts or low-cost—if not completely free—rental of land, buildings, and machinery" (Bluestone and Harrison 1982:246)? They comment on public ownership in other mature industrial states in this manner:

> Throughout Western Europe there exists an entire sector consisting of "public enterprises": partly or wholly-owned government corporations that engage in the production of a wide range of basic industrial and consumer commodities. In most cases, there is nothing especially "socialistic" about these public enterprises in their operational objectives, in their day-to-day management, or even in the character of those who run them. Rather, they represent a mature form of what is often called "state capitalism." (Bluestone and Harrison 1982:246)

Perhaps even more important than who owns what is who controls the decision making. Public ownership at the local, state, or national level should facilitate participation in decision making. Mechanisms for community- and worker-owned buyouts and start-ups should be put in place. The private sector also needs to alter management practices to allow employees some participation in planning for new products and processes and economic conversion. If we do not develop and use our human resources, we are the poorer for it, they contend.

Where do the authors suggest this program start? It should start with public information and debate. Without public knowledge of what the issues are and what alternatives exist, there is no ground swell to force change. If what we have noted in Chapter 5 is true, in general, about the mass media, a major reorientation would have to occur. The prospect for this is not encouraging.

Another Democratic Left Model: Reich

A different tripartite planning idea comes from Robert Reich of the John F. Kennedy School of Government at Harvard University. Reich (1983) helped bring to the public's attention the problem of short-run corporate planning and popularized the term *paper entrepreneurialism*. In addition to being more critical of corporate management than Rohatyn, he seems to be criticizing narrow interest groups, that is, big business political clout, rather than the social program interest groups. He also brought to public attention that the choice between social justice (handled by government) and prosperity (handled by the private economy) was a false choice in the modern political economy when such decisions are interlocked. Unfortunately, U.S. historical background has contributed to the country's cultural ideology that the two areas are somehow separate. U.S. cyclical ideological swings demonstrate this pattern—first business has its way, then the social ills must be taken care of by government regulation and laws, then follows disillusionment with expectations, followed by a swing back to business priorities.

Thus, we are back to tripartite planning, which tries to balance the two needs of society with a holistic view, particularly since the matter of global interdependence has arisen. Other mature industrial nations are less suspicious of government since they used it earlier to throw off vestiges of feudalism. In those countries, after-tax income is more evenly dispersed than in the United States; government-sponsored training, health care, and unemployment benefits are taken for granted; and national level tripartite boards are becoming commonplace (Reich 1983:16). In Japan, community, consensus and long-term security for its privileged workers "appears to have spurred its citizens to greater feats of production than has the rugged individualism of modern America" (Reich 1983:16). Other industrial countries have higher productivity, longer life expectancy, less unemployment, less pollution, and better support policies for working women and their children, apparently through negotiations by parties concerned and taking a wider and more long-run view when planning.

How does Reich's tripartite planning board differ from Rohatyn's? Reich sees his plan as an open forum for debate and input from all interest groups, as well as a data collection agency, with the basic criterion that the total picture must be observed as each industry is considered, including suppliers, employees, consumers, the relationship of companies in the industry to each other, the communities and regions involved, and the foreign competition. His hope is to preserve the democratic nature of the decision-making process. He views the closed-door nature of Rohatyn's professionals as possibly tending toward fascism and definitely not including all parties and all facets of the social picture (Rothenberg 1982:99). He anticipates that this open democratic institutional setting will encourage warring parties entrenched in beggar-thy-neighbor cultural attitudes to see their wider interests and negotiate.

Besides this need for planning, what is Reich's program? The plan is to (1) restructure in a flexible manner within industry so human resources can be fully used through participation in decision making; (2) promote sunrise growth industries—small batch speciality items and high tech areas, such as fiber optics, lasers, biotechnology, and robotics—while preserving some of the older smokestack industries in diminished form; and (3) promote worker- and community-owned enterprises. The latter are particularly important if we are to promote a climate of trust in which workers, managers, and communities are to cooperate on the innovation it will take to better society as a whole (Reich 1987).

In other words, Reich's emphasis is on competing efficiently and creatively. "No view of the government's proper role in the economy can claim legitimacy in America unless it carries with it the promise of prosperity" (Reich 1983:17). Reagonomics, Reich says, reflects the ascendancy of the business ideology that gives short shrift to the public goods sector, consumers, and social justice. According to Reich we must be able to have both prosperity and social justice, as other industrial nations are trying to do through tripartite planning. We short-circuit our future economic growth by not paying attention to social issues and by allowing the gap between rich and poor to widen.

> I don't think that social justice is a charity that can be traded off against economic growth. I think it actually *undergirds* future economic growth. (Quoted in Rothenberg 1983:97, emphasis in the original)

Another difference Reich finds between ourselves and other countries is in the nature of our MNCS. U.S. and British MNCs are of the pure type, with no allegiance to any country. Other industrial nations, he contends, have MNCs with policies intended to assist the workers at home—exporting low-wage work and reinvesting in industry at home to keep up employment in the higher-wage jobs, such as making components for foreign assembly (Reich 1983: 260–267). Another means of upgrading home workers is through tying joint ventures and licensing with U.S. MNCs to acquire R&D and technology for their nationals. The aims of our national planning should be to encourage a link-up of foreign investment with job betterment and to acquire R&D ourselves, rather than job loss, wage competition, or limiting long-run growth for short-run corporate gain. In other words, pure MNCs are not investing in long-run human capital improvements in their home countries. In the long run, then, "national governments . . . thus become bargaining agents for the least mobile factor of international production—human capital" (Reich 1983:266). The United States is getting shortchanged in this area, due to the orientation of MNCs and the failure of the political will to do something about it. This failure of political will is the result of the way U.S. culture and structure developed historically. These are not just economic issues or political issues, but broader social issues in the political economy. These issues ought to be debated and decided openly by all people concerned, with long-run national priorities in mind.

Reich gives a serious blow to U.S. managerialism—inflexibility and centralization of decision making. He criticizes narrow economism— making technical decisions based on profits only while ignoring society at large and human capital. With these two arguments he is clearly separating himself from the postindustrial liberals. However, he himself is criticized by those on his left about his optimism that the powerful will be willing to deal democratically and to negotiate. As with Thurow's plans for encouraging high-tech industries, Reich also has not been popular with AFL-CIO leaders who want to hear more about revitalizing old smokestack industries.

A Third Democratic Left Program: Bowles, Gordon, and Weisskopf

Economists Bowles, Gordon, and Weisskopf (1984) have an interesting version of the problems of the U.S. political economy. Rather than seeing society as a zero-sum entity, they see it as full of wastefulness, inefficiency, and slack—ready to offer more to everybody, if properly structured and inspired. In their view the problem stems from this wasteful lack of productivity. The factors involved in creating this slack are:

1. a decline in work intensity by dissatisfied workers and a proliferation of low-productivity jobs because of a large pool of low-wage workers
2. a reduced inspiration to innovate and invest—partly from lack of demand caused by low wages, unemployment, misallocation of resources
3. excess supervision—one supervisor for each six workers
4. a scare to the business community from citizen pressure for safety and environmental protection—which appears to have stimulated a failure of nerve instead of creativity
5. failure to use existing capacity
6. useless output—such as excess military spending, nuclear production, food packaging and processing, excessive crime control rather than creating jobs to employ people, excessive health costs stemming from profit-dominated health system, and unnecessary advertising.

Corporate response to the problems of decline was repression—tight money, cutbacks in social spending, antiunionism, induced recession, capital flight, and emerging corporatism. These measures hurt both labor and business. They estimate that this slack in production resulted in a loss of $1.2 trillion to GNP in 1980 alone.

As an alternative to repression and antidemocratic tendencies being used, the authors suggest three broad goals: (1) saving capitalism from strangling itself, (2) extending public ownership in some basic areas, and (3) extending democracy in the workplace, the community, and in overall planning. The specifics of their program for achieving these goals include these twelve items:

1. an increase in wages, particularly for low-wage workers; full employment to stimulate demand; and equal pay for jobs of comparable worth. The higher labor costs will be offset by higher productivity.

2. price controls
3. public control of all banks and insurance companies and a re-structuring of the Federal Reserve Bank with election of its board every four years by the House of Representatives
4. publicly controlled energy and military production and reduction in military spending
5. public supported child care
6. plant closing legislation to reduce capital flight and soften its impact
7. a national health care system
8. public support of community-owned enterprises and democratically elected community investment boards
9. more worker information and control on the job
10. worker re-training for high-productivity jobs
11. a reduced three-tier tax structure—including elimination of corporate income tax, but a higher rate for property produced income
12. some overall planning at the national and supranational level for allocating resources to public as well as individual needs.

To summarize, with the proper restructuring of the political economy and the allocation of resources to provide socially useful goods and services, everyone should benefit and the quality of life should improve. Like Bluestone, Harrison, Reich, and others on the democratic left, economic recovery is only one part of the agenda. Just as important is what the program means for people—their development, their participation in decision making, and their improvement in quality of life, which is more than just quantity of income.

The egalitarianism and populism of this overall wage-led productivity growth program have a great deal of appeal for many people. The antipathy from corporate management or union leaders entrenched in adversarial tactics is not discussed (Lewis 1983:41; Moberg 1983:20). Increased production is to help defray the costs of some programs, and the profits from publicly owned companies and the savings from military budget cuts are intended to pick up the rest. These problems—how to get cooperation and whether various aspects of the program will operate and balance as planned—are thorny matters.

More from the Democratic Left: Kuttner

The title of Kuttner's book, *The Economic Illusion: False Choices between Prosperity and Social Justice* (1985), is reminiscent of the arguments we have seen from all of the democratic left in one way or another—that U.S. culture has deluded people into believing they must have either guns or butter but not both; that is, somehow social justice is inimical to economic prosperity. The democratic left is asking people to suspend that belief for a minute and examine what can be done. The contribution of Kuttner's book is that he gives us data from other countries where both are being emphasized in various ways. Other mature industrial countries do have problems and do make mistakes, but they also have apparently managed to have higher growth rates along with more social justice than the United States has.

For example, the two nations with the highest taxes on capital are the two fastest growing in the industrial world—West Germany and Japan. The countries with the lowest corporate tax rates are also the lowest in growth rate—Great Britain and the United States. The three countries with the largest growth in government spending from 1973 to 1981 also had the highest economic growth rates—Japan, Italy, and France. The countries with the slowest government growth rates (although their spending was relatively high) were Great Britain and the United States. Countries with the most unified and strongest labor movement— Austria, Sweden, Norway, Holland, and West Germany—have been the most successful in holding down inflation while maintaining rapid economic growth. Other industrial nations also have more stringent early warning laws, and more demanding health and safety and environmental requirements. Chapter 3 noted that, with the exception of Japan, these industrial nations also offered more income equity and social support services for women workers.

From the More Orthodox-Marxian Side

From this model come various proposals of letting the right and center fail so completely to solve U.S. problems that the people will insist on a completely new structure oriented to egalitarian concepts and public ownership. In this model private ownership and the promotion of individual greed are the basic problems. We have not discussed this model in the text because the premises of a revolutionary restructuring of the political economy seem remote from the possibilities of the future of the United States, given the U.S. historical structural and cultural base.

THE BOTTOM LINE

As discussed in this and earlier chapters, conservatives and old-line liberals have given these reasons for economic problems in the United States: lack of capital accumulation, unions, government laws and regulations and taxes, foreign competition, and low-productivity in the undereducated or recalcitrant workforce. Less democratic government intervention has been called for—either laissez faire of the Reaganomics type or corporatist planning by industrial leaders of the Rohatyn style. According to this end of the spectrum, social benefits are incompatible with economic prosperity. More social equality, in this view, means less prosperity. As Judy Gregory of Cleveland 925 (9 to 5) described the followers of these programs: "they believe the shibboleths that Americans have asked too much and live too well" (quoted in Kramer 1984:12).

Kuttner, with his data from other mature industrial countries, questions this reasoning. He and other democratic left political economists argue that U.S. inflexibility and lack of re-examining the myths built up in its past have led to problems—namely, not using human resources and not being willing to experiment with more democratic organizational structures.

Economist Ray Marshall says essentially the same—U.S. failure is in the lack of public investment in infrastructure, people, and research and development, and in the "amazing amount of pessimism about our political system and our ability to undertake effective programs, despite the evidence to the contrary" (Marshall 1984:19).

Behind their arguments it seems Kuttner and Marshall are saying the United States is dealing with a paralysis of fear. The powerful individuals, still viewing society as zero-sum, fear the loss of power if workers and consumers are empowered to participate in the knowledge of what is going on and in the decision making. The public fears what they do not yet know about the situation and that a change, still thinking zero-sum society, means they might lose what little they have, particularly at the hands of the corporatists.

Cooperation and reciprocity appear to be ideals suited for hunting and gathering societies. Or do they? Democratic, people-oriented experiements in other mature industrial societies, faulted and incomplete though they be, have not done badly.

People who argue for productivity's being related to commitment to a larger picture of human betterment may be onto something. We have frequently been wrong in the past projections of the future because our vision has been limited to what appears to have worked historically. The real trajectory has often been made somewhere between apparent accident and the actions of people who dared see different visions of the possible.

To compete with the rest of the mature industrial world in an interdependent global economy, it appears that the United States is being pushed or pulled into some kind of national planning. The questions are what kinds of planning and who will control it? If a ground swell for democratic participation does not materialize, despite the apparent readiness for democratic populism that continues to show up in opinion polls, we can expect a continuation for a while along the lines toward corporatist planning and a continued lessening of democracy for what people involved perceive to be the needs of big business.

The point to consider here is information. Democratic alternatives and what might become public issues are out-mediaed by people who have the power and who fear change in what they take to be a zero-sum society. This might conceivably be a loss in the long run for them and for all of us, in terms of what could be, in a society with more resilience than we give it credit for.

BIBLIOGRAPHY

Banks, William C. 1985. The way we'll work: Shorter hours, bigger bonuses (The year 2000; On the job). *Money* 14, 11:153–165 (November).

Baumol, William J., and Alan S. Blinder. 1985. *Economics: Principles and policies*, 3rd ed. New York: Harcourt Brace Jovanovich.

Blakely, Edward J., and Philip Shapira. 1984. Industrial restructuring: Public policies for investment in advanced industrial society. *Annals of the American Academy of Political and Social Science* 475:96–109 (September).

Bluestone, Barry, and Bennett Harrison. 1982. *The deindustrialization of America: Plant closings, community abandonment, and the dismantling of basic industry.* New York: Basic Books.

Bowles, Samuel, David M. Gordon, and Thomas E. Weisskopf. 1984. *Beyond the waste land: A democratic alternative to economic decline.* Garden City, N.Y.: Doubleday (Anchor).

Deindustrialization: Restructuring the economy. 1984. *Annals of the American Academy of Political and Social Science*, Special issue, 475:1–229 (September).

Edsall, Thomas Byrne. 1984. *The new politics of inequality.* New York: W. W. Norton.

Ford, Ramona L. 1983. Revitalizing the distressed community: GSOC and ESOP alternatives to enterprise zones. *Growth and Change* 14, 4:22–31 (October).

Friedman, Milton, and Rose Friedman. 1979. *Free to choose: A personal statement.* New York: Harcourt Brace Jovanovich.

Harrington, Michael. 1986. Progressive economics for 1988. *The Nation* 242, 17:601, 612–617 (May 3).

Kemp, Jack. 1979. *An American renaissance: A strategy for the 1980s.* New York: Harper & Row.

Kramer, Lawrence. 1984. Economic future of U.S. explored. *In These Times* 8, 10:12 (February 1–7).

Kuttner, Robert. 1985. *The economic illusion: False choices between prosperity and social justice.* New York: Houghton Mifflin.

Lawrence, Robert Z. 1983. "Is trade deindustrializing America? A medium-term perspective." *In Brookings papers on economic activity, Vol. 1* edited by William C. Brainard and George L. Perry, 129–172. Washington, D.C.: Brookings Institution.

Lekachman, Robert. 1984. An economic agenda. *The Progressive* 48, 5:40–41 (May).

Lembcke, Jerry, and Martin Hart-Landsberg. 1985. Reindustrialization and the logic of class politics in late 20th century America. *Insurgent Sociologist* 13, 1–2:7–21 (Summer-Fall).

Lewis, J. Patrick. 1983. An economic bill of rights. *The Progressive* 47, 12:40–41 (December).

Livingston, James. 1981. Democracy interferes with free enterprise. *In These Times* 5, 10:11 (January 28–February 3).

Marshall, Ray. 1984. Building an economic consensus for the future. *The Texas Observer* 76, 13:15–19 (June 29).

Moberg, David. 1983. A blueprint to fix economy. *In These Times* 7, 30:19–20 (July 27–August 9).

Morf, Martin. 1983. Eight scenarios for work in the future. *Futurist* 17, 3:24–29 (June).

Naisbitt, John. 1984. *Megatrends: Ten new directions transforming our lives.* New York: Warner.

Noble, David F. 1984. *Forces of production: A social history of industrial automation.* New York: Alfred A. Knopf.

Reich, Robert B. 1983. *The next American frontier: A provocative program for economic renewal.* New York: Penguin.

———. 1987. Enterprise and double cross. *Washington Monthly* 18, 12:13–19 (January).

Rohatyn, Felix. 1983. *The twenty year century.* New York: Random.

———. 1984. *Restoring America's competitiveness: Proposals for an industrial policy.* Washington, D.C.: Center for National Policy.

Rothenberg, Randall. 1983. Mr. Industrial Policy: The Democrats' latest answer to Reaganomics is the brainchild of a diminutive Harvard professor named Robert Reich. *Esquire* 99, 5:94–99 (May).

Solomon, Ezra. 1982. *Beyond the turning point: The U.S. economy in the 1980s.* San Francisco: W. H. Freeman.

Thurow, Lester C. 1982. *Dangerous currents: The state of economics.* New York: Random.

———. 1983. The need to work smarter. *Newsweek* 102, 4:80 (October 3).

Wanniski, J. 1978. *The way the world works, how economies fail—and succeed.* New York: Basic Books.

Watkins, Alfred J. 1981. Felix Rohatyn's biggest deal. *Working Papers for a New Society* 8, 5:44–52 (September/October).

———. 1984. Rohatyn's new corporatism offers no real solutions. *The Texas Observer* 76, 15: 14–17 (August 3).

Index

447